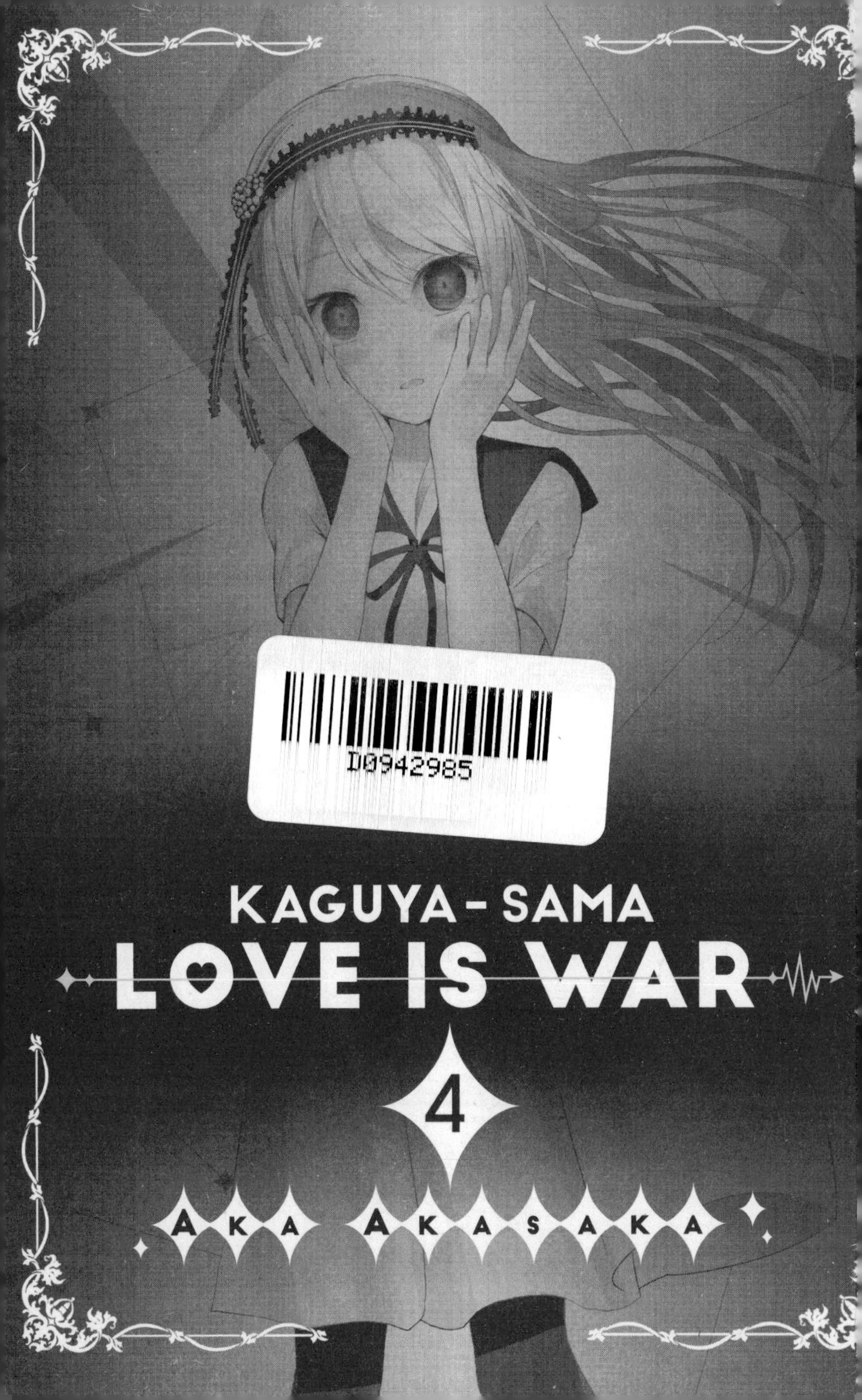
KAGUYA-SAMA
LOVE IS WAR
4
AKA AKASAKA

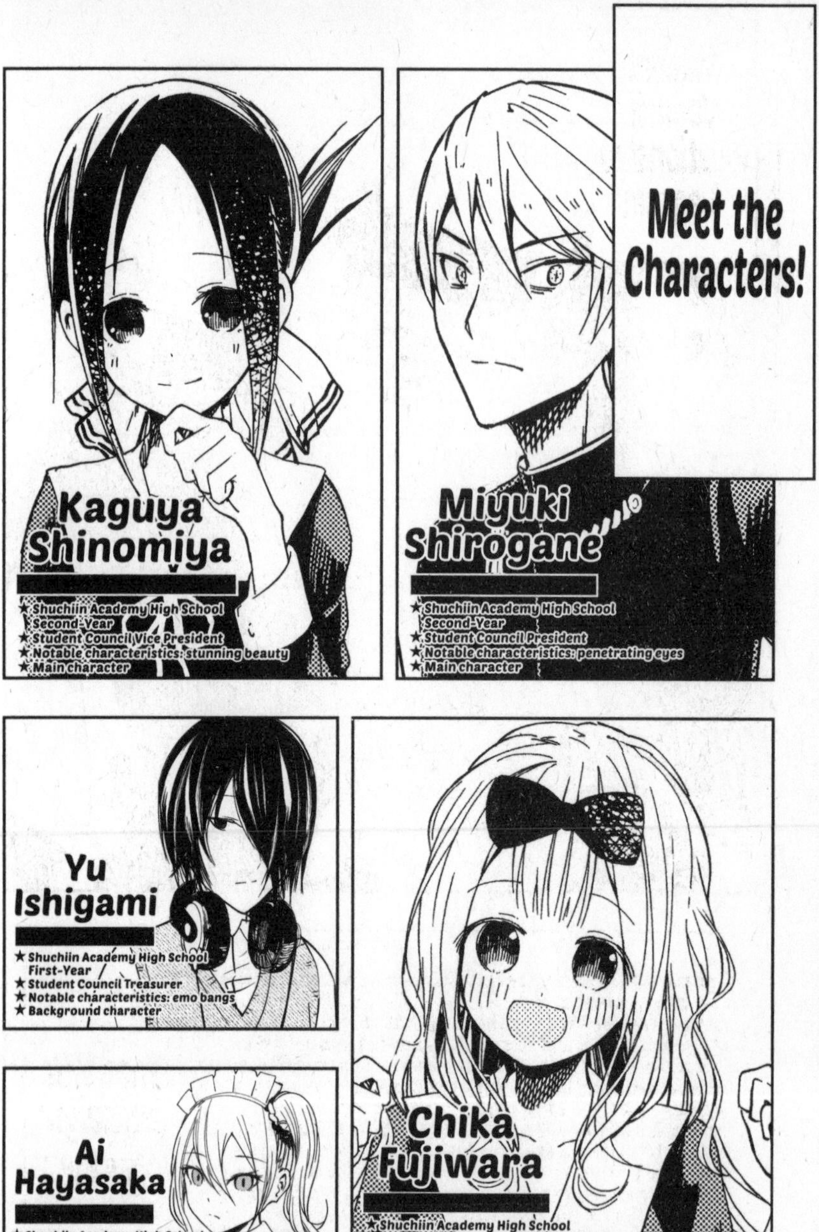
Meet the Characters!
Miyuki Shirogane
★ Shuchiin Academy High School Second-Year
★ Student Council President
★ Notable characteristics: penetrating eyes
★ Main character
Kaguya Shinomiya
★ Shuchiin Academy High School Second-Year
★ Student Council Vice President
★ Notable characteristics: stunning beauty
★ Main character
Chika Fujiwara
★ Shuchiin Academy High School Second-Year
★ Student Council Secretary
★ Notable characteristics: soft, poofy, large boobs
★ Main character
Yu Ishigami
★ Shuchiin Academy High School First-Year
★ Student Council Treasurer
★ Notable characteristics: emo bangs
★ Background character
Ai Hayasaka
★ Shuchiin Academy High School Second-Year
★ Notable characteristics: one-quarter Irish
★ Profession: Kaguya Shinomiya's personal assistant

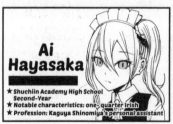

Student Council Relationship Diagram

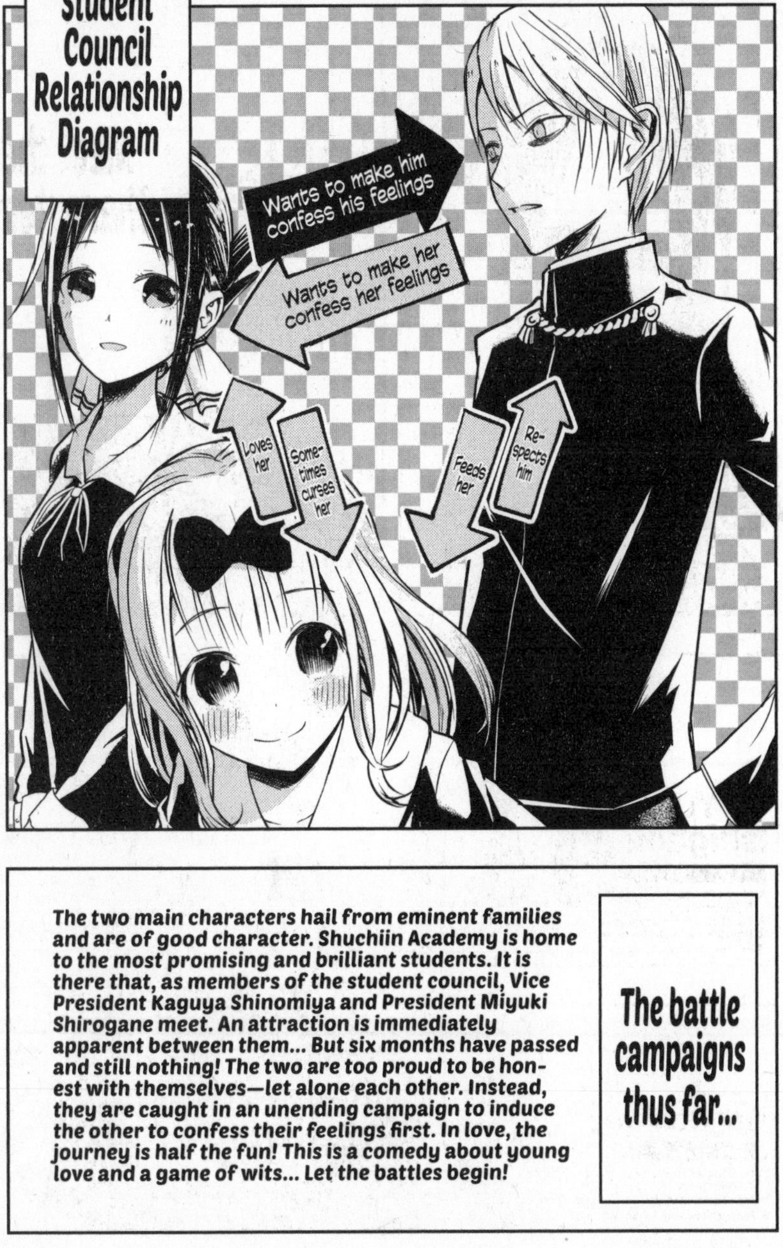
Wants to make him confess his feelings
Wants to make her confess her feelings
Loves her
Sometimes curses her
Feeds her
Respects him

The battle campaigns thus far...

The two main characters hail from eminent families and are of good character. Shuchiin Academy is home to the most promising and brilliant students. It is there that, as members of the student council, Vice President Kaguya Shinomiya and President Miyuki Shirogane meet. An attraction is immediately apparent between them... But six months have passed and still nothing! The two are too proud to be honest with themselves—let alone each other. Instead, they are caught in an unending campaign to induce the other to confess their feelings first. In love, the journey is half the fun! This is a comedy about young love and a game of wits... Let the battles begin!

KAGUYA-SAMA LOVE IS WAR

BATTLE CAMPAIGNS 4

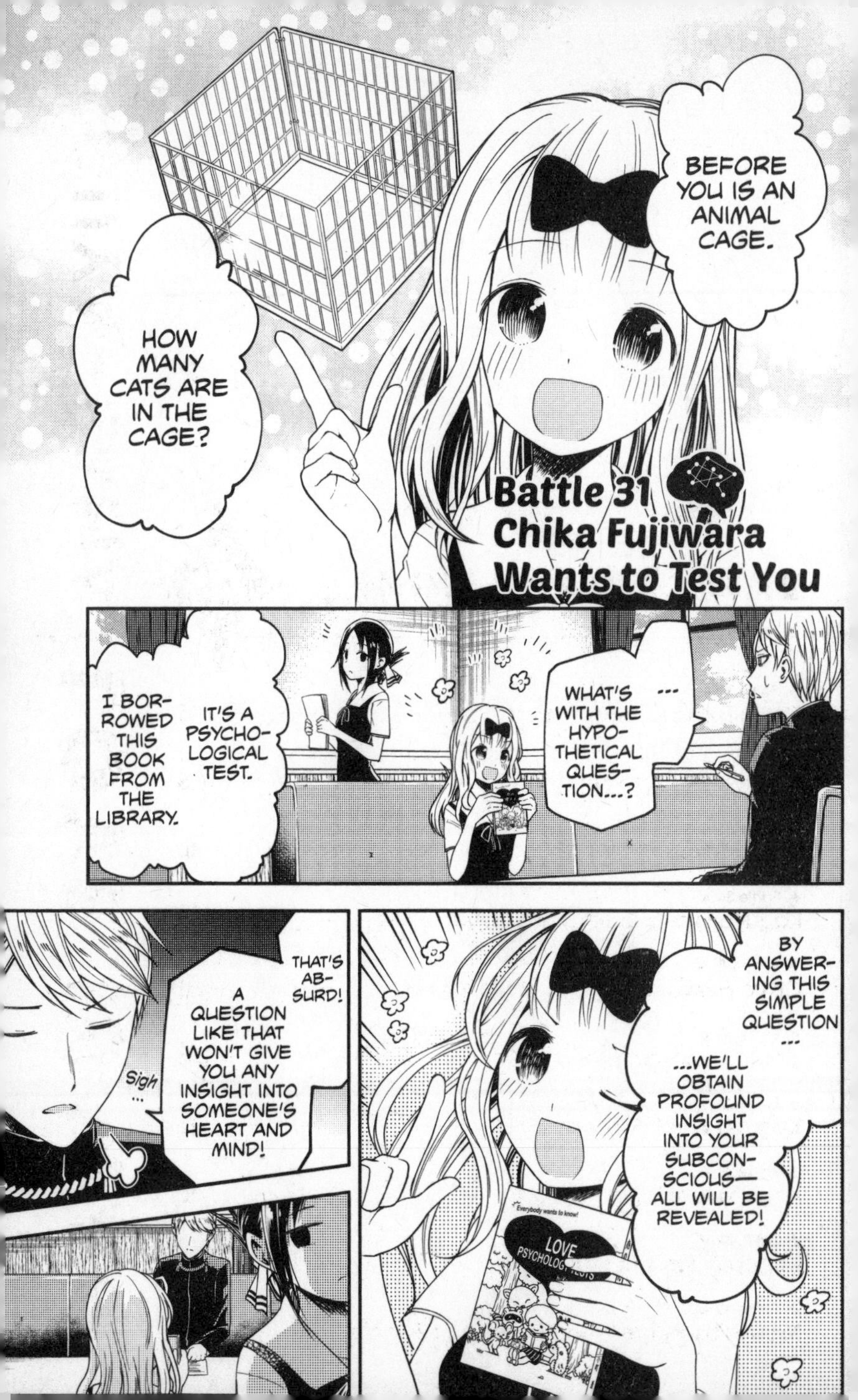
BEFORE YOU IS AN ANIMAL CAGE.
HOW MANY CATS ARE IN THE CAGE?
Battle 31 Chika Fujiwara Wants to Test You
WHAT'S WITH THE HYPOTHETICAL QUESTION...?
...
IT'S A PSYCHOLOGICAL TEST.
I BORROWED THIS BOOK FROM THE LIBRARY.
BY ANSWERING THIS SIMPLE QUESTION...
...WE'LL OBTAIN PROFOUND INSIGHT INTO YOUR SUBCONSCIOUS—ALL WILL BE REVEALED!
Everybody wants to know!
LOVE PSYCHOLOGY TESTS
THAT'S ABSURD!
A QUESTION LIKE THAT WON'T GIVE YOU ANY INSIGHT INTO SOMEONE'S HEART AND MIND!
Sigh...

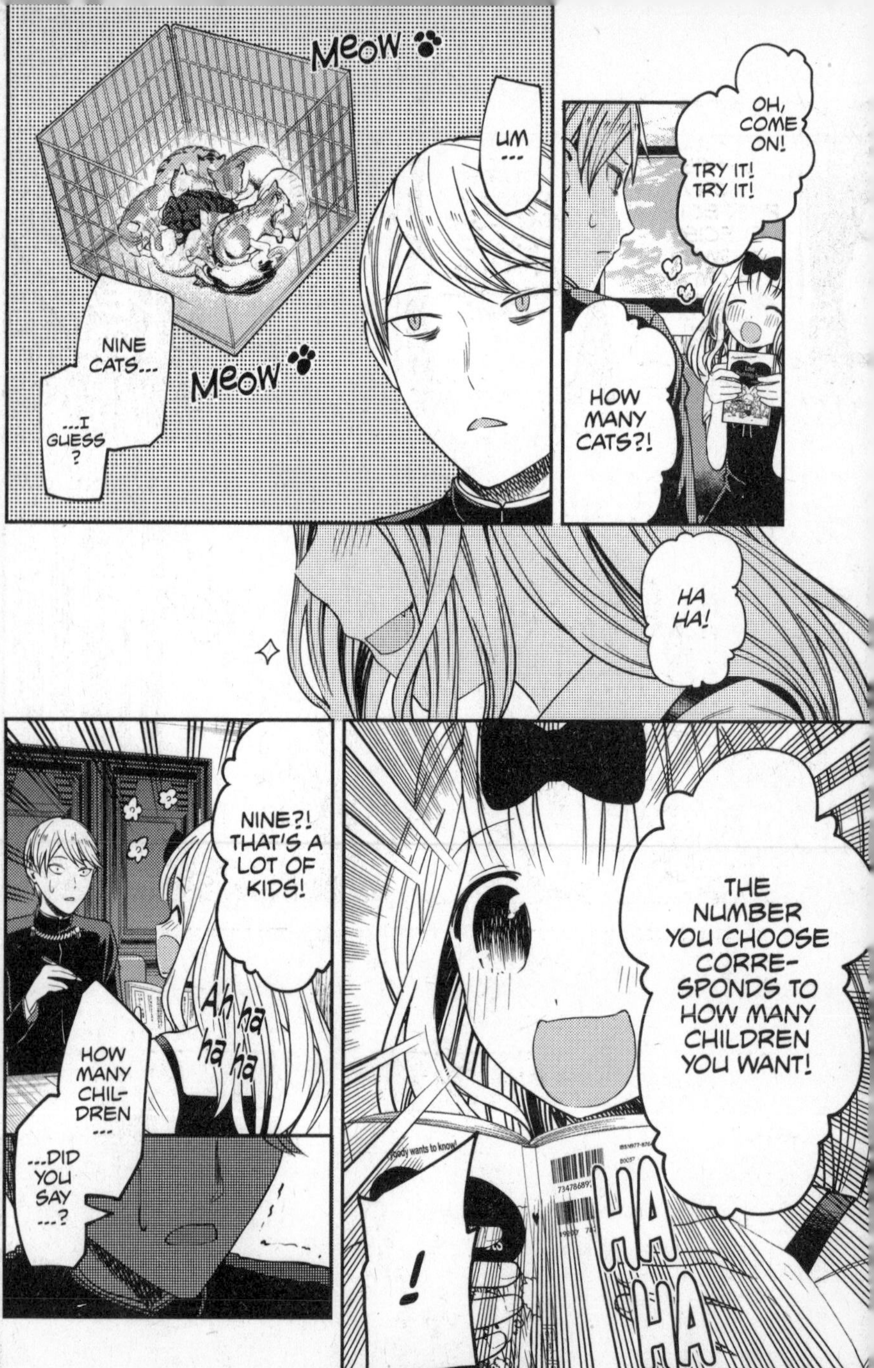
OH, COME ON!
TRY IT! TRY IT!
HOW MANY CATS?!
UM...
MEOW
NINE CATS...
...I GUESS?
MEOW
HA HA!
THE NUMBER YOU CHOOSE CORRE-SPONDS TO HOW MANY CHILDREN YOU WANT!
HA HA-
!
NINE?! THAT'S A LOT OF KIDS!
Ah ha ha ha
HOW MANY CHIL-DREN...
...DID YOU SAY...?

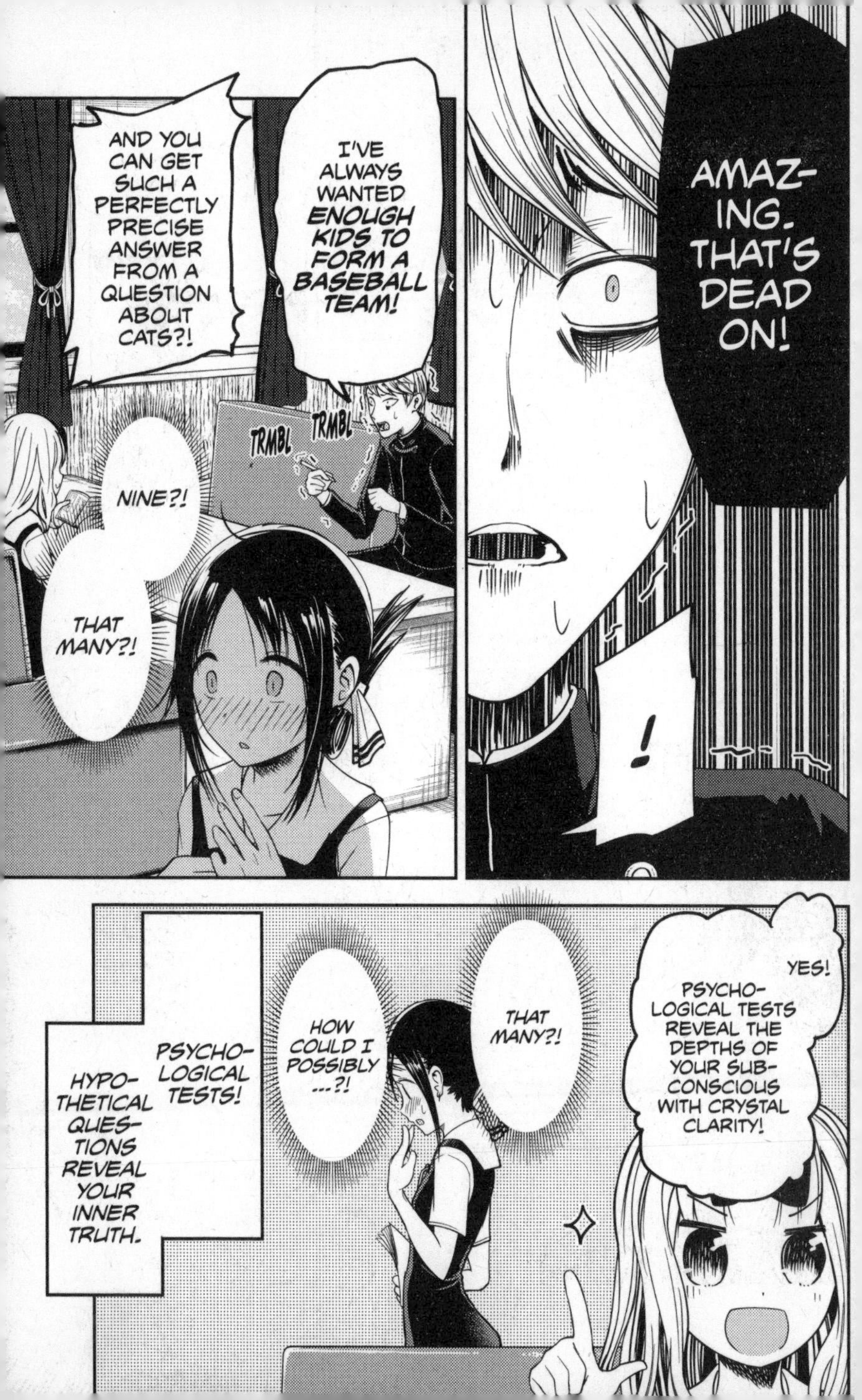
AMAZING. THAT'S DEAD ON!
!
I'VE ALWAYS WANTED ENOUGH KIDS TO FORM A BASEBALL TEAM!
AND YOU CAN GET SUCH A PERFECTLY PRECISE ANSWER FROM A QUESTION ABOUT CATS?!
TRMBL
TRMBL
NINE?!
THAT MANY?!
YES!
PSYCHOLOGICAL TESTS REVEAL THE DEPTHS OF YOUR SUBCONSCIOUS WITH CRYSTAL CLARITY!
THAT MANY?!
HOW COULD I POSSIBLY ...?!
PSYCHOLOGICAL TESTS!
HYPOTHETICAL QUESTIONS REVEAL YOUR INNER TRUTH.

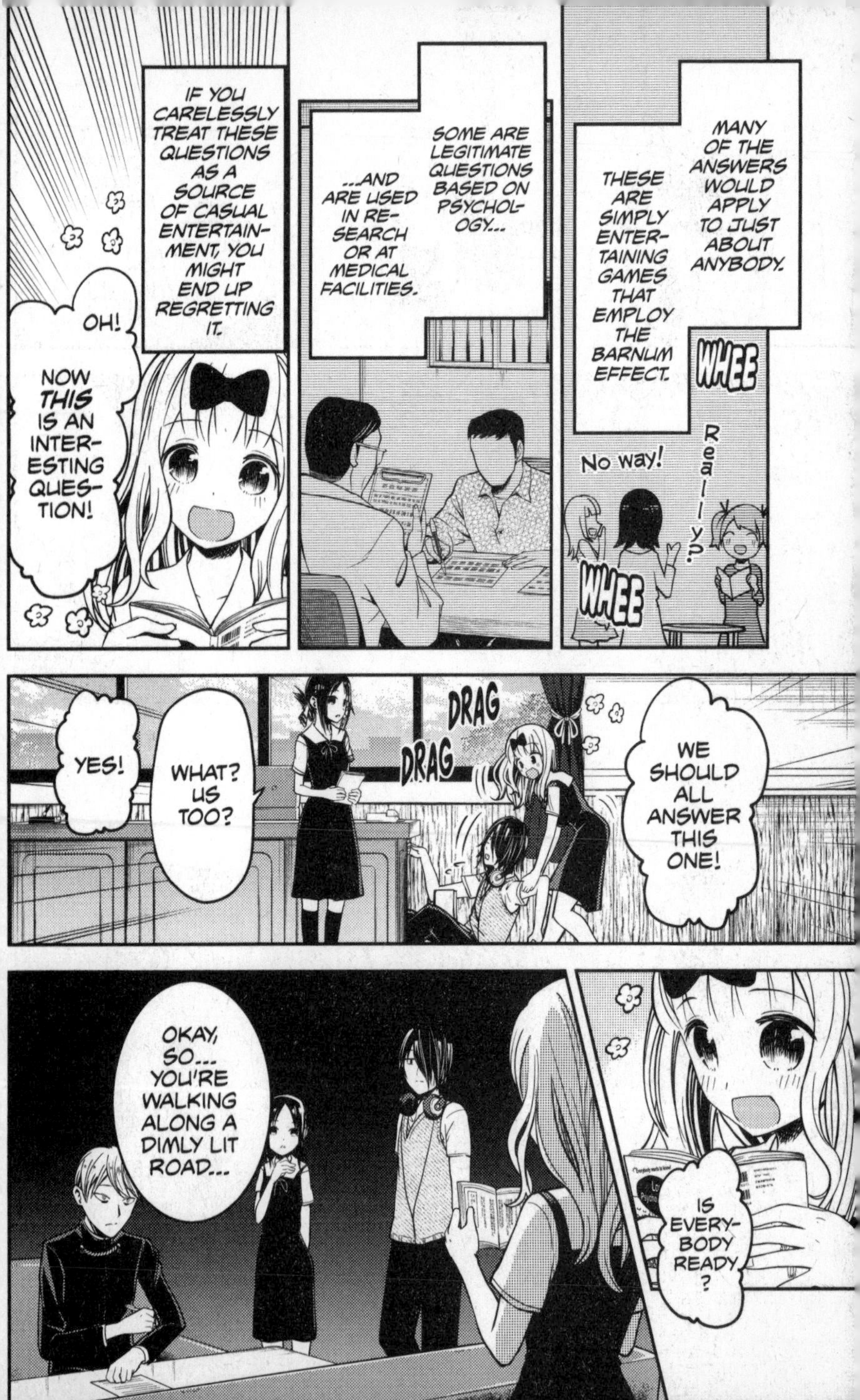
MANY OF THE ANSWERS WOULD APPLY TO JUST ABOUT ANYBODY.
THESE ARE SIMPLY ENTERTAINING GAMES THAT EMPLOY THE BARNUM EFFECT.
WHEE
Really?
No way!
WHEE
SOME ARE LEGITIMATE QUESTIONS BASED ON PSYCHOLOGY...
...AND ARE USED IN RESEARCH OR AT MEDICAL FACILITIES.
IF YOU CARELESSLY TREAT THESE QUESTIONS AS A SOURCE OF CASUAL ENTERTAINMENT, YOU MIGHT END UP REGRETTING IT.
OH!
NOW THIS IS AN INTERESTING QUESTION!
WE SHOULD ALL ANSWER THIS ONE!
DRAG
DRAG
WHAT? US TOO?
YES!
IS EVERYBODY READY?
OKAY, SO... YOU'RE WALKING ALONG A DIMLY LIT ROAD...

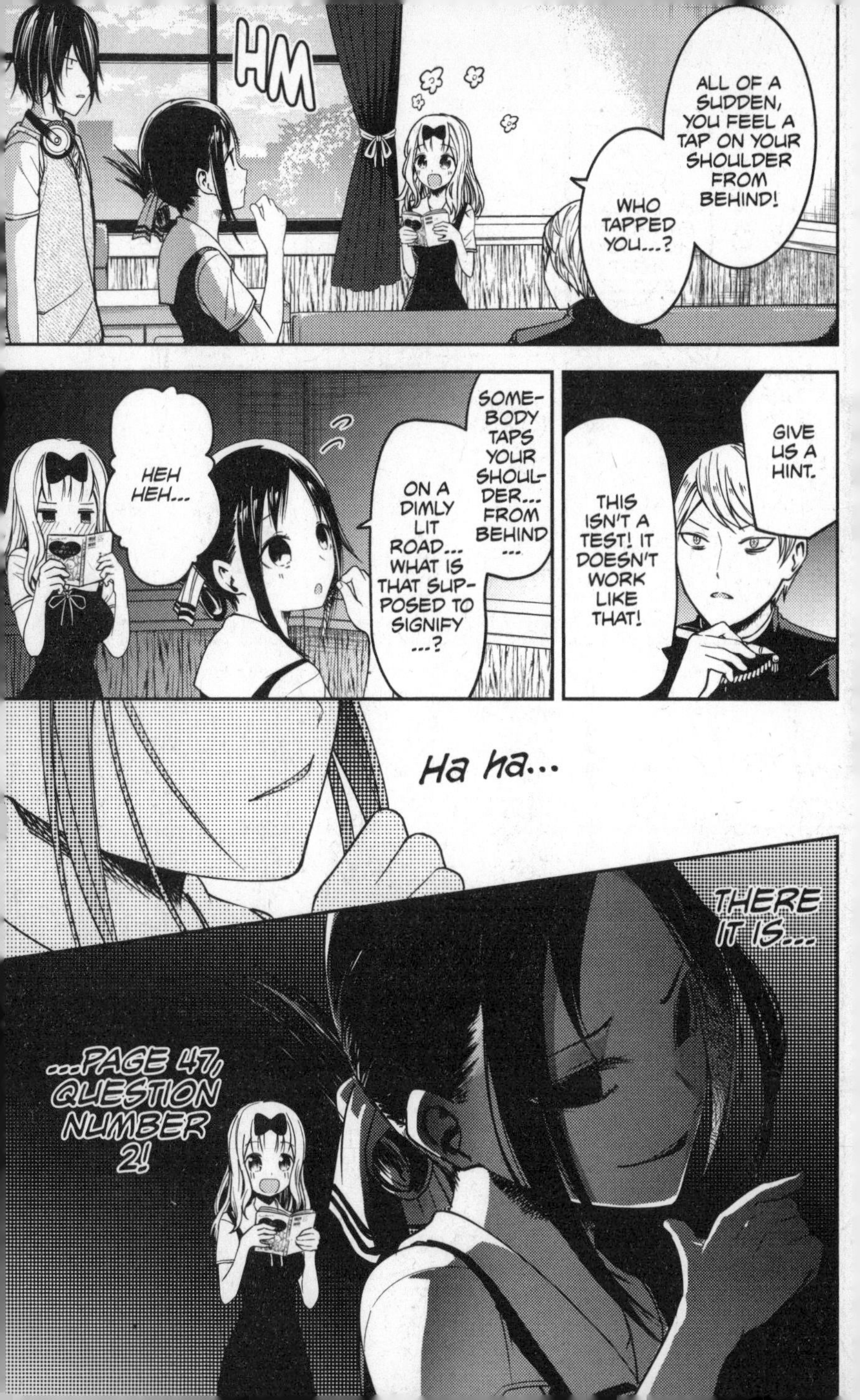
ALL OF A SUDDEN, YOU FEEL A TAP ON YOUR SHOULDER FROM BEHIND!
WHO TAPPED YOU...?
HM
GIVE US A HINT.
THIS ISN'T A TEST! IT DOESN'T WORK LIKE THAT!
SOMEBODY TAPS YOUR SHOULDER... FROM BEHIND...
ON A DIMLY LIT ROAD... WHAT IS THAT SUPPOSED TO SIGNIFY...?
HEH HEH...
Ha ha...
THERE IT IS...
...PAGE 47, QUESTION NUMBER 2!

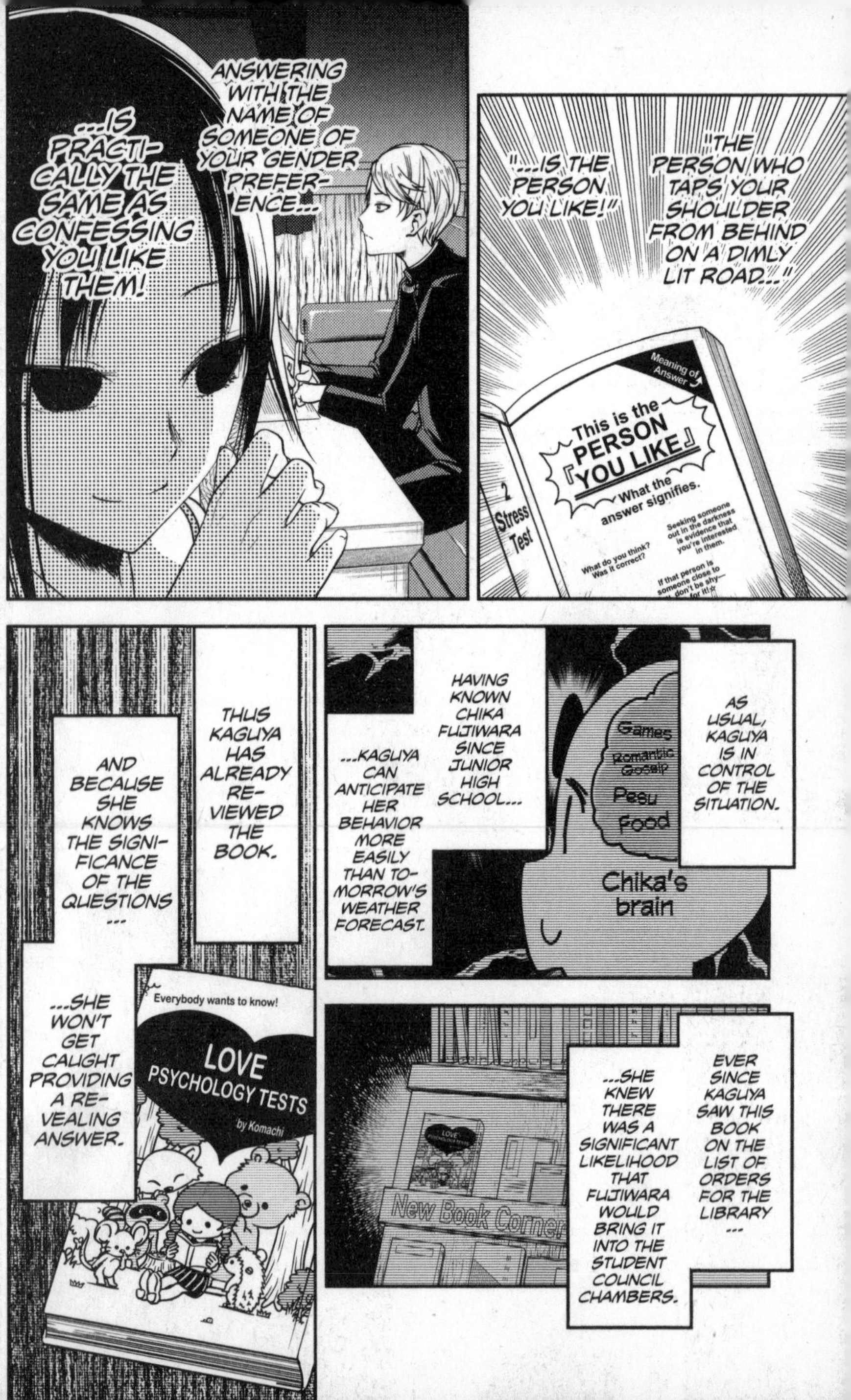
"THE PERSON WHO TAPS YOUR SHOULDER FROM BEHIND ON A DIMLY LIT ROAD..."
"...IS THE PERSON YOU LIKE!"
Meaning of Answer
2 Stress Test
This is the PERSON 『YOU LIKE』
What the answer signifies.
Seeking someone out in the darkness is evidence that you're interested in them.
What do you think? Was it correct?
If that person is someone close to
ANSWERING WITH THE NAME OF SOMEONE OF YOUR GENDER PREFERENCE...
...IS PRACTICALLY THE SAME AS CONFESSING YOU LIKE THEM!
AS USUAL, KAGUYA IS IN CONTROL OF THE SITUATION.
Games
Romantic Gossip
Pesu
Food
Chika's brain
HAVING KNOWN CHIKA FUJIWARA SINCE JUNIOR HIGH SCHOOL...
...KAGUYA CAN ANTICIPATE HER BEHAVIOR MORE EASILY THAN TOMORROW'S WEATHER FORECAST.
EVER SINCE KAGUYA SAW THIS BOOK ON THE LIST OF ORDERS FOR THE LIBRARY...
...SHE KNEW THERE WAS A SIGNIFICANT LIKELIHOOD THAT FUJIWARA WOULD BRING IT INTO THE STUDENT COUNCIL CHAMBERS.
New Book Corner
THUS KAGUYA HAS ALREADY REVIEWED THE BOOK.
AND BECAUSE SHE KNOWS THE SIGNIFICANCE OF THE QUESTIONS...
...SHE WON'T GET CAUGHT PROVIDING A REVEALING ANSWER.
Everybody wants to know!
LOVE PSYCHOLOGY TESTS
by Komachi

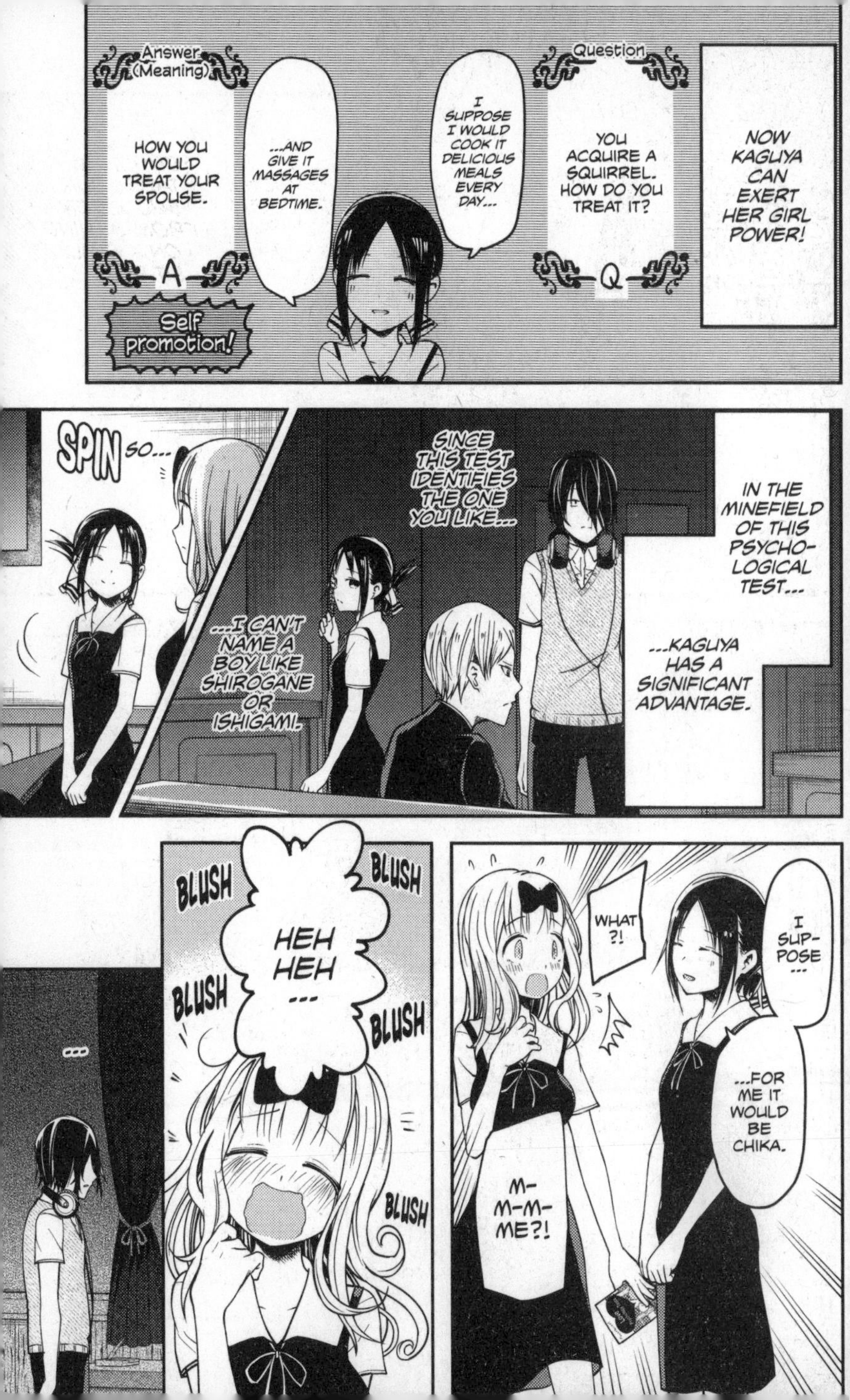
NOW KAGUYA CAN EXERT HER GIRL POWER!
Question
YOU ACQUIRE A SQUIRREL. HOW DO YOU TREAT IT?
Q
I SUPPOSE I WOULD COOK IT DELICIOUS MEALS EVERY DAY...
...AND GIVE IT MASSAGES AT BEDTIME.
Answer (Meaning)
HOW YOU WOULD TREAT YOUR SPOUSE.
A
Self promotion!
IN THE MINEFIELD OF THIS PSYCHOLOGICAL TEST...
...KAGUYA HAS A SIGNIFICANT ADVANTAGE.
SINCE THIS TEST IDENTIFIES THE ONE YOU LIKE...
...I CAN'T NAME A BOY LIKE SHIROGANE OR ISHIGAMI.
SO...
SPIN
I SUPPOSE...
...FOR ME IT WOULD BE CHIKA.
WHAT?!
M-M-M-ME?!
BLUSH
BLUSH
HEH HEH...
BLUSH
BLUSH
BLUSH
...

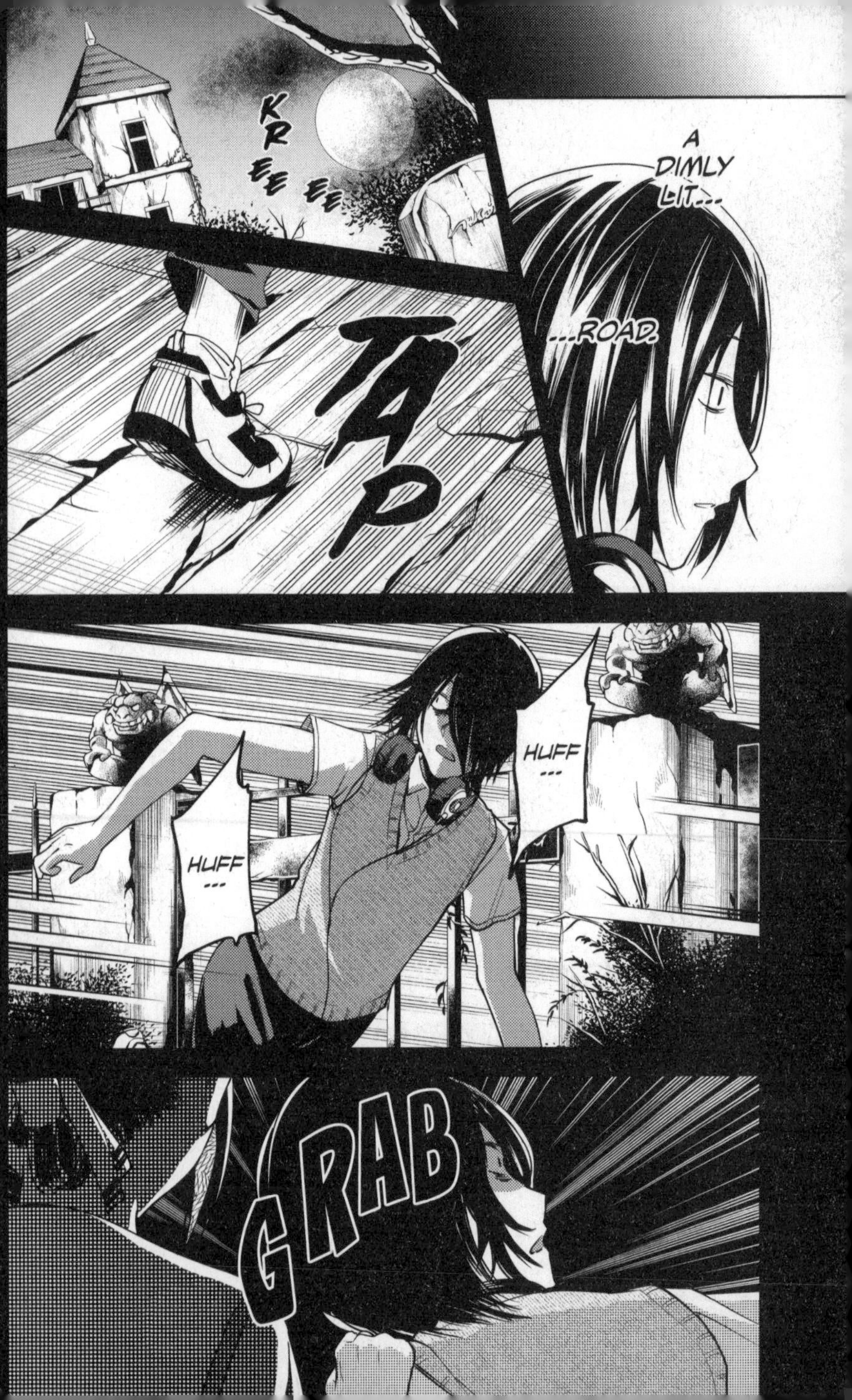
A DIMLY LIT...
...ROAD.
KREEEEE
TAP
HUFF...
HUFF...
GRAB

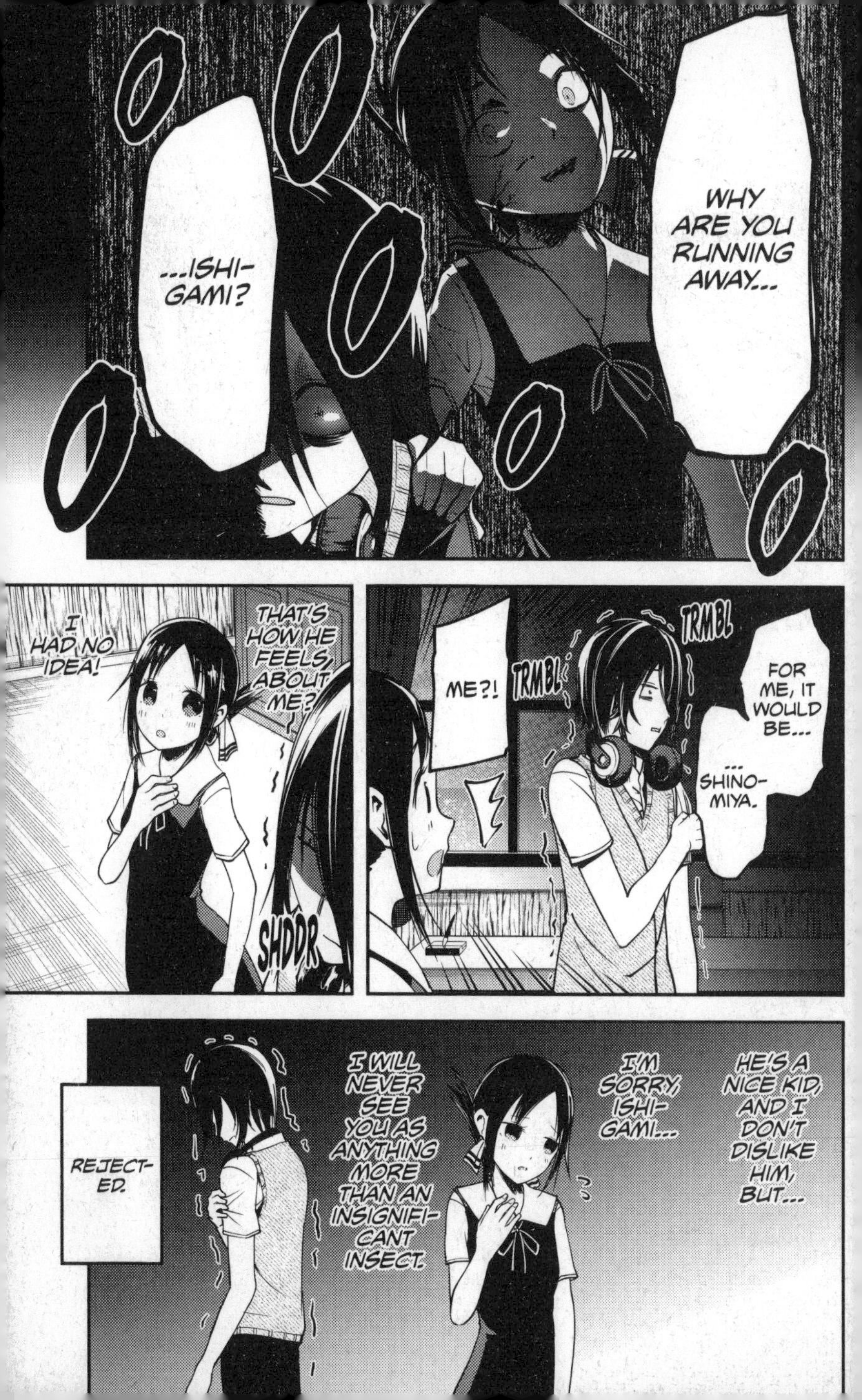
WHY ARE YOU RUNNING AWAY...
...ISHI-GAMI?
TRMBL
FOR ME, IT WOULD BE...
...SHINO-MIYA.
TRMBL
ME?!
THAT'S HOW HE FEELS, ABOUT ME?
I HAD NO IDEA!
SHDDR
HE'S A NICE KID, AND I DON'T DISLIKE HIM, BUT...
I'M SORRY, ISHI-GAMI...
I WILL NEVER SEE YOU AS ANYTHING MORE THAN AN INSIGNIFI-CANT INSECT.
REJECT-ED.

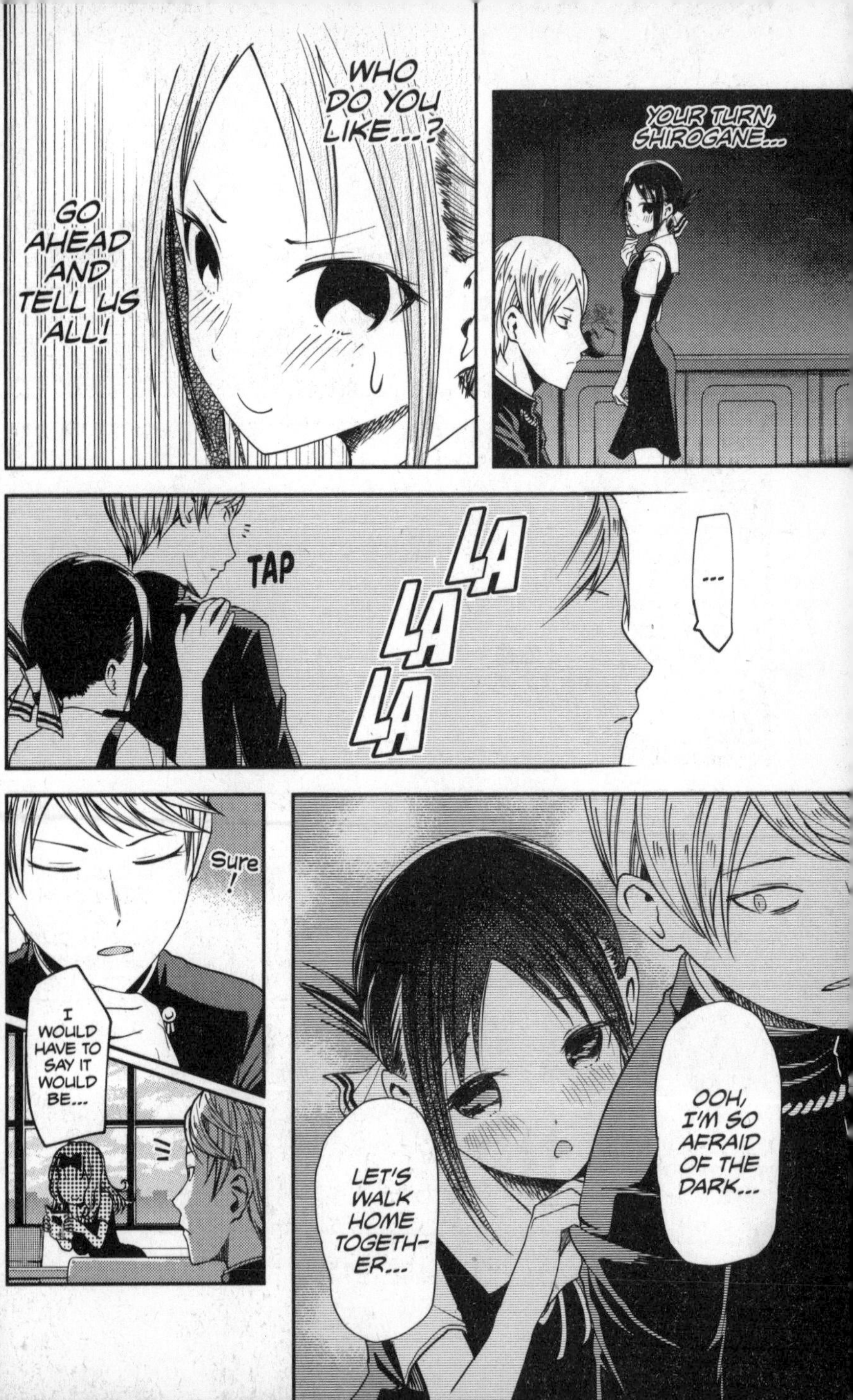
YOUR TURN, SHIROGANE...
WHO DO YOU LIKE...?
GO AHEAD AND TELL US ALL!
...
LA LA LA
TAP
OOH, I'M SO AFRAID OF THE DARK...
LET'S WALK HOME TOGETH-ER...
Sure!
I WOULD HAVE TO SAY IT WOULD BE...

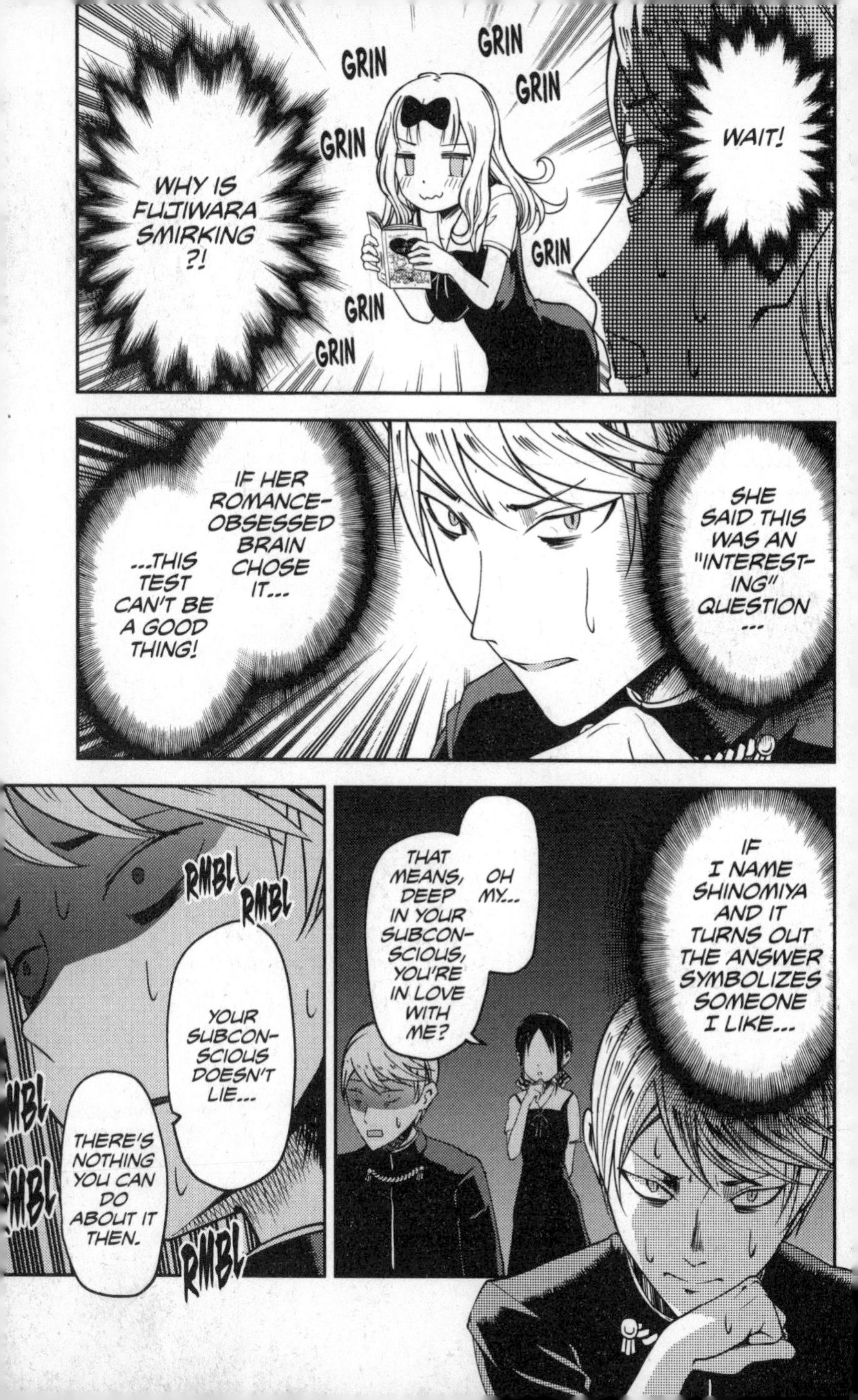
WAIT!
GRIN
GRIN
GRIN
GRIN
GRIN
GRIN
GRIN
WHY IS FUJIWARA SMIRKING ?!
SHE SAID THIS WAS AN "INTERESTING" QUESTION...
IF HER ROMANCE-OBSESSED BRAIN CHOSE IT...
...THIS TEST CAN'T BE A GOOD THING!
IF I NAME SHINOMIYA AND IT TURNS OUT THE ANSWER SYMBOLIZES SOMEONE I LIKE...
OH MY...
THAT MEANS, DEEP IN YOUR SUBCONSCIOUS, YOU'RE IN LOVE WITH ME?
RMBL
RMBL
YOUR SUBCONSCIOUS DOESN'T LIE...
THERE'S NOTHING YOU CAN DO ABOUT IT THEN.
RMBL

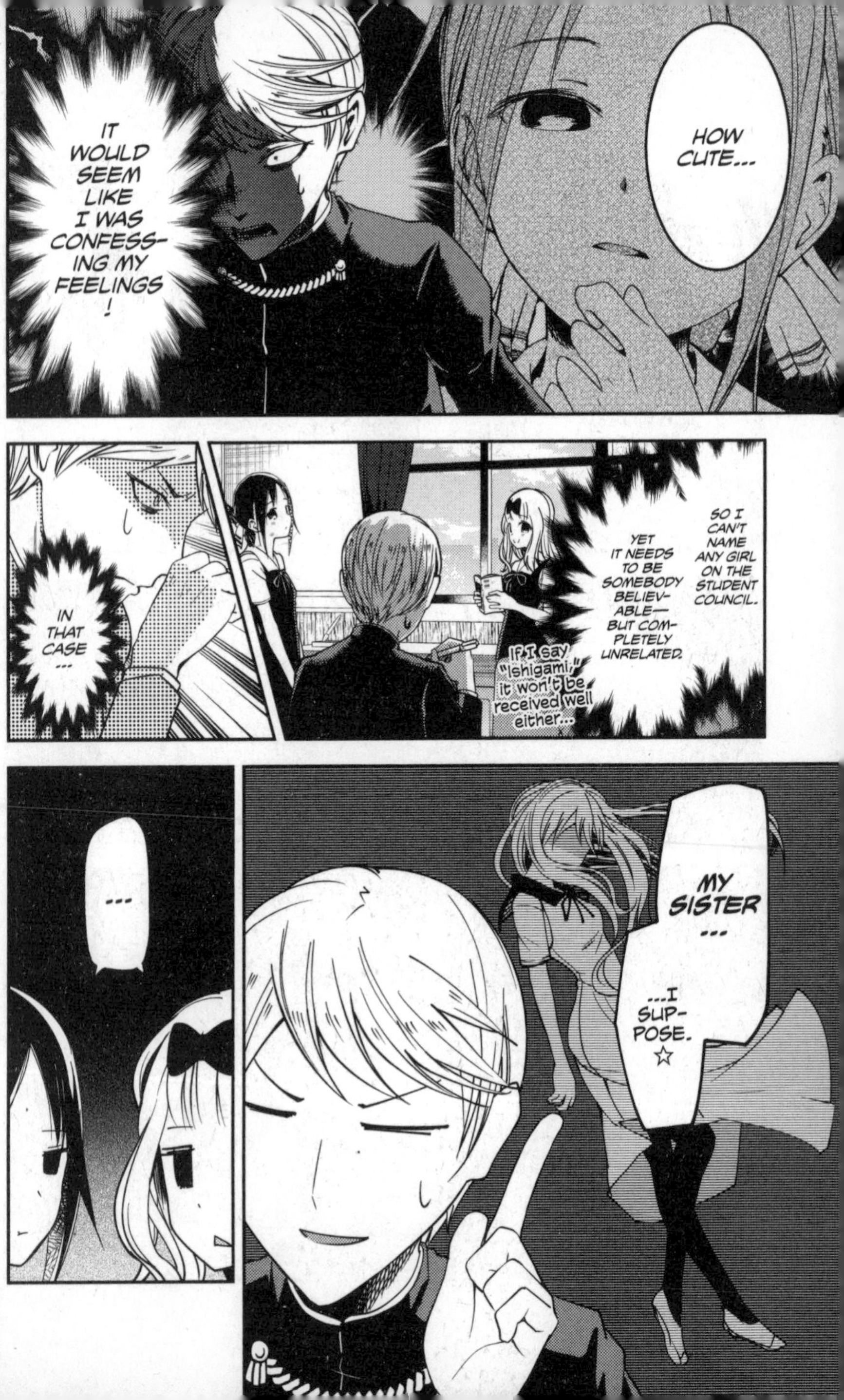
HOW CUTE...
IT WOULD SEEM LIKE I WAS CONFESSING MY FEELINGS!
SO I CAN'T NAME ANY GIRL ON THE STUDENT COUNCIL.
YET IT NEEDS TO BE SOMEBODY BELIEVABLE—BUT COMPLETELY UNRELATED.
If I say "Ishigami," it won't be received well either...
IN THAT CASE...
MY SISTER... ...I SUPPOSE.☆
...

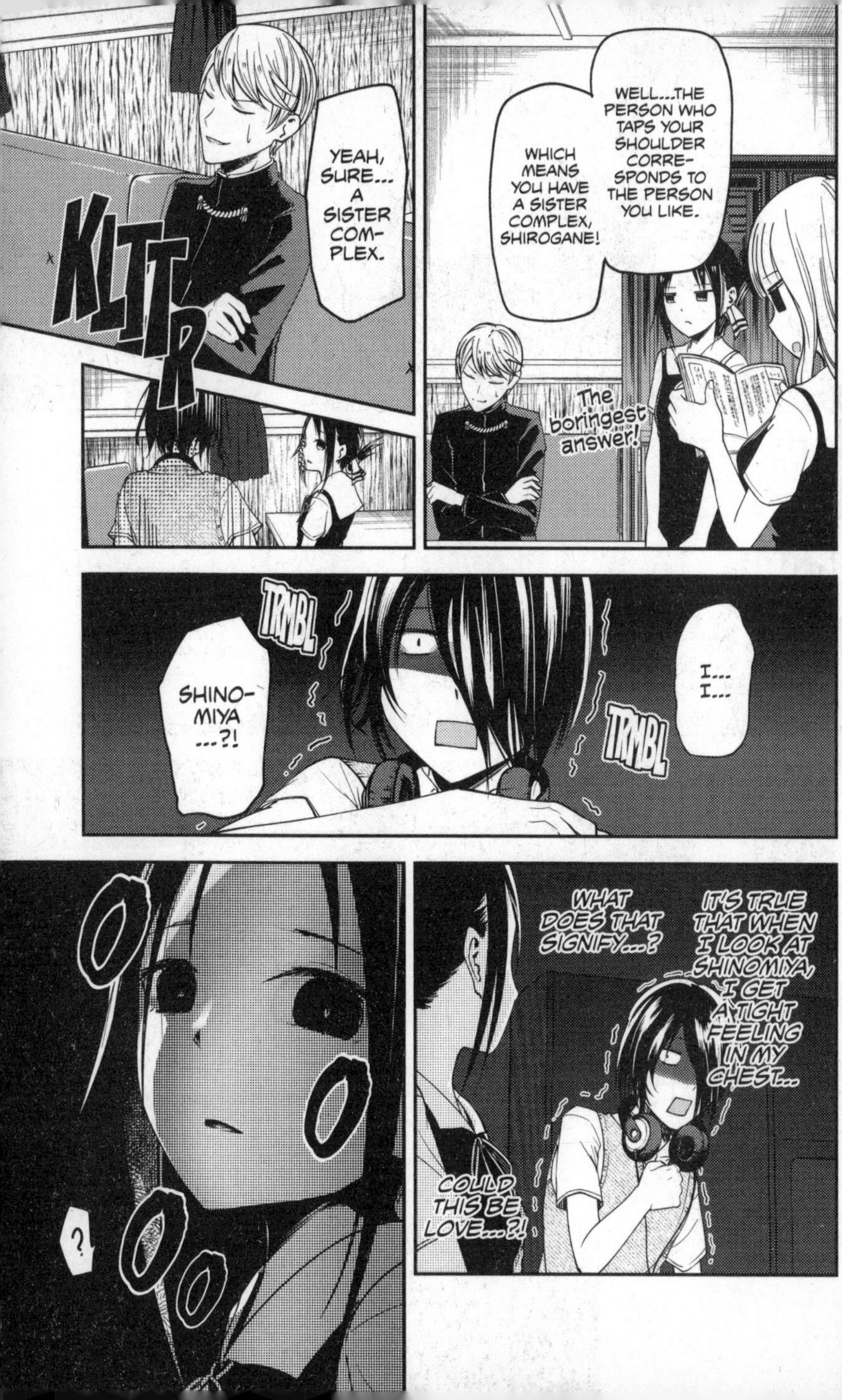
WELL...THE PERSON WHO TAPS YOUR SHOULDER CORRE-SPONDS TO THE PERSON YOU LIKE.
WHICH MEANS YOU HAVE A SISTER COMPLEX, SHIROGANE!
The boringest answer!
YEAH, SURE... A SISTER COM-PLEX.
KLTTR
I... I...
TRMBL
TRMBL
SHINO-MIYA ...?!
IT'S TRUE THAT WHEN I LOOK AT SHINOMIYA, I GET A TIGHT FEELING IN MY CHEST...
WHAT DOES THAT SIGNIFY...?
COULD THIS BE LOVE...?!
?

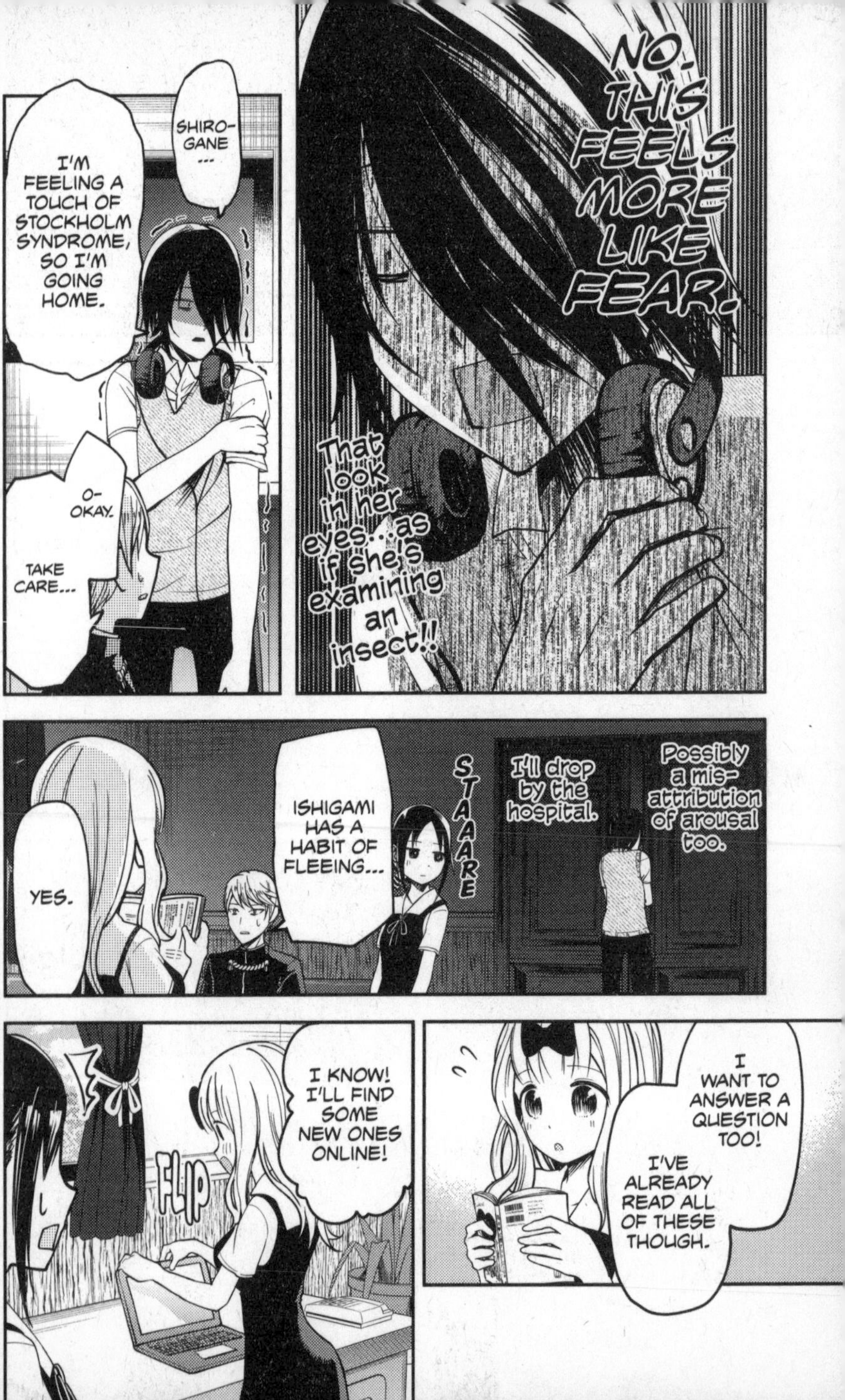
NO-THIS FEELS MORE LIKE FEAR.
That look in her eyes...as if she's examining an insect!!
SHIRO-GANE...
I'M FEELING A TOUCH OF STOCKHOLM SYNDROME, SO I'M GOING HOME.
O-OKAY.
TAKE CARE...
Possibly a mis-attribution of arousal too.
I'll drop by the hospital.
STAAAARE
ISHIGAMI HAS A HABIT OF FLEEING...
YES.
I WANT TO ANSWER A QUESTION TOO!
I'VE ALREADY READ ALL OF THESE THOUGH.
I KNOW! I'LL FIND SOME NEW ONES ONLINE!
FLIP

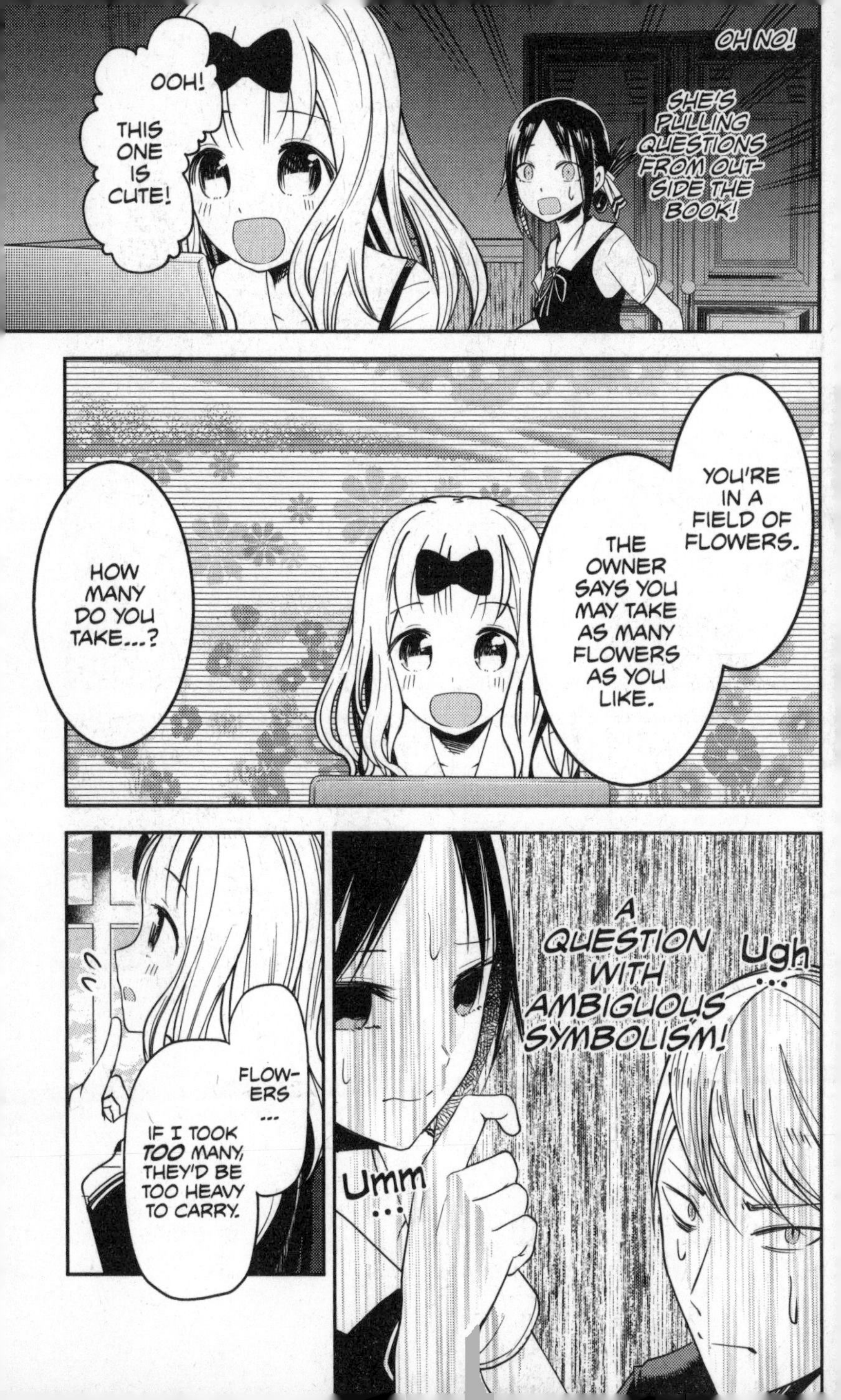
OH NO!
SHE'S PULLING QUESTIONS FROM OUT-SIDE THE BOOK!
OOH!
THIS ONE IS CUTE!
YOU'RE IN A FIELD OF FLOWERS.
THE OWNER SAYS YOU MAY TAKE AS MANY FLOWERS AS YOU LIKE.
HOW MANY DO YOU TAKE...?
Ugh...
A QUESTION WITH AMBIGUOUS SYMBOLISM!
Umm...
FLOW-ERS...
IF I TOOK *TOO* MANY, THEY'D BE TOO HEAVY TO CARRY.

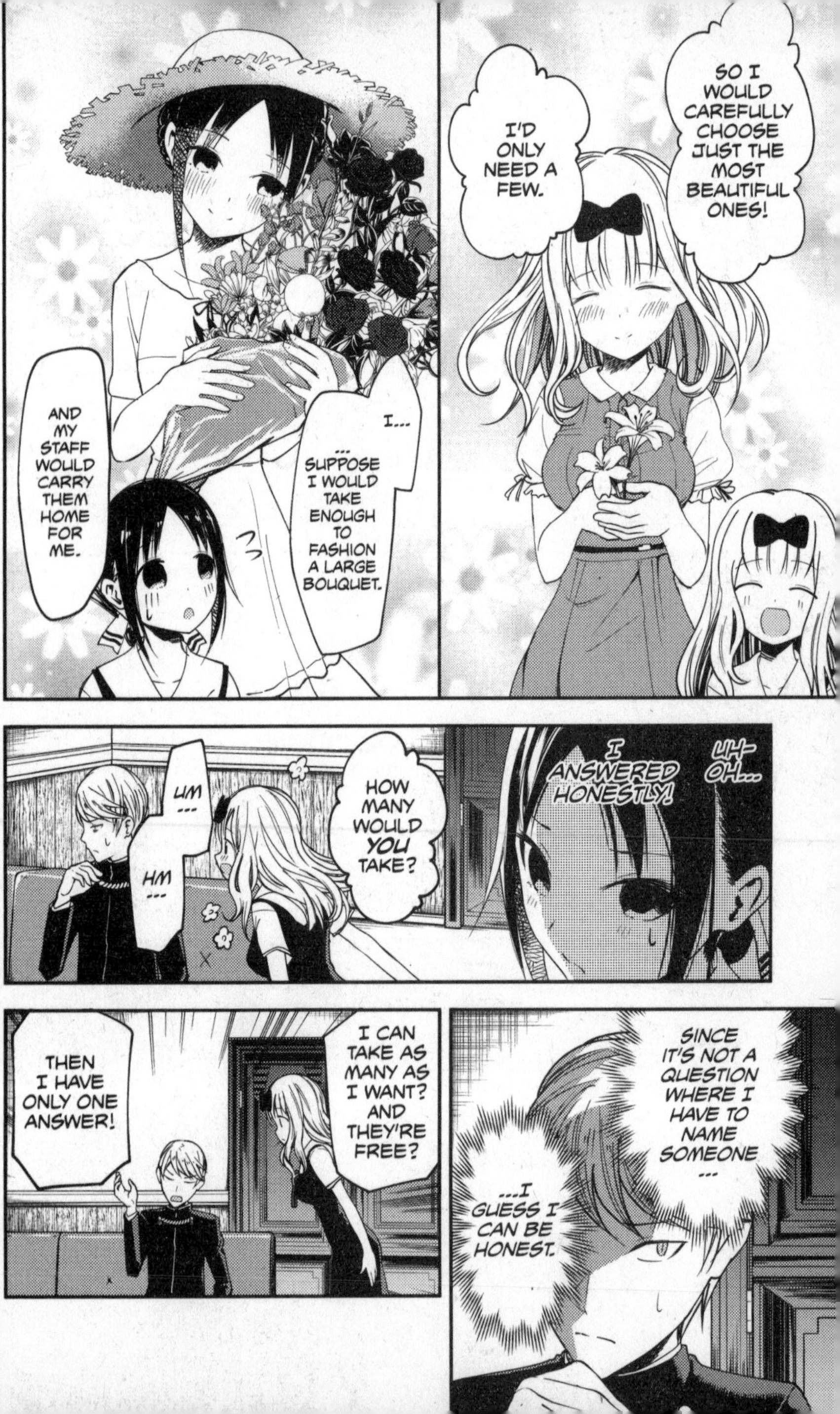
SO I WOULD CAREFULLY CHOOSE JUST THE MOST BEAUTIFUL ONES!
I'D ONLY NEED A FEW.
I...
...SUPPOSE I WOULD TAKE ENOUGH TO FASHION A LARGE BOUQUET.
AND MY STAFF WOULD CARRY THEM HOME FOR ME.
UH-OH...
I ANSWERED HONESTLY!
HOW MANY WOULD YOU TAKE?
UM...
HM...
SINCE IT'S NOT A QUESTION WHERE I HAVE TO NAME SOMEONE...
...I GUESS I CAN BE HONEST.
I CAN TAKE AS MANY AS I WANT? AND THEY'RE FREE?
THEN I HAVE ONLY ONE ANSWER!

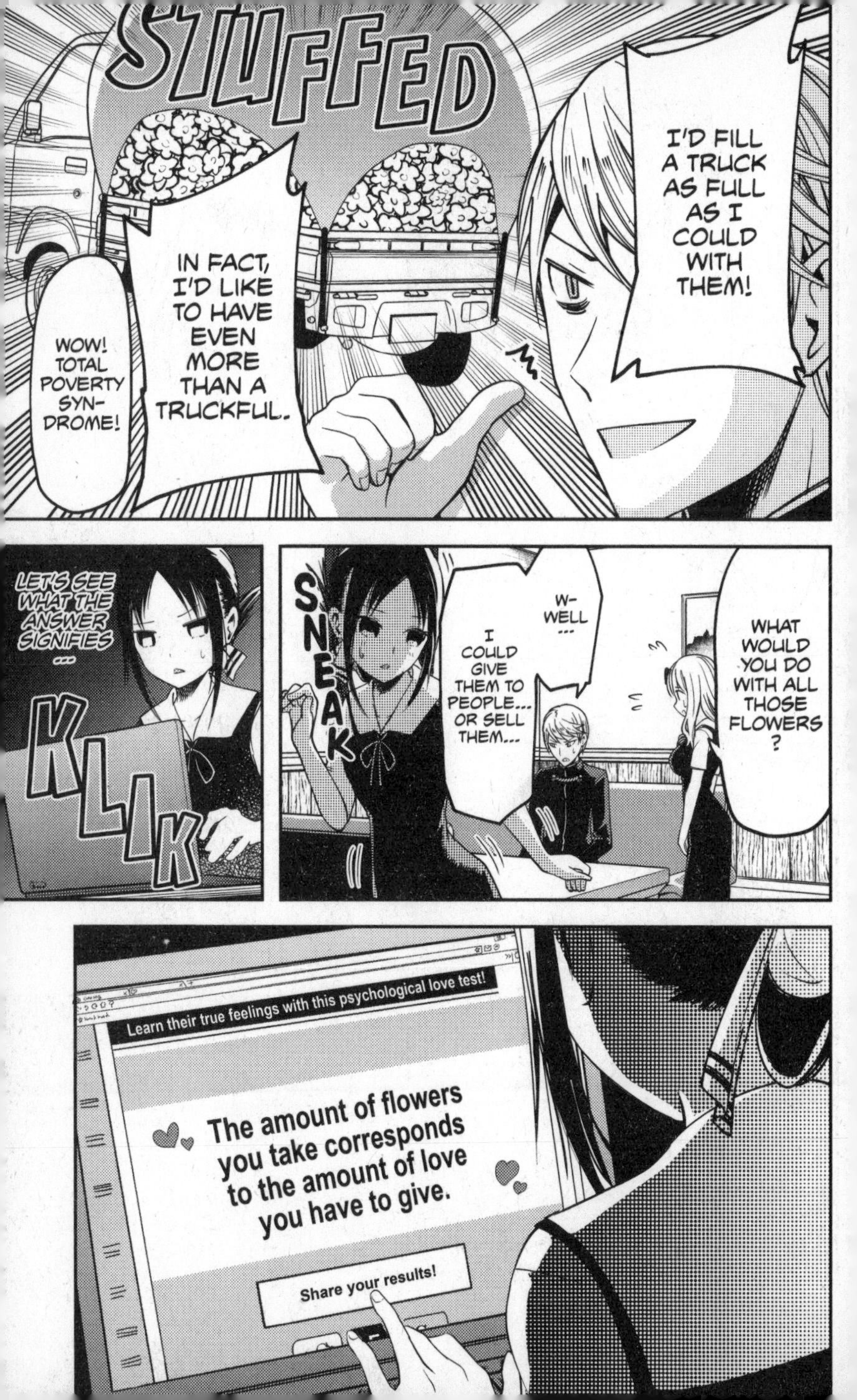
I'D FILL A TRUCK AS FULL AS I COULD WITH THEM!
STUFFED
IN FACT, I'D LIKE TO HAVE EVEN MORE THAN A TRUCKFUL.
WOW! TOTAL POVERTY SYNDROME!
WHAT WOULD YOU DO WITH ALL THOSE FLOWERS?
W-WELL...
I COULD GIVE THEM TO PEOPLE... OR SELL THEM...
SNEAK
LET'S SEE WHAT THE ANSWER SIGNIFIES...
KLIK
Learn their true feelings with this psychological love test!
The amount of flowers you take corresponds to the amount of love you have to give.
Share your results!

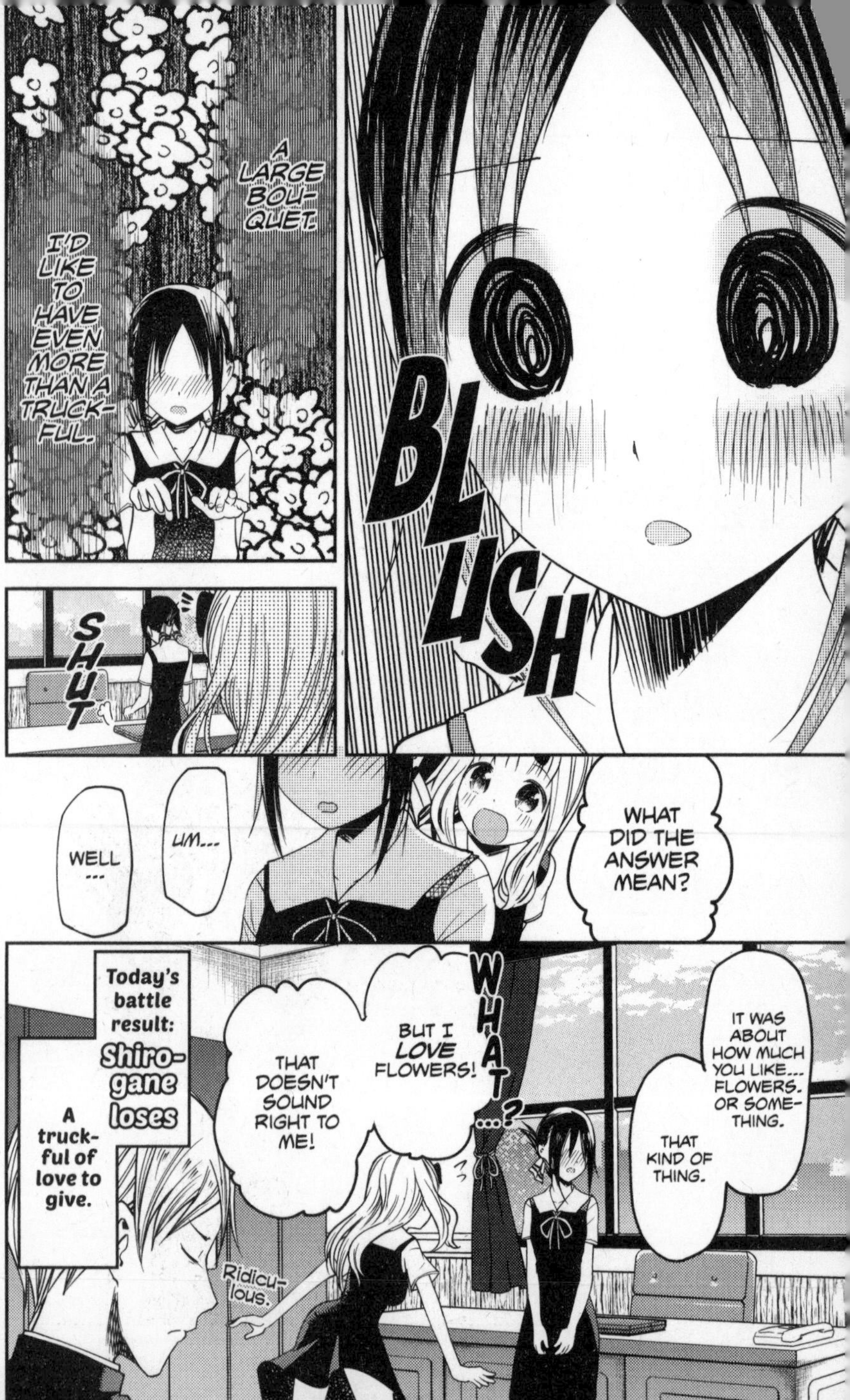
BLUSH
A LARGE BOUQUET.
I'D LIKE TO HAVE EVEN MORE THAN A TRUCKFUL.
SHUT
WHAT DID THE ANSWER MEAN?
UM...
WELL...
IT WAS ABOUT HOW MUCH YOU LIKE... FLOWERS. OR SOMETHING.
THAT KIND OF THING.
WHAT...?
BUT I LOVE FLOWERS!
THAT DOESN'T SOUND RIGHT TO ME!
Ridiculous.
Today's battle result: Shirogane loses
A truckful of love to give.

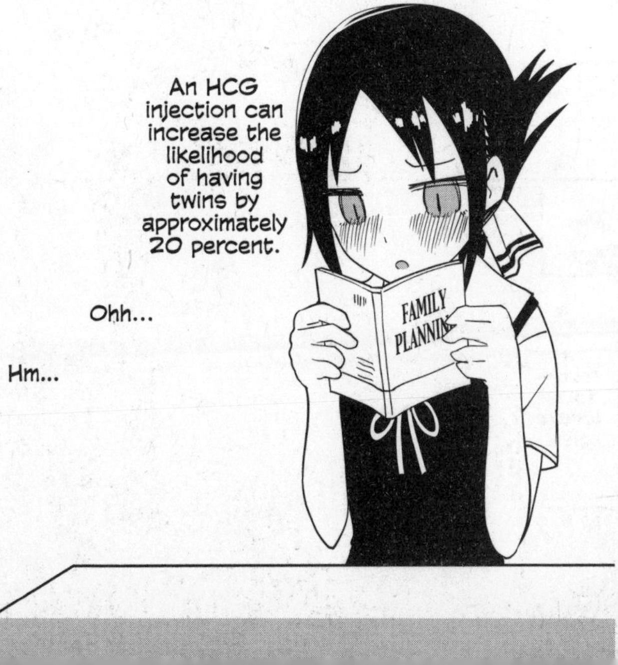
An HCG injection can increase the likelihood of having twins by approximately 20 percent.
FAMILY PLANNIN
Ohh...
Hm...

KAGUYA-SAMA

LOVE IS WAR

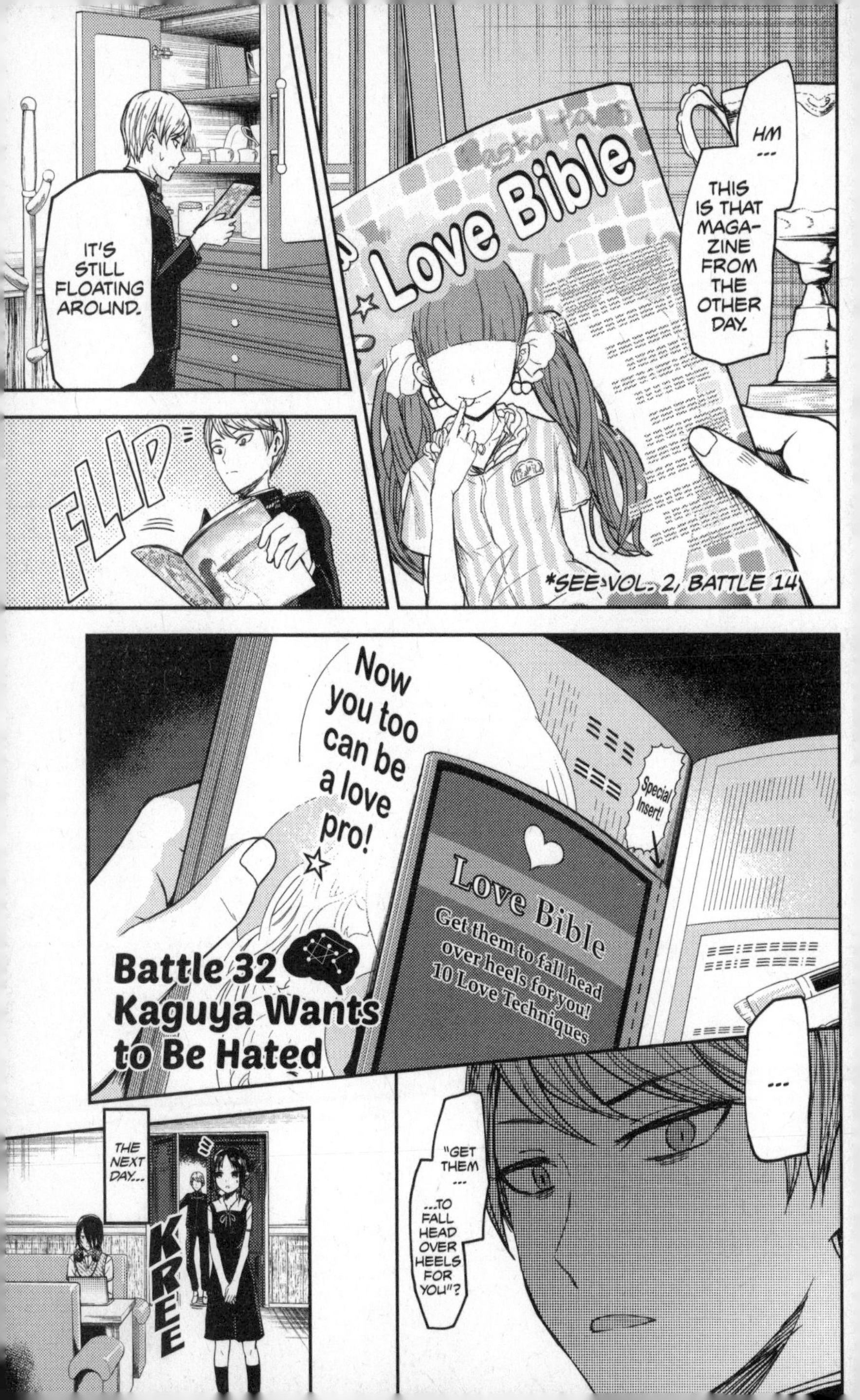
HM...
THIS IS THAT MAGAZINE FROM THE OTHER DAY.
Love Bible
*SEE VOL. 2, BATTLE 14
IT'S STILL FLOATING AROUND.
FLIP
Now you too can be a love pro!
Special Insert!
Love Bible
Get them to fall head over heels for you! 10 Love Techniques
Battle 32 Kaguya Wants to Be Hated
...
"GET THEM...
...TO FALL HEAD OVER HEELS FOR YOU"?
THE NEXT DAY...
KREE

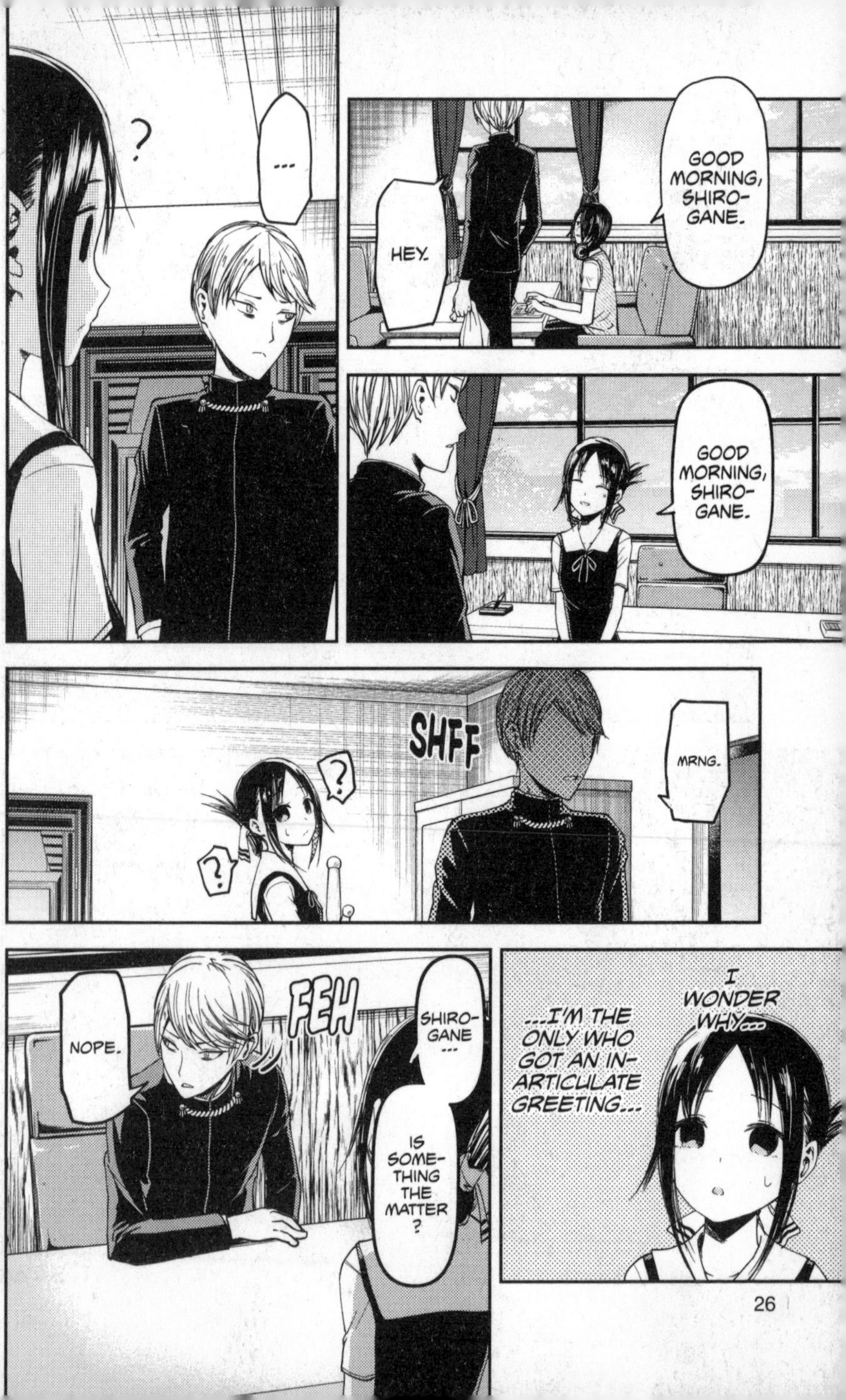
GOOD MORNING, SHIRO-GANE.
HEY.
GOOD MORNING, SHIRO-GANE.
...
?
MRNG.
SHFF
?
?
I WONDER WHY...
...I'M THE ONLY WHO GOT AN IN-ARTICULATE GREETING...
SHIRO-GANE ...
IS SOME-THING THE MATTER ?
FEH
NOPE.

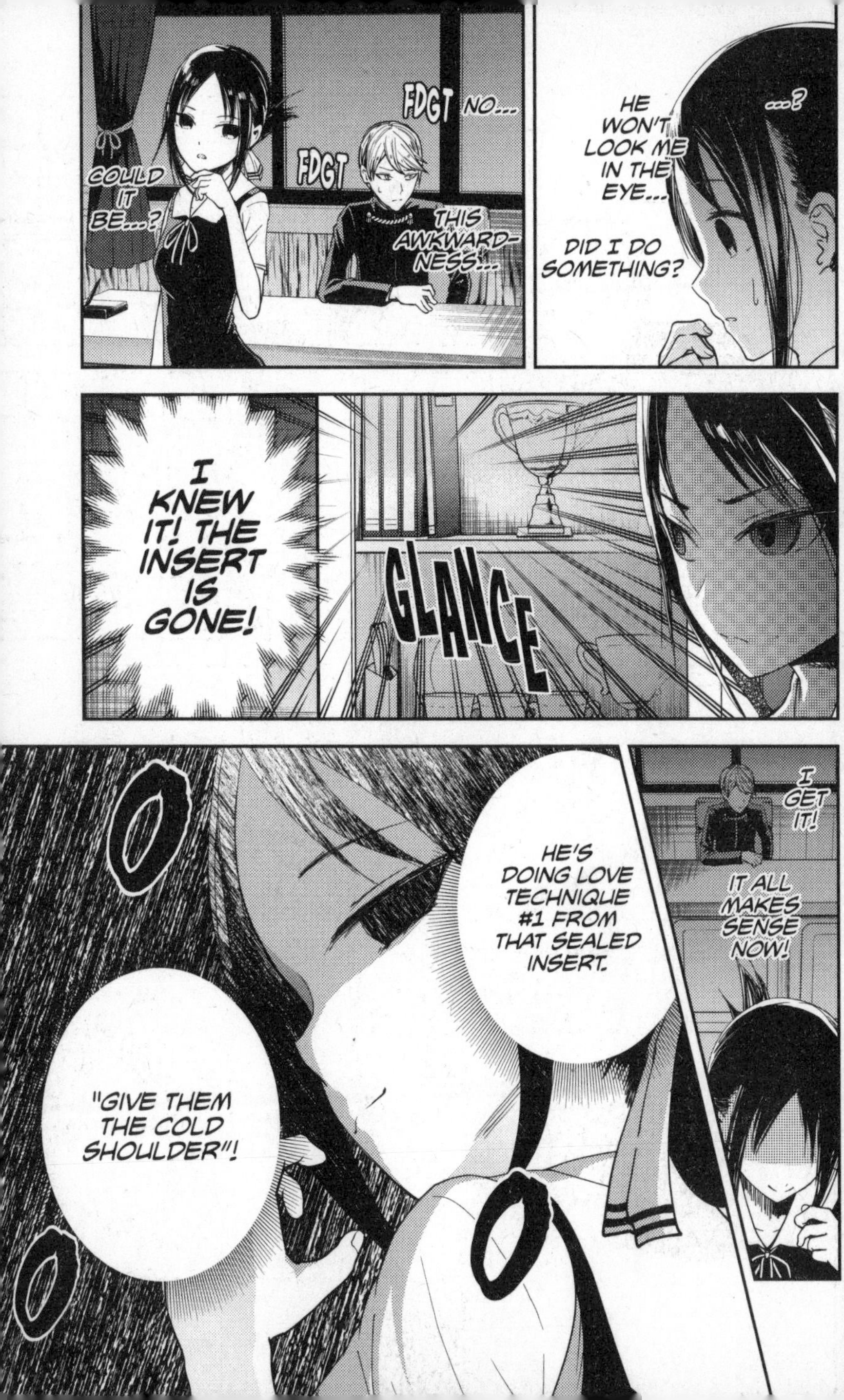
...?
HE WON'T LOOK ME IN THE EYE...
DID I DO SOMETHING?
FDGT
NO...
FDGT
THIS AWKWARD-NESS...
COULD IT BE...?
GLANCE
I KNEW IT! THE INSERT IS GONE!
I GET IT!
IT ALL MAKES SENSE NOW!
HE'S DOING LOVE TECHNIQUE #1 FROM THAT SEALED INSERT.
"GIVE THEM THE COLD SHOULDER"!

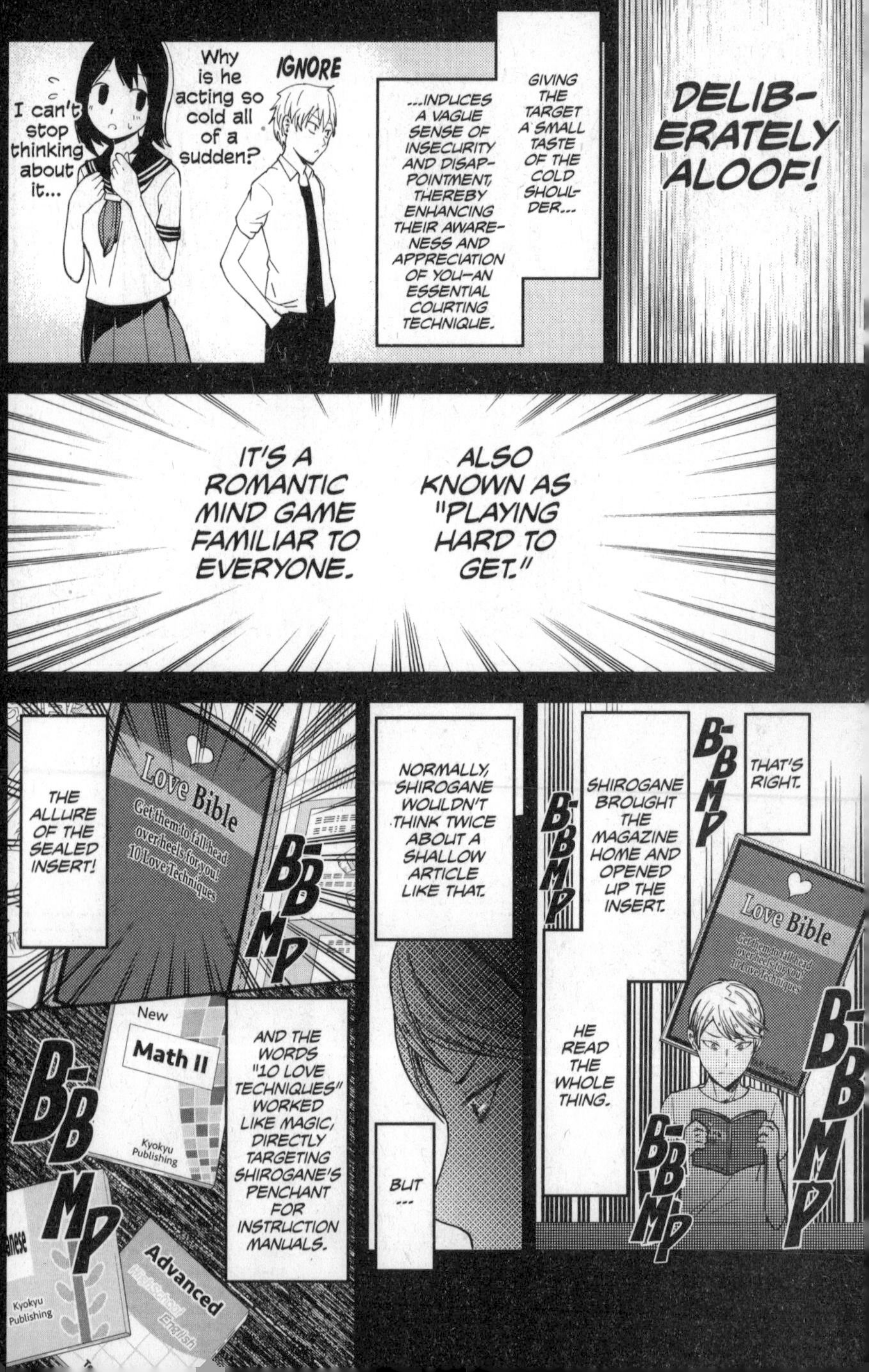
DELIB-ERATELY ALOOF!
GIVING THE TARGET A SMALL TASTE OF THE COLD SHOULDER...
...INDUCES A VAGUE SENSE OF INSECURITY AND DISAPPOINTMENT, THEREBY ENHANCING THEIR AWARENESS AND APPRECIATION OF YOU—AN ESSENTIAL COURTING TECHNIQUE.
IGNORE
Why is he acting so cold all of a sudden?
I can't stop thinking about it...
IT'S A ROMANTIC MIND GAME FAMILIAR TO EVERYONE.
ALSO KNOWN AS "PLAYING HARD TO GET."
THAT'S RIGHT.
B-B-BMP
SHIROGANE BROUGHT THE MAGAZINE HOME AND OPENED UP THE INSERT.
B-B-BMP
Love Bible
HE READ THE WHOLE THING.
B-B-BMP
B-B-BMP
NORMALLY, SHIROGANE WOULDN'T THINK TWICE ABOUT A SHALLOW ARTICLE LIKE THAT.
BUT ---
THE ALLURE OF THE SEALED INSERT!
Love Bible
Get them to fall head over heels for you!
10 Love Techniques
B-B-BMP
AND THE WORDS "10 LOVE TECHNIQUES" WORKED LIKE MAGIC, DIRECTLY TARGETING SHIROGANE'S PENCHANT FOR INSTRUCTION MANUALS.
New
Math II
Kyokyu Publishing
B-B-BMP
Kyokyu Publishing
Advanced
High School English

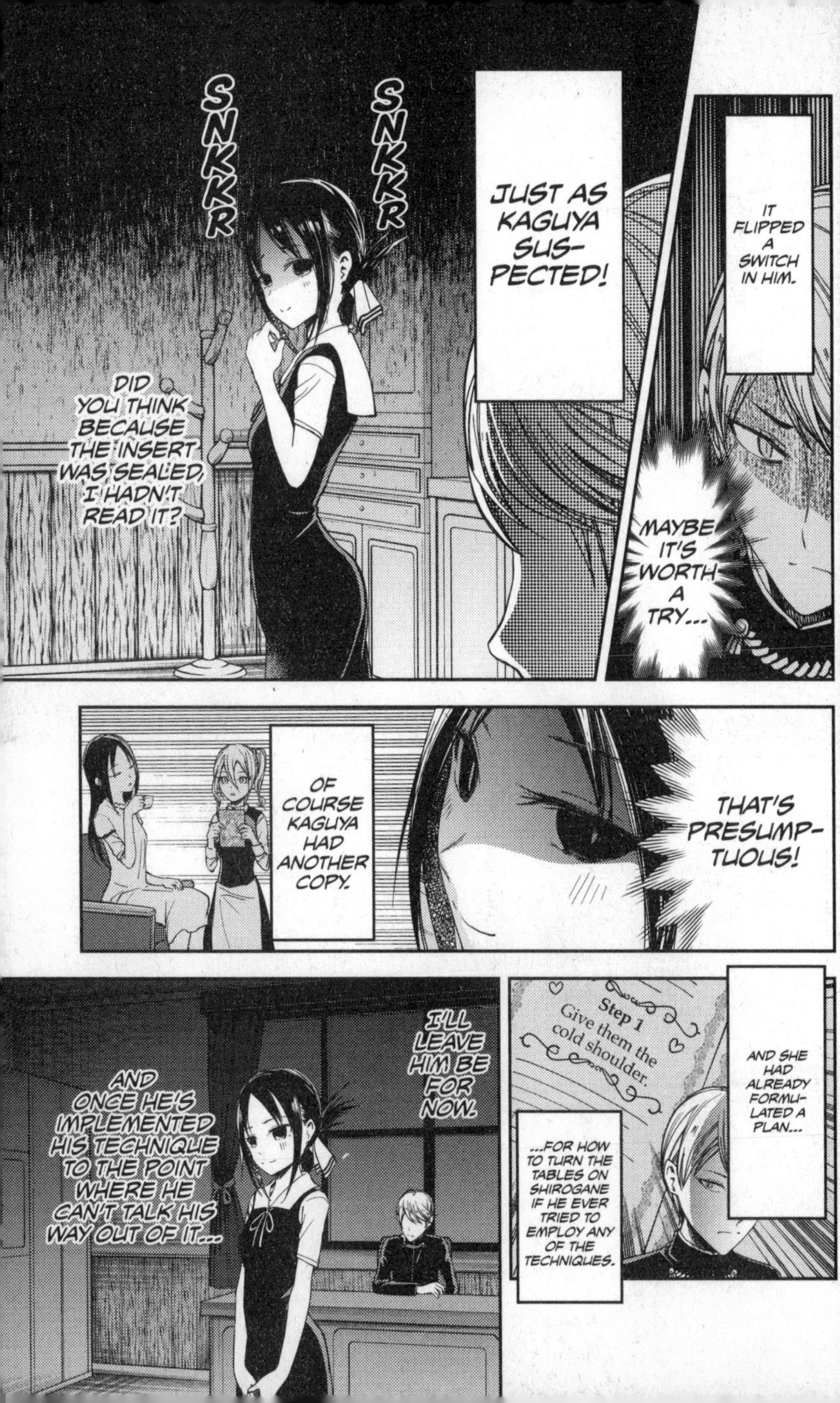
IT FLIPPED A SWITCH IN HIM.
MAYBE IT'S WORTH A TRY...
JUST AS KAGUYA SUS-PECTED!
SNKKR
SNKKR
DID YOU THINK BECAUSE THE INSERT WAS SEALED, I HADN'T READ IT?
THAT'S PRESUMP-TUOUS!
OF COURSE KAGUYA HAD ANOTHER COPY.
AND SHE HAD ALREADY FORMU-LATED A PLAN...
Step 1 Give them the cold shoulder.
...FOR HOW TO TURN THE TABLES ON SHIROGANE IF HE EVER TRIED TO EMPLOY ANY OF THE TECHNIQUES.
I'LL LEAVE HIM BE FOR NOW.
AND ONCE HE'S IMPLEMENTED HIS TECHNIQUE TO THE POINT WHERE HE CAN'T TALK HIS WAY OUT OF IT...

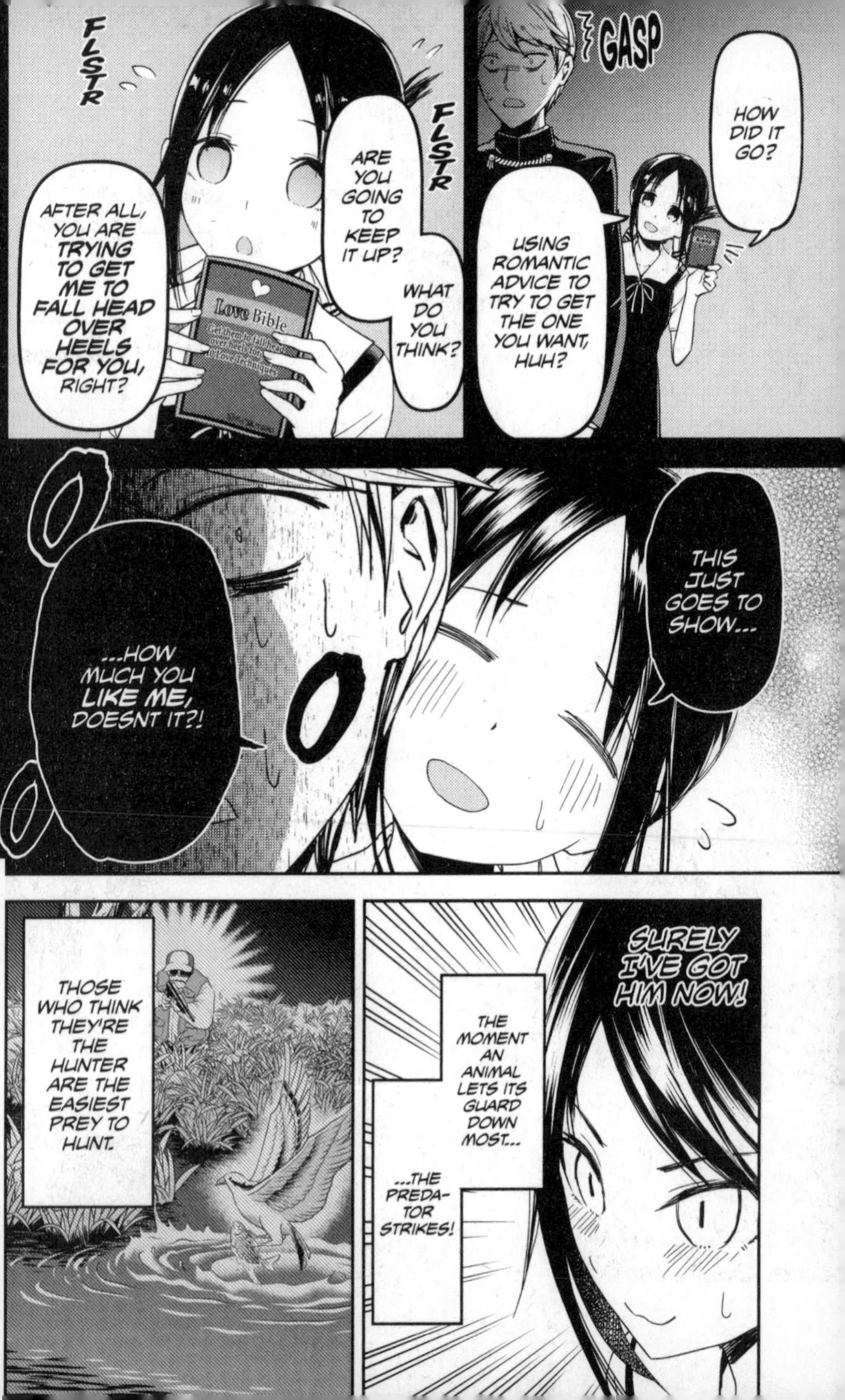
GASP
HOW DID IT GO?
USING ROMANTIC ADVICE TO TRY TO GET THE ONE YOU WANT, HUH?
FLSTR
ARE YOU GOING TO KEEP IT UP?
WHAT DO YOU THINK?
AFTER ALL, YOU ARE TRYING TO GET ME TO FALL HEAD OVER HEELS FOR YOU, RIGHT?
FLSTR
Love Bible
THIS JUST GOES TO SHOW...
...HOW MUCH YOU LIKE ME, DOESNT IT?!
SURELY I'VE GOT HIM NOW!
THE MOMENT AN ANIMAL LETS ITS GUARD DOWN MOST...
...THE PREDATOR STRIKES!
THOSE WHO THINK THEY'RE THE HUNTER ARE THE EASIEST PREY TO HUNT.

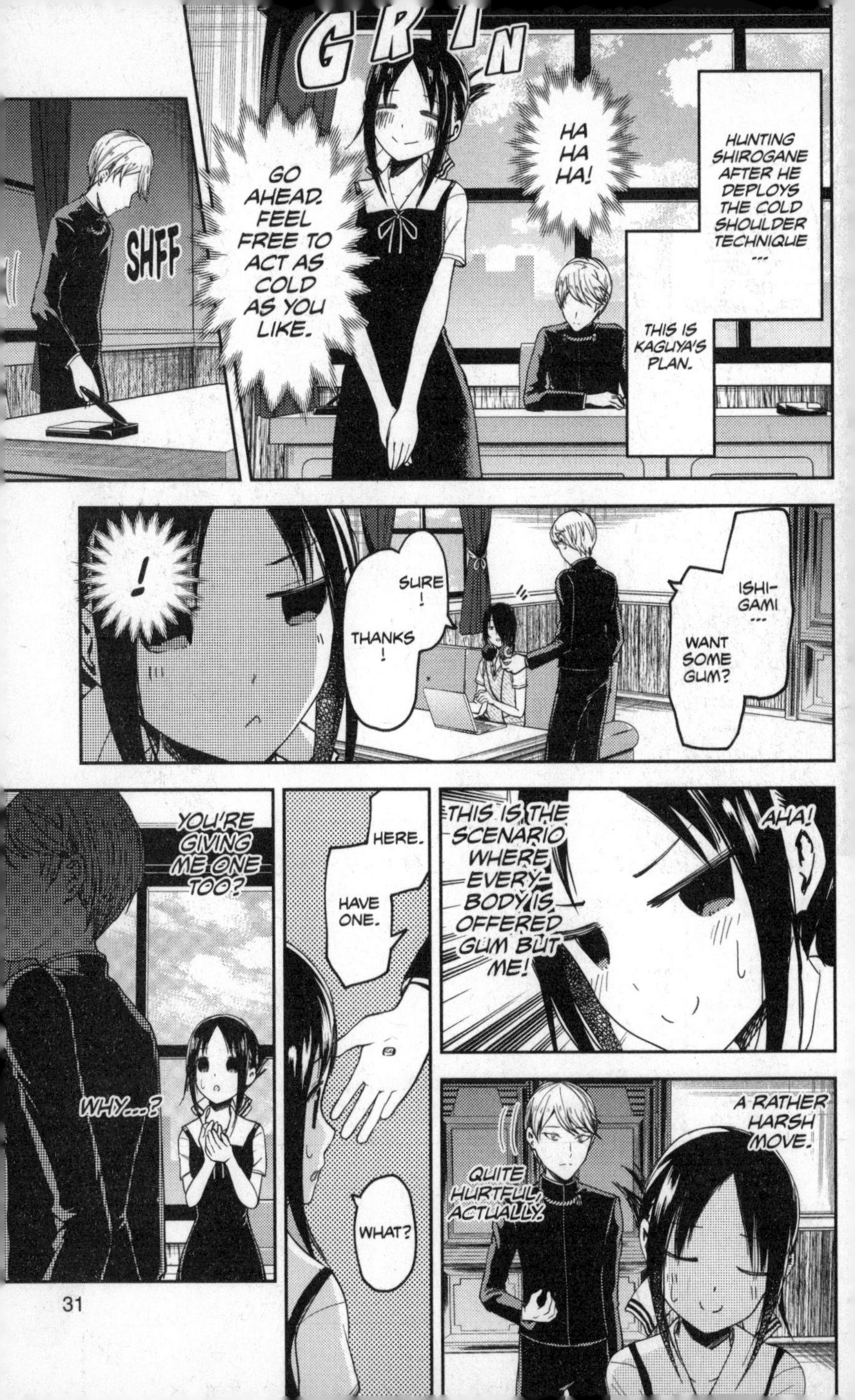
GRIN
HUNTING SHIROGANE AFTER HE DEPLOYS THE COLD SHOULDER TECHNIQUE...
THIS IS KAGUYA'S PLAN.
HA HA HA!
GO AHEAD. FEEL FREE TO ACT AS COLD AS YOU LIKE.
SHFF
ISHIGAMI... WANT SOME GUM?
SURE! THANKS!
!
AHA!
THIS IS THE SCENARIO WHERE EVERYBODY IS OFFERED GUM BUT ME!
A RATHER HARSH MOVE.
QUITE HURTFUL, ACTUALLY.
HERE. HAVE ONE.
WHAT?
YOU'RE GIVING ME ONE TOO?
WHY...?

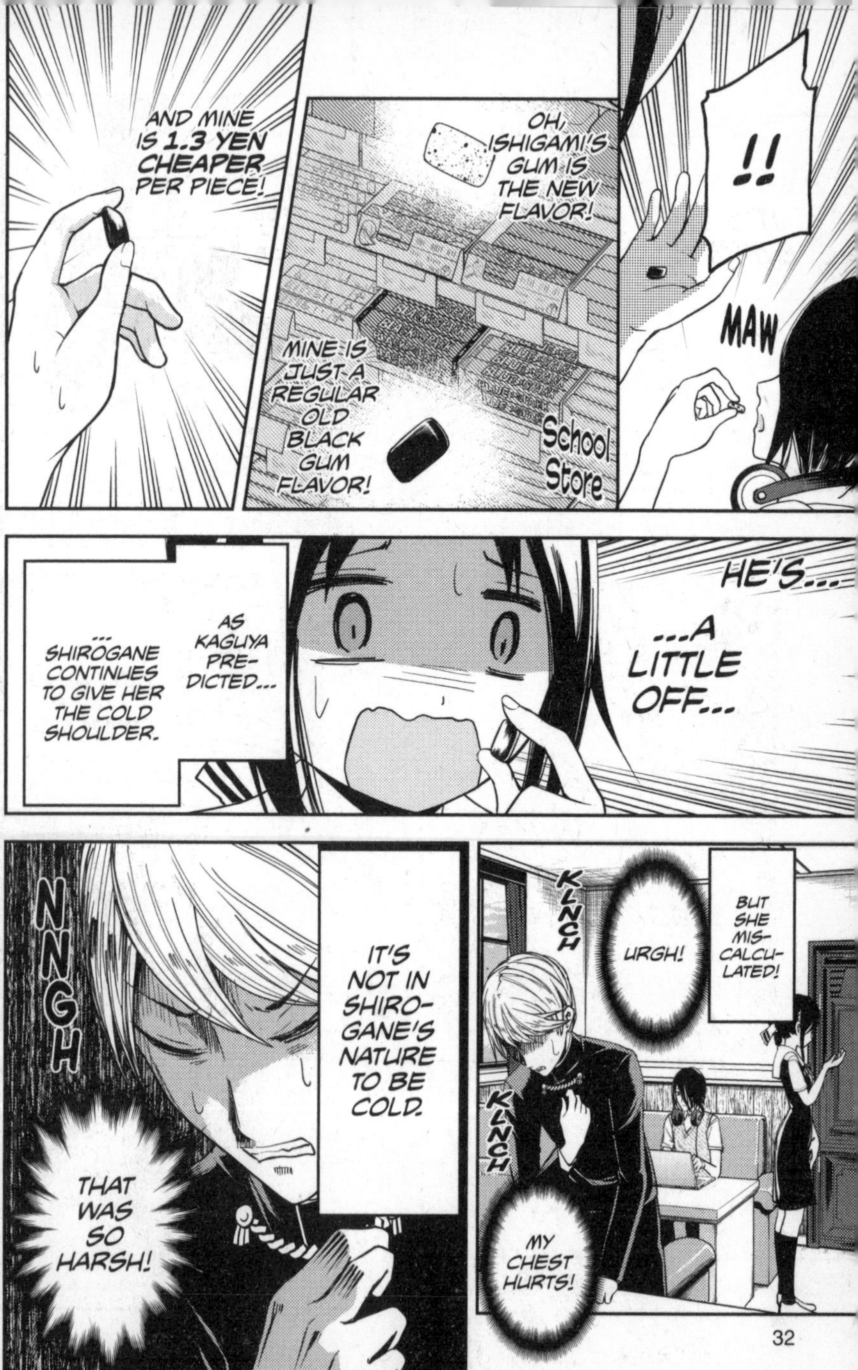
!!
MAW
OH, ISHIGAMI'S GUM IS THE NEW FLAVOR!
MINE IS JUST A REGULAR OLD BLACK GUM FLAVOR!
School Store
AND MINE IS 1.3 YEN CHEAPER PER PIECE!
HE'S...
...A LITTLE OFF...
AS KAGUYA PREDICTED...
...SHIROGANE CONTINUES TO GIVE HER THE COLD SHOULDER.
BUT SHE MISCALCULATED!
KLINCH
URGH!
KLINCH
MY CHEST HURTS!
IT'S NOT IN SHIROGANE'S NATURE TO BE COLD.
NNGH
THAT WAS SO HARSH!

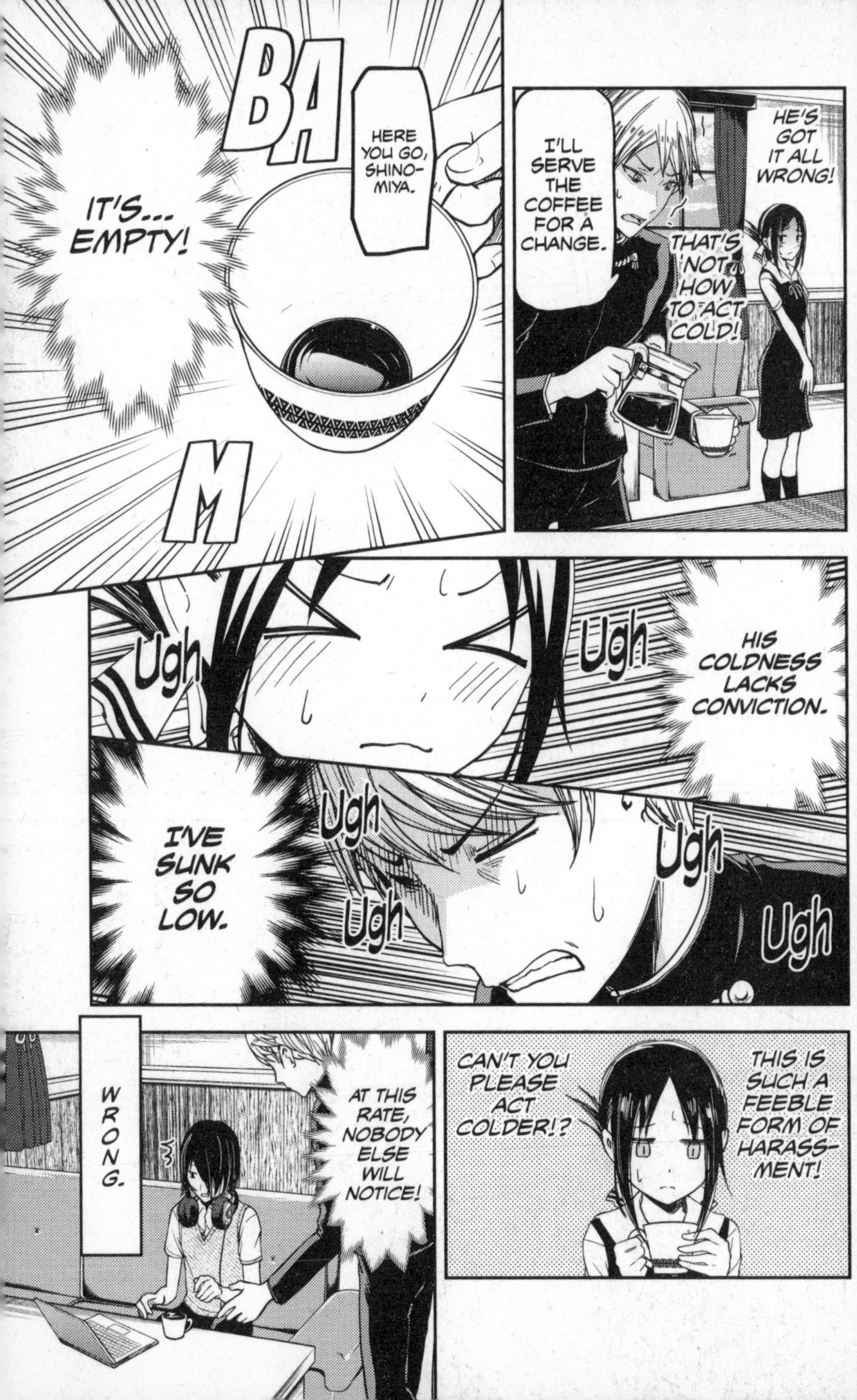
I'LL SERVE THE COFFEE FOR A CHANGE.
HE'S GOT IT ALL WRONG!
THAT'S NOT HOW TO ACT COLD!
BA
HERE YOU GO, SHINOMIYA.
IT'S... EMPTY!
M
HIS COLDNESS LACKS CONVICTION.
Ugh
Ugh
Ugh
Ugh
Ugh
Ugh
I'VE SUNK SO LOW.
THIS IS SUCH A FEEBLE FORM OF HARASSMENT!
CAN'T YOU PLEASE ACT COLDER!?
AT THIS RATE, NOBODY ELSE WILL NOTICE!
WRONG.

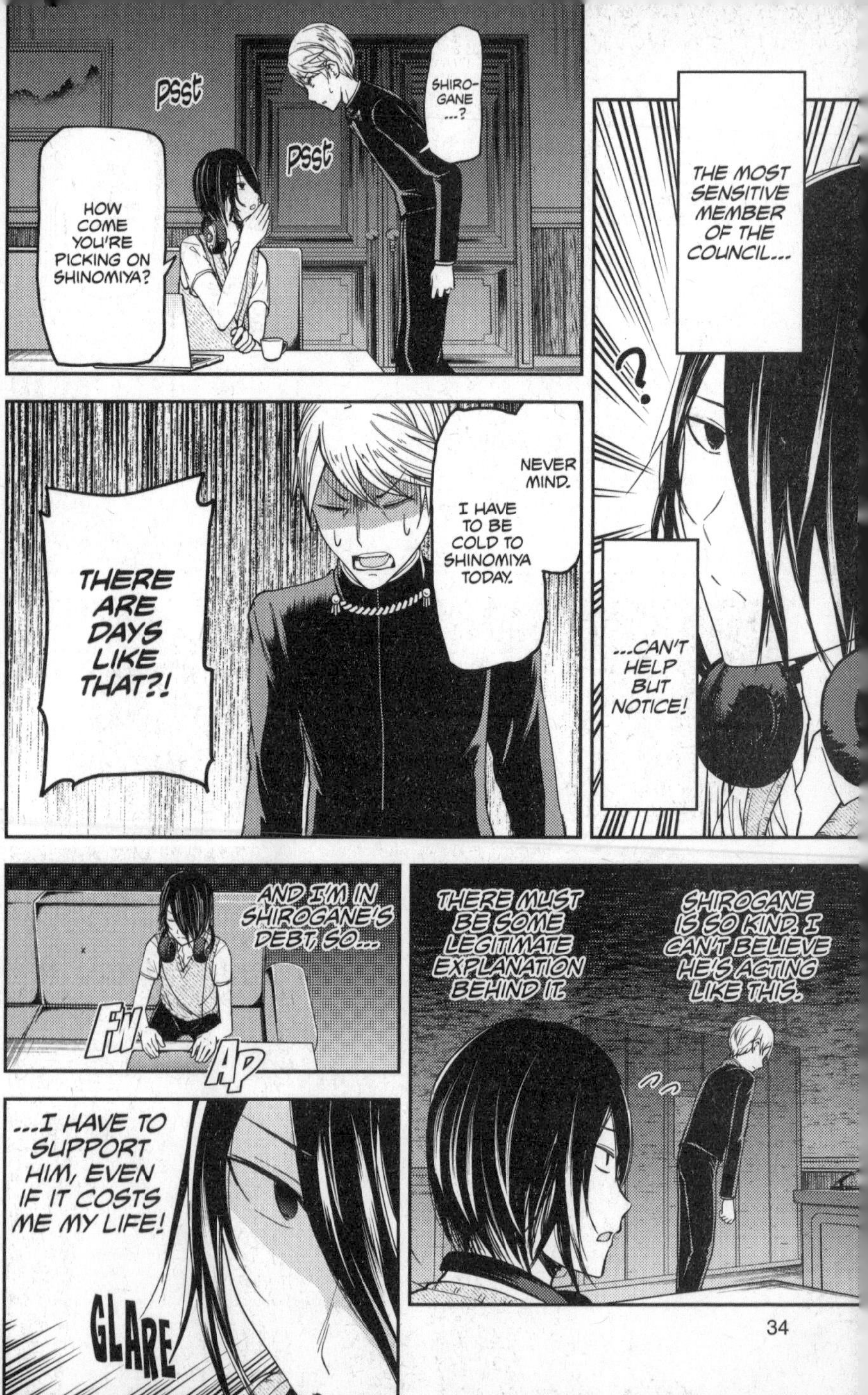

THE MOST SENSITIVE MEMBER OF THE COUNCIL...
?
...CAN'T HELP BUT NOTICE!
SHIRO-GANE ...?
PSST
PSST
HOW COME YOU'RE PICKING ON SHINOMIYA?
NEVER MIND.
I HAVE TO BE COLD TO SHINOMIYA TODAY.
THERE ARE DAYS LIKE THAT?!
SHIROGANE IS SO KIND. I CAN'T BELIEVE HE'S ACTING LIKE THIS.
THERE MUST BE SOME LEGITIMATE EXPLANATION BEHIND IT.
AND I'M IN SHIROGANE'S DEBT, SO...
FWAP
...I HAVE TO SUPPORT HIM, EVEN IF IT COSTS ME MY LIFE!
GLARE

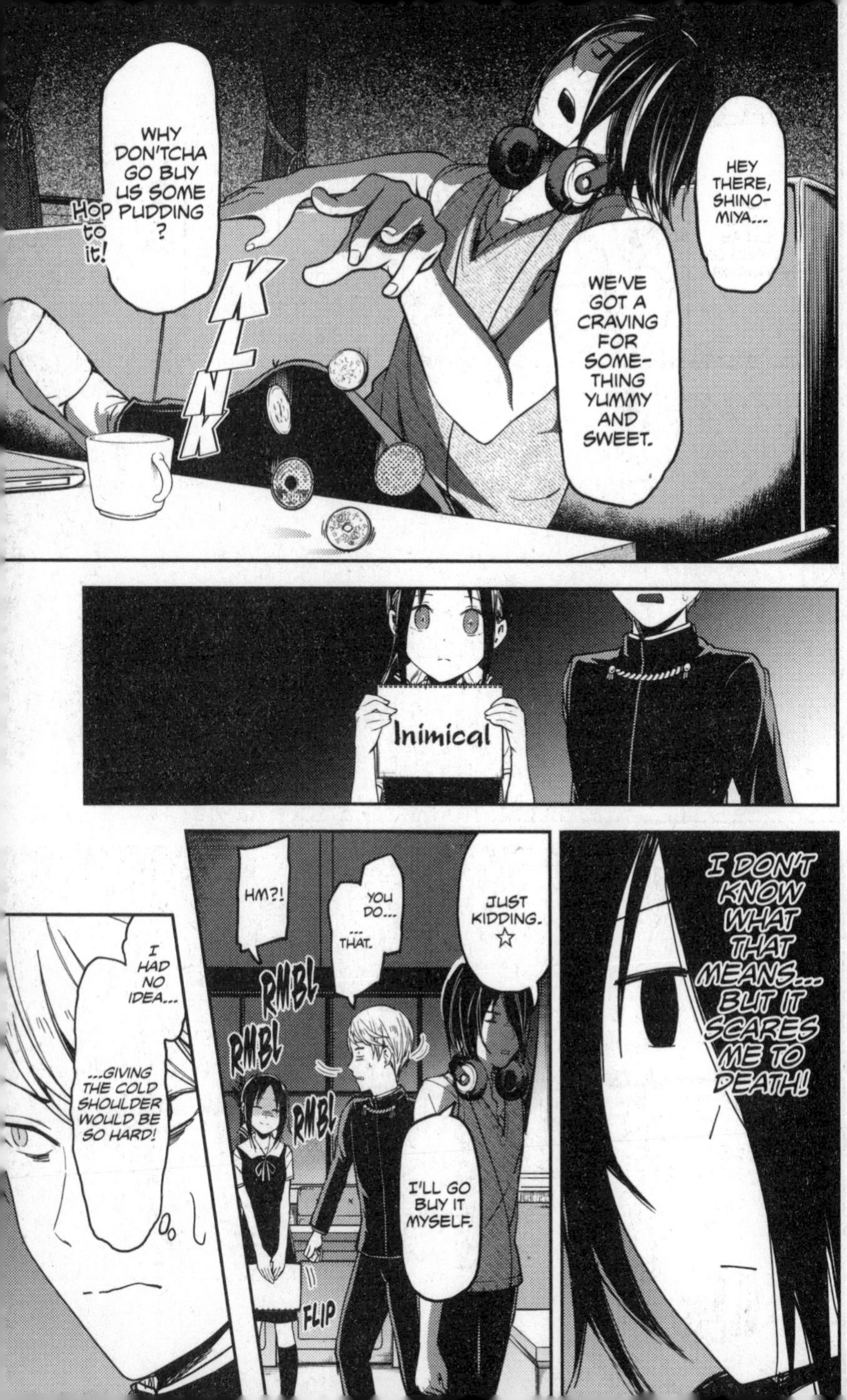
HEY THERE, SHINO-MIYA...
WE'VE GOT A CRAVING FOR SOME-THING YUMMY AND SWEET.
WHY DON'TCHA GO BUY US SOME PUDDING?
Hop to it!
KLNK
Inimical
I DON'T KNOW WHAT THAT MEANS... BUT IT SCARES ME TO DEATH!
JUST KIDDING. ☆
YOU DO... ...THAT.
HM?!
RMBL
RMBL
RMBL
I'LL GO BUY IT MYSELF.
FLIP
I HAD NO IDEA...
...GIVING THE COLD SHOULDER WOULD BE SO HARD!

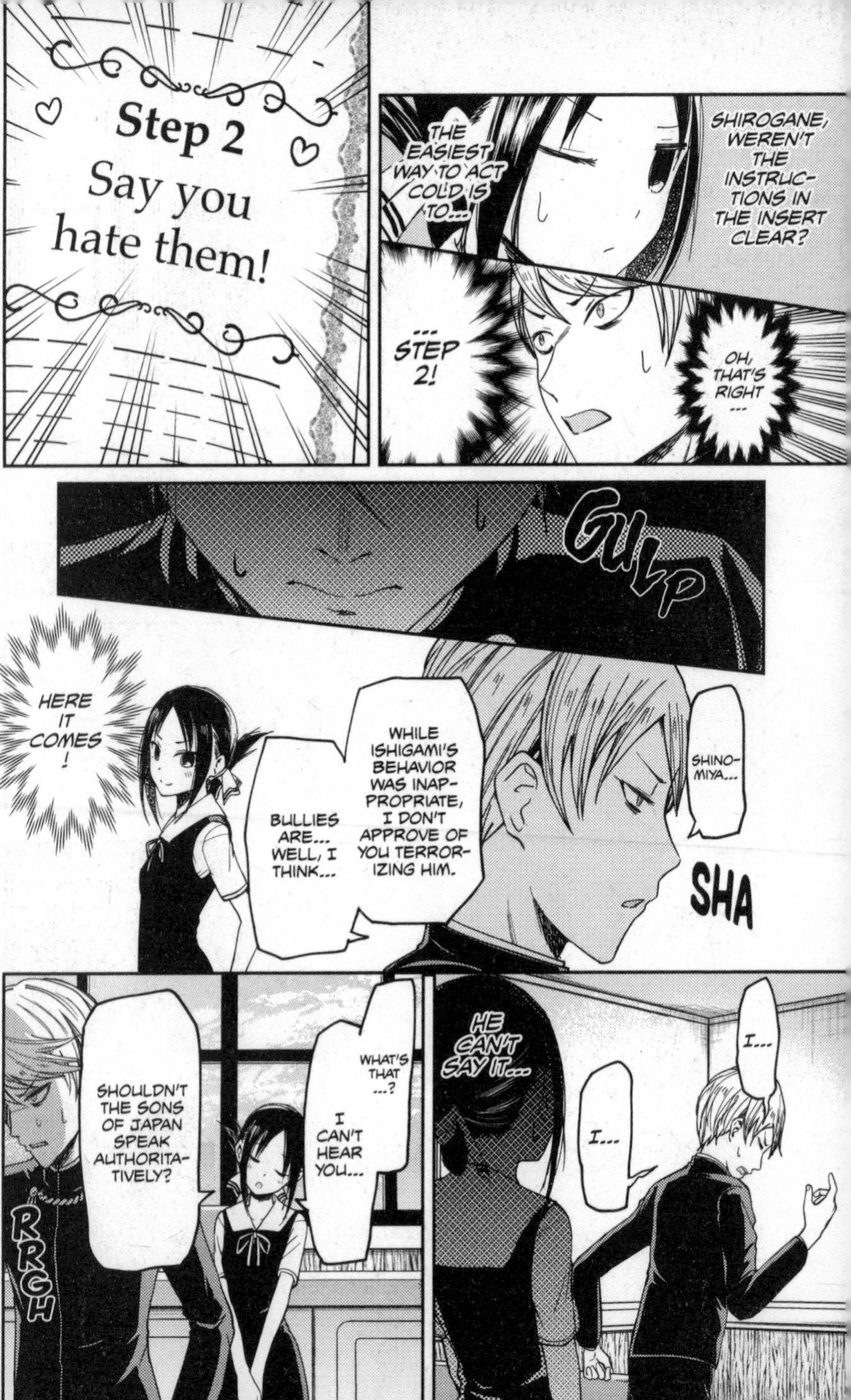
SHIROGANE, WEREN'T THE INSTRUCTIONS IN THE INSERT CLEAR?
THE EASIEST WAY TO ACT COLD IS TO...
OH, THAT'S RIGHT...
...STEP 2!
Step 2
Say you hate them!
GULP
SHINOMIYA...
SHA
WHILE ISHIGAMI'S BEHAVIOR WAS INAPPROPRIATE, I DON'T APPROVE OF YOU TERRORIZING HIM.
BULLIES ARE... WELL, I THINK...
HERE IT COMES!
I...
I...
HE CAN'T SAY IT...
WHAT'S THAT...?
I CAN'T HEAR YOU...
SHOULDN'T THE SONS OF JAPAN SPEAK AUTHORITATIVELY?
RRGH

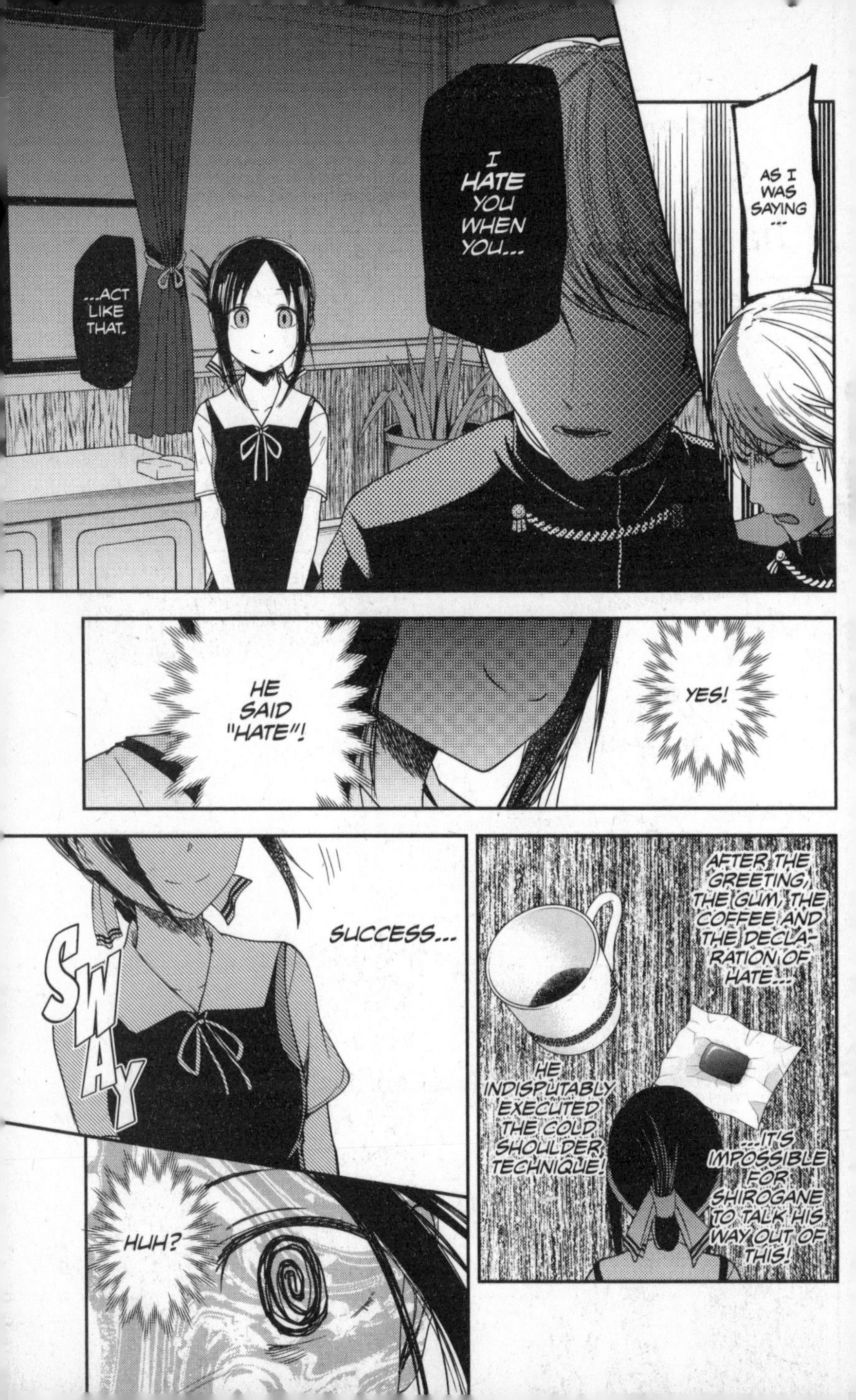
AS I WAS SAYING...
I HATE YOU WHEN YOU...
...ACT LIKE THAT.
YES!
HE SAID "HATE"!
AFTER THE GREETING, THE GUM, THE COFFEE AND THE DECLA-RATION OF HATE...
HE INDISPUTABLY EXECUTED THE COLD SHOULDER TECHNIQUE!
...IT'S IMPOSSIBLE FOR SHIROGANE TO TALK HIS WAY OUT OF THIS!
SUCCESS...
SWAY
HUH?

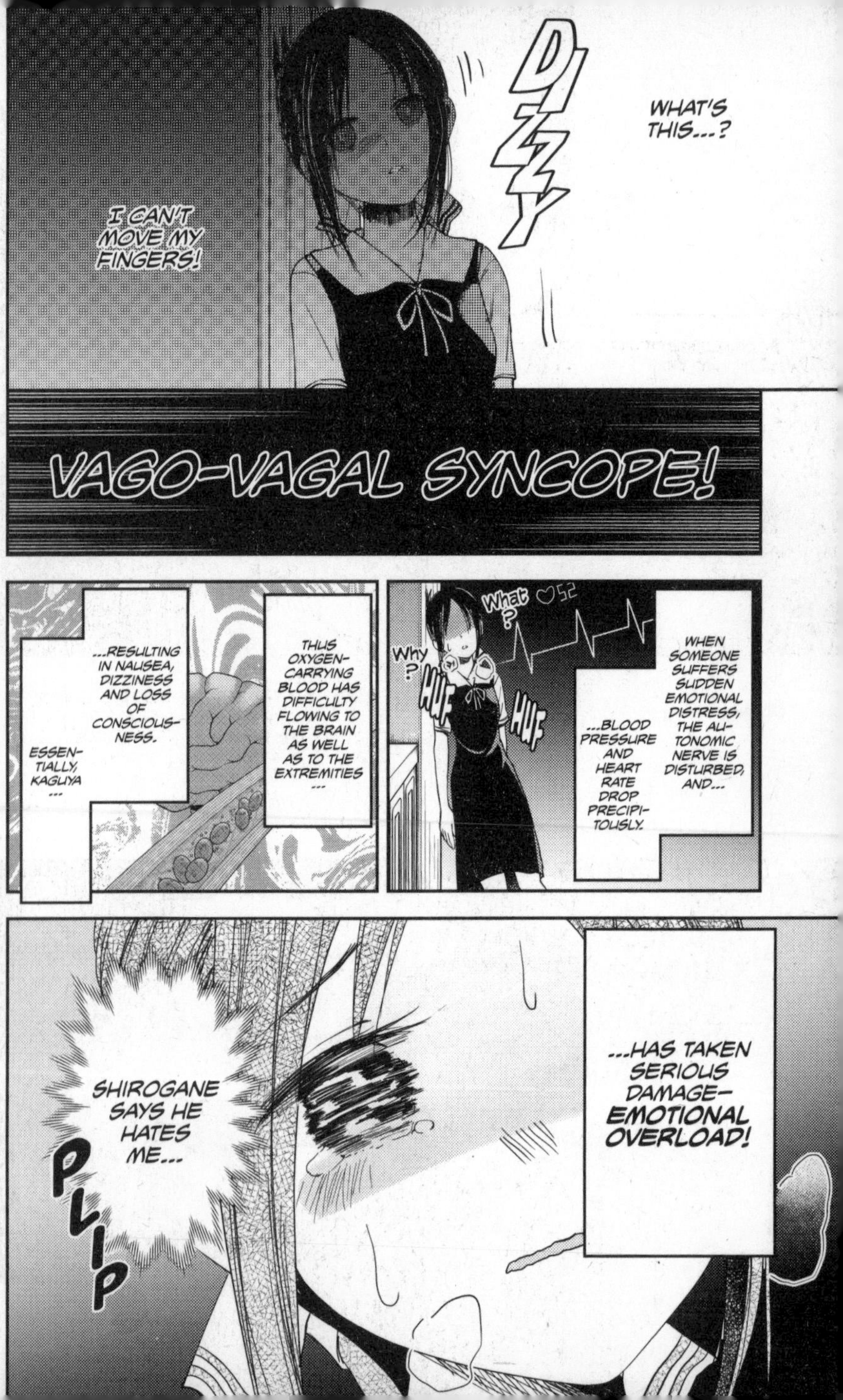
WHAT'S THIS...?
DIZZY
I CAN'T MOVE MY FINGERS!
VAGO-VAGAL SYNCOPE!
WHEN SOMEONE SUFFERS SUDDEN EMOTIONAL DISTRESS, THE AUTONOMIC NERVE IS DISTURBED, AND...
...BLOOD PRESSURE AND HEART RATE DROP PRECIPITOUSLY.
What ?
♡52
HUF
HUF
Why ?
THUS OXYGEN-CARRYING BLOOD HAS DIFFICULTY FLOWING TO THE BRAIN AS WELL AS TO THE EXTREMITIES...
...RESULTING IN NAUSEA, DIZZINESS AND LOSS OF CONSCIOUSNESS.
ESSENTIALLY, KAGUYA...
...HAS TAKEN SERIOUS DAMAGE—EMOTIONAL OVERLOAD!
SHIROGANE SAYS HE HATES ME...
PLIP

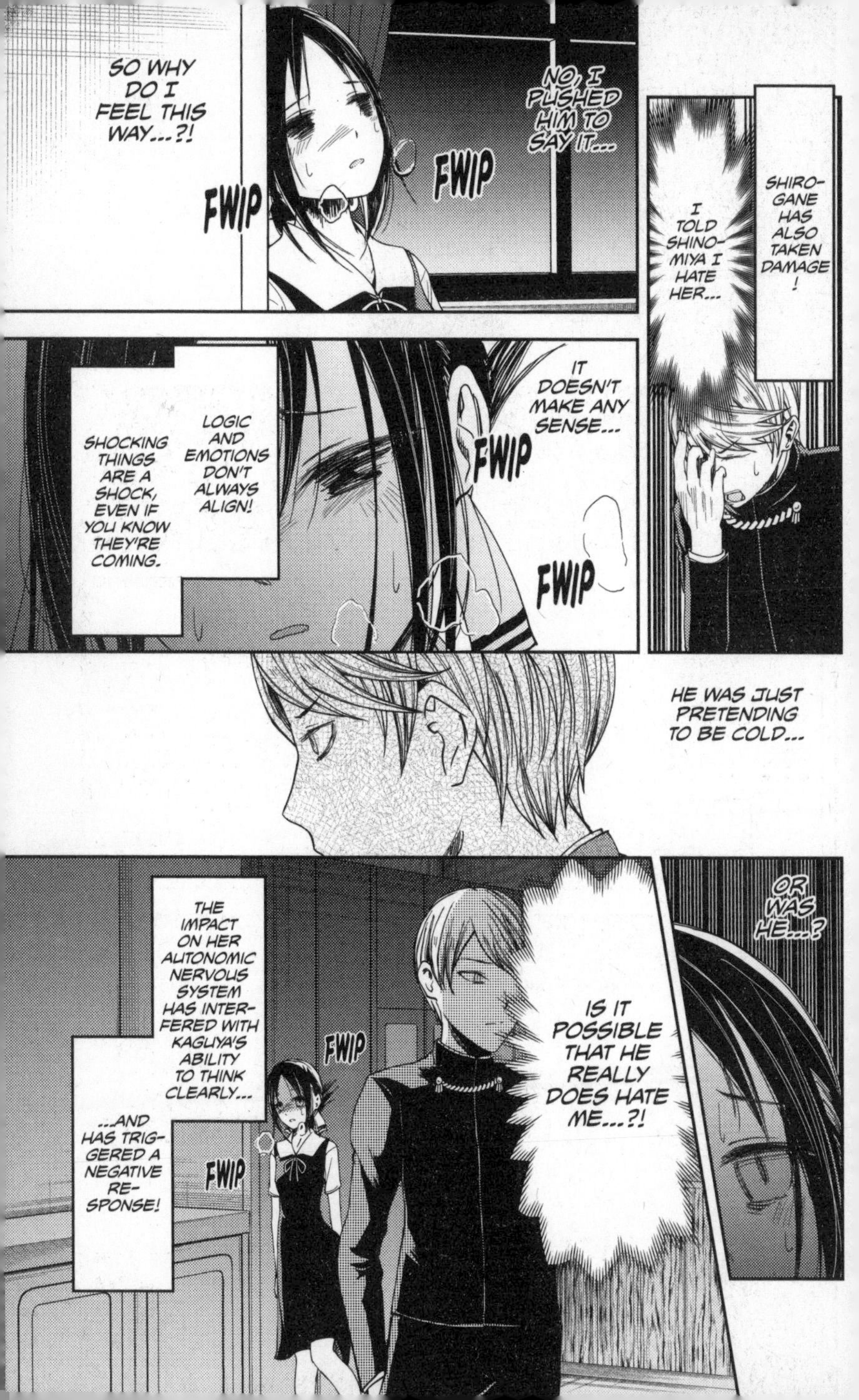
SHIRO-GANE HAS ALSO TAKEN DAMAGE!
I TOLD SHINO-MIYA I HATE HER...
NO, I PUSHED HIM TO SAY IT...
FWIP
SO WHY DO I FEEL THIS WAY...?!
FWIP
IT DOESN'T MAKE ANY SENSE...
FWIP
FWIP
LOGIC AND EMOTIONS DON'T ALWAYS ALIGN!
SHOCKING THINGS ARE A SHOCK, EVEN IF YOU KNOW THEY'RE COMING.
HE WAS JUST PRETENDING TO BE COLD...
OR WAS HE...?
IS IT POSSIBLE THAT HE REALLY DOES HATE ME...?!
THE IMPACT ON HER AUTONOMIC NERVOUS SYSTEM HAS INTER-FERED WITH KAGUYA'S ABILITY TO THINK CLEARLY...
FWIP
...AND HAS TRIG-GERED A NEGATIVE RE-SPONSE!
FWIP

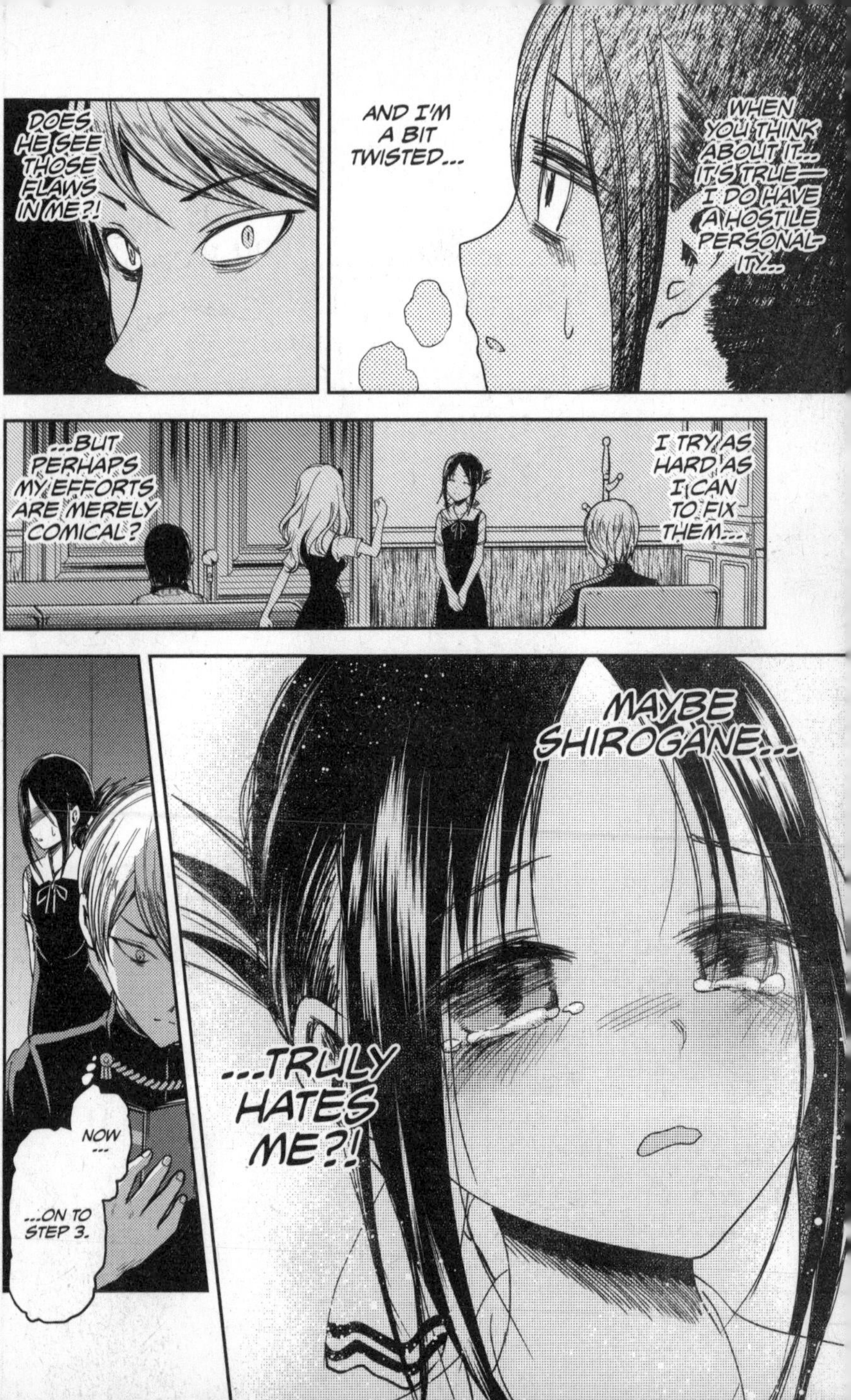
WHEN YOU THINK ABOUT IT... IT'S TRUE— I DO HAVE A HOSTILE PERSONALITY...
AND I'M A BIT TWISTED...
DOES HE SEE THOSE FLAWS IN ME?!
I TRY AS HARD AS I CAN TO FIX THEM...
...BUT PERHAPS MY EFFORTS ARE MERELY COMICAL?
MAYBE SHIROGANE...
...TRULY HATES ME?!
NOW...
...ON TO STEP 3.

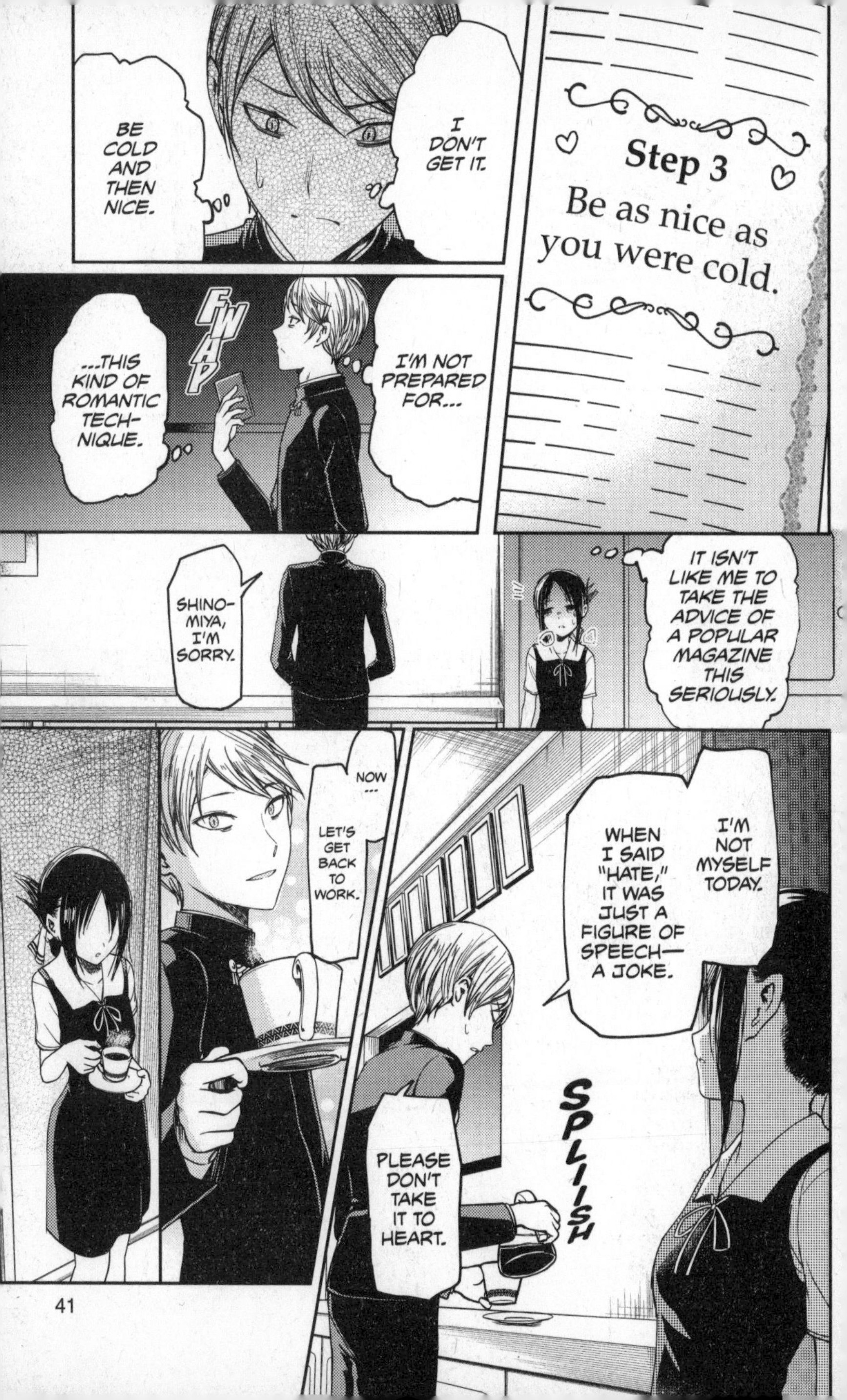
Step 3
Be as nice as you were cold.
I DON'T GET IT.
BE COLD AND THEN NICE.
FWAP
I'M NOT PREPARED FOR...
...THIS KIND OF ROMANTIC TECH-NIQUE.
IT ISN'T LIKE ME TO TAKE THE ADVICE OF A POPULAR MAGAZINE THIS SERIOUSLY.
SHINO-MIYA, I'M SORRY.
I'M NOT MYSELF TODAY.
WHEN I SAID "HATE," IT WAS JUST A FIGURE OF SPEECH— A JOKE.
SPLISH
PLEASE DON'T TAKE IT TO HEART.
NOW...
LET'S GET BACK TO WORK.

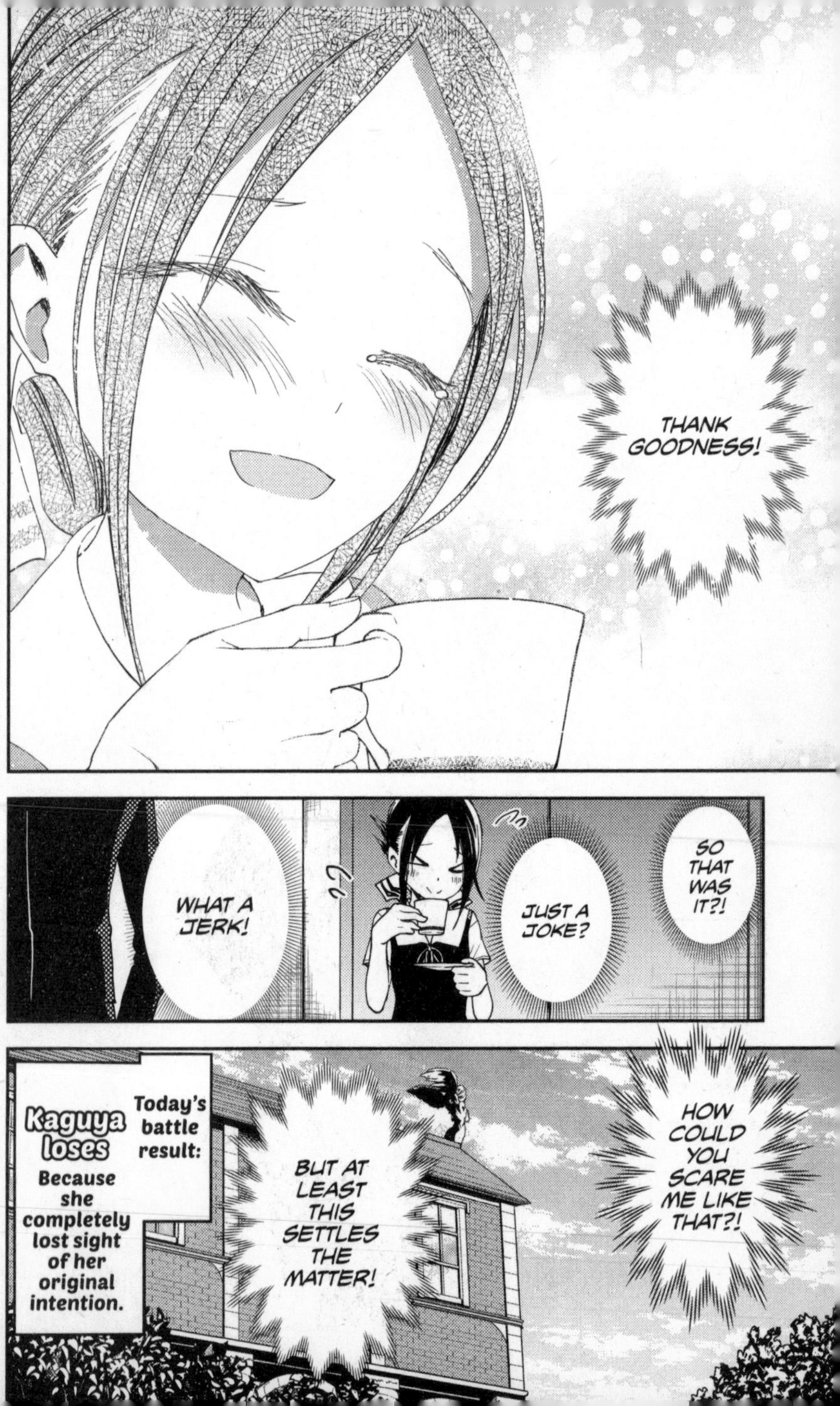
THANK GOODNESS!
SO THAT WAS IT?!
JUST A JOKE?
WHAT A JERK!
HOW COULD YOU SCARE ME LIKE THAT?!
BUT AT LEAST THIS SETTLES THE MATTER!
Today's battle result:
Kaguya loses
Because she completely lost sight of her original intention.

I feel like I'm forgetting something. But no matter.

PERHAPS IT'S TIME TO STOP CALLING THIS A BATTLE BETWEEN TWO GENIUSES ...

Battle 33 Miyuki Shirogane Wants to Sing

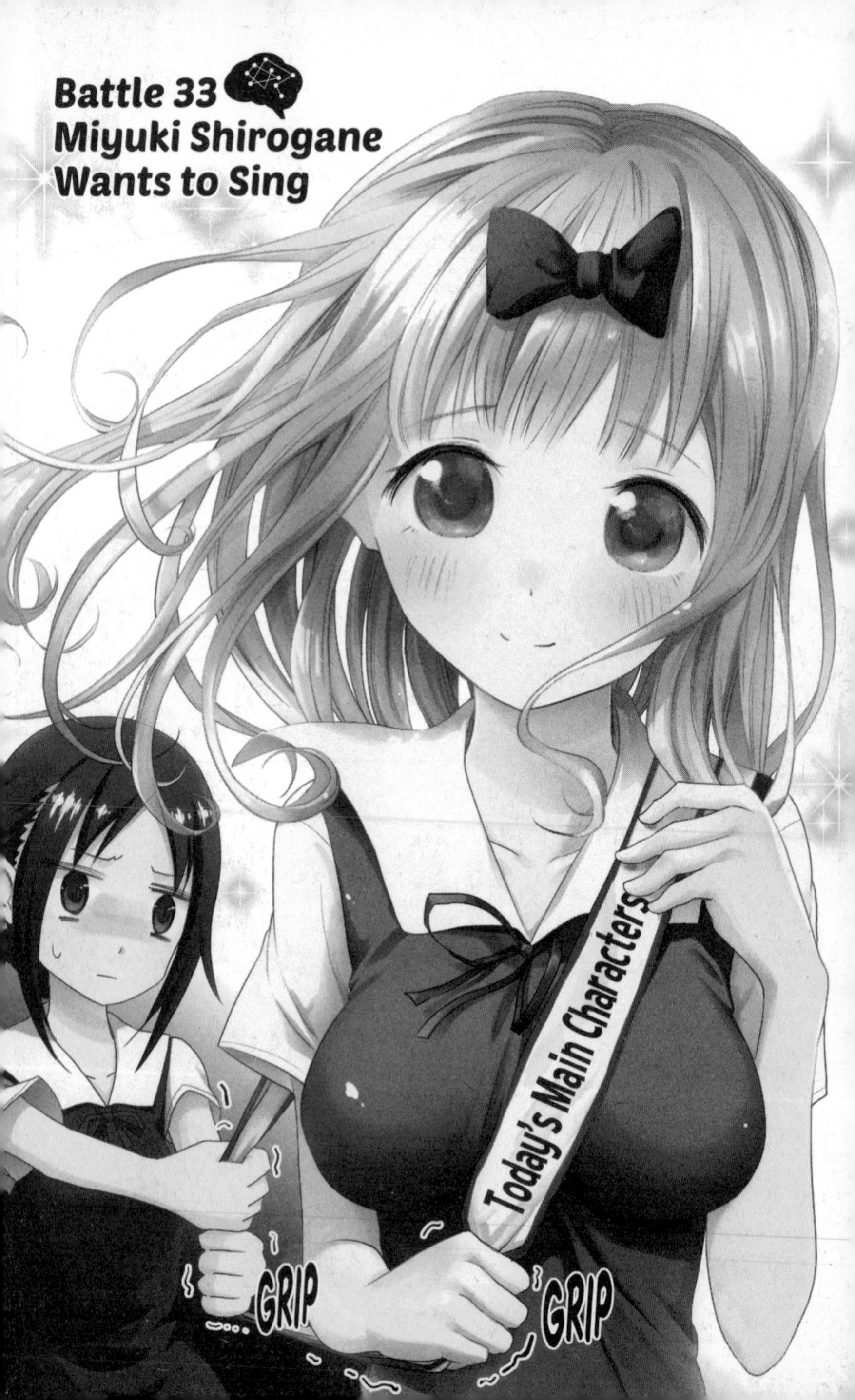
Today's Main Characters
GRIP
GRIP

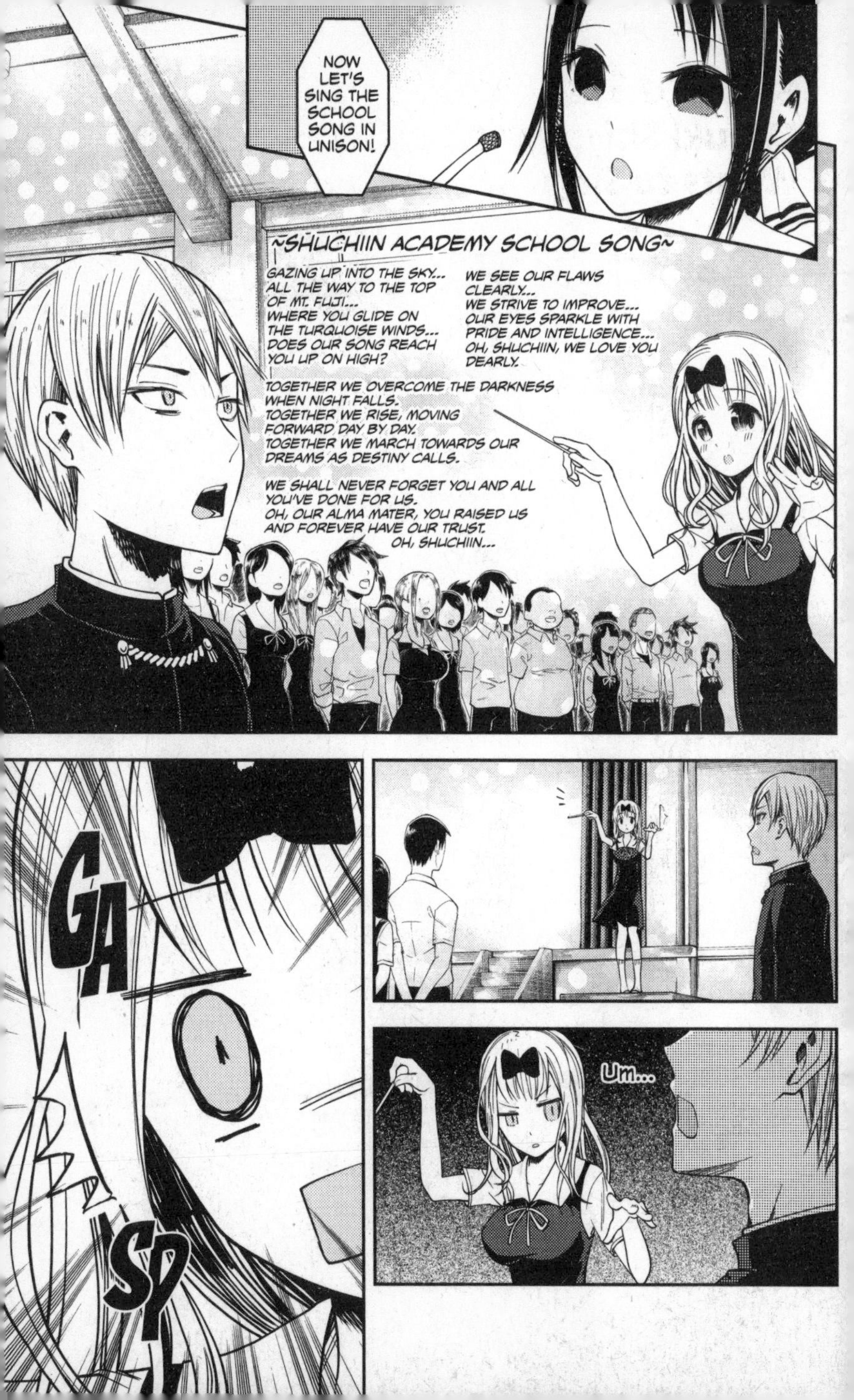
NOW LET'S SING THE SCHOOL SONG IN UNISON!
~SHUCHIIN ACADEMY SCHOOL SONG~
GAZING UP INTO THE SKY... ALL THE WAY TO THE TOP OF MT. FUJI... WHERE YOU GLIDE ON THE TURQUOISE WINDS... DOES OUR SONG REACH YOU UP ON HIGH?
WE SEE OUR FLAWS CLEARLY... WE STRIVE TO IMPROVE... OUR EYES SPARKLE WITH PRIDE AND INTELLIGENCE... OH, SHUCHIIN, WE LOVE YOU DEARLY.
TOGETHER WE OVERCOME THE DARKNESS WHEN NIGHT FALLS. TOGETHER WE RISE, MOVING FORWARD DAY BY DAY. TOGETHER WE MARCH TOWARDS OUR DREAMS AS DESTINY CALLS.
WE SHALL NEVER FORGET YOU AND ALL YOU'VE DONE FOR US. OH, OUR ALMA MATER, YOU RAISED US AND FOREVER HAVE OUR TRUST. OH, SHUCHIIN...
Um...
GASP

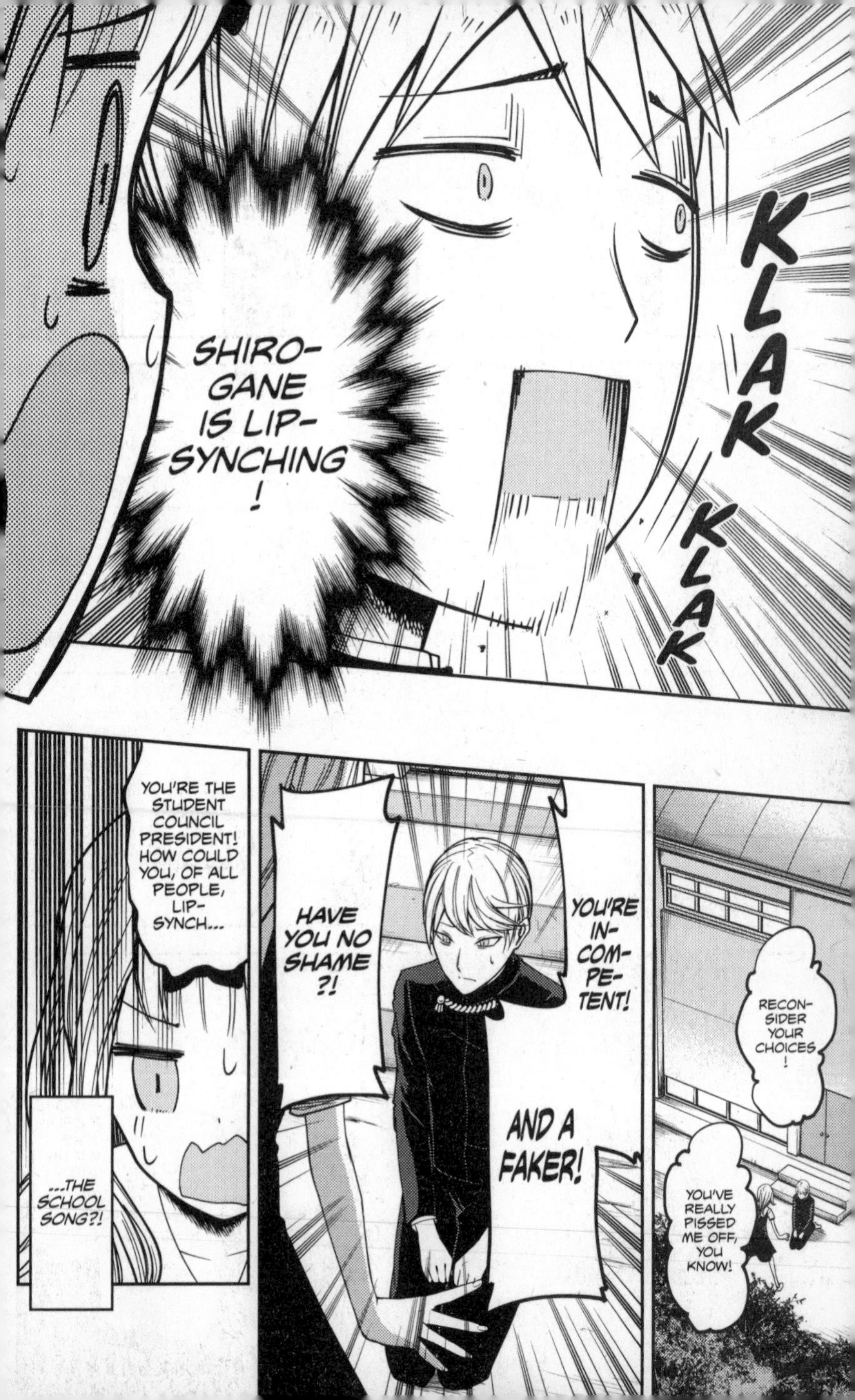
KLAK
KLAK
SHIRO-GANE IS LIP-SYNCHING!
RECON-SIDER YOUR CHOICES!
YOU'VE REALLY PISSED ME OFF, YOU KNOW!
YOU'RE IN-COM-PE-TENT!
HAVE YOU NO SHAME?!
AND A FAKER!
YOU'RE THE STUDENT COUNCIL PRESIDENT! HOW COULD YOU, OF ALL PEOPLE, LIP-SYNCH...
...THE SCHOOL SONG?!

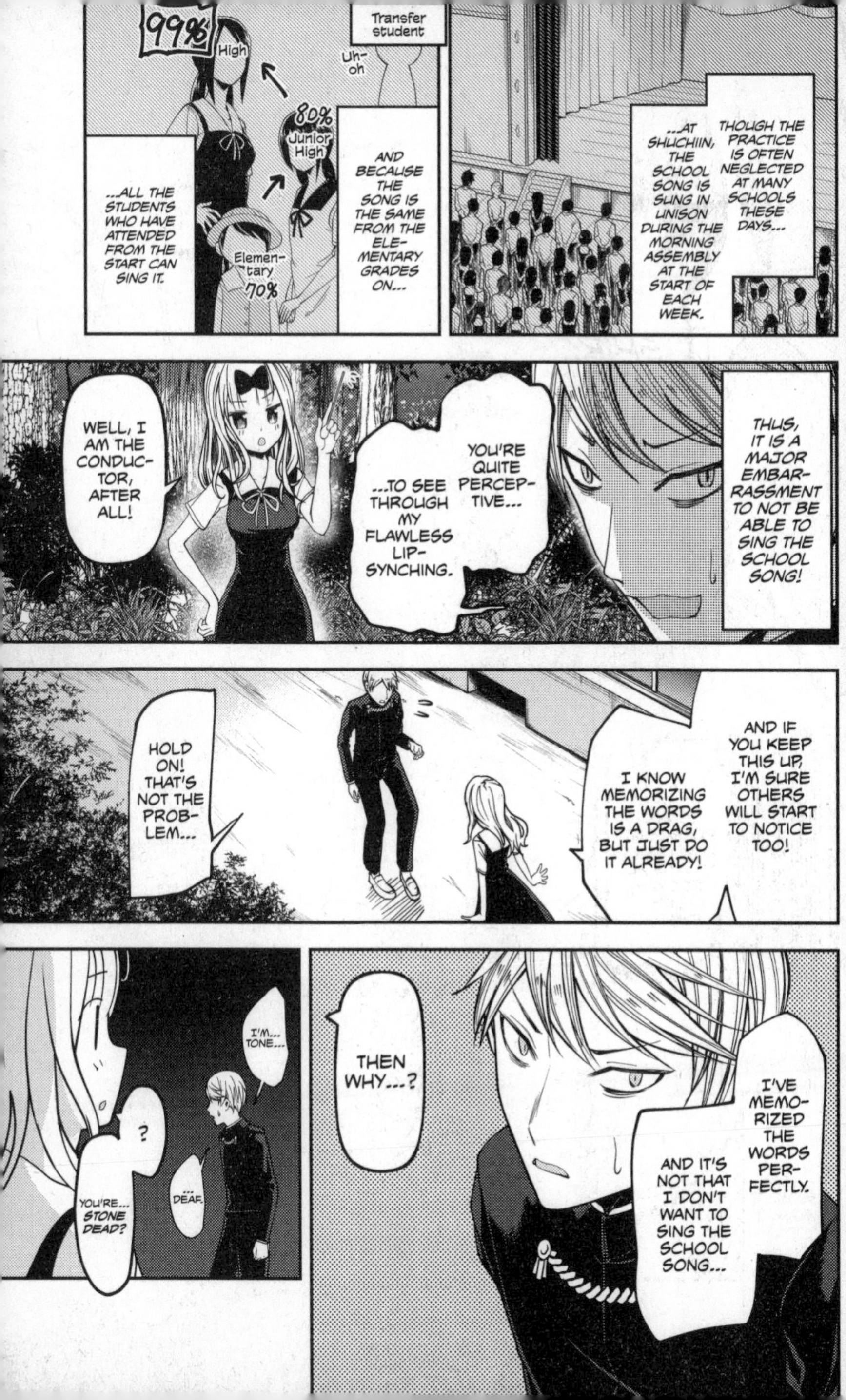
THOUGH THE PRACTICE IS OFTEN NEGLECTED AT MANY SCHOOLS THESE DAYS...
...AT SHUCHIIN, THE SCHOOL SONG IS SUNG IN UNISON DURING THE MORNING ASSEMBLY AT THE START OF EACH WEEK.
Transfer student
Uh-oh
AND BECAUSE THE SONG IS THE SAME FROM THE ELEMENTARY GRADES ON...
99%
High
80%
Junior High
Elementary
70%
...ALL THE STUDENTS WHO HAVE ATTENDED FROM THE START CAN SING IT.
THUS, IT IS A MAJOR EMBARRASSMENT TO NOT BE ABLE TO SING THE SCHOOL SONG!
YOU'RE QUITE PERCEPTIVE...
...TO SEE THROUGH MY FLAWLESS LIP-SYNCHING.
WELL, I AM THE CONDUCTOR, AFTER ALL!
AND IF YOU KEEP THIS UP, I'M SURE OTHERS WILL START TO NOTICE TOO!
I KNOW MEMORIZING THE WORDS IS A DRAG, BUT JUST DO IT ALREADY!
HOLD ON! THAT'S NOT THE PROBLEM...
I'VE MEMORIZED THE WORDS PERFECTLY.
AND IT'S NOT THAT I DON'T WANT TO SING THE SCHOOL SONG...
THEN WHY...?
I'M... TONE...
?
...DEAF.
YOU'RE... STONE DEAD?

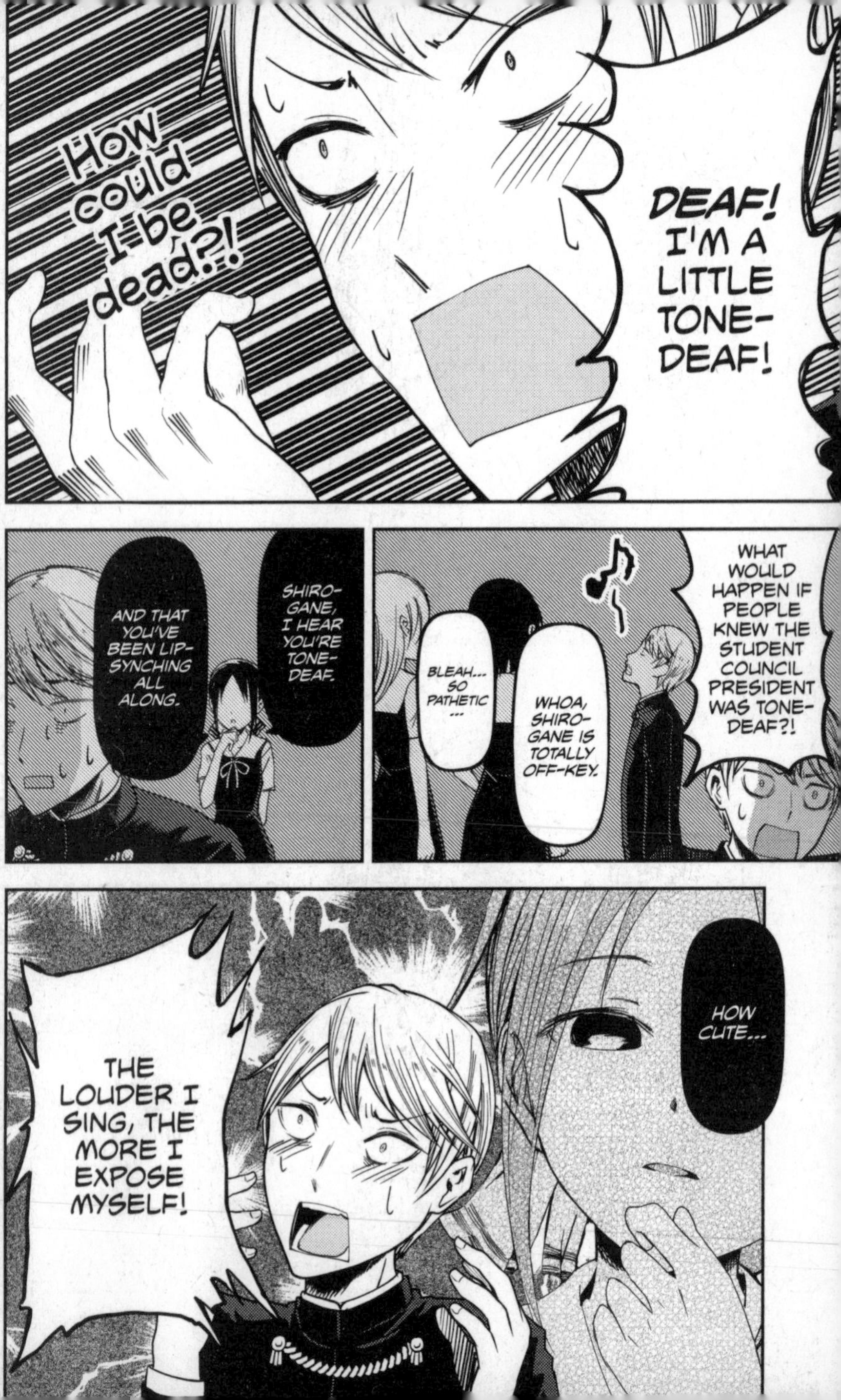
DEAF! I'M A LITTLE TONE-DEAF!
How could I be dead?!
WHAT WOULD HAPPEN IF PEOPLE KNEW THE STUDENT COUNCIL PRESIDENT WAS TONE-DEAF?!
WHOA, SHIROGANE IS TOTALLY OFF-KEY.
BLEAH... SO PATHETIC...
SHIROGANE, I HEAR YOU'RE TONE-DEAF.
AND THAT YOU'VE BEEN LIP-SYNCHING ALL ALONG.
HOW CUTE...
THE LOUDER I SING, THE MORE I EXPOSE MYSELF!

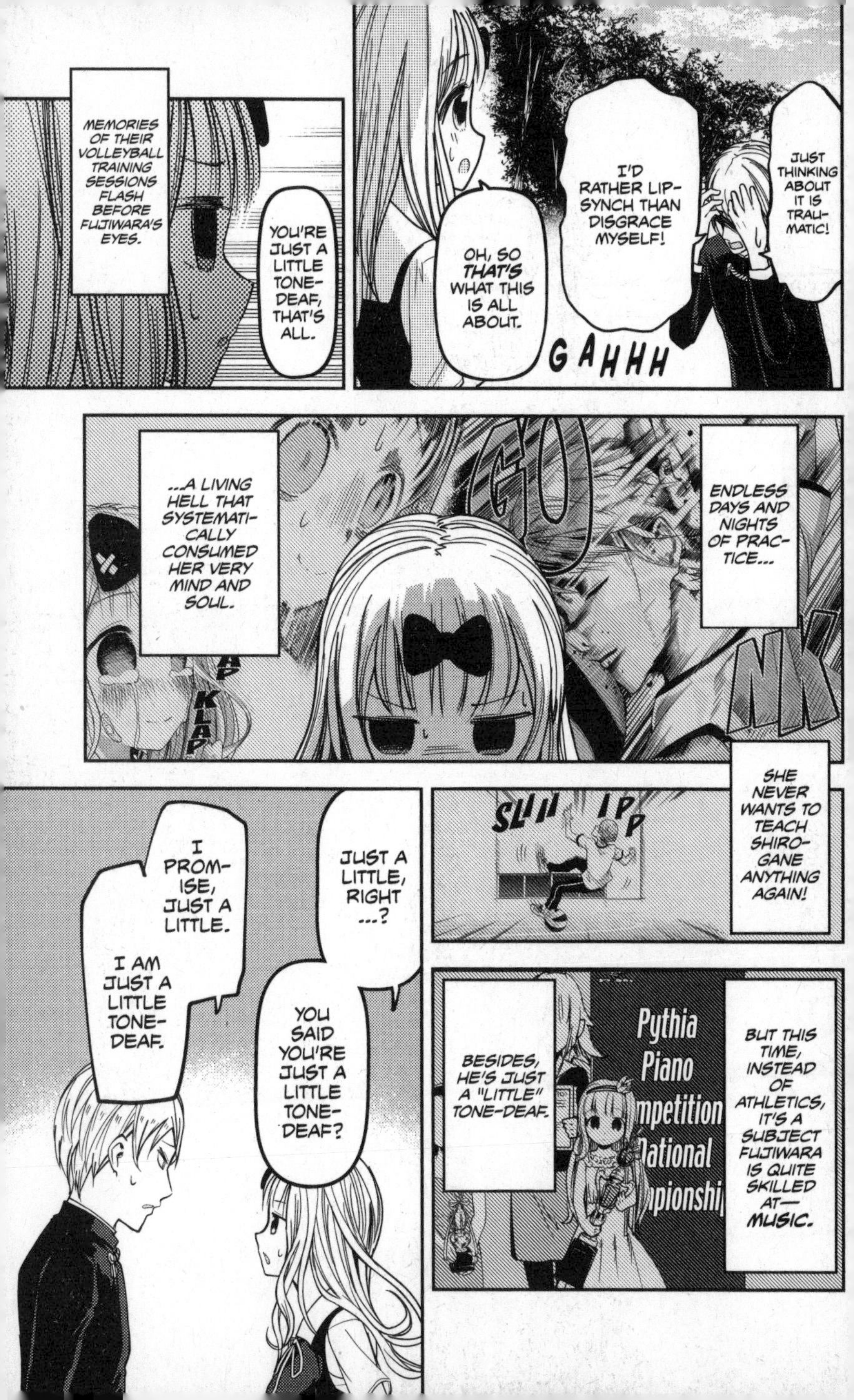
JUST THINKING ABOUT IT IS TRAUMATIC!
I'D RATHER LIP-SYNCH THAN DISGRACE MYSELF!
GAHHH
OH, SO THAT'S WHAT THIS IS ALL ABOUT.
YOU'RE JUST A LITTLE TONE-DEAF, THAT'S ALL.
MEMORIES OF THEIR VOLLEYBALL TRAINING SESSIONS FLASH BEFORE FUJIWARA'S EYES.
ENDLESS DAYS AND NIGHTS OF PRACTICE...
...A LIVING HELL THAT SYSTEMATICALLY CONSUMED HER VERY MIND AND SOUL.
KLAP
SHE NEVER WANTS TO TEACH SHIROGANE ANYTHING AGAIN!
BUT THIS TIME, INSTEAD OF ATHLETICS, IT'S A SUBJECT FUJIWARA IS QUITE SKILLED AT— MUSIC.
Pythia
Piano
BESIDES, HE'S JUST A "LITTLE" TONE-DEAF.
JUST A LITTLE, RIGHT...?
I PROMISE, JUST A LITTLE.
I AM JUST A LITTLE TONE-DEAF.
YOU SAID YOU'RE JUST A LITTLE TONE-DEAF?

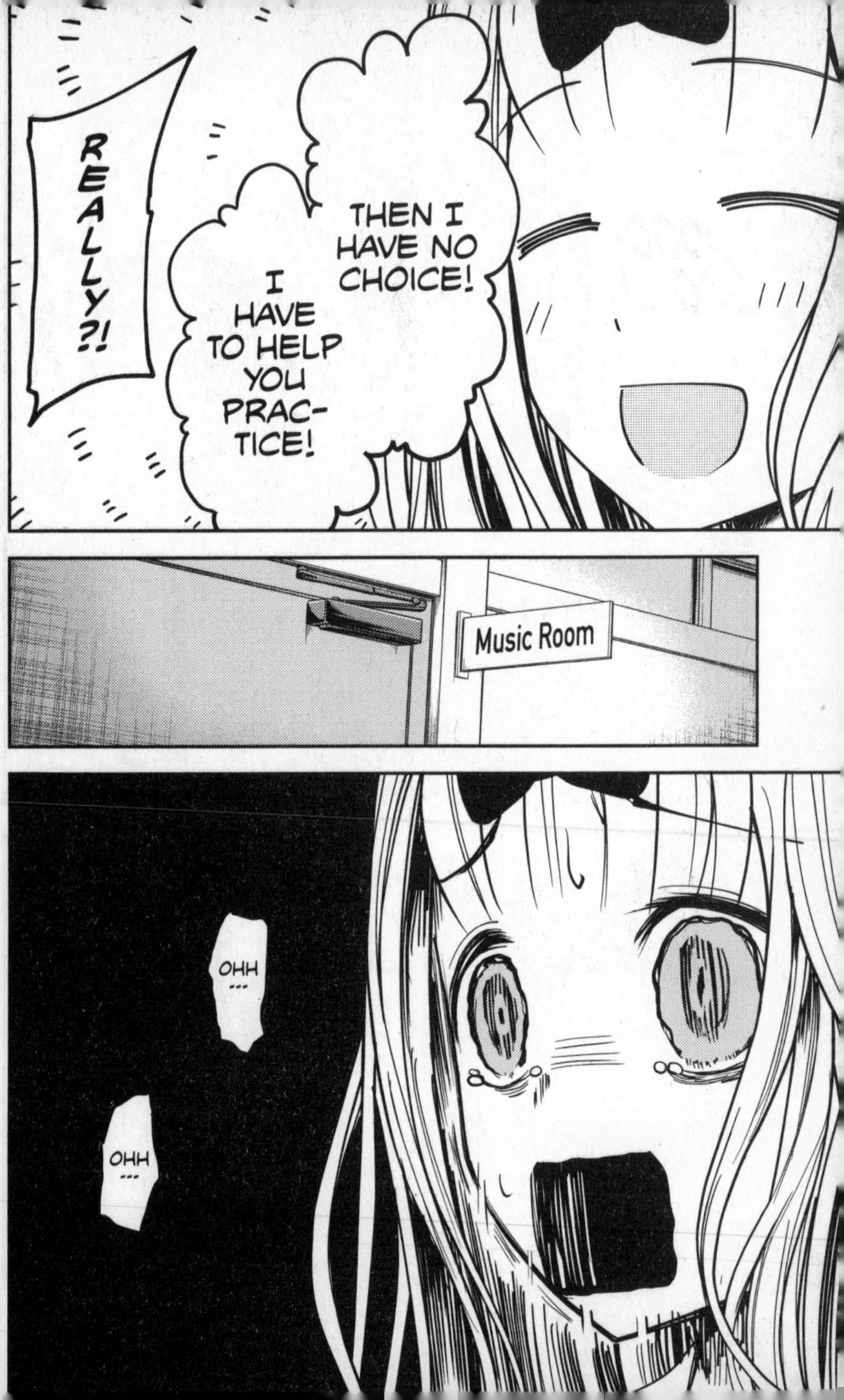
THEN I HAVE NO CHOICE!
I HAVE TO HELP YOU PRACTICE!
REALLY?!
Music Room
OHH...
OHH...

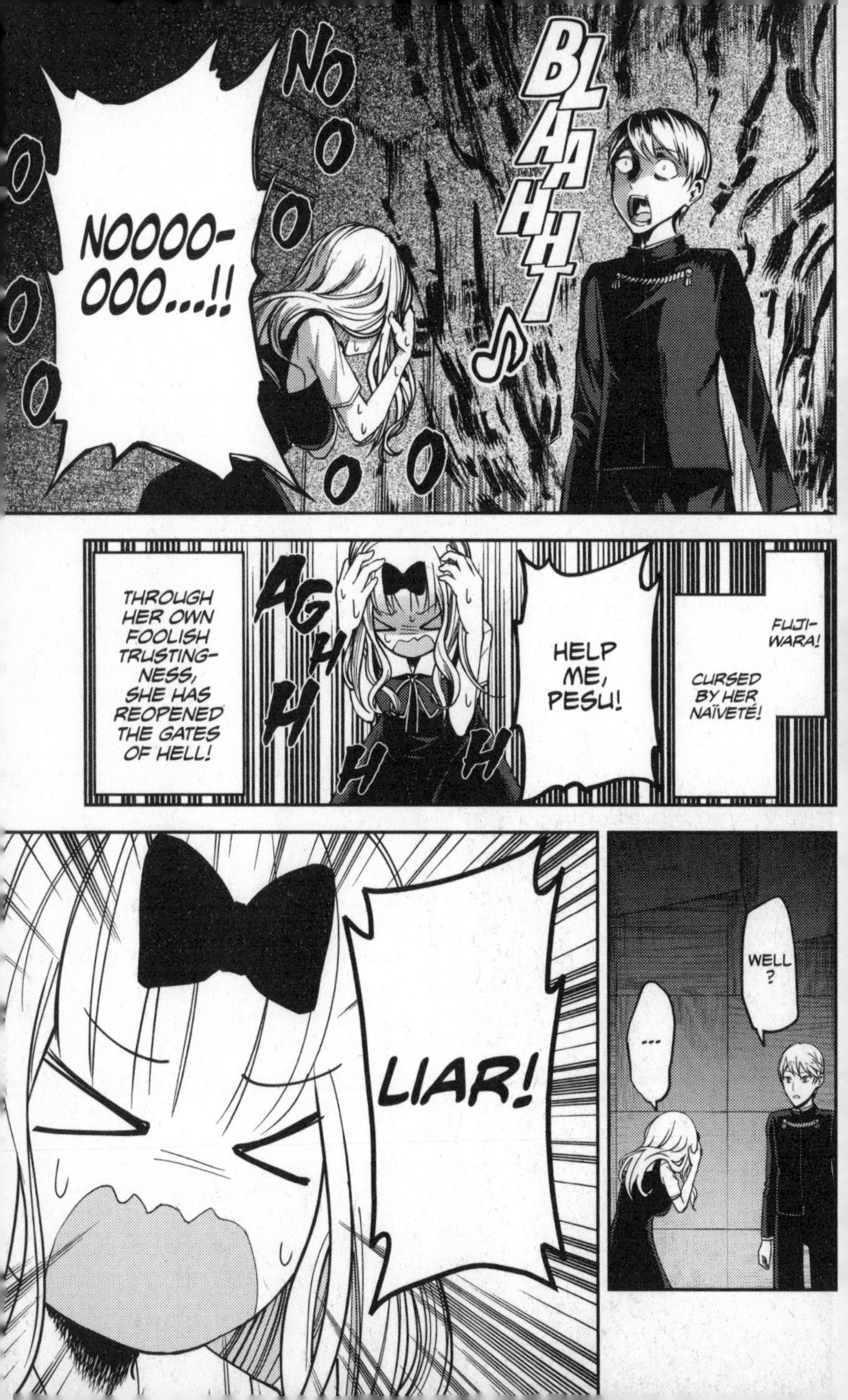
BLAAHHHT ♪
NOOOO-OOO...!!
NOOOOOO
OOOOO
FUJI-WARA!
CURSED BY HER NAÏVETÉ!
HELP ME, PESU!
AGHHHHH
THROUGH HER OWN FOOLISH TRUSTING-NESS, SHE HAS REOPENED THE GATES OF HELL!
WELL?
...
LIAR!

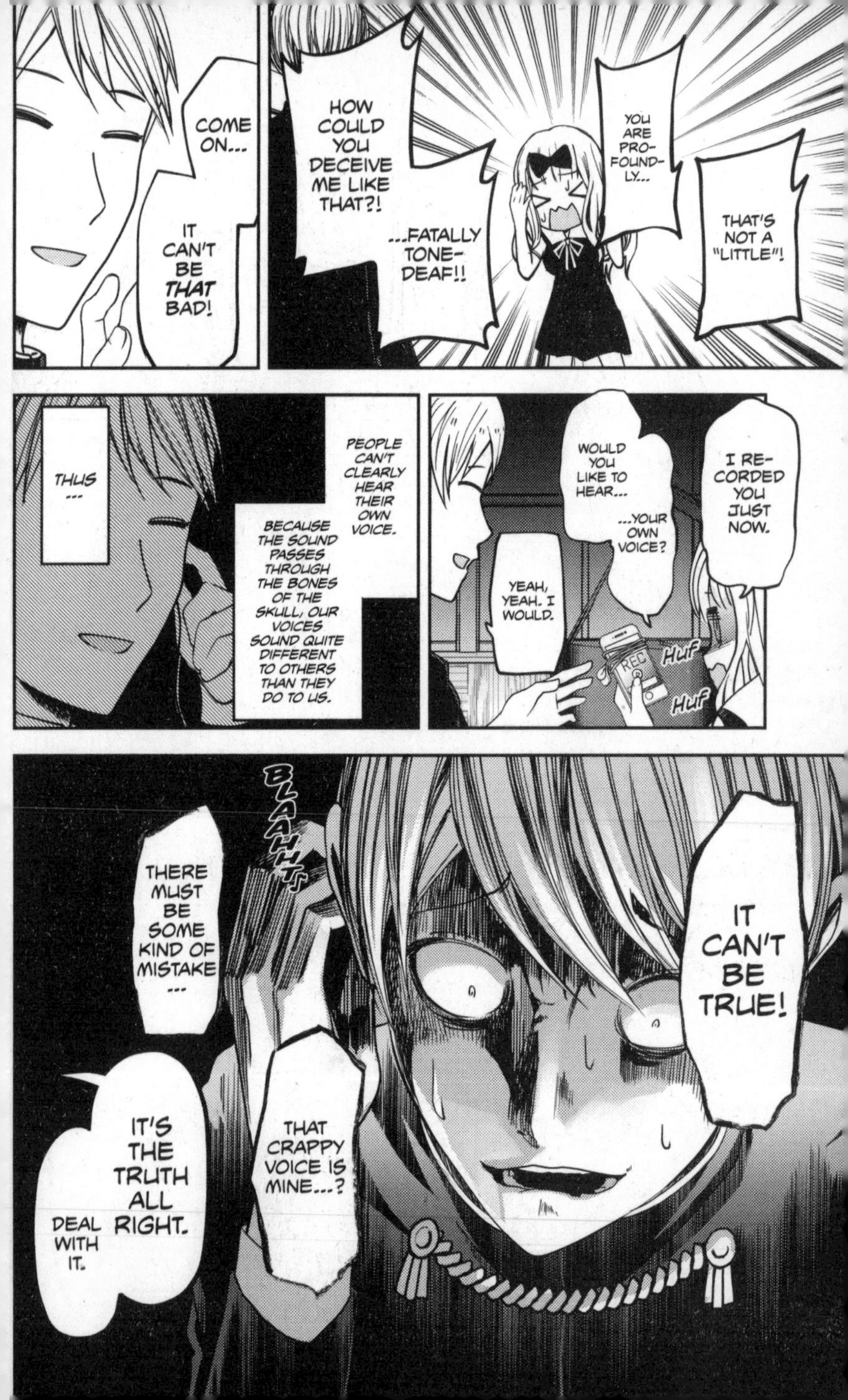
THAT'S NOT A "LITTLE"!
YOU ARE PROFOUNDLY...
...FATALLY TONE-DEAF!!
HOW COULD YOU DECEIVE ME LIKE THAT?!
COME ON...
IT CAN'T BE *THAT* BAD!
I RECORDED YOU JUST NOW.
WOULD YOU LIKE TO HEAR...
...YOUR OWN VOICE?
YEAH, YEAH. I WOULD.
Huf
Huf
REC
PEOPLE CAN'T CLEARLY HEAR THEIR OWN VOICE.
BECAUSE THE SOUND PASSES THROUGH THE BONES OF THE SKULL, OUR VOICES SOUND QUITE DIFFERENT TO OTHERS THAN THEY DO TO US.
THUS...
IT CAN'T BE TRUE!
BLAAHHTS
THERE MUST BE SOME KIND OF MISTAKE...
THAT CRAPPY VOICE IS MINE...?
IT'S THE TRUTH ALL RIGHT.
DEAL WITH IT.

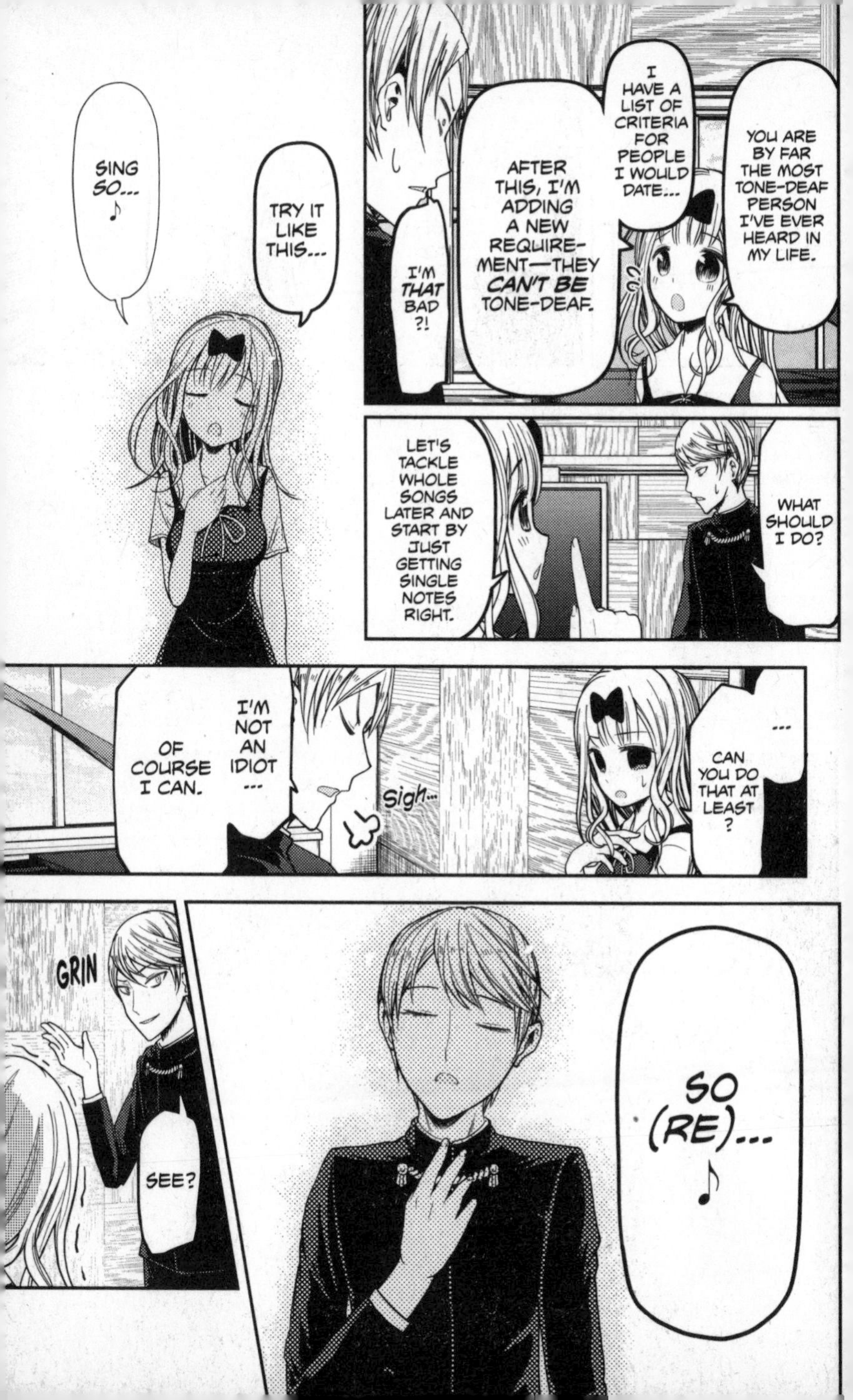
YOU ARE BY FAR THE MOST TONE-DEAF PERSON I'VE EVER HEARD IN MY LIFE.
I HAVE A LIST OF CRITERIA FOR PEOPLE I WOULD DATE...
AFTER THIS, I'M ADDING A NEW REQUIREMENT—THEY *CAN'T BE* TONE-DEAF.
I'M *THAT* BAD?!
WHAT SHOULD I DO?
LET'S TACKLE WHOLE SONGS LATER AND START BY JUST GETTING SINGLE NOTES RIGHT.
TRY IT LIKE THIS...
SING SO... ♪
... CAN YOU DO THAT AT LEAST?
Sigh...
I'M NOT AN IDIOT...
OF COURSE I CAN.
SO (RE)... ♪
GRIN
SEE?

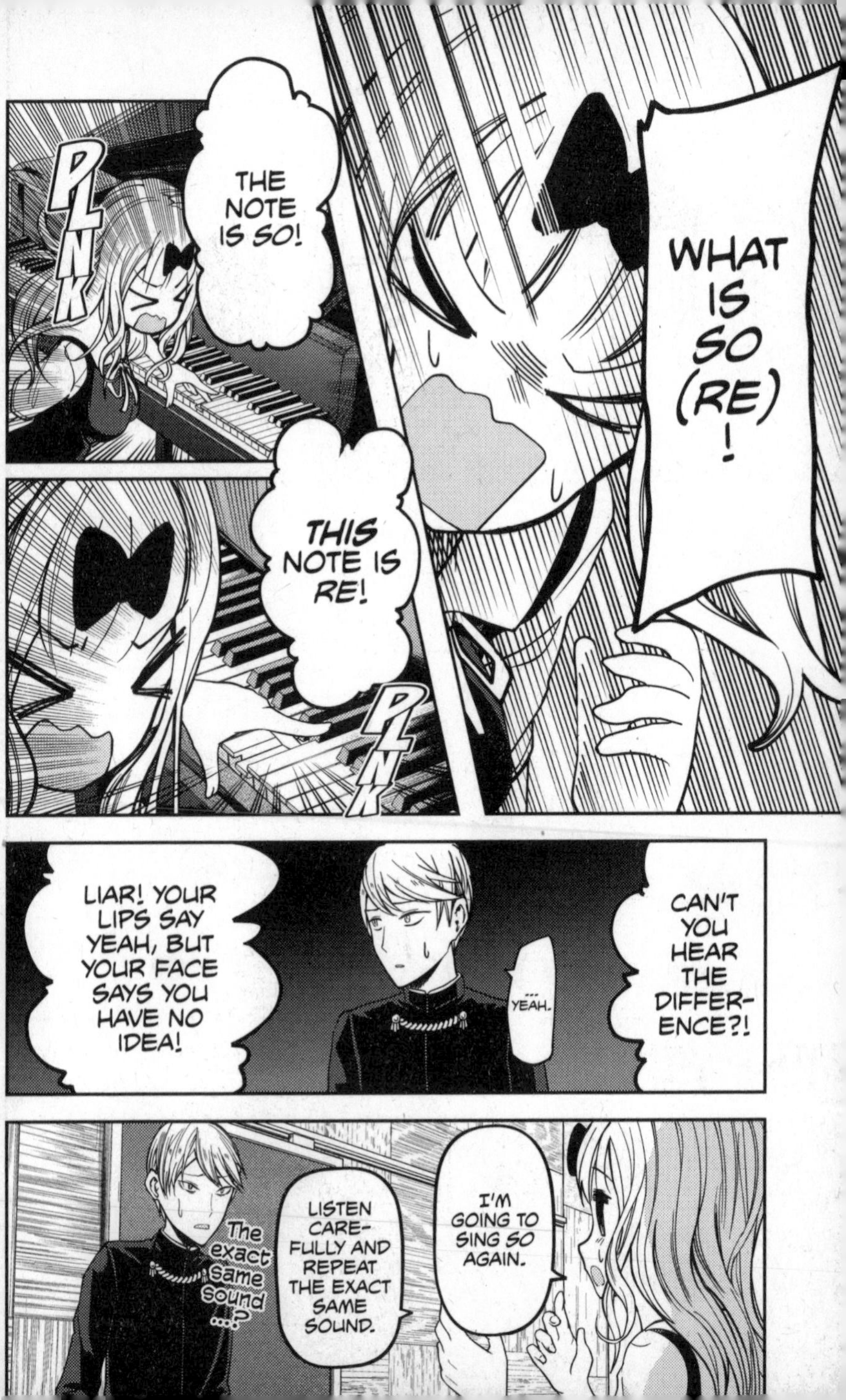
WHAT IS SO (RE)!
THE NOTE IS SO!
PLNK
THIS NOTE IS RE!
PLNK
CAN'T YOU HEAR THE DIFFER-ENCE?!
...YEAH.
LIAR! YOUR LIPS SAY YEAH, BUT YOUR FACE SAYS YOU HAVE NO IDEA!
I'M GOING TO SING SO AGAIN.
LISTEN CARE-FULLY AND REPEAT THE EXACT SAME SOUND.
The exact same sound...?

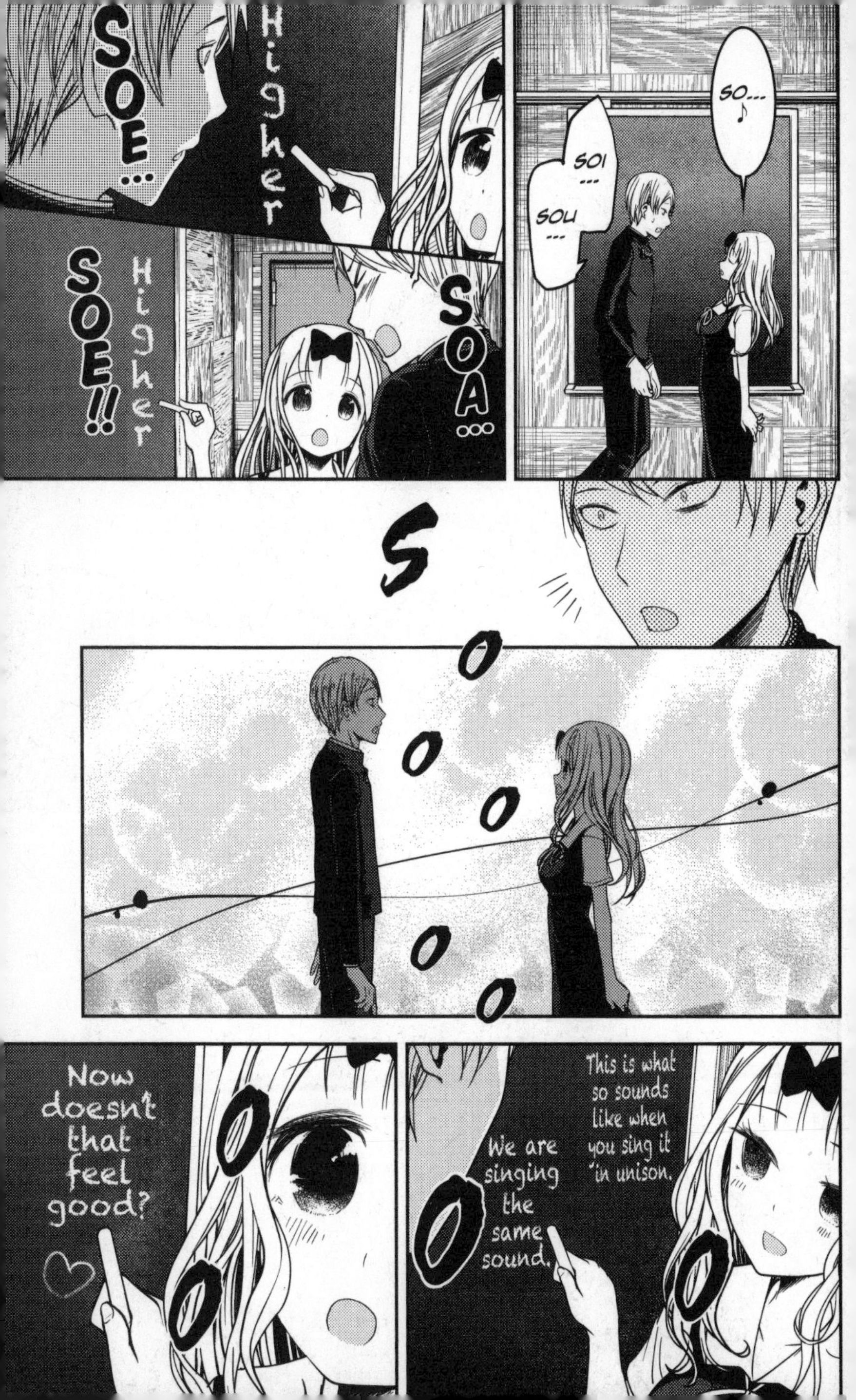
SO... ♪
SOI... SOU...
SOE...
Higher
SOA...
Higher
SOE!!
SOOOOOO
This is what so sounds like when you sing it in unison.
We are singing the same sound.
Now doesn't that feel good?

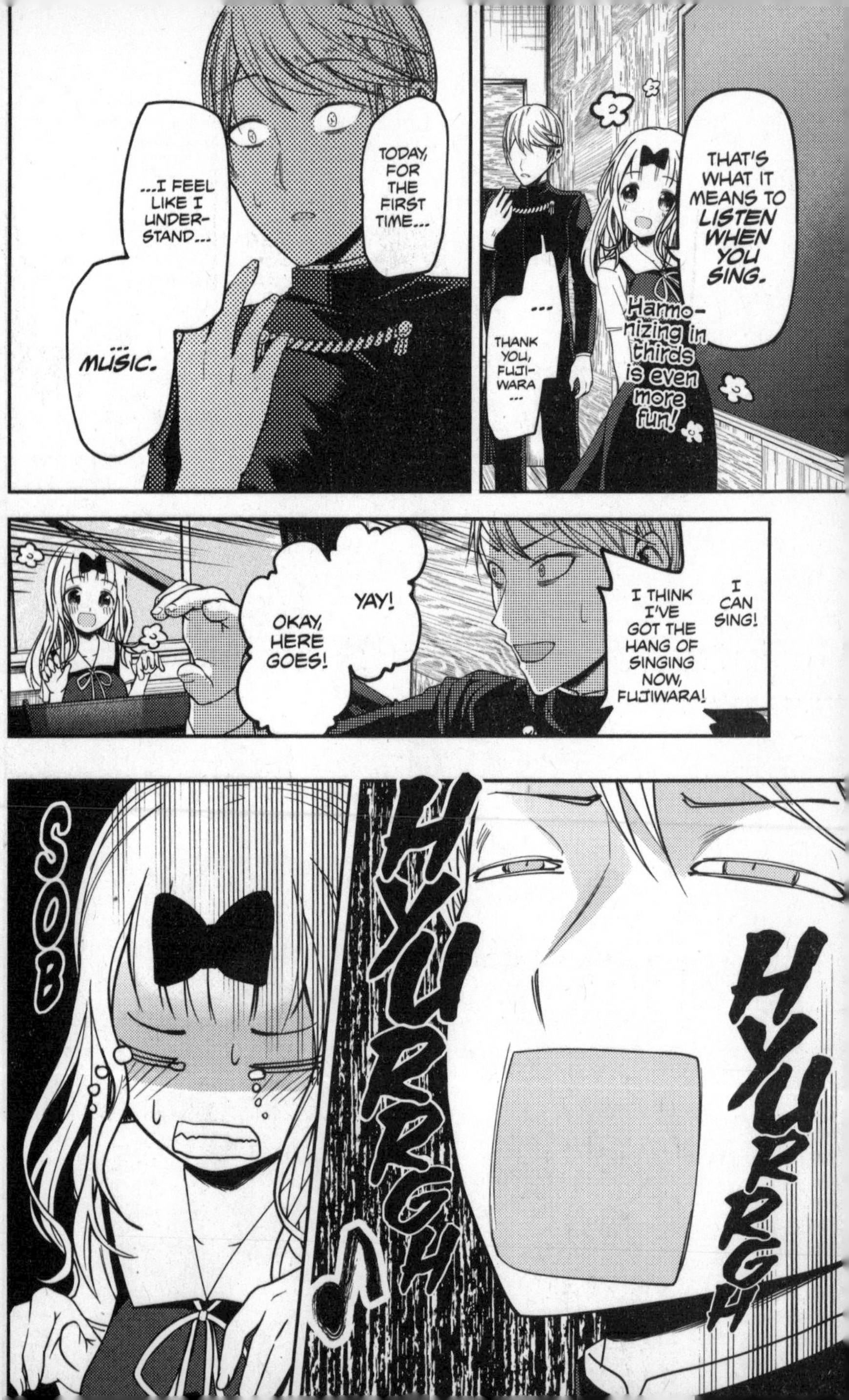
THAT'S WHAT IT MEANS TO LISTEN WHEN YOU SING.
Harmonizing in thirds is even more fun!
...
THANK YOU, FUJIWARA...
TODAY, FOR THE FIRST TIME...
...I FEEL LIKE I UNDERSTAND...
...MUSIC.
I CAN SING!
I THINK I'VE GOT THE HANG OF SINGING NOW, FUJIWARA!
YAY!
OKAY, HERE GOES!
HYURRGH
HYURRGH
SOB

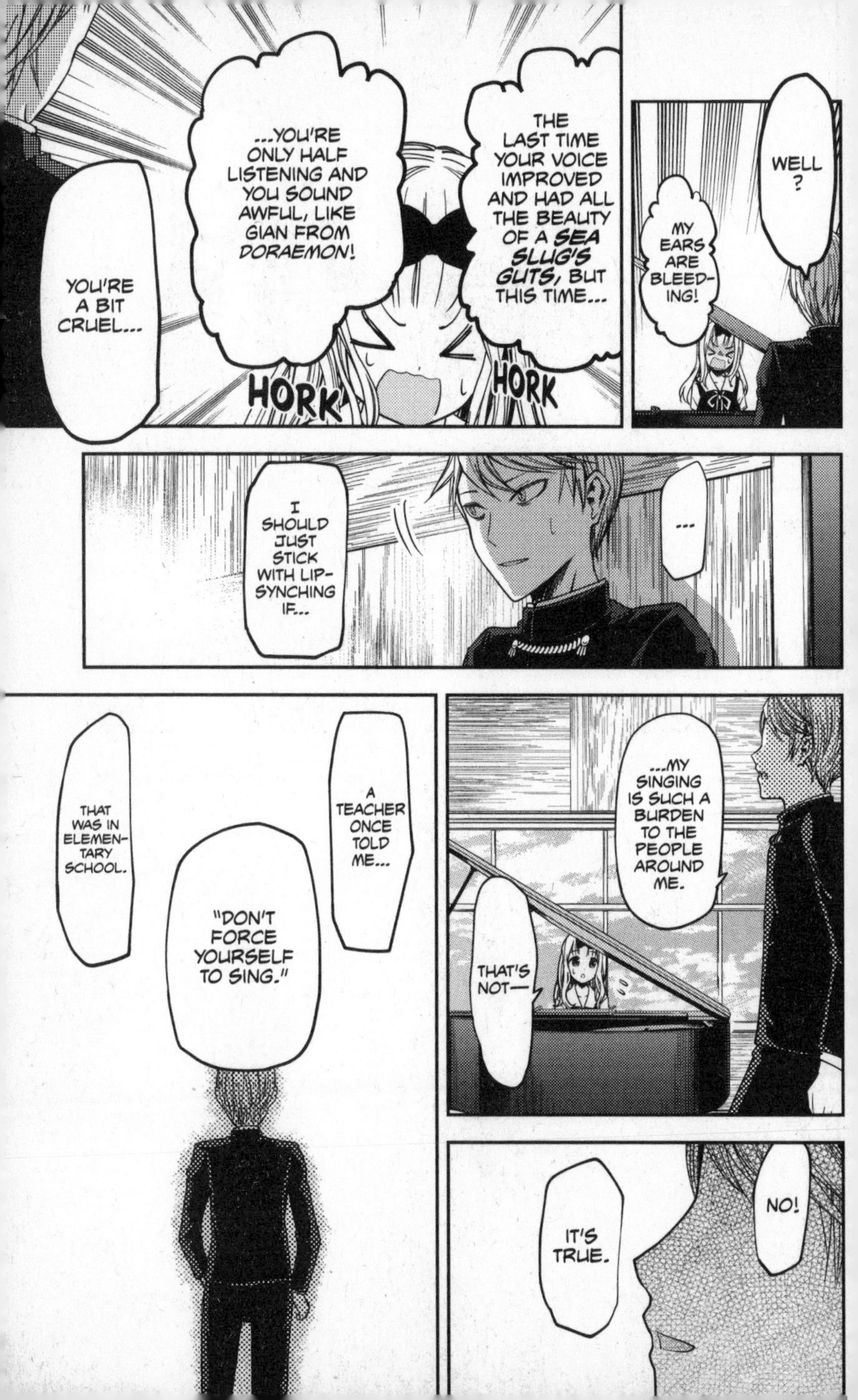
WELL?
MY EARS ARE BLEEDING!
THE LAST TIME YOUR VOICE IMPROVED AND HAD ALL THE BEAUTY OF A SEA SLUG'S GUTS, BUT THIS TIME...
...YOU'RE ONLY HALF LISTENING AND YOU SOUND AWFUL, LIKE GIAN FROM DORAEMON!
HORK
HORK
YOU'RE A BIT CRUEL...
...
I SHOULD JUST STICK WITH LIP-SYNCHING IF...
...MY SINGING IS SUCH A BURDEN TO THE PEOPLE AROUND ME.
THAT'S NOT—
NO!
IT'S TRUE.
A TEACHER ONCE TOLD ME...
THAT WAS IN ELEMENTARY SCHOOL.
"DON'T FORCE YOURSELF TO SING."

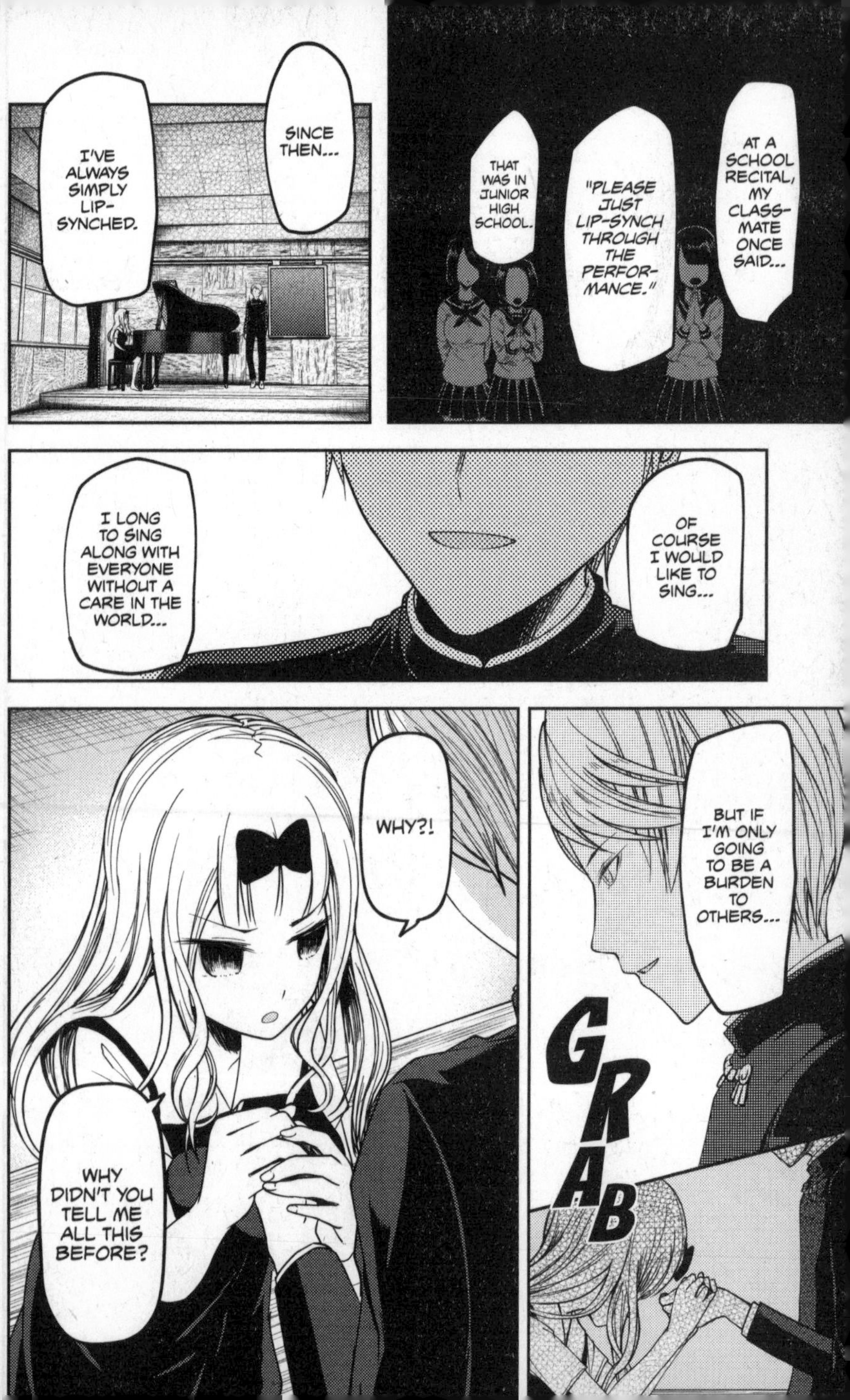
AT A SCHOOL RECITAL, MY CLASSMATE ONCE SAID...
"PLEASE JUST LIP-SYNCH THROUGH THE PERFORMANCE."
THAT WAS IN JUNIOR HIGH SCHOOL.
SINCE THEN...
I'VE ALWAYS SIMPLY LIP-SYNCHED.
OF COURSE I WOULD LIKE TO SING...
I LONG TO SING ALONG WITH EVERYONE WITHOUT A CARE IN THE WORLD...
BUT IF I'M ONLY GOING TO BE A BURDEN TO OTHERS...
GRAB
WHY?!
WHY DIDN'T YOU TELL ME ALL THIS BEFORE?

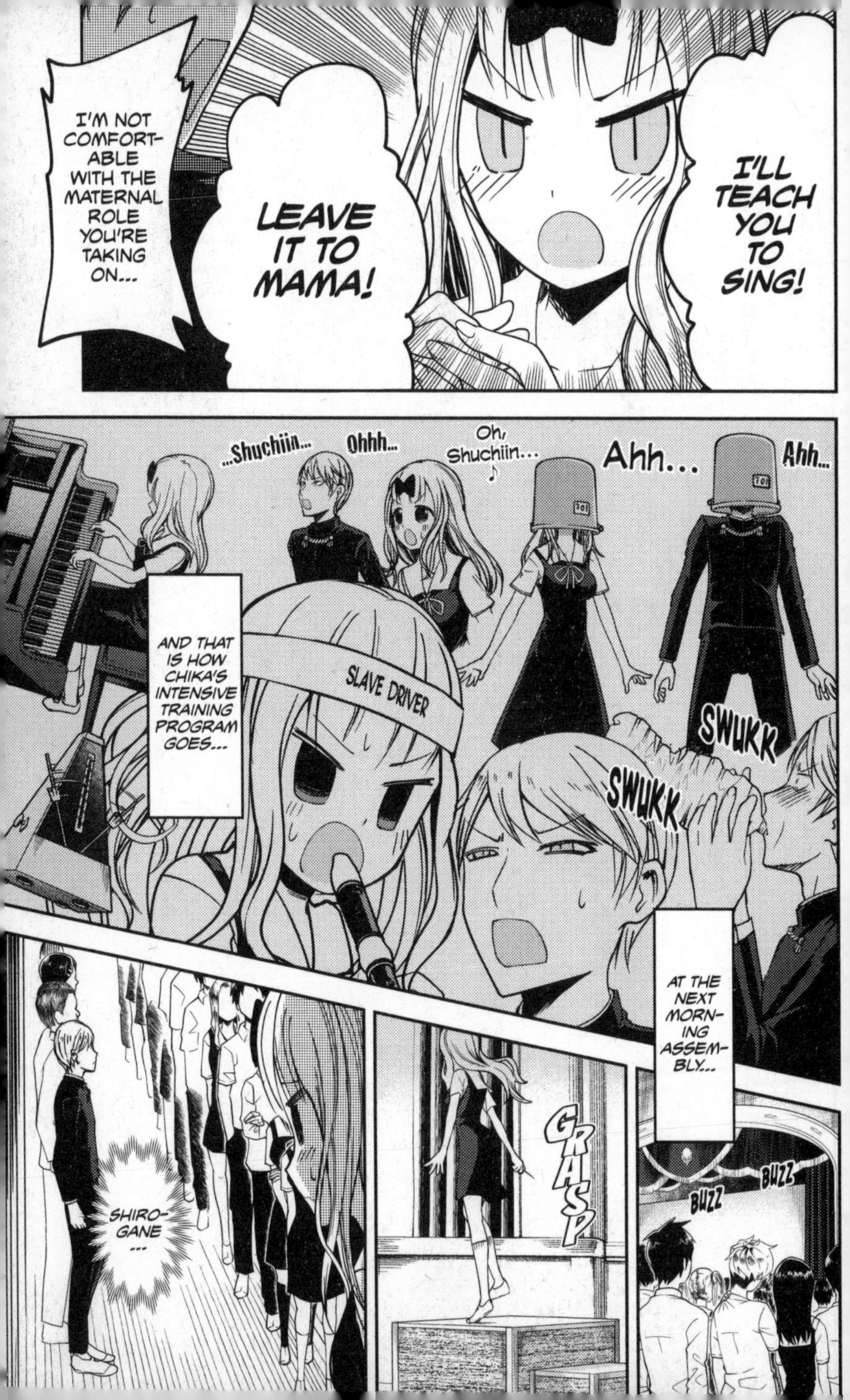

I'LL TEACH YOU TO SING!
LEAVE IT TO MAMA!
I'M NOT COMFORTABLE WITH THE MATERNAL ROLE YOU'RE TAKING ON...
Ahh...
Ahh...
Oh, Shuchiin... ♪
Ohhh...
...Shuchiin...
AND THAT IS HOW CHIKA'S INTENSIVE TRAINING PROGRAM GOES...
SLAVE DRIVER
SWUKK
SWUKK
AT THE NEXT MORNING ASSEMBLY...
BUZZ
BUZZ
GRASP
SHIROGANE ...

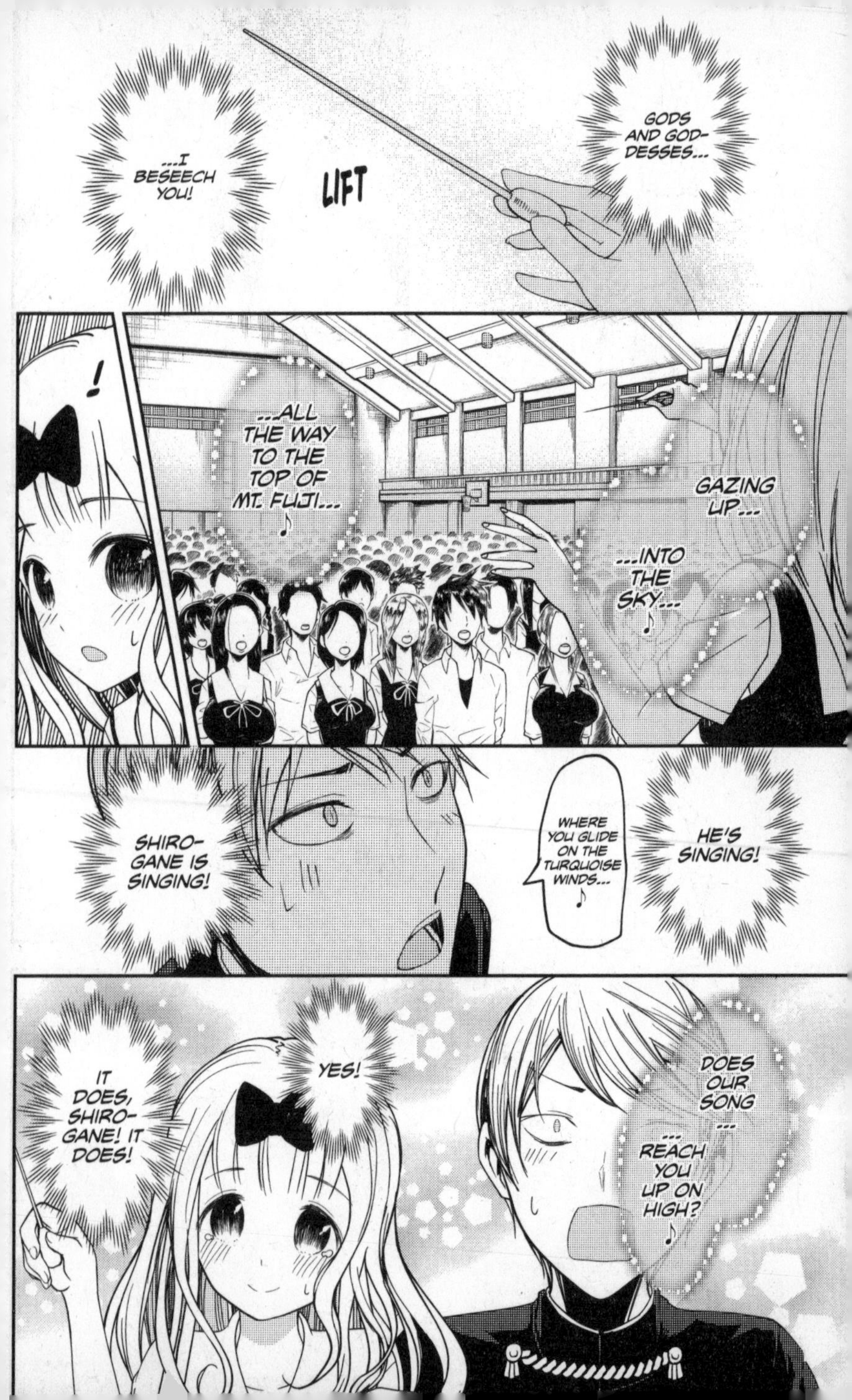
GODS AND GODDESSES...
LIFT
...I BESEECH YOU!
GAZING UP...
...INTO THE SKY... ♪
...ALL THE WAY TO THE TOP OF MT. FUJI... ♪
!
HE'S SINGING!
WHERE YOU GLIDE ON THE TURQUOISE WINDS... ♪
SHIROGANE IS SINGING!
DOES OUR SONG... ...REACH YOU UP ON HIGH? ♪
YES!
IT DOES, SHIROGANE! IT DOES!

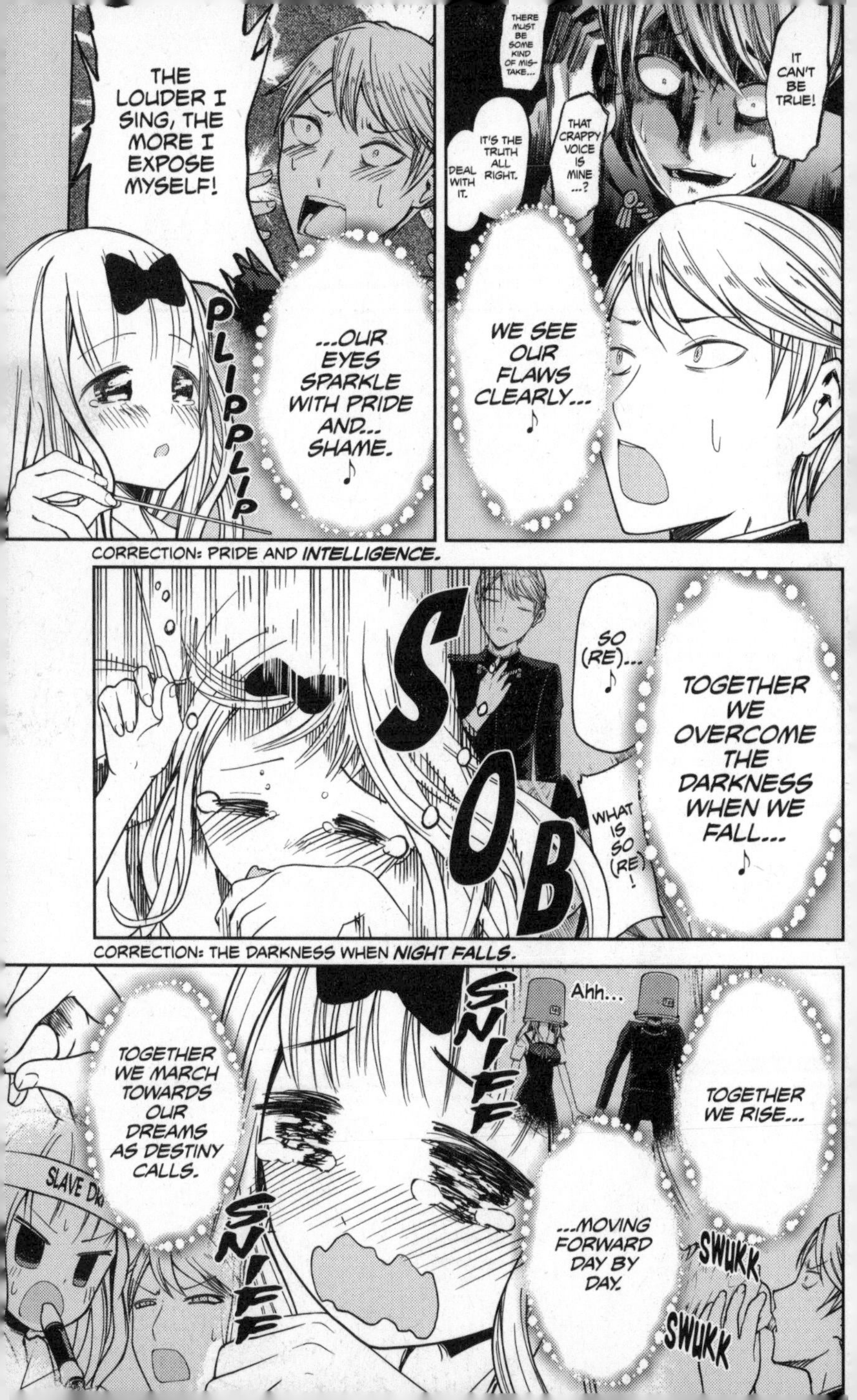
IT CAN'T BE TRUE!
THERE MUST BE SOME KIND OF MIS-TAKE...
THAT CRAPPY VOICE IS MINE ...?
IT'S THE TRUTH ALL RIGHT.
DEAL WITH IT.
WE SEE OUR FLAWS CLEARLY... ♪
THE LOUDER I SING, THE MORE I EXPOSE MYSELF!
...OUR EYES SPARKLE WITH PRIDE AND... SHAME. ♪
PLIP PLIP
CORRECTION: PRIDE AND INTELLIGENCE.
TOGETHER WE OVERCOME THE DARKNESS WHEN WE FALL... ♪
SO (RE)... ♪
WHAT IS SO (RE)!
SOB
CORRECTION: THE DARKNESS WHEN NIGHT FALLS.
TOGETHER WE RISE...
Ahh...
...MOVING FORWARD DAY BY DAY.
SWUKK
SWUKK
SNIFF
SNIFF
TOGETHER WE MARCH TOWARDS OUR DREAMS AS DESTINY CALLS.

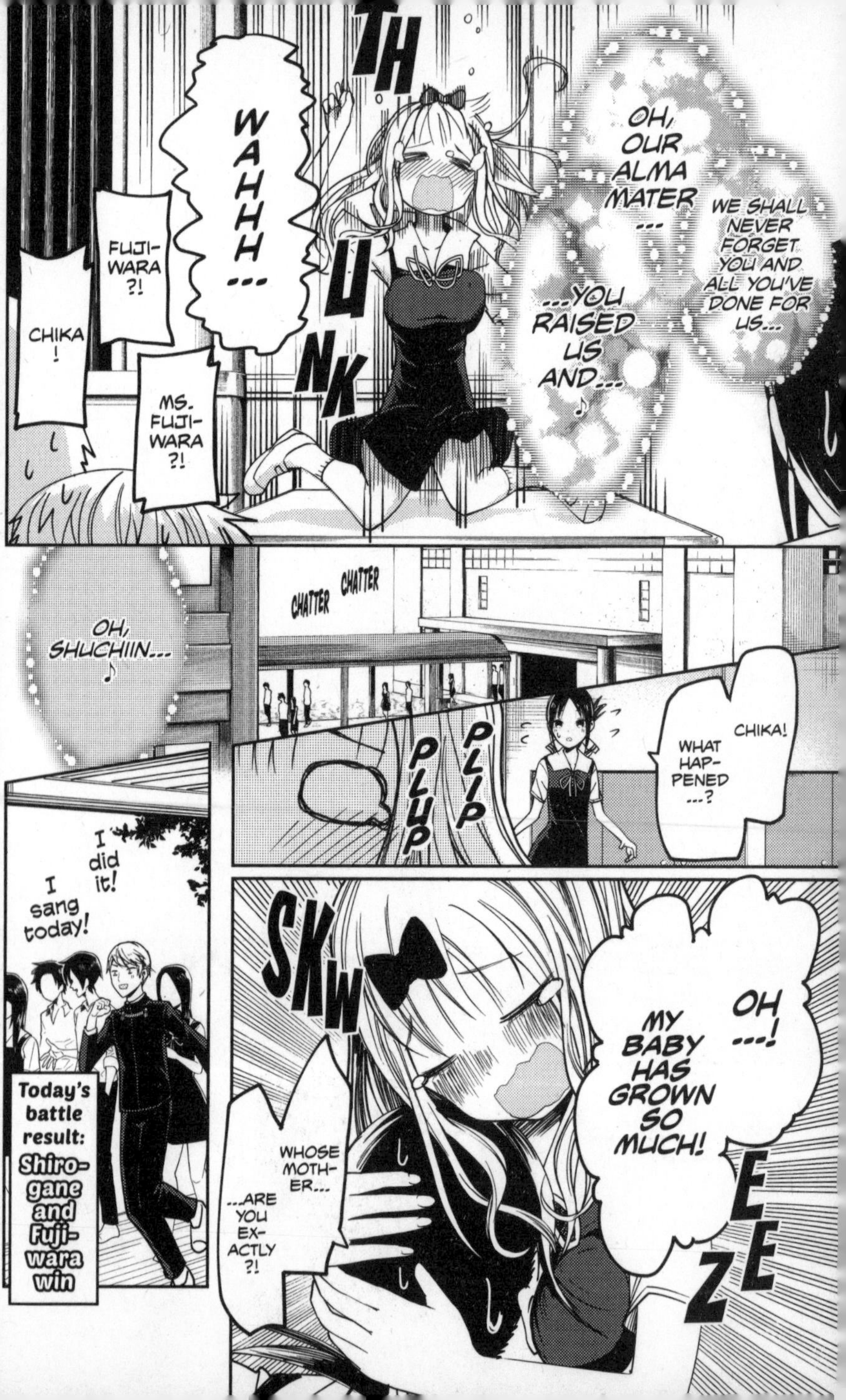
WE SHALL NEVER FORGET YOU AND ALL YOU'VE DONE FOR US...
OH, OUR ALMA MATER...
...YOU RAISED US AND... ♪
THUNK
WAHHH...
FUJI-WARA?!
MS. FUJI-WARA?!
CHIKA!
CHATTER CHATTER
OH, SHUCHIIN... ♪
CHIKA!
WHAT HAP-PENED...?
PLIP PLUP
OH...!
MY BABY HAS GROWN SO MUCH!
SKWEEZE
WHOSE MOTH-ER...
...ARE YOU EX-ACTLY?!
I did it!
I sang today!
Today's battle result:
Shiro-gane and Fuji-wara win

There
isn't
going
to be
any
more
of
this,
is
there
?!

Because
I'm not
doing
this
again!!

TO BE
CONTIN-
UED...

KAGUYA-SAMA
LOVE IS WAR

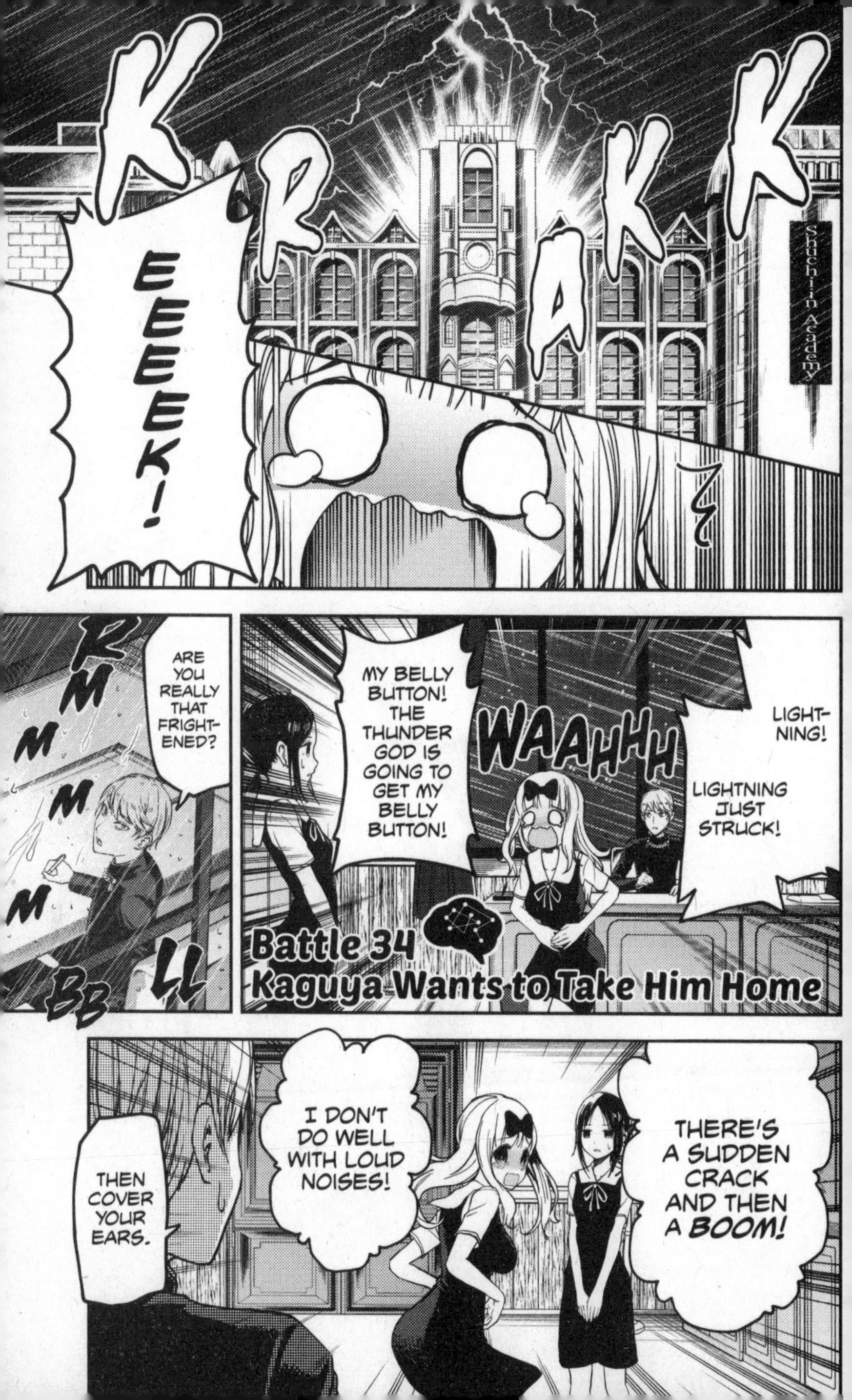
KRAKK
Shuchiin Academy
EEEEEK!
LIGHTNING!
LIGHTNING JUST STRUCK!
WAAHHH
MY BELLY BUTTON! THE THUNDER GOD IS GOING TO GET MY BELLY BUTTON!
Battle 34
Kaguya Wants to Take Him Home
RMMMMM
ARE YOU REALLY THAT FRIGHTENED?
BBLL
THERE'S A SUDDEN CRACK AND THEN A BOOM!
I DON'T DO WELL WITH LOUD NOISES!
THEN COVER YOUR EARS.

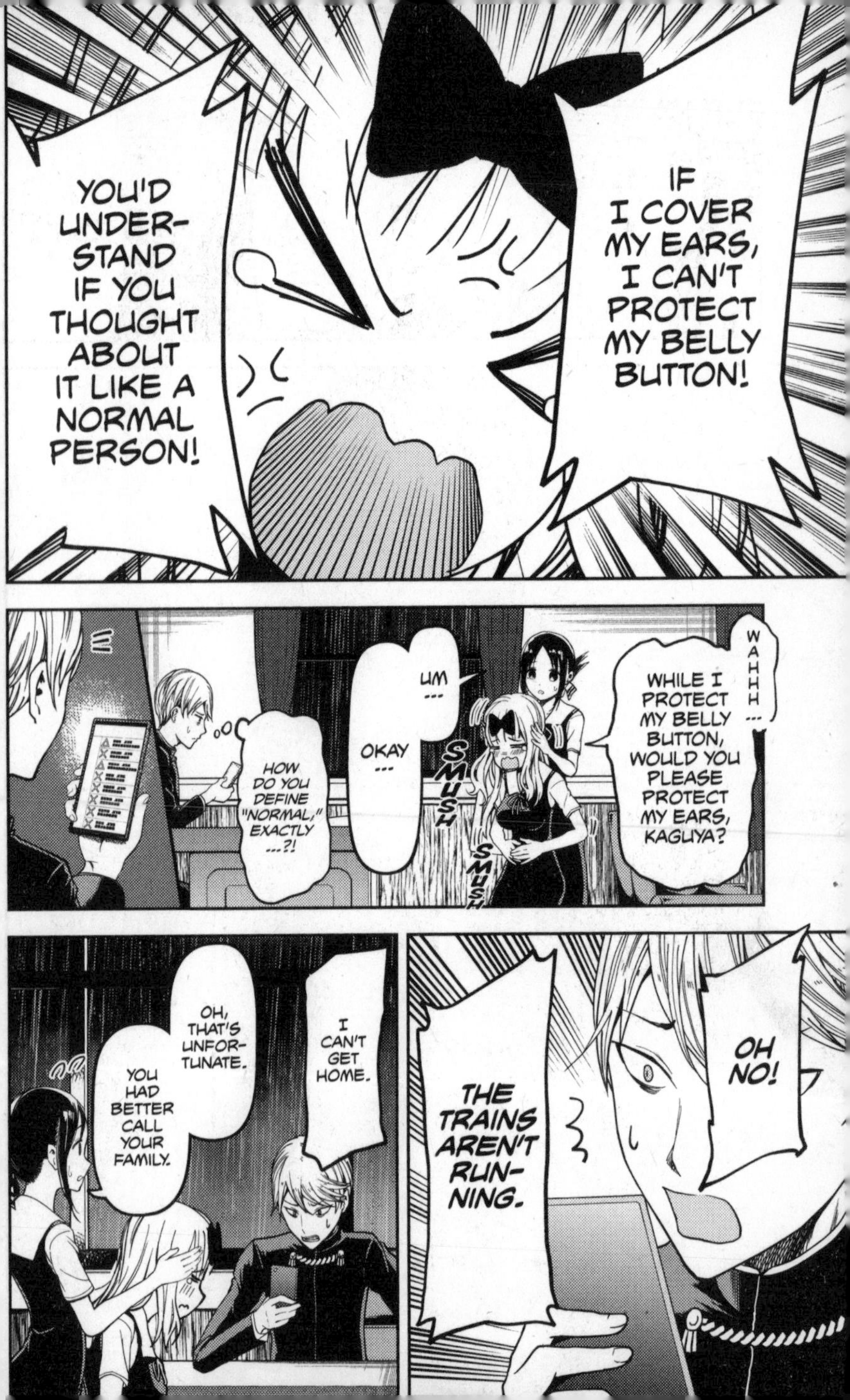
IF I COVER MY EARS, I CAN'T PROTECT MY BELLY BUTTON!
YOU'D UNDERSTAND IF YOU THOUGHT ABOUT IT LIKE A NORMAL PERSON!
WAHHH...
WHILE I PROTECT MY BELLY BUTTON, WOULD YOU PLEASE PROTECT MY EARS, KAGUYA?
SMUSH
SMUSH
UM...
OKAY...
HOW DO YOU DEFINE "NORMAL," EXACTLY...?!
OH NO!
THE TRAINS AREN'T RUNNING.
I CAN'T GET HOME.
OH, THAT'S UNFORTUNATE.
YOU HAD BETTER CALL YOUR FAMILY.

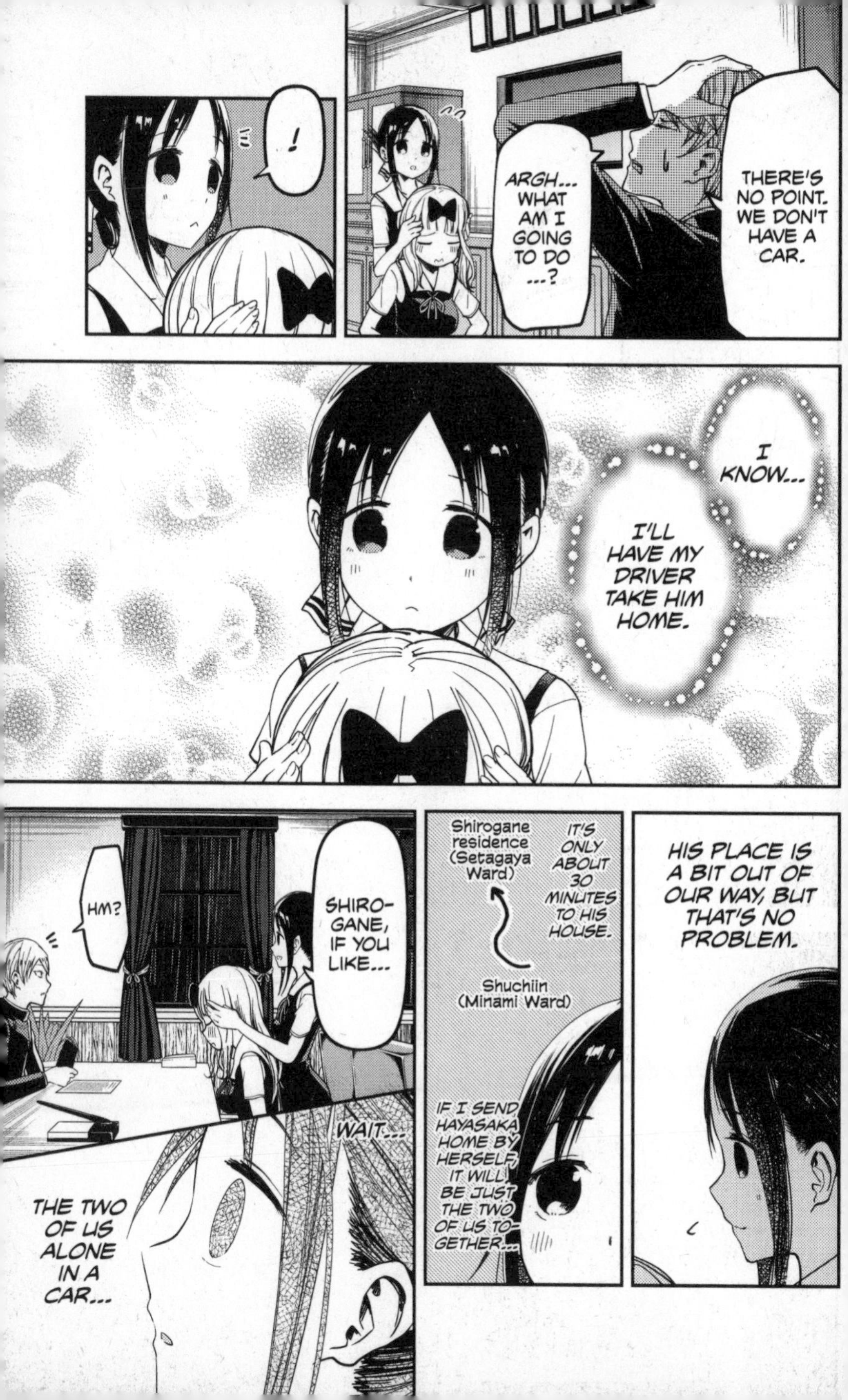
THERE'S NO POINT. WE DON'T HAVE A CAR.
ARGH... WHAT AM I GOING TO DO ...?
!
I KNOW...
I'LL HAVE MY DRIVER TAKE HIM HOME.
HIS PLACE IS A BIT OUT OF OUR WAY, BUT THAT'S NO PROBLEM.
IT'S ONLY ABOUT 30 MINUTES TO HIS HOUSE.
Shirogane residence (Setagaya Ward)
Shuchiin (Minami Ward)
IF I SEND HAYASAKA HOME BY HERSELF, IT WILL BE JUST THE TWO OF US TOGETHER...
SHIRO-GANE, IF YOU LIKE...
HM?
WAIT...
THE TWO OF US ALONE IN A CAR...

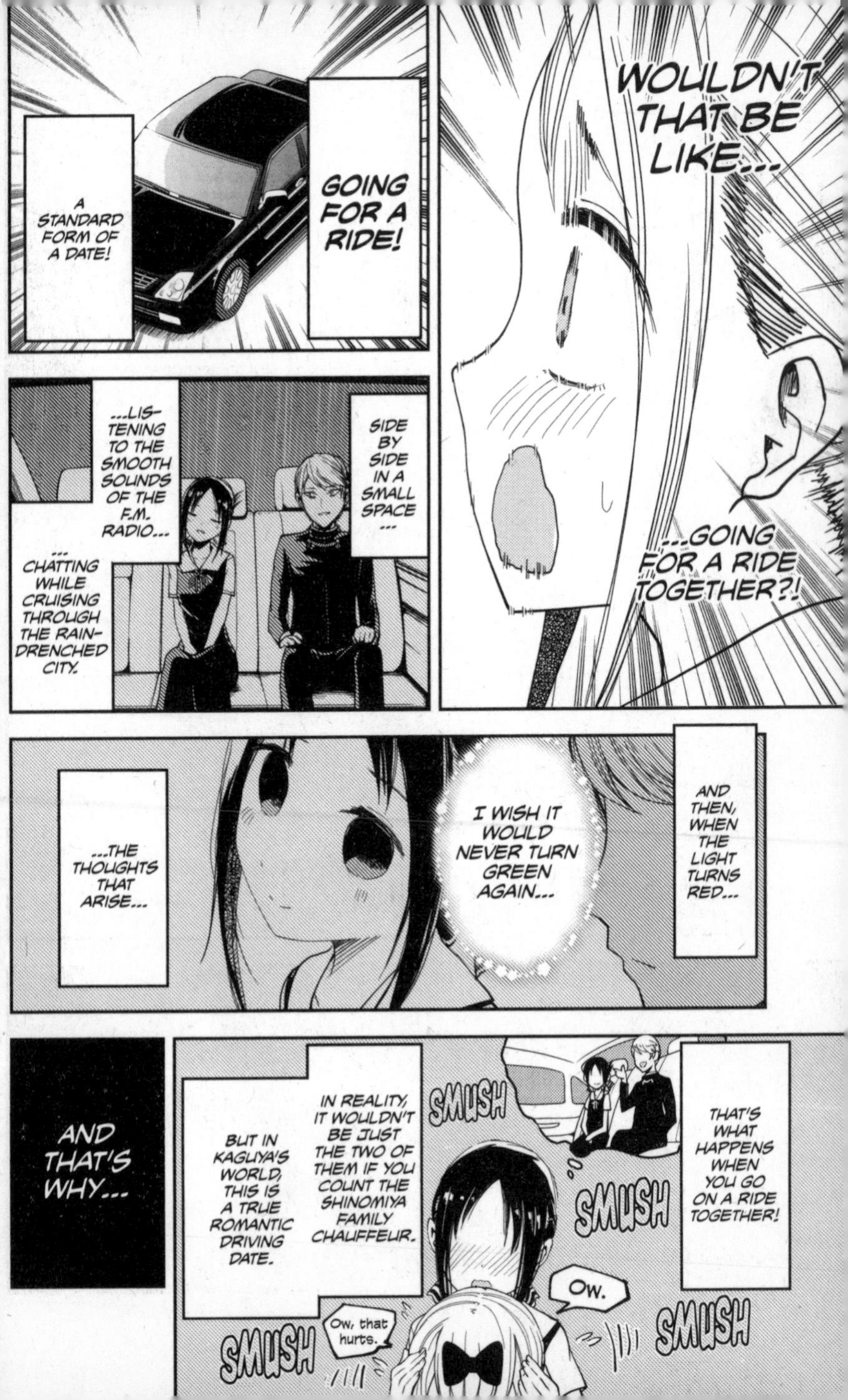
WOULDN'T THAT BE LIKE...
...GOING FOR A RIDE TOGETHER?!
GOING FOR A RIDE!
A STANDARD FORM OF A DATE!
SIDE BY SIDE IN A SMALL SPACE...
...LISTENING TO THE SMOOTH SOUNDS OF THE F.M. RADIO...
...CHATTING WHILE CRUISING THROUGH THE RAIN-DRENCHED CITY.
AND THEN, WHEN THE LIGHT TURNS RED...
I WISH IT WOULD NEVER TURN GREEN AGAIN...
...THE THOUGHTS THAT ARISE...
THAT'S WHAT HAPPENS WHEN YOU GO ON A RIDE TOGETHER!
SMUSH
IN REALITY, IT WOULDN'T BE JUST THE TWO OF THEM IF YOU COUNT THE SHINOMIYA FAMILY CHAUFFEUR.
BUT IN KAGUYA'S WORLD, THIS IS A TRUE ROMANTIC DRIVING DATE.
SMUSH
Ow.
SMUSH
Ow, that hurts.
SMUSH
AND THAT'S WHY...

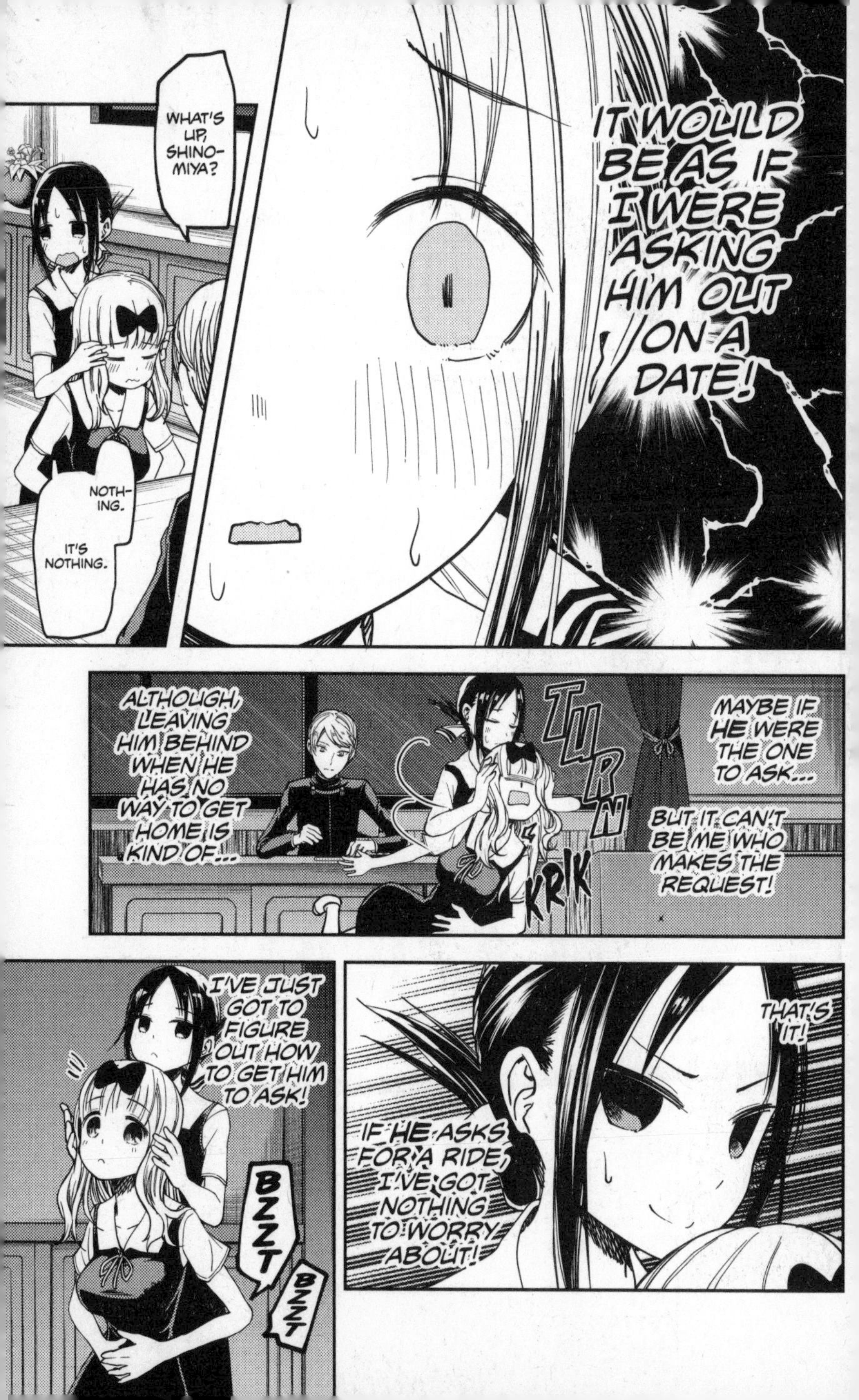
IT WOULD BE AS IF I WERE ASKING HIM OUT ON A DATE!
WHAT'S UP, SHINO-MIYA?
NOTH-ING.
IT'S NOTHING.
MAYBE IF HE WERE THE ONE TO ASK...
BUT IT CAN'T BE ME WHO MAKES THE REQUEST!
TURN
KRIK
ALTHOUGH, LEAVING HIM BEHIND WHEN HE HAS NO WAY TO GET HOME IS KIND OF...
THAT'S IT!
IF HE ASKS FOR A RIDE, I'VE GOT NOTHING TO WORRY ABOUT!
I'VE JUST GOT TO FIGURE OUT HOW TO GET HIM TO ASK!
BZZT
BZZT

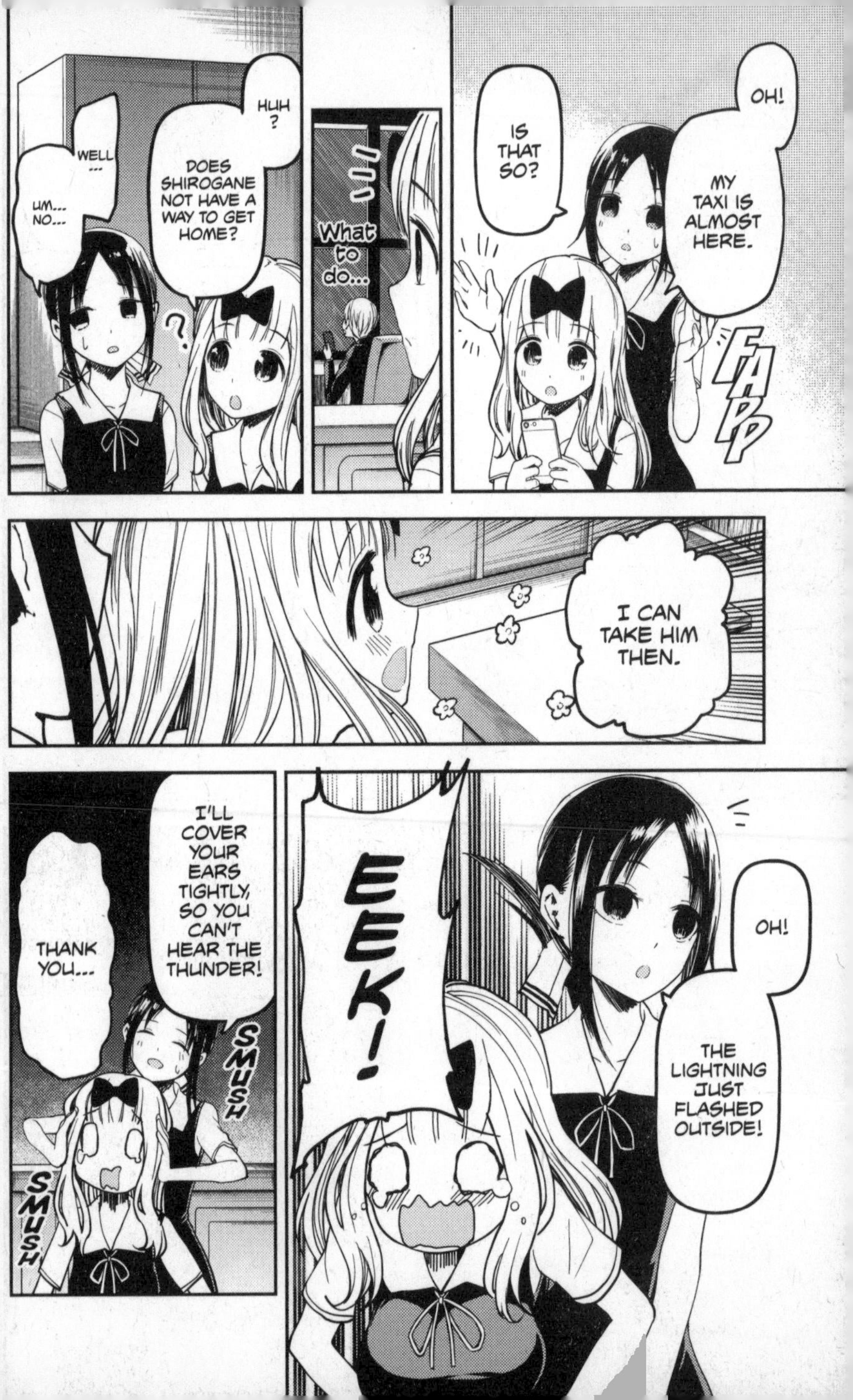
OH!
MY TAXI IS ALMOST HERE.
FAPP
IS THAT SO?
What to do...
HUH?
DOES SHIROGANE NOT HAVE A WAY TO GET HOME?
WELL...
UM... NO...
I CAN TAKE HIM THEN.
OH!
THE LIGHTNING JUST FLASHED OUTSIDE!
EEK!
I'LL COVER YOUR EARS TIGHTLY, SO YOU CAN'T HEAR THE THUNDER!
SMUSH
THANK YOU...
SMUSH

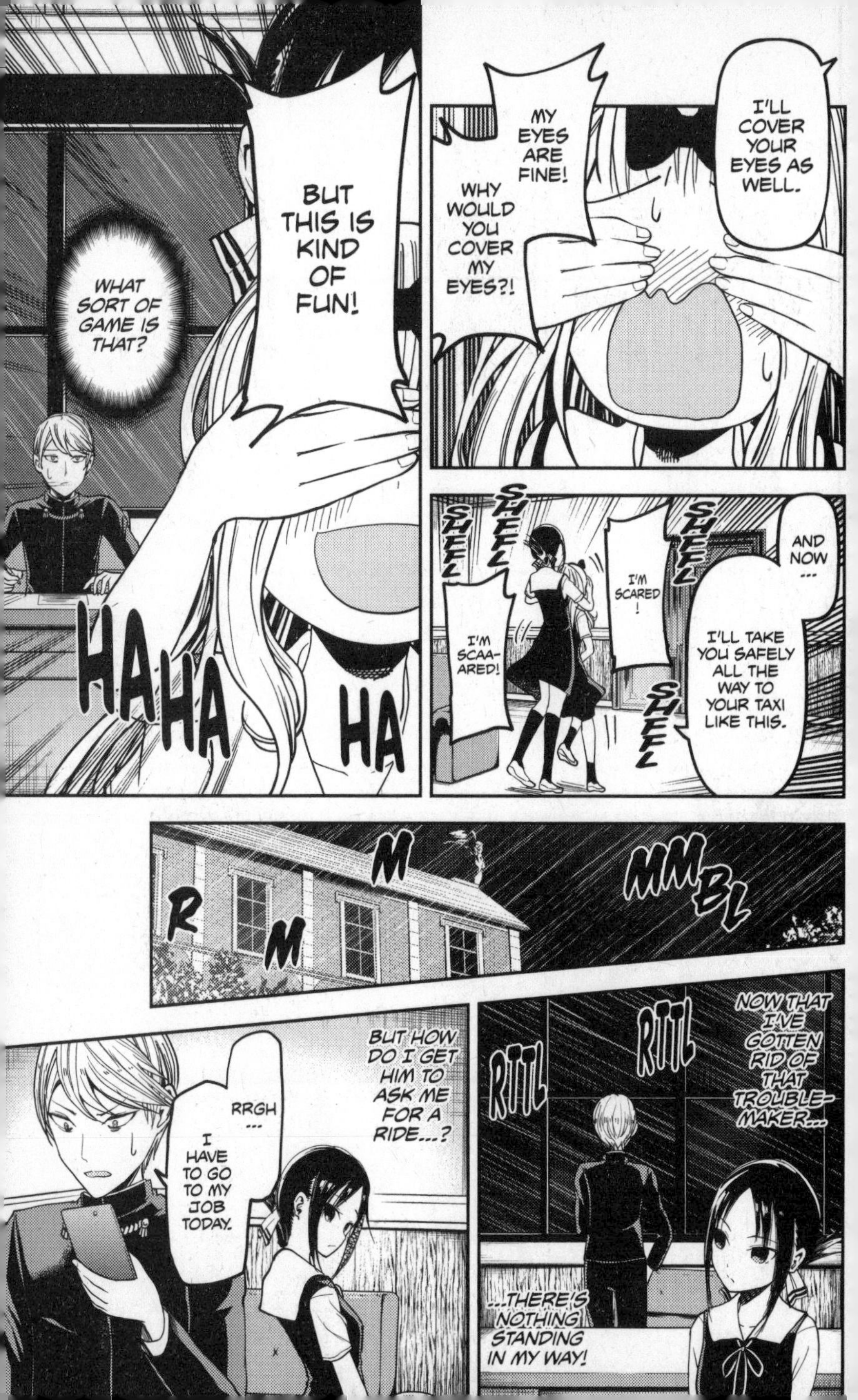
I'LL COVER YOUR EYES AS WELL.
MY EYES ARE FINE!
WHY WOULD YOU COVER MY EYES?!
AND NOW...
I'LL TAKE YOU SAFELY ALL THE WAY TO YOUR TAXI LIKE THIS.
SHFFL
SHFFL
I'M SCARED!
SHFFL
SHFFL
I'M SCAAA-ARED!
BUT THIS IS KIND OF FUN!
WHAT SORT OF GAME IS THAT?
HA HA HA HA
MMBL
RMMM
NOW THAT I'VE GOTTEN RID OF THAT TROUBLE-MAKER...
RTTL
RTTL
...THERE'S NOTHING STANDING IN MY WAY!
BUT HOW DO I GET HIM TO ASK ME FOR A RIDE...?
RRGH...
I HAVE TO GO TO MY JOB TODAY.

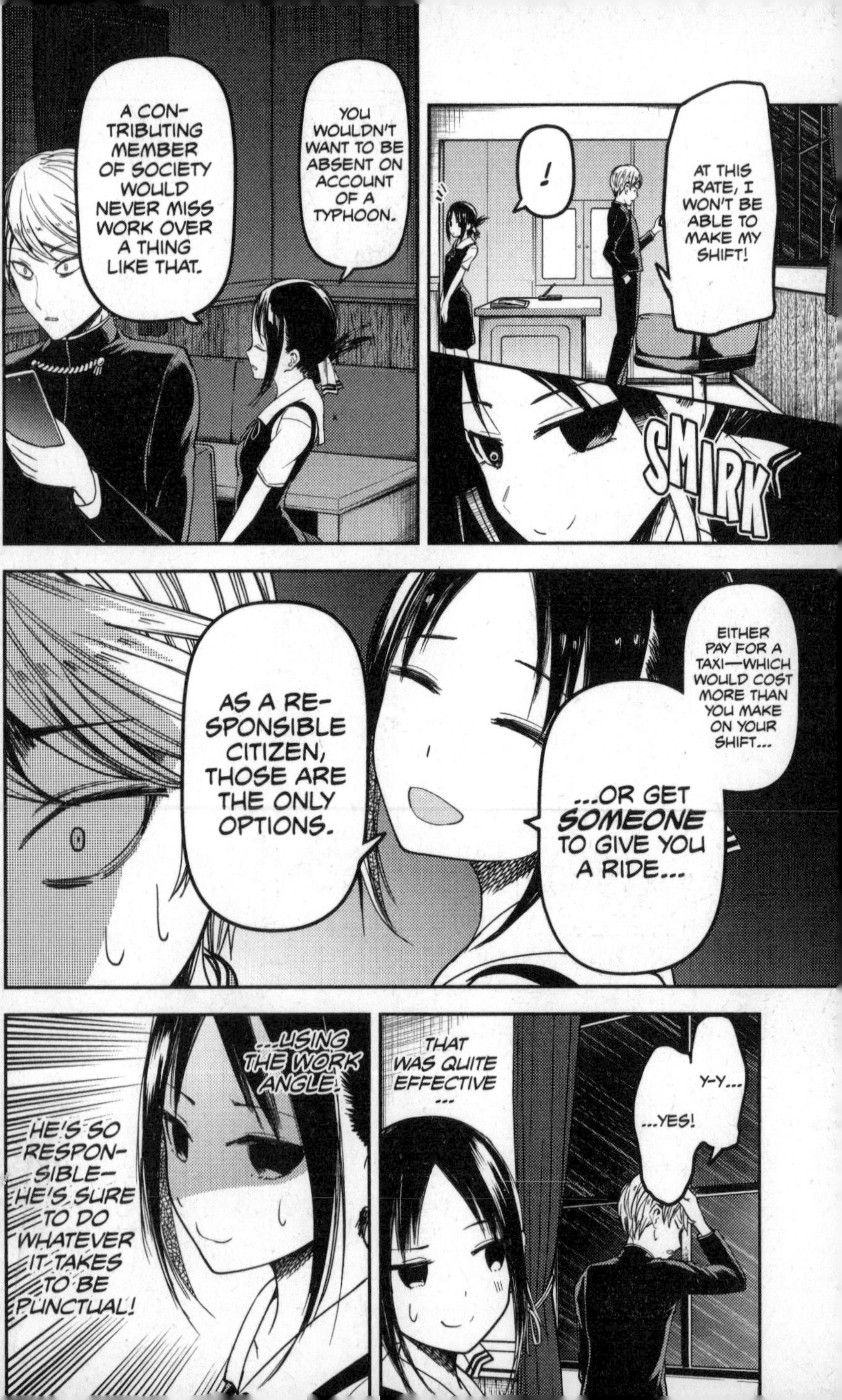
AT THIS RATE, I WON'T BE ABLE TO MAKE MY SHIFT!
!
SMIRK
YOU WOULDN'T WANT TO BE ABSENT ON ACCOUNT OF A TYPHOON.
A CONTRIBUTING MEMBER OF SOCIETY WOULD NEVER MISS WORK OVER A THING LIKE THAT.
EITHER PAY FOR A TAXI—WHICH WOULD COST MORE THAN YOU MAKE ON YOUR SHIFT...
...OR GET *SOMEONE* TO GIVE YOU A RIDE...
AS A RESPONSIBLE CITIZEN, THOSE ARE THE ONLY OPTIONS.
Y-Y... ...YES!
THAT WAS QUITE EFFECTIVE ...
...USING THE WORK ANGLE.
HE'S SO RESPONSIBLE—HE'S SURE TO DO WHATEVER IT TAKES TO BE PUNCTUAL!

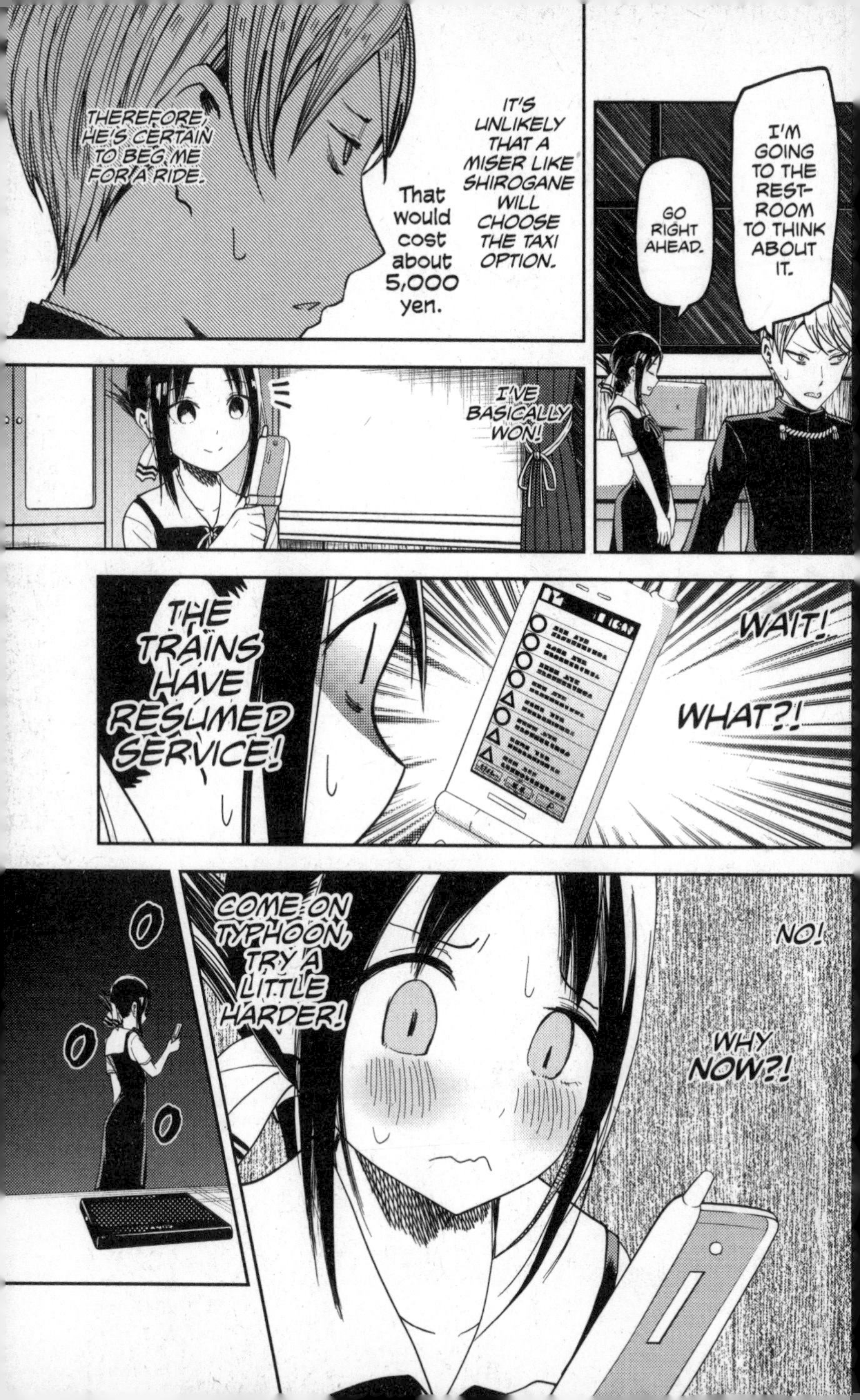
I'M GOING TO THE REST-ROOM TO THINK ABOUT IT.
GO RIGHT AHEAD.
IT'S UNLIKELY THAT A MISER LIKE SHIROGANE WILL CHOOSE THE TAXI OPTION.
That would cost about 5,000 yen.
THEREFORE, HE'S CERTAIN TO BEG ME FOR A RIDE.
I'VE BASICALLY WON!
WAIT!
WHAT?!
THE TRAINS HAVE RESUMED SERVICE!
NO!
WHY NOW?!
COME ON TYPHOON, TRY A LITTLE HARDER!

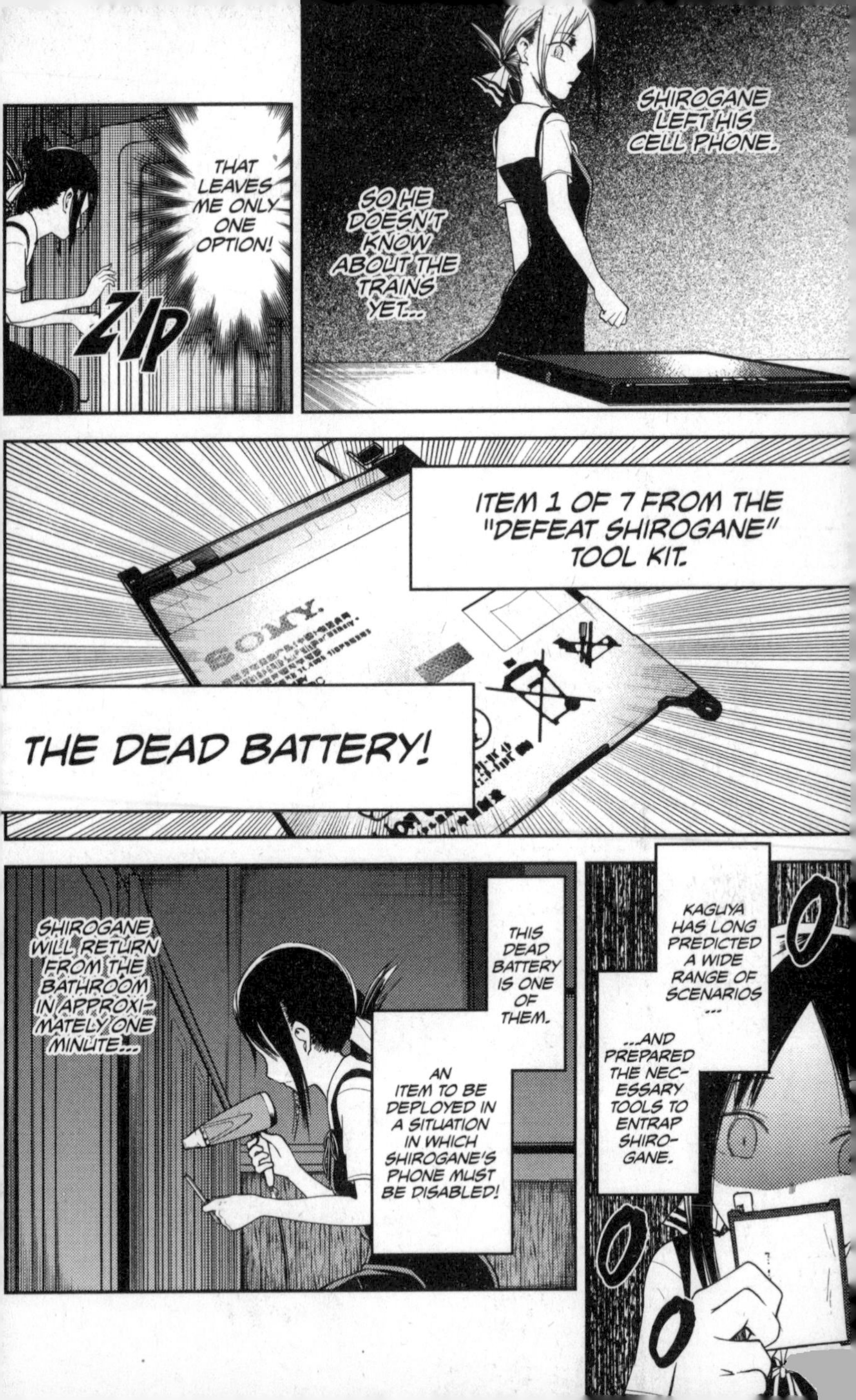
SHIROGANE LEFT HIS CELL PHONE.
SO HE DOESN'T KNOW ABOUT THE TRAINS YET...
THAT LEAVES ME ONLY ONE OPTION!
ZIP
ITEM 1 OF 7 FROM THE "DEFEAT SHIROGANE" TOOL KIT.
THE DEAD BATTERY!
KAGUYA HAS LONG PREDICTED A WIDE RANGE OF SCENARIOS...
...AND PREPARED THE NECESSARY TOOLS TO ENTRAP SHIROGANE.
THIS DEAD BATTERY IS ONE OF THEM.
AN ITEM TO BE DEPLOYED IN A SITUATION IN WHICH SHIROGANE'S PHONE MUST BE DISABLED!
SHIROGANE WILL RETURN FROM THE BATHROOM IN APPROXIMATELY ONE MINUTE...

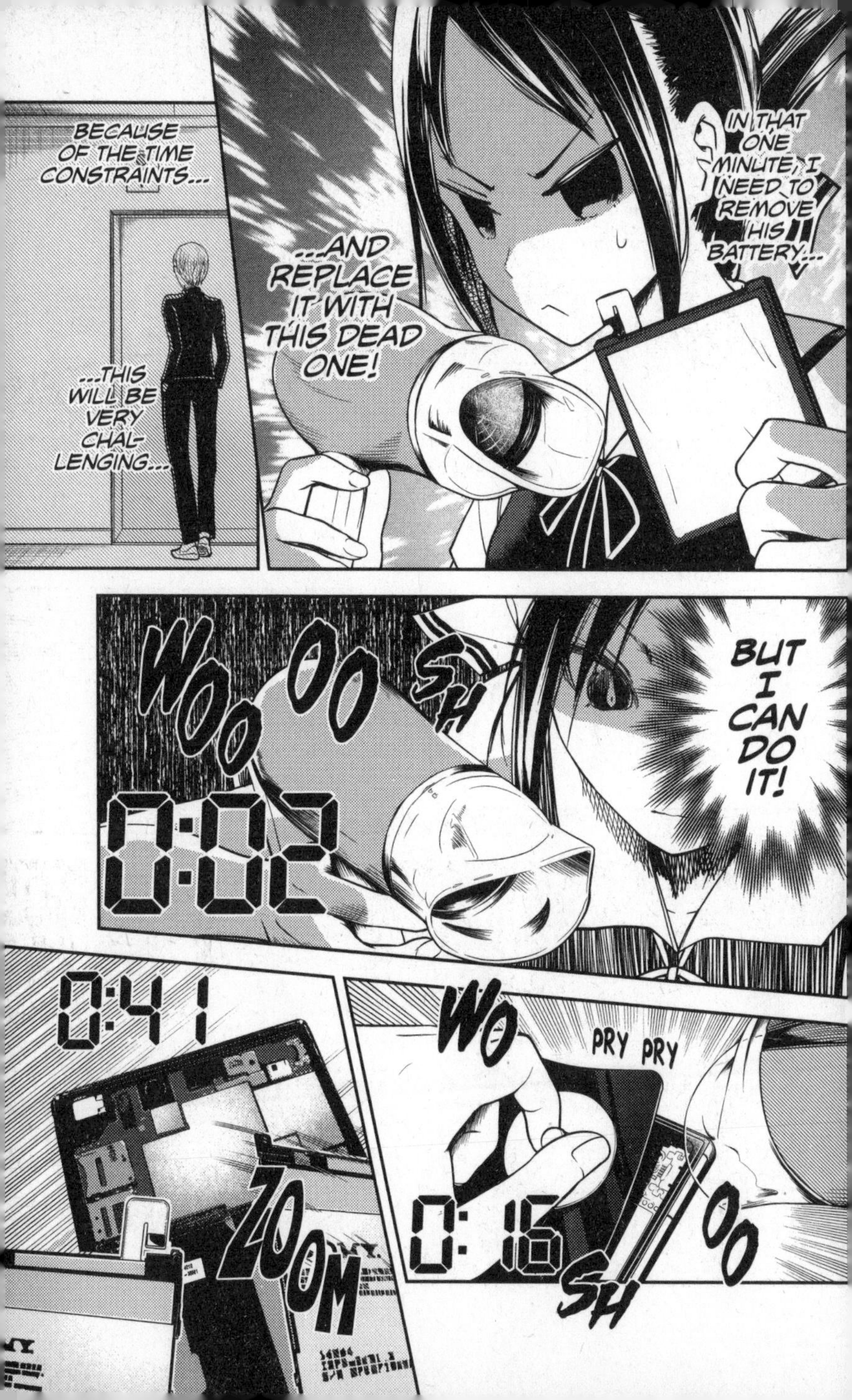
IN THAT ONE MINUTE, I NEED TO REMOVE HIS BATTERY...
...AND REPLACE IT WITH THIS DEAD ONE!
BECAUSE OF THE TIME CONSTRAINTS...
...THIS WILL BE VERY CHAL-LENGING...
BUT I CAN DO IT!
WOOOOSH
0:02
WO
PRY PRY
0:16
OOSH
0:41
ZOOM

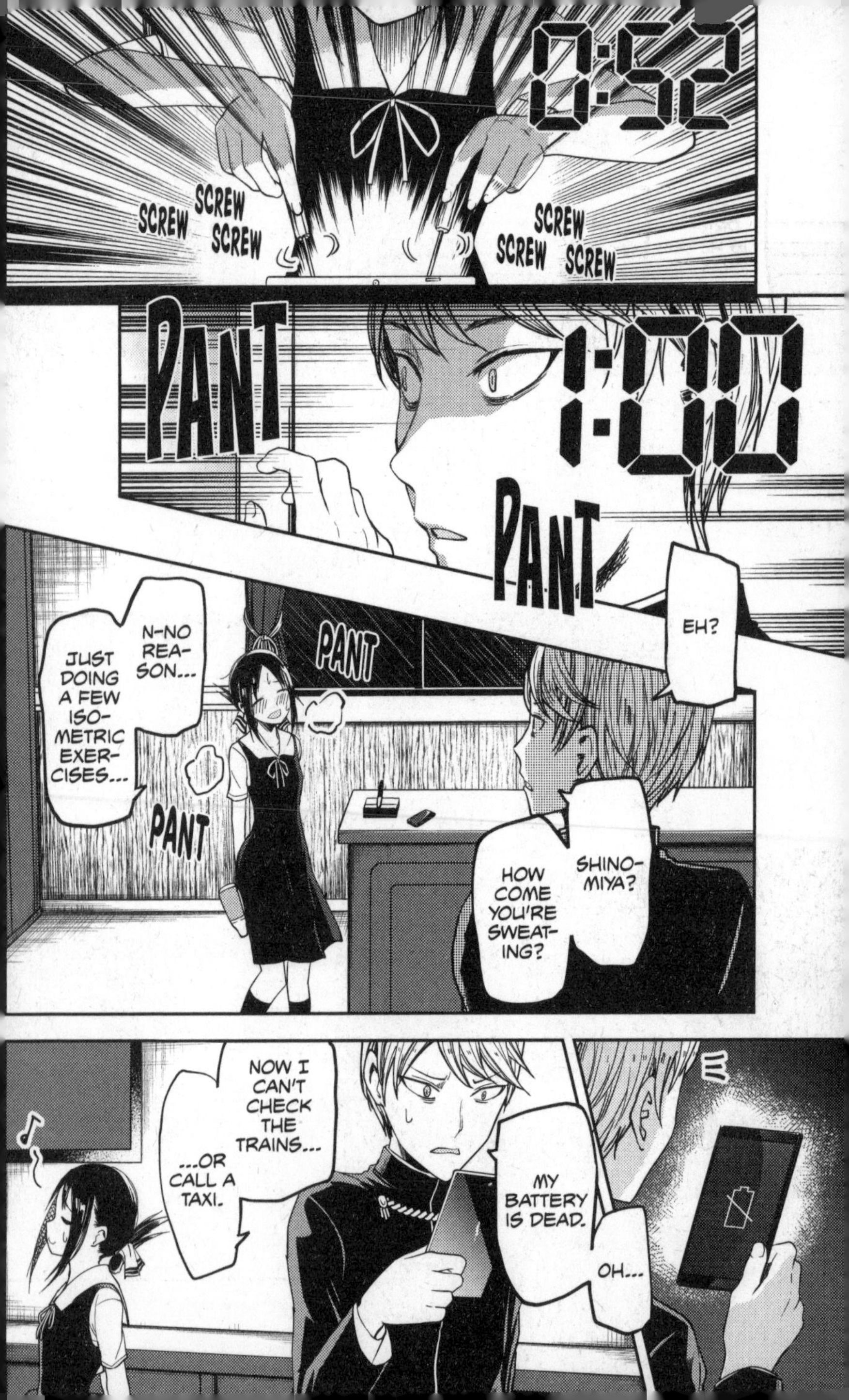
0:52
SCREW
SCREW
SCREW
SCREW
SCREW
SCREW
1:00
PANT
PANT
EH?
SHINOMIYA?
HOW COME YOU'RE SWEATING?
PANT
N-NO REASON...
JUST DOING A FEW ISOMETRIC EXERCISES...
PANT
OH...
MY BATTERY IS DEAD.
NOW I CAN'T CHECK THE TRAINS...
...OR CALL A TAXI.

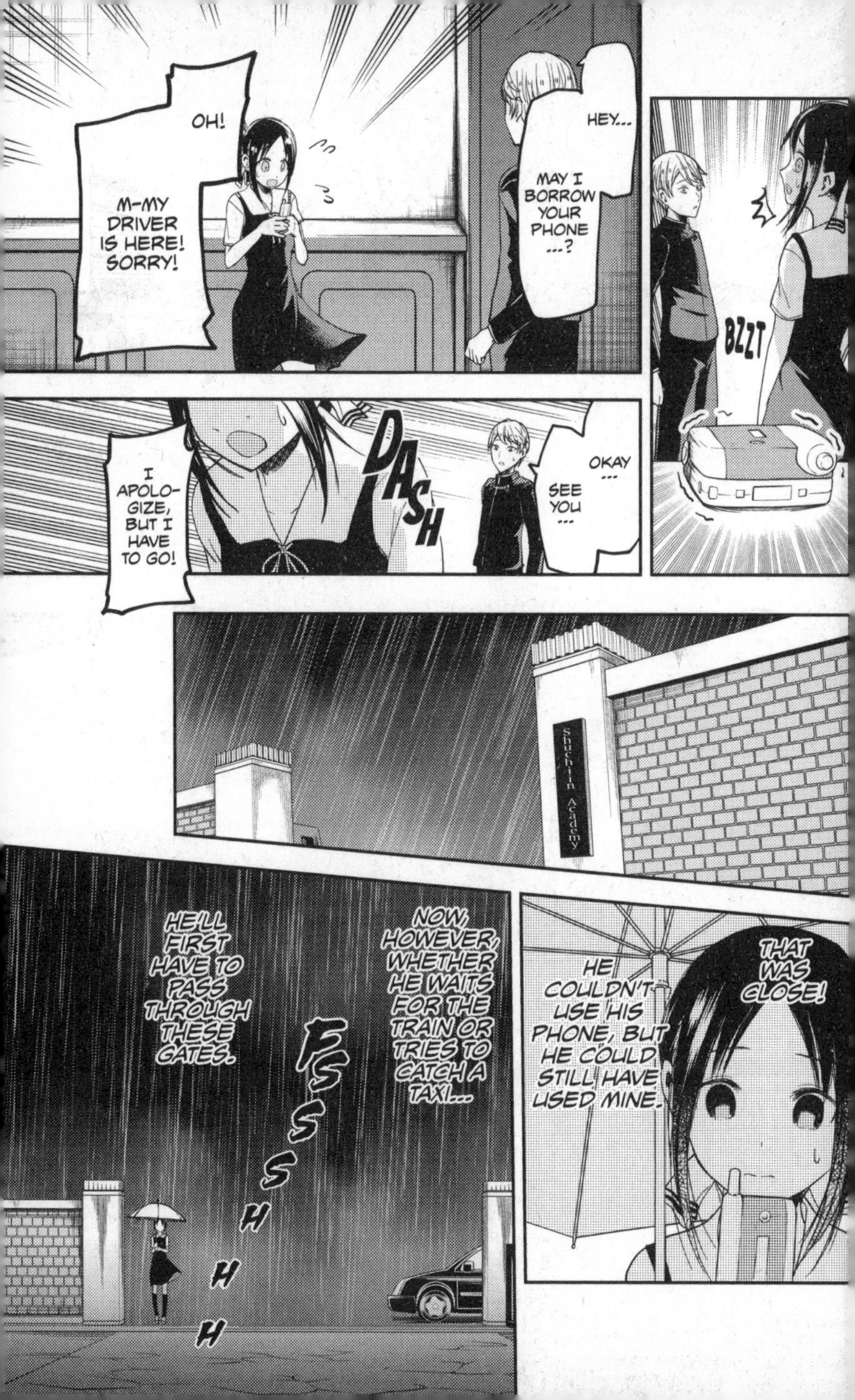
BZZT
HEY... MAY I BORROW YOUR PHONE ...?
OH!
M-MY DRIVER IS HERE! SORRY!
OKAY ... SEE YOU ...
DASH
I APOLOGIZE, BUT I HAVE TO GO!
Shuchiin Academy
THAT WAS CLOSE!
HE COULDN'T USE HIS PHONE, BUT HE COULD STILL HAVE USED MINE.
NOW, HOWEVER, WHETHER HE WAITS FOR THE TRAIN OR TRIES TO CATCH A TAXI...
FSSSHHHH
HE'LL FIRST HAVE TO PASS THROUGH THESE GATES.

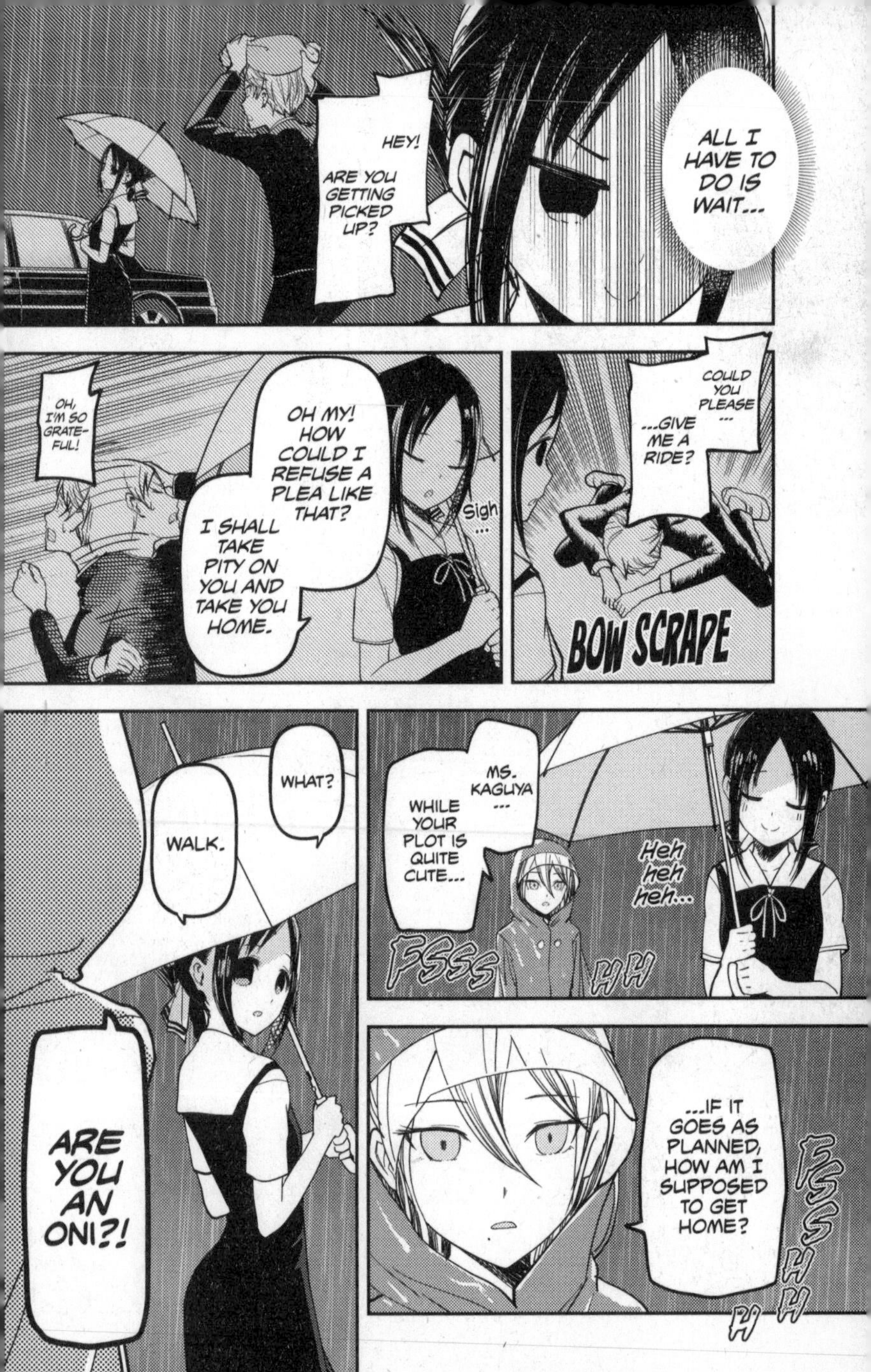
ALL I HAVE TO DO IS WAIT...
HEY!
ARE YOU GETTING PICKED UP?
COULD YOU PLEASE... ...GIVE ME A RIDE?
BOW SCRAPE
Sigh...
OH MY! HOW COULD I REFUSE A PLEA LIKE THAT?
I SHALL TAKE PITY ON YOU AND TAKE YOU HOME.
OH, I'M SO GRATEFUL!
Heh heh heh...
MS. KAGUYA...
WHILE YOUR PLOT IS QUITE CUTE...
FSSSHH
...IF IT GOES AS PLANNED, HOW AM I SUPPOSED TO GET HOME?
FSSSHHH
WHAT?
WALK.
ARE YOU AN ONI?!

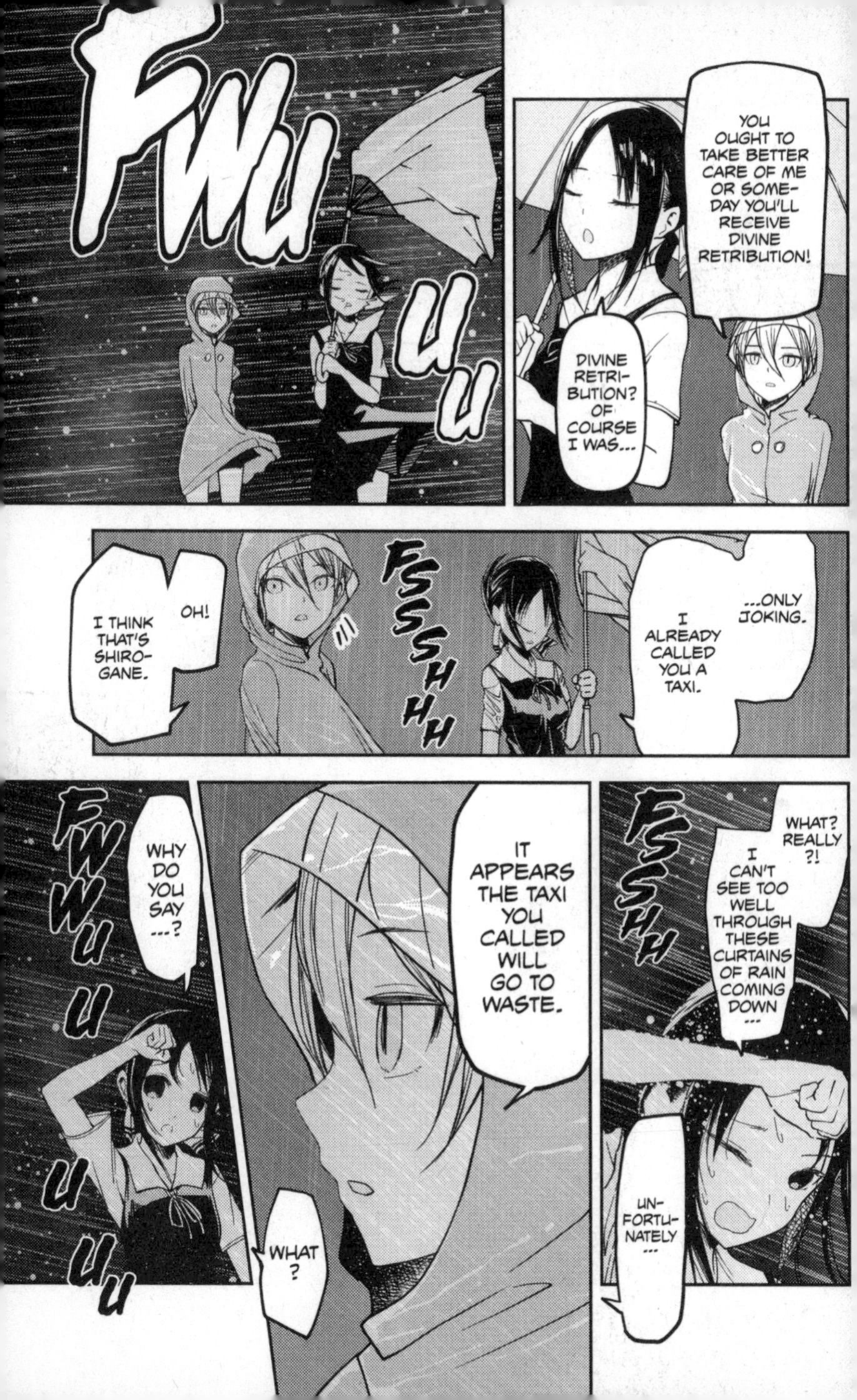
YOU OUGHT TO TAKE BETTER CARE OF ME OR SOME-DAY YOU'LL RECEIVE DIVINE RETRIBUTION!
DIVINE RETRI-BUTION? OF COURSE I WAS...
FWUUUUU
...ONLY JOKING.
I ALREADY CALLED YOU A TAXI.
FSSSHHH
OH!
I THINK THAT'S SHIRO-GANE.
FSSHH
WHAT? REALLY?!
I CAN'T SEE TOO WELL THROUGH THESE CURTAINS OF RAIN COMING DOWN...
UN-FORTU-NATELY...
IT APPEARS THE TAXI YOU CALLED WILL GO TO WASTE.
WHAT?
FWWUUUUUU
WHY DO YOU SAY...?

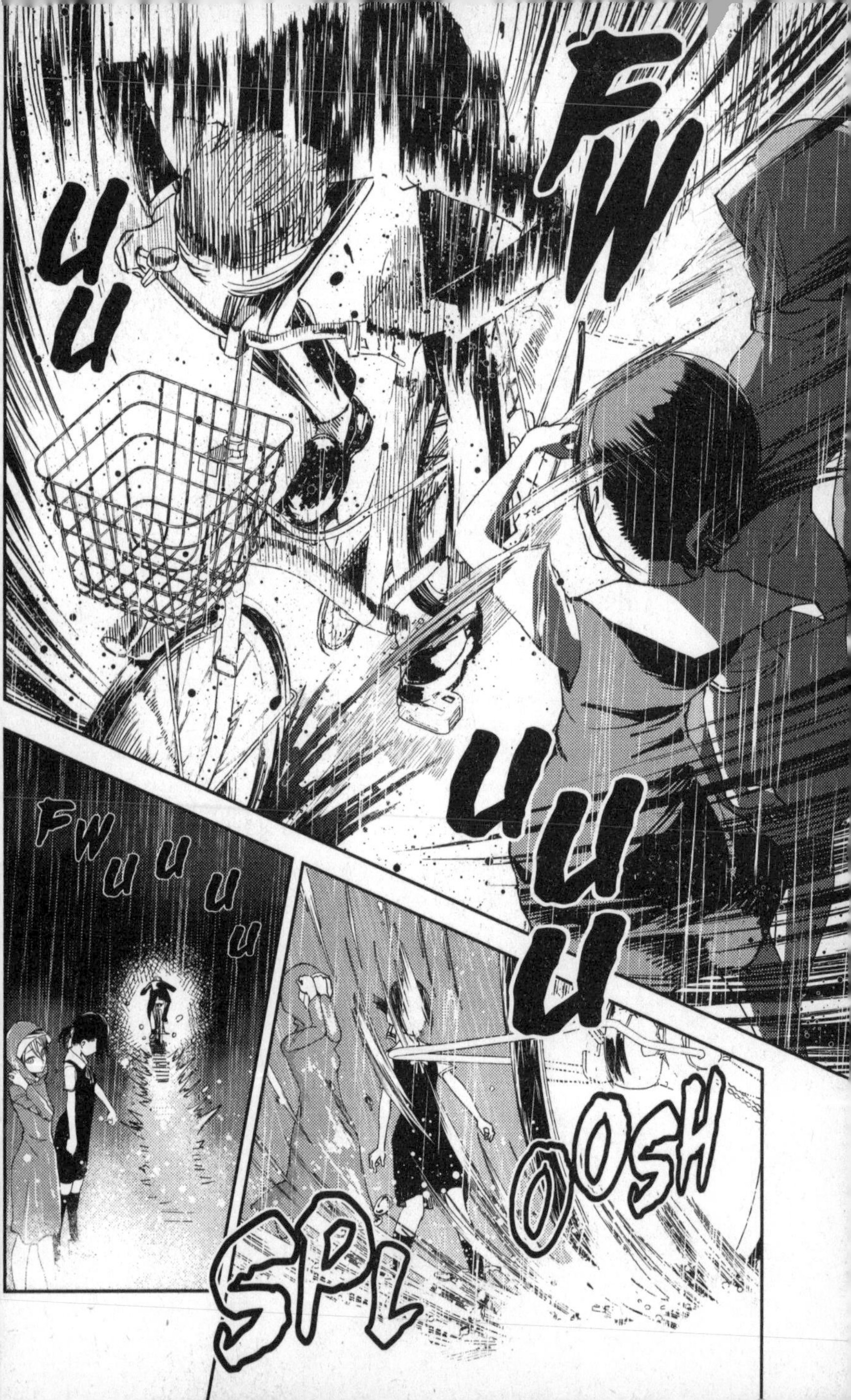
FWUUUUU
SPLOOSH
FWUUUUU

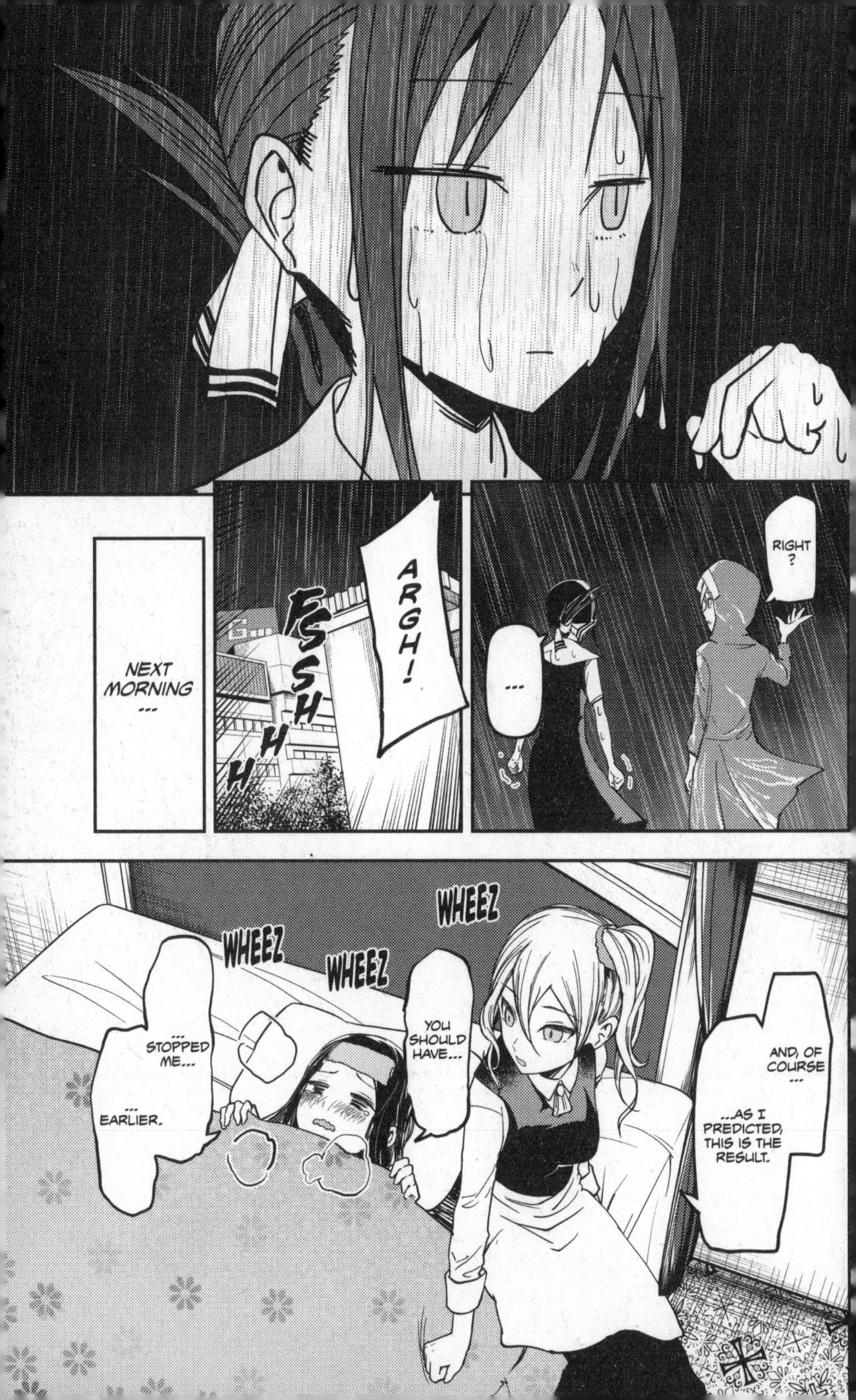

RIGHT?
...
ARGH!
FSSHHH
NEXT MORNING...
AND, OF COURSE...
...AS I PREDICTED, THIS IS THE RESULT.
WHEEZ
YOU SHOULD HAVE...
WHEEZ
WHEEZ
...STOPPED ME...
...EARLIER.

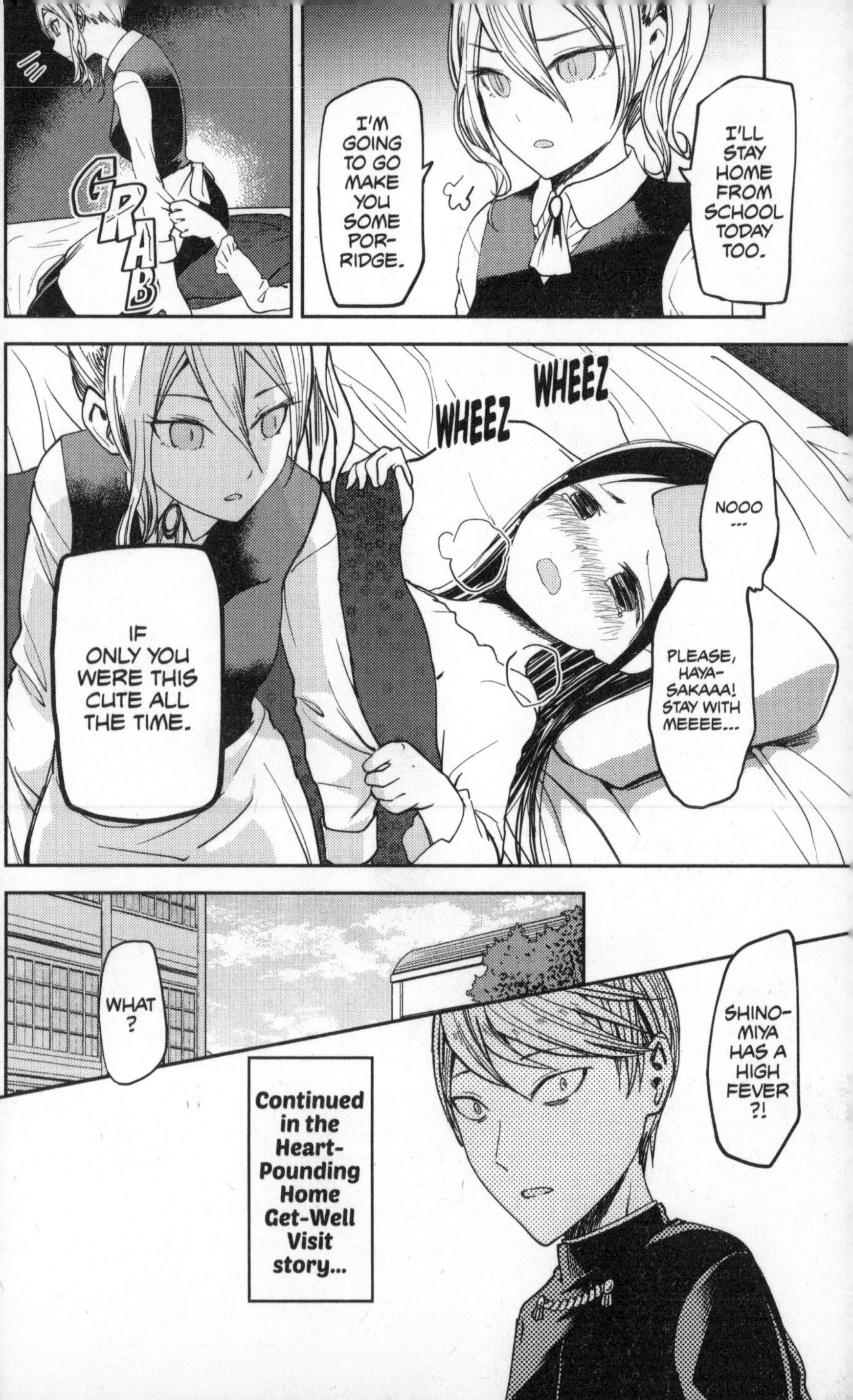
I'LL STAY HOME FROM SCHOOL TODAY TOO.
I'M GOING TO GO MAKE YOU SOME POR-RIDGE.
GRAB
WHEEZ
WHEEZ
NOOO...
PLEASE, HAYA-SAKAAA! STAY WITH MEEEE...
IF ONLY YOU WERE THIS CUTE ALL THE TIME.
SHINO-MIYA HAS A HIGH FEVER?!
WHAT?
Continued in the Heart-Pounding Home Get-Well Visit story...

SHIROGANE'S SMARTPHONE (USED, NO WARRANTY) GETS A NEW BATTERY.

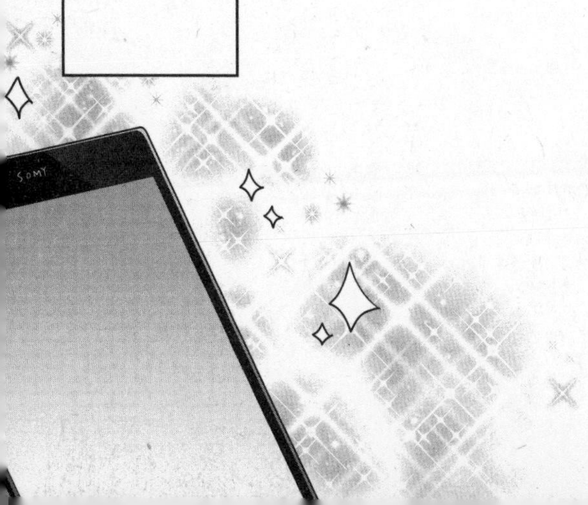
SOMY

KAGUYA-SAMA
LOVE IS WAR

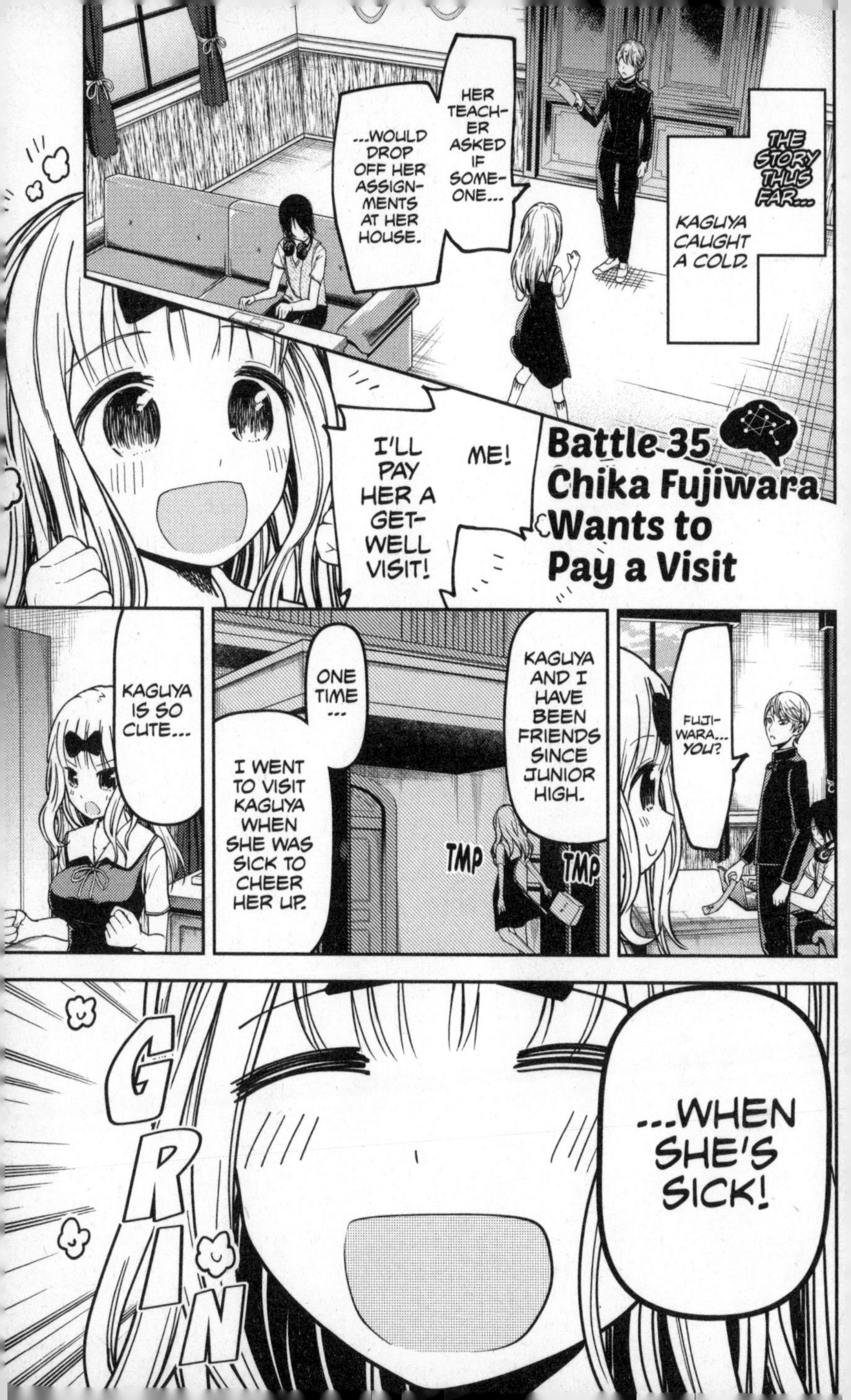
THE STORY THUS FAR...
KAGUYA CAUGHT A COLD.
HER TEACHER ASKED IF SOMEONE...
...WOULD DROP OFF HER ASSIGNMENTS AT HER HOUSE.
ME!
I'LL PAY HER A GET-WELL VISIT!
Battle 35 Chika Fujiwara Wants to Pay a Visit
FUJIWARA... YOU?
KAGUYA AND I HAVE BEEN FRIENDS SINCE JUNIOR HIGH.
TMP
TMP
ONE TIME...
I WENT TO VISIT KAGUYA WHEN SHE WAS SICK TO CHEER HER UP.
KAGUYA IS SO CUTE...
...WHEN SHE'S SICK!
GRIN

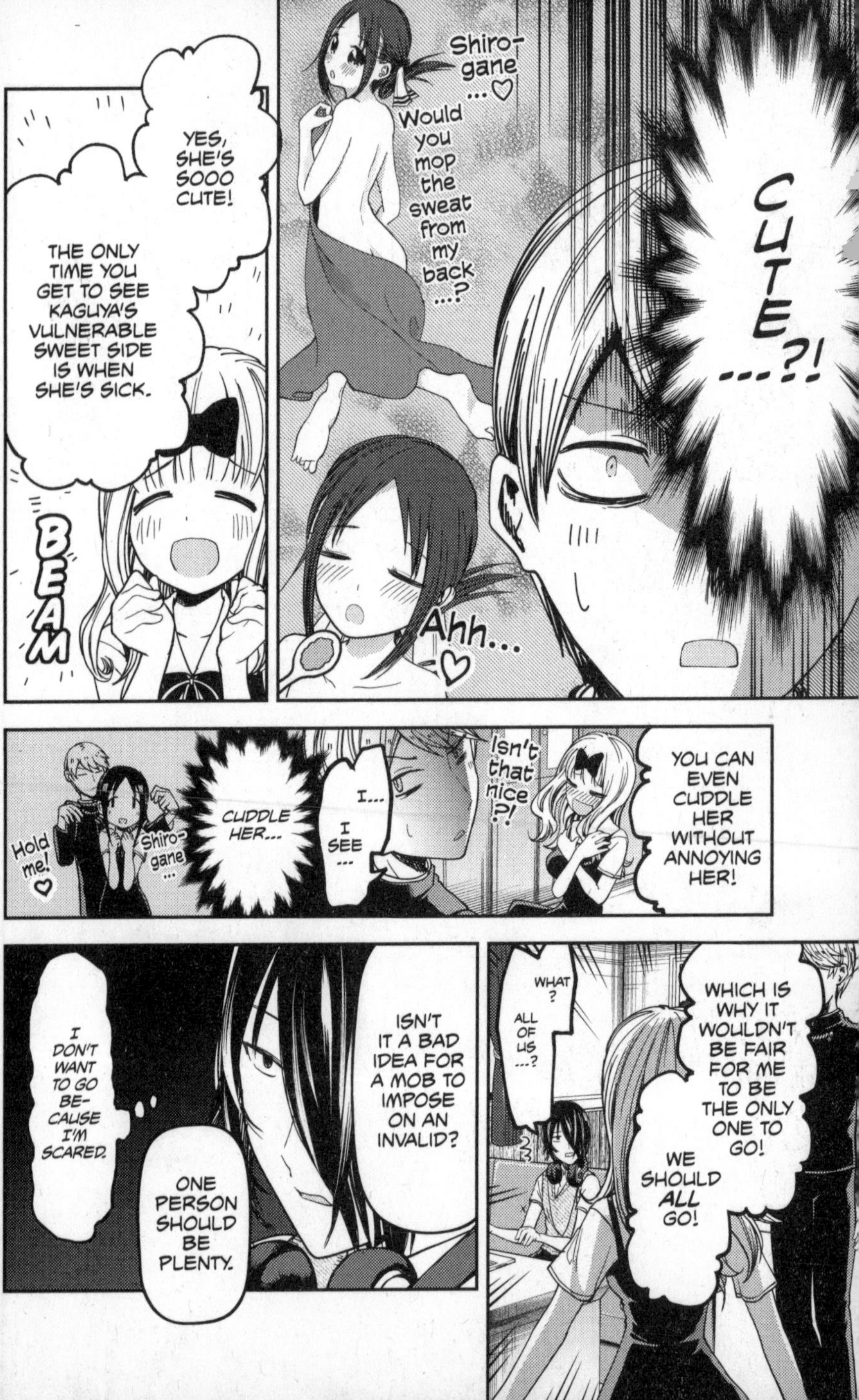
CUTE...?!
Shirogane...♡
Would you mop the sweat from my back...?
Ahh...♡
YES, SHE'S SOOO CUTE!
THE ONLY TIME YOU GET TO SEE KAGUYA'S VULNERABLE SWEET SIDE IS WHEN SHE'S SICK.
BEAM
YOU CAN EVEN CUDDLE HER WITHOUT ANNOYING HER!
Isn't that nice?!
I... I SEE...
CUDDLE HER...
Shirogane...
Hold me! ♡
WHICH IS WHY IT WOULDN'T BE FAIR FOR ME TO BE THE ONLY ONE TO GO!
WE SHOULD ALL GO!
WHAT?
ALL OF US...?
ISN'T IT A BAD IDEA FOR A MOB TO IMPOSE ON AN INVALID?
ONE PERSON SHOULD BE PLENTY.
I DON'T WANT TO GO BECAUSE I'M SCARED.

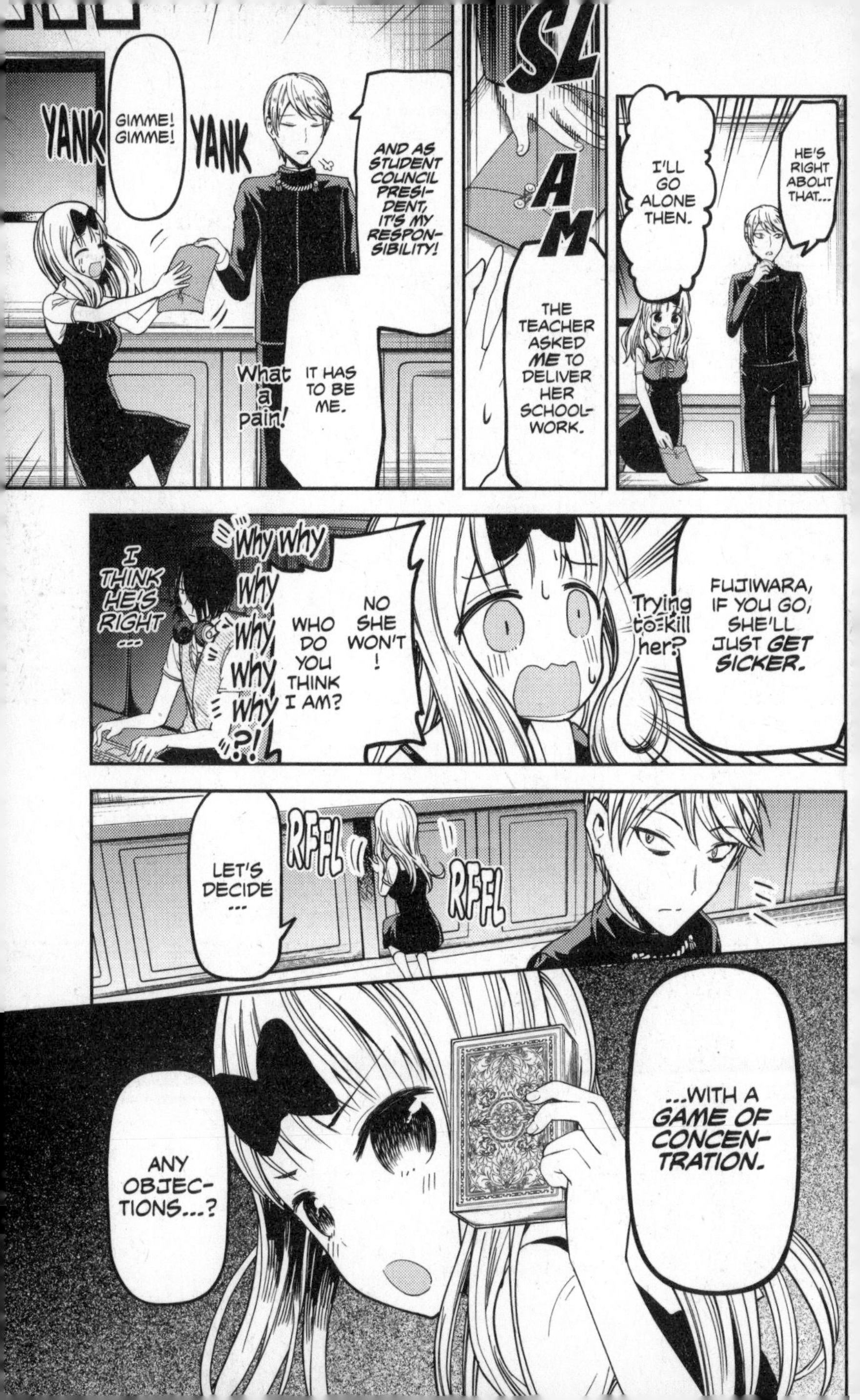
HE'S RIGHT ABOUT THAT...
I'LL GO ALONE THEN.
SLAM
THE TEACHER ASKED ME TO DELIVER HER SCHOOLWORK.
AND AS STUDENT COUNCIL PRESIDENT, IT'S MY RESPONSIBILITY!
IT HAS TO BE ME.
What a pain!
YANK
GIMME! GIMME!
YANK
FUJIWARA, IF YOU GO, SHE'LL JUST GET SICKER.
Trying to kill her?
NO SHE WON'T!
WHO DO YOU THINK I AM?
Why why why why why why?!
I THINK HE'S RIGHT...
RFFL
RFFL
LET'S DECIDE...
...WITH A GAME OF CONCENTRATION.
ANY OBJECTIONS...?

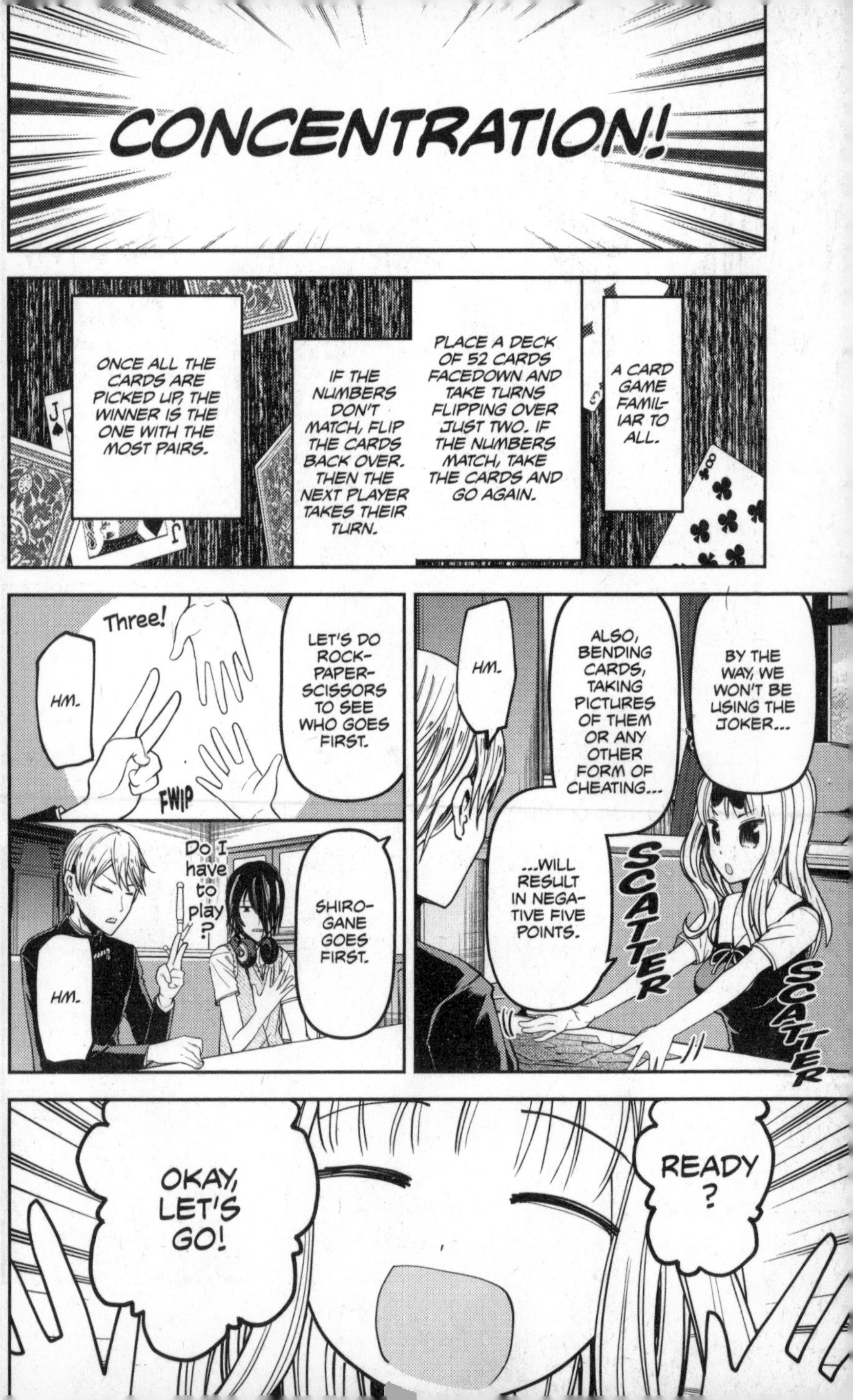
CONCENTRATION!
A CARD GAME FAMILIAR TO ALL.
PLACE A DECK OF 52 CARDS FACEDOWN AND TAKE TURNS FLIPPING OVER JUST TWO. IF THE NUMBERS MATCH, TAKE THE CARDS AND GO AGAIN.
IF THE NUMBERS DON'T MATCH, FLIP THE CARDS BACK OVER. THEN THE NEXT PLAYER TAKES THEIR TURN.
ONCE ALL THE CARDS ARE PICKED UP, THE WINNER IS THE ONE WITH THE MOST PAIRS.
BY THE WAY, WE WON'T BE USING THE JOKER...
ALSO, BENDING CARDS, TAKING PICTURES OF THEM OR ANY OTHER FORM OF CHEATING...
HM.
...WILL RESULT IN NEGATIVE FIVE POINTS.
SCATTER
SCATTER
LET'S DO ROCK-PAPER-SCISSORS TO SEE WHO GOES FIRST.
Three!
HM.
FWIP
SHIROGANE GOES FIRST.
Do I have to play?
HM.
READY?
OKAY, LET'S GO!

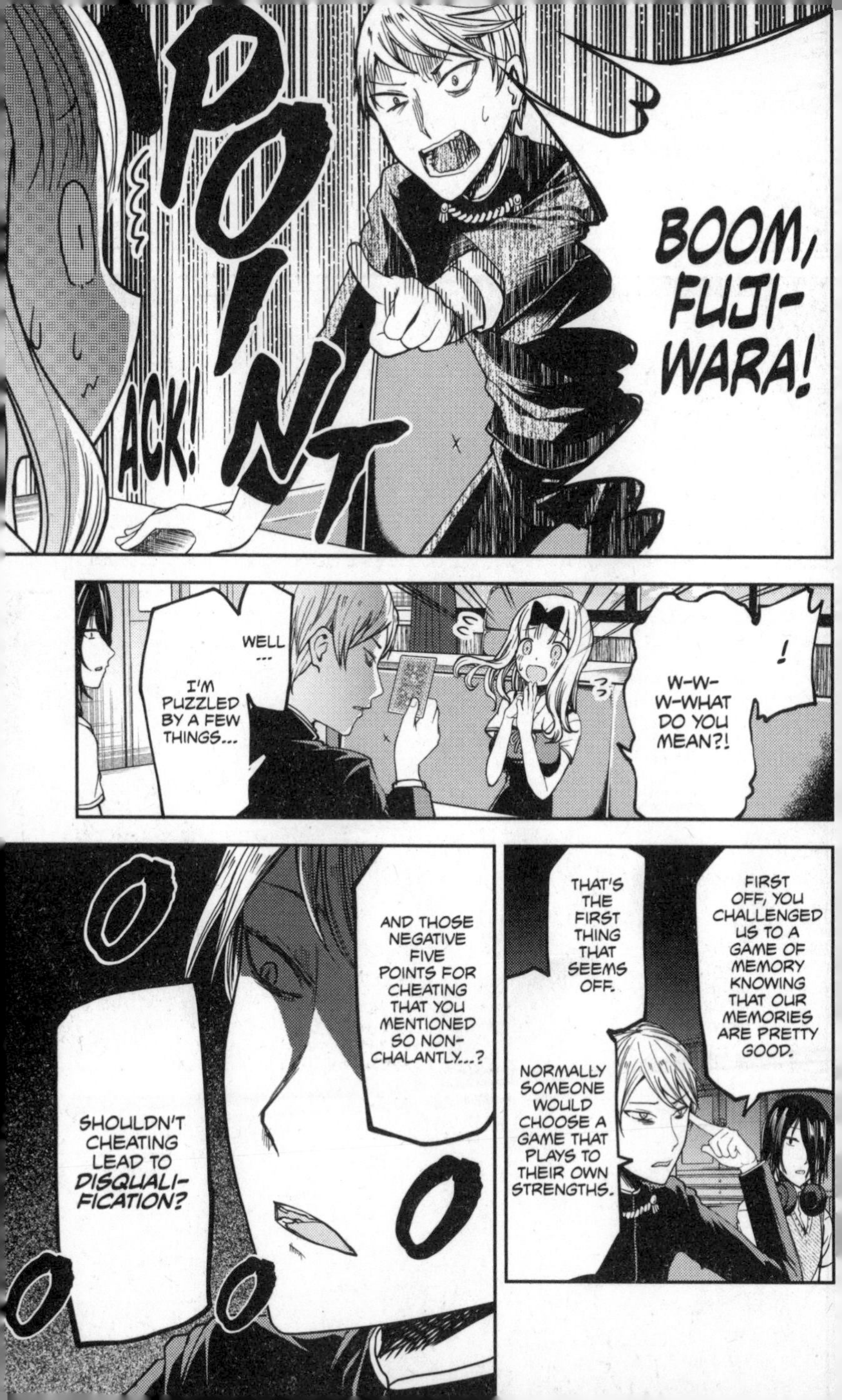
BOOM, FUJI-WARA!
POINT
ACK!
!
W-W-W-WHAT DO YOU MEAN?!
WELL... I'M PUZZLED BY A FEW THINGS...
FIRST OFF, YOU CHALLENGED US TO A GAME OF MEMORY KNOWING THAT OUR MEMORIES ARE PRETTY GOOD.
THAT'S THE FIRST THING THAT SEEMS OFF.
NORMALLY SOMEONE WOULD CHOOSE A GAME THAT PLAYS TO THEIR OWN STRENGTHS.
AND THOSE NEGATIVE FIVE POINTS FOR CHEATING THAT YOU MENTIONED SO NON-CHALANTLY...?
SHOULDN'T CHEATING LEAD TO *DISQUALIFICATION?*

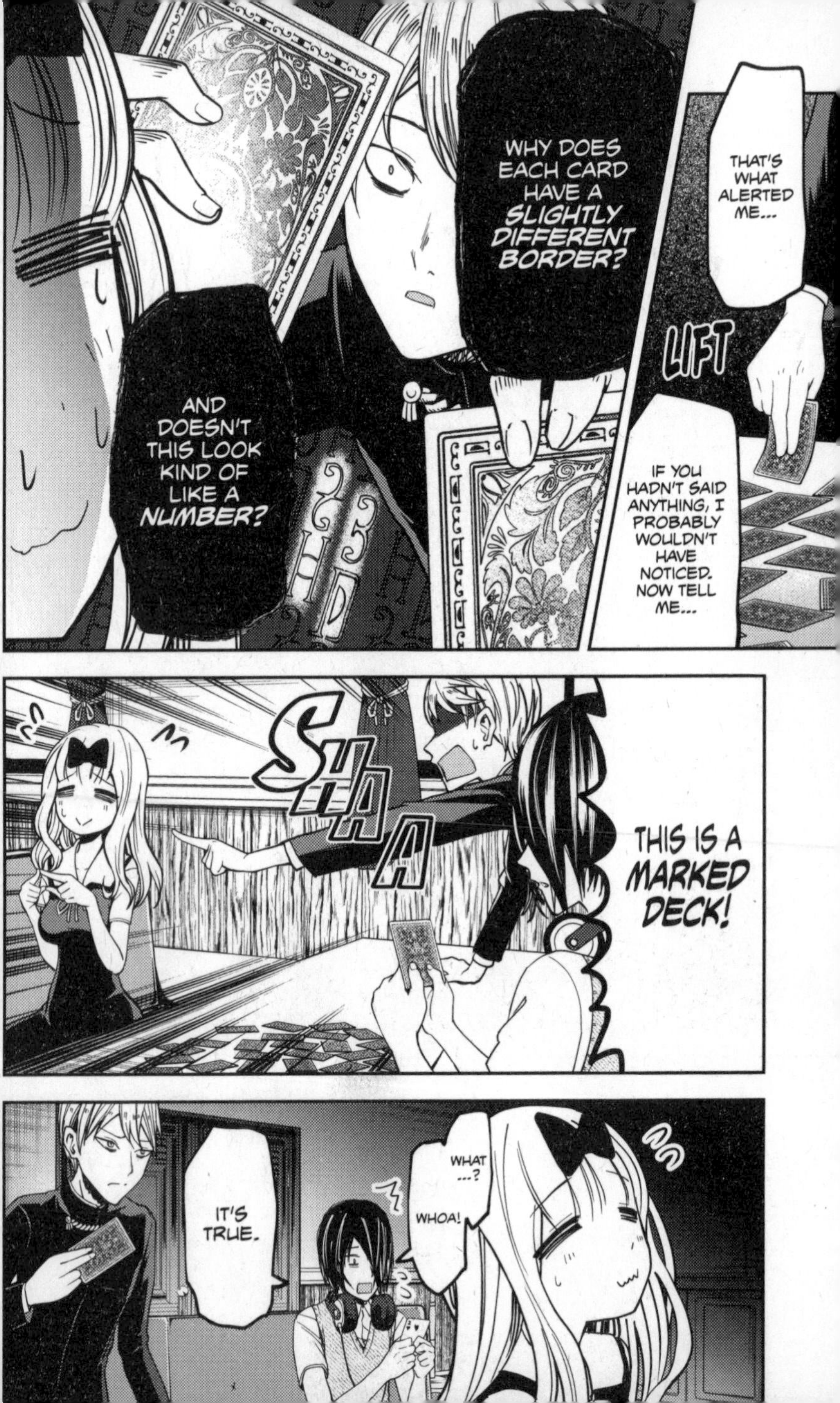
THAT'S WHAT ALERTED ME...
LIFT
IF YOU HADN'T SAID ANYTHING, I PROBABLY WOULDN'T HAVE NOTICED. NOW TELL ME...
WHY DOES EACH CARD HAVE A SLIGHTLY DIFFERENT BORDER?
AND DOESN'T THIS LOOK KIND OF LIKE A NUMBER?
THIS IS A MARKED DECK!
SHAA
WHAT ...?
WHOA!
IT'S TRUE.

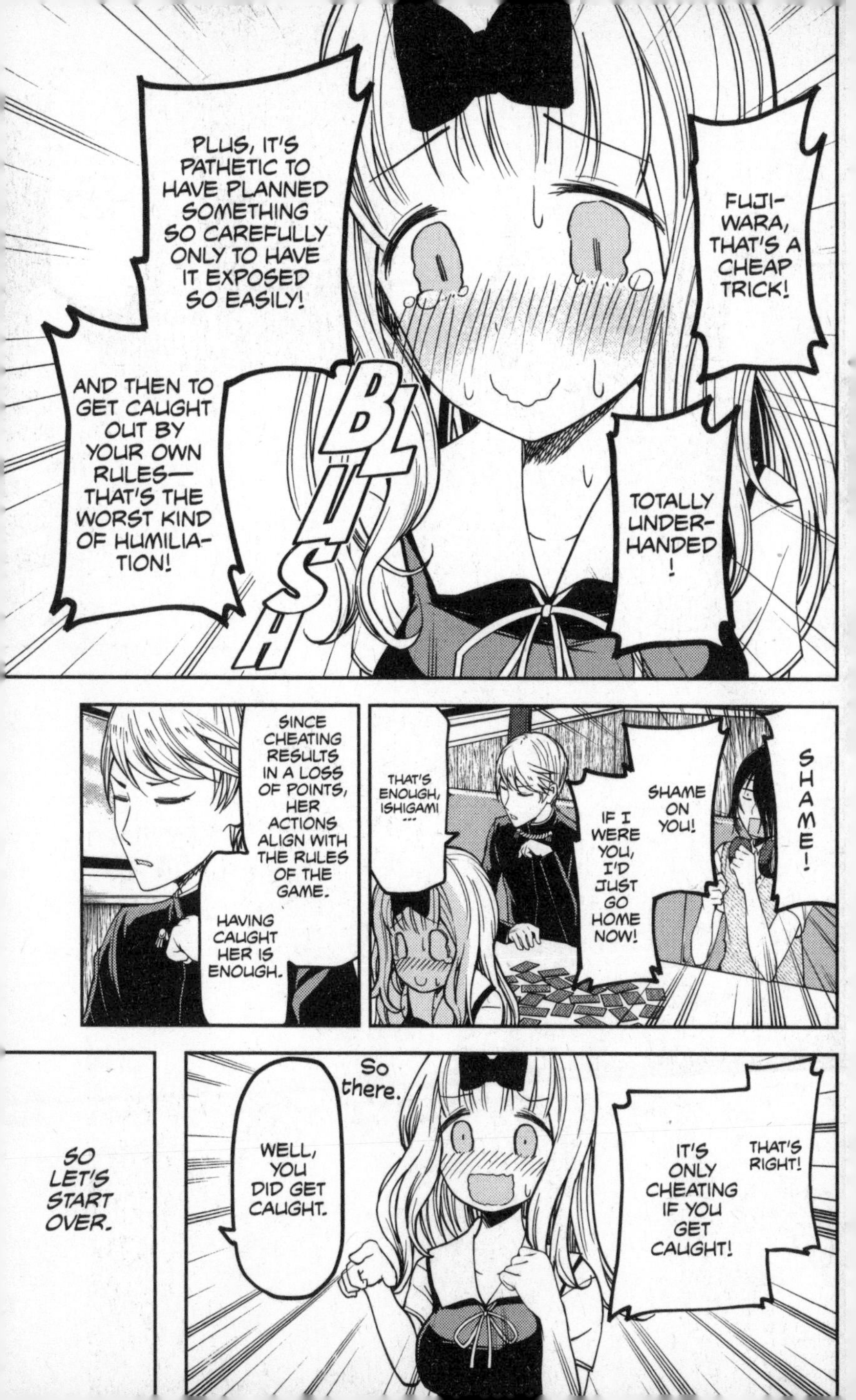
FUJIWARA, THAT'S A CHEAP TRICK!
TOTALLY UNDERHANDED!
PLUS, IT'S PATHETIC TO HAVE PLANNED SOMETHING SO CAREFULLY ONLY TO HAVE IT EXPOSED SO EASILY!
AND THEN TO GET CAUGHT OUT BY YOUR OWN RULES—THAT'S THE WORST KIND OF HUMILIATION!
BLUSH
SHAME SHAME!
SHAME ON YOU!
IF I WERE YOU, I'D JUST GO HOME NOW!
THAT'S ENOUGH, ISHIGAMI...
SINCE CHEATING RESULTS IN A LOSS OF POINTS, HER ACTIONS ALIGN WITH THE RULES OF THE GAME.
HAVING CAUGHT HER IS ENOUGH.
THAT'S RIGHT!
IT'S ONLY CHEATING IF YOU GET CAUGHT!
So there.
WELL, YOU DID GET CAUGHT.
SO LET'S START OVER.

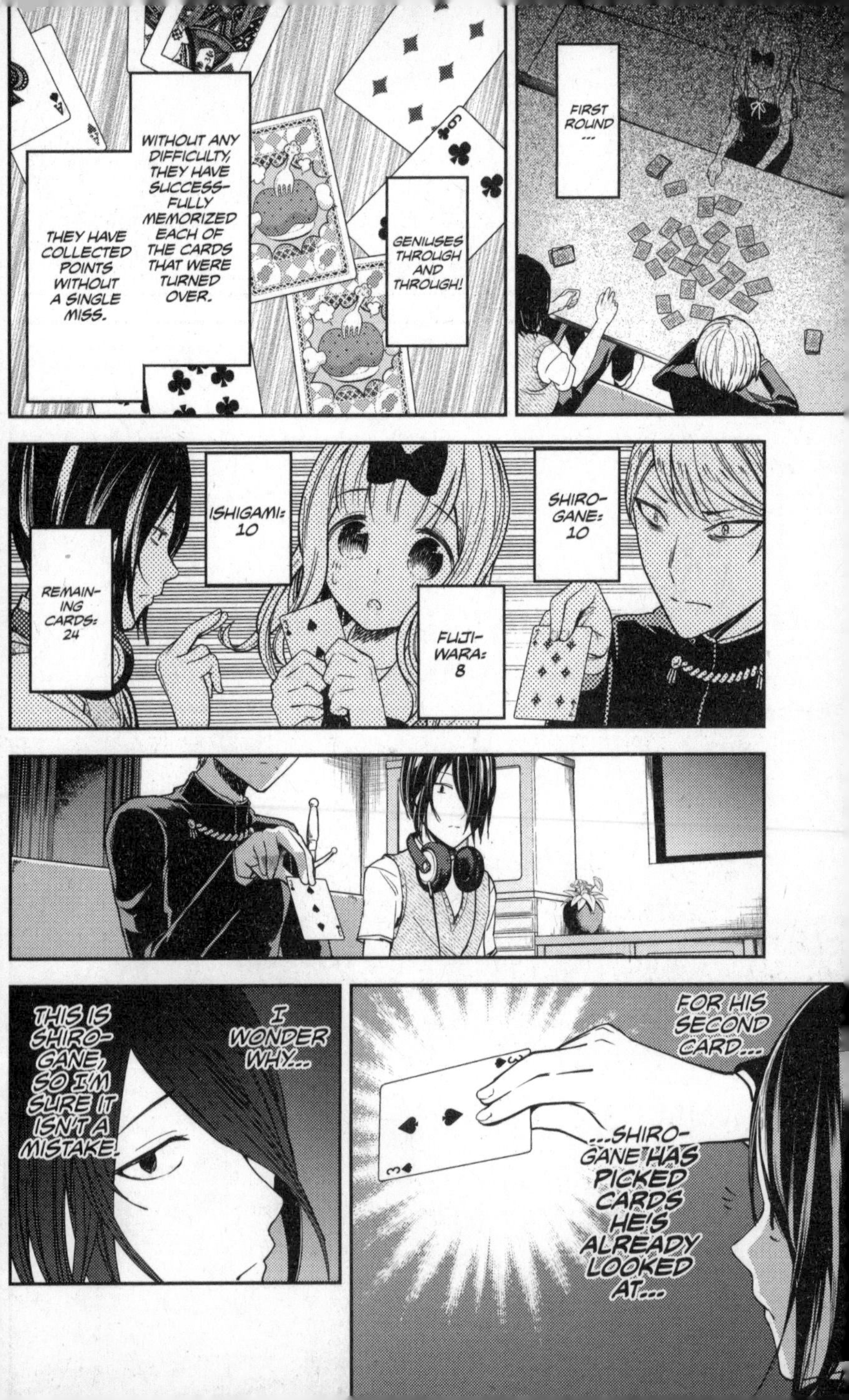
FIRST ROUND...
GENIUSES THROUGH AND THROUGH!
WITHOUT ANY DIFFICULTY, THEY HAVE SUCCESSFULLY MEMORIZED EACH OF THE CARDS THAT WERE TURNED OVER.
THEY HAVE COLLECTED POINTS WITHOUT A SINGLE MISS.
SHIROGANE: 10
FUJIWARA: 8
ISHIGAMI: 10
REMAINING CARDS: 24
FOR HIS SECOND CARD...
...SHIROGANE HAS PICKED CARDS HE'S ALREADY LOOKED AT...
I WONDER WHY...
THIS IS SHIROGANE, SO I'M SURE IT ISN'T A MISTAKE.

THE PROBLEM...

EIGHT CARDS REMAIN (ALL TWO-CARD PAIRS). ASSUMING ALL PLAYERS HAVE MEMORIZED THE REVEALED CARDS, AND THE ONLY CARD REVEALED IS ♡1, I FLIP A CARD AND SHOW ♡2.

IN THIS CASE, WHAT'S THE OPTIMAL MOVE FOR THE NEXT PLAYER?

Memorized

1st

SO THAT'S WHAT HE'S DOING...

OH, I SEE!

*Skipping turns is permitted.

I SEE...

DEPENDING ON THE SITUATION, IT CAN BE USEFUL TO PASS!

Hm...

BUT, IF I DRAW THE ♡1 THAT I ALREADY DREW BEFORE...

...AN ACTION WHICH IS ESSENTIALLY THE SAME AS PASSING ON MY TURN...

...I CAN LOWER THE LIKELIHOOD THAT THE NEXT PLAYER WILL MAKE A PAIR TO TWO IN SIX FOR THEIR FIRST CARD (33.3 PERCENT) AND ONE IN FIVE (20 PERCENT) FOR THEIR SECOND CARD.

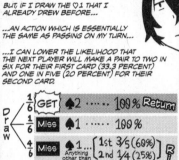

Draw	$\frac{1}{6}$	GET ♠2	100% Return
	$\frac{1}{6}$	Miss ♠1	100%
	$\frac{4}{6}$	Miss ♠1 Anything other than	1st 3/5 (60%) / 2nd 1/4 (25%)
Pass		♡1 ...	1st 2/6 (33.3%) / 2nd 1/5 (20%)

Risk

THERE IS A ONE IN SIX CHANCE THAT I WILL DRAW (♠2) AND GET A PAIR.

GET!

BUT IF I DON'T... THE NEXT PLAYER CAN GET A PAIR IN THE FOLLOWING WAYS...

IF I DRAW A ♠1, THEY CAN FLIP THE ♡1.

100 PERCENT CHANCE

IF I DRAW ANYTHING BESIDES A ♠1... THEIR FIRST DRAW WILL HAVE A THREE IN FIVE CHANCE (60 PERCENT), AND THEIR SECOND DRAW WILL HAVE A ONE IN FOUR CHANCE (25 PERCENT).

VERY NICE.

YOUR RECOLLECTION IS POWERFUL.

Would you wipe the sweat from my front too?

Shiro-gane

HIS FOCUS IS STRONG AND HE MAKES NO UNNECESSARY MOVES!

A TRUE GENIUS...

BA M

TIME TO RAISE THE DIFFICULTY LEVEL!

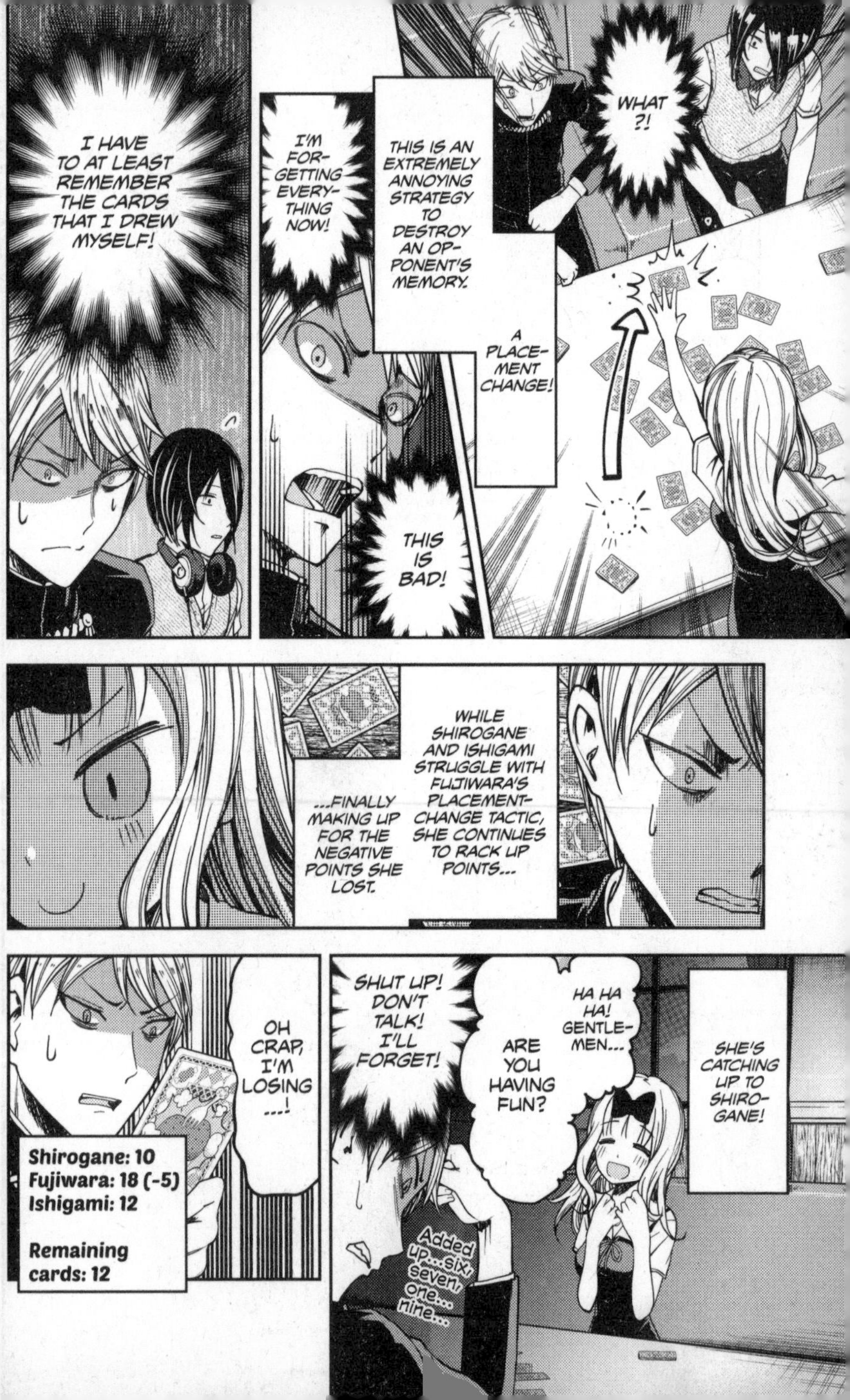
WHAT ?!
THIS IS AN EXTREMELY ANNOYING STRATEGY TO DESTROY AN OPPONENT'S MEMORY.
A PLACEMENT CHANGE!
I'M FORGETTING EVERYTHING NOW!
THIS IS BAD!
I HAVE TO AT LEAST REMEMBER THE CARDS THAT I DREW MYSELF!
WHILE SHIROGANE AND ISHIGAMI STRUGGLE WITH FUJIWARA'S PLACEMENT-CHANGE TACTIC, SHE CONTINUES TO RACK UP POINTS...
...FINALLY MAKING UP FOR THE NEGATIVE POINTS SHE LOST.
SHE'S CATCHING UP TO SHIROGANE!
HA HA HA! GENTLEMEN...
ARE YOU HAVING FUN?
SHUT UP! DON'T TALK! I'LL FORGET!
Added up... six, seven, one... nine...
OH CRAP, I'M LOSING ...!
Shirogane: 10
Fujiwara: 18 (-5)
Ishigami: 12
Remaining cards: 12

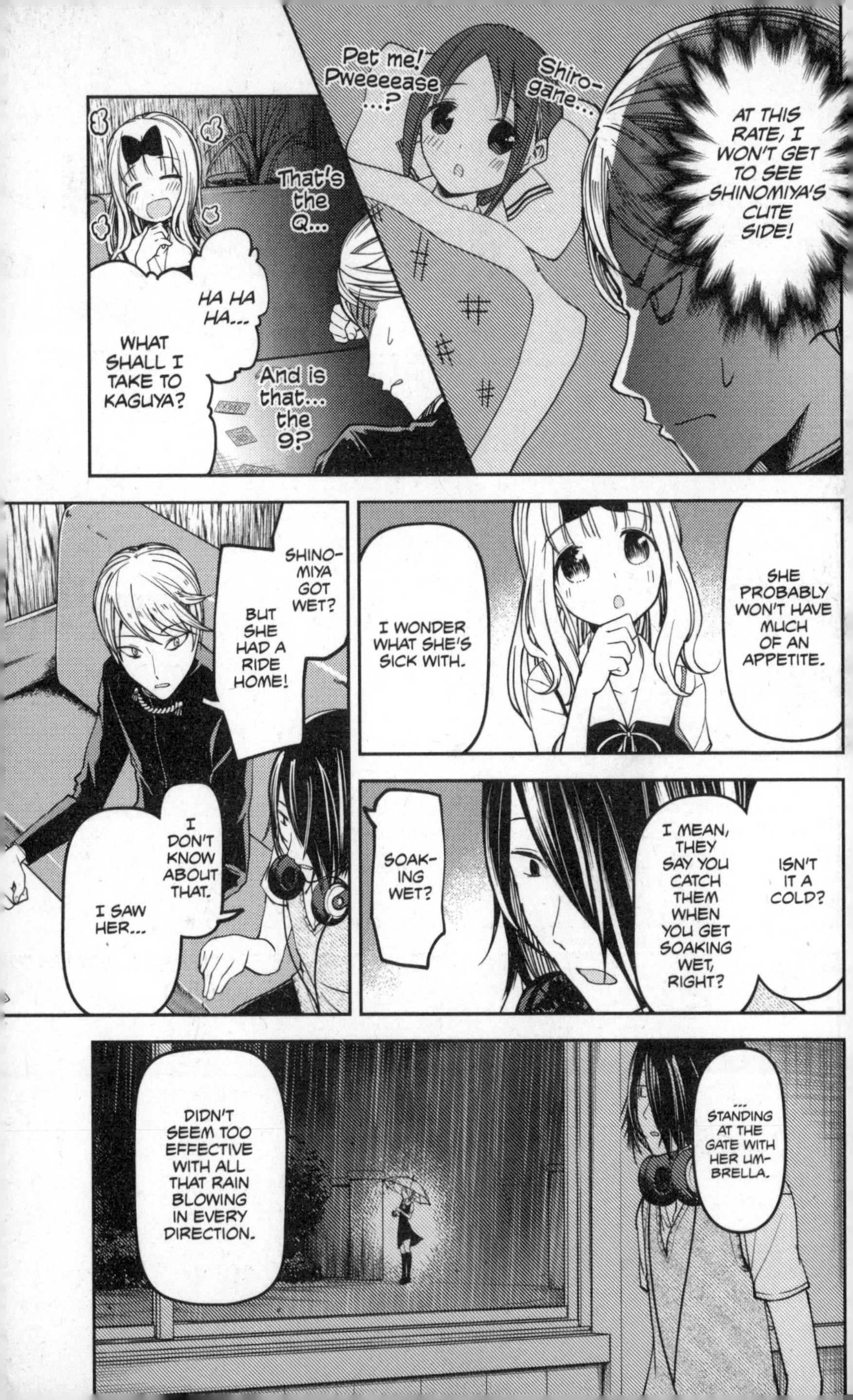
AT THIS RATE, I WON'T GET TO SEE SHINOMIYA'S CUTE SIDE!
Shiro-gane...
Pet me! Pweeeease ...?
That's the Q...
HA HA HA...
WHAT SHALL I TAKE TO KAGUYA?
And is that... the 9?
SHE PROBABLY WON'T HAVE MUCH OF AN APPETITE.
I WONDER WHAT SHE'S SICK WITH.
ISN'T IT A COLD?
I MEAN, THEY SAY YOU CATCH THEM WHEN YOU GET SOAKING WET, RIGHT?
SOAK-ING WET?
SHINO-MIYA GOT WET?
BUT SHE HAD A RIDE HOME!
I DON'T KNOW ABOUT THAT.
I SAW HER...
...STANDING AT THE GATE WITH HER UM-BRELLA.
DIDN'T SEEM TOO EFFECTIVE WITH ALL THAT RAIN BLOWING IN EVERY DIRECTION.

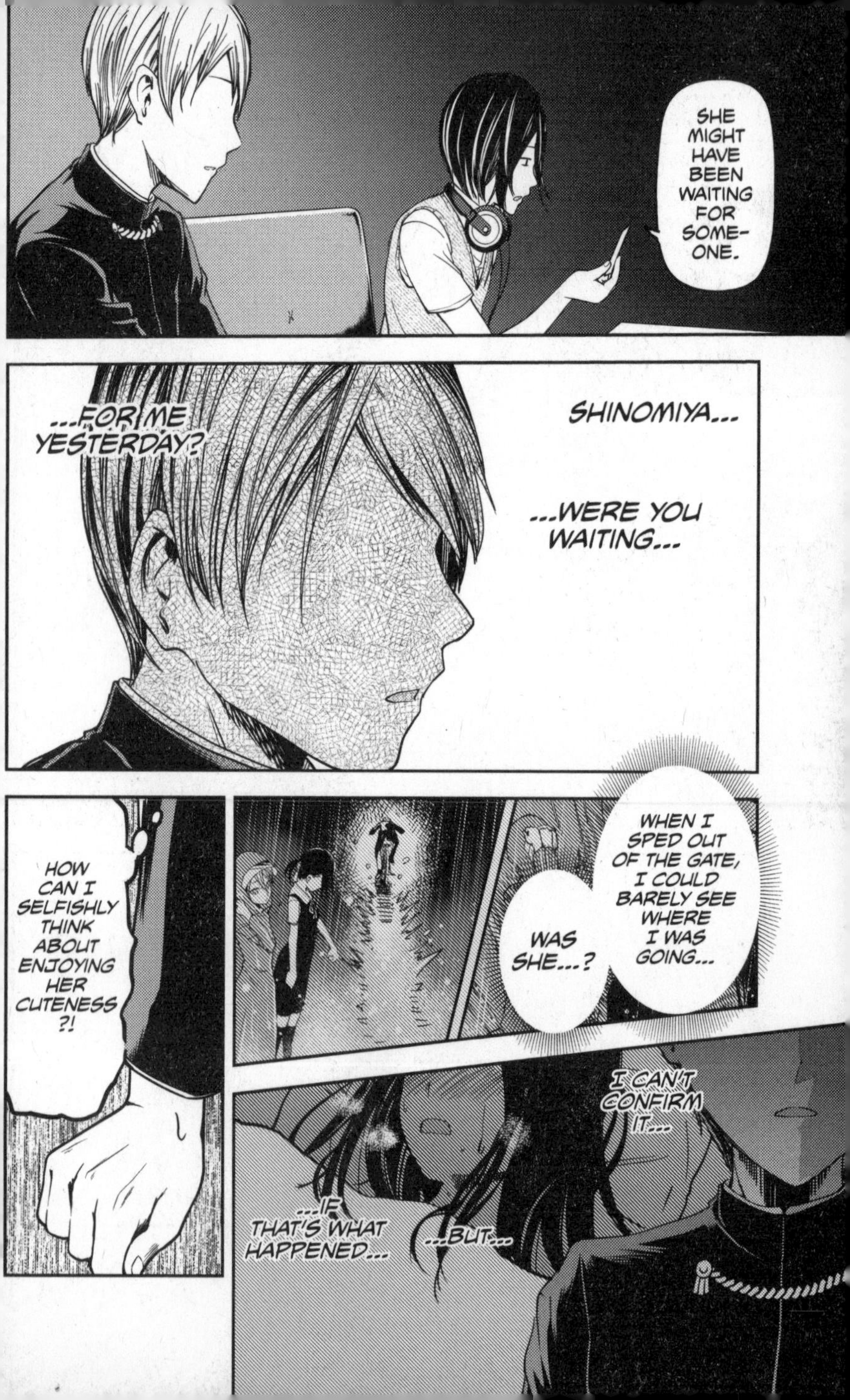
SHE MIGHT HAVE BEEN WAITING FOR SOME-ONE.
SHINOMIYA...
...WERE YOU WAITING...
...FOR ME YESTERDAY?
WHEN I SPED OUT OF THE GATE, I COULD BARELY SEE WHERE I WAS GOING...
WAS SHE...?
I CAN'T CONFIRM IT...
...BUT...
...IF THAT'S WHAT HAPPENED...
HOW CAN I SELFISHLY THINK ABOUT ENJOYING HER CUTENESS?!

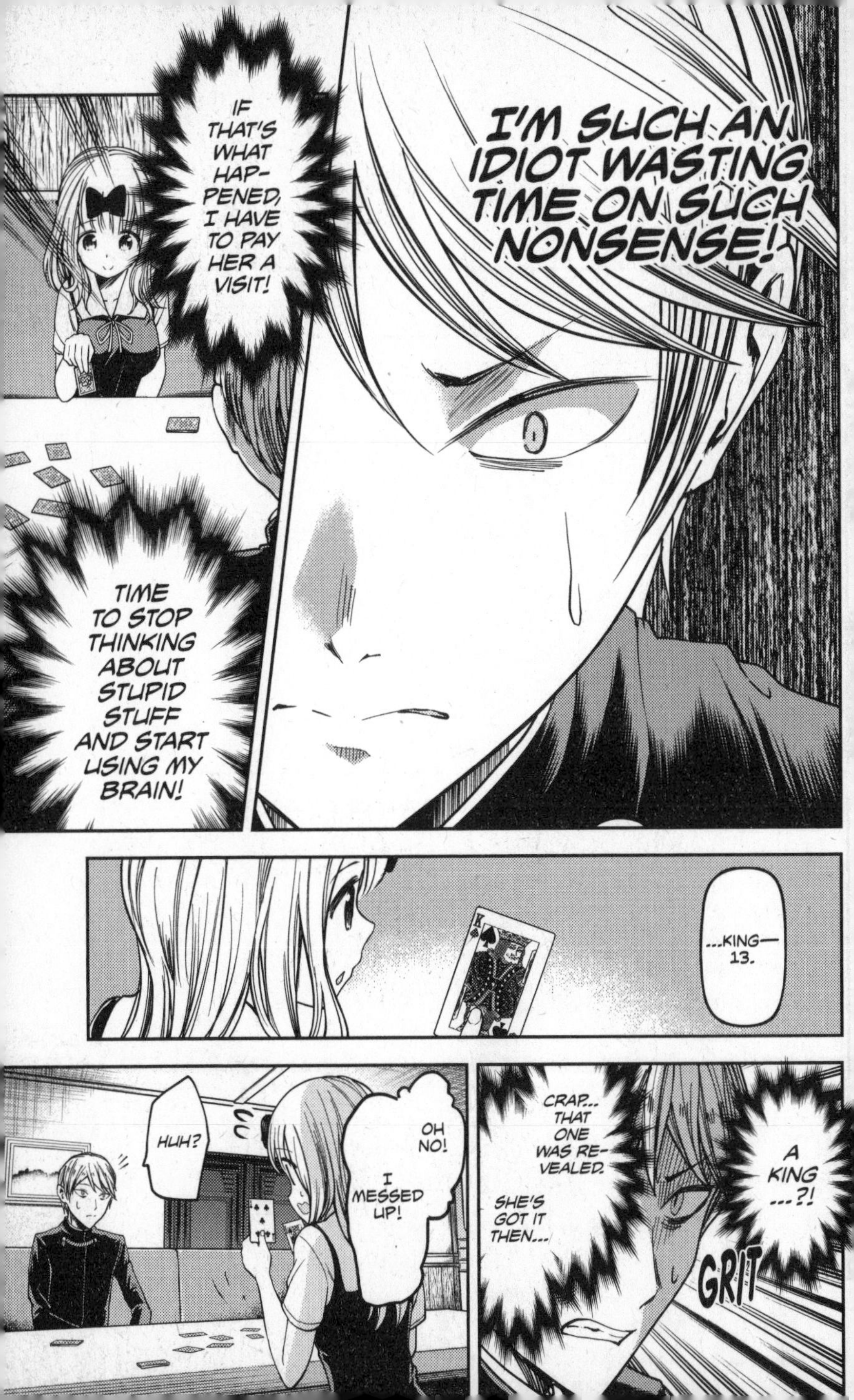
I'M SUCH AN IDIOT WASTING TIME ON SUCH NONSENSE!
IF THAT'S WHAT HAP-PENED, I HAVE TO PAY HER A VISIT!
TIME TO STOP THINKING ABOUT STUPID STUFF AND START USING MY BRAIN!
...KING— 13.
A KING ...?!
CRAP... THAT ONE WAS RE-VEALED.
SHE'S GOT IT THEN...
GRIT
OH NO!
I MESSED UP!
HUH?

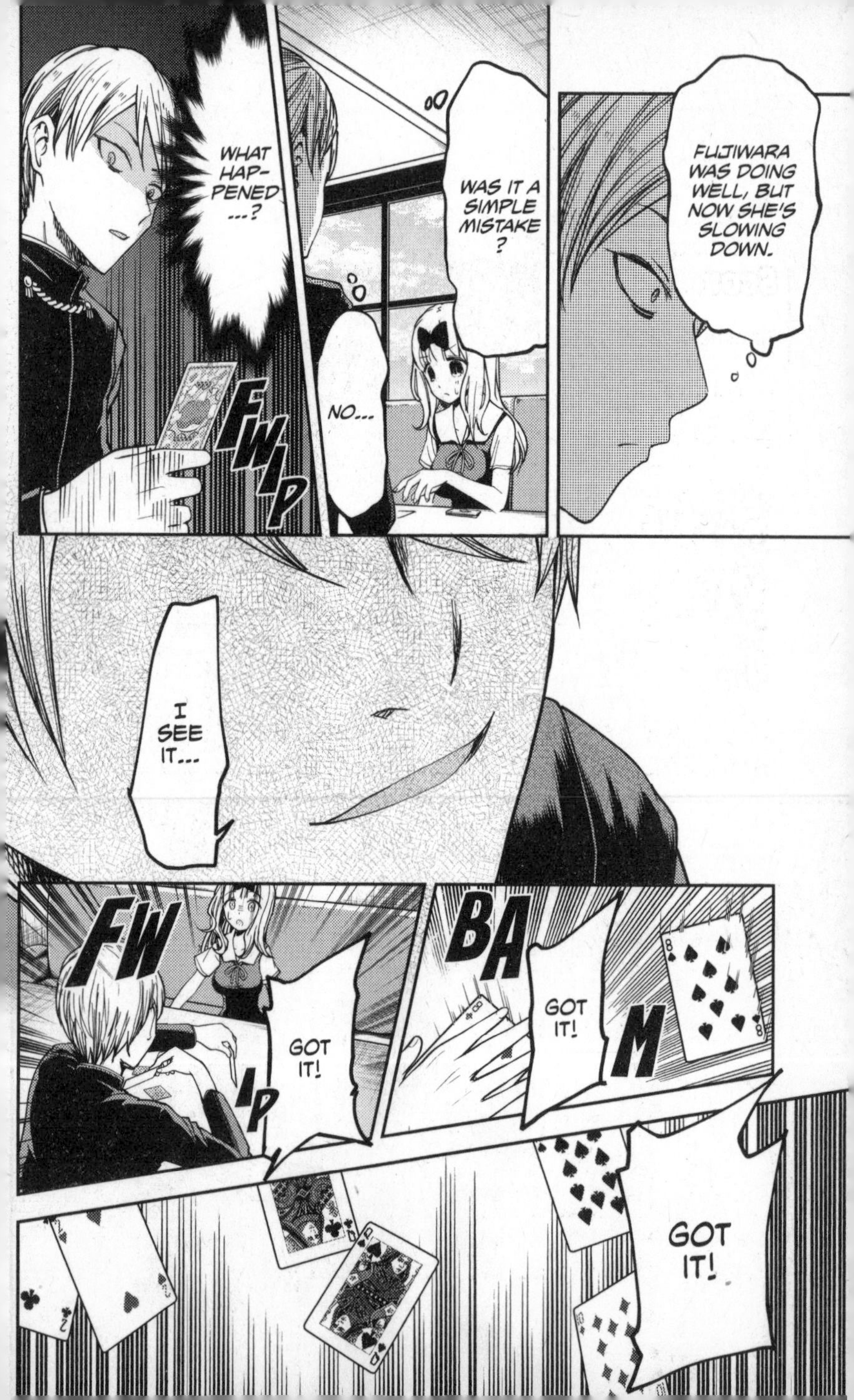
FUJIWARA WAS DOING WELL, BUT NOW SHE'S SLOWING DOWN.
WAS IT A SIMPLE MISTAKE?
NO...
WHAT HAP-PENED---?
FWIP
I SEE IT...
BAM
GOT IT!
FWIP
GOT IT!
GOT IT!

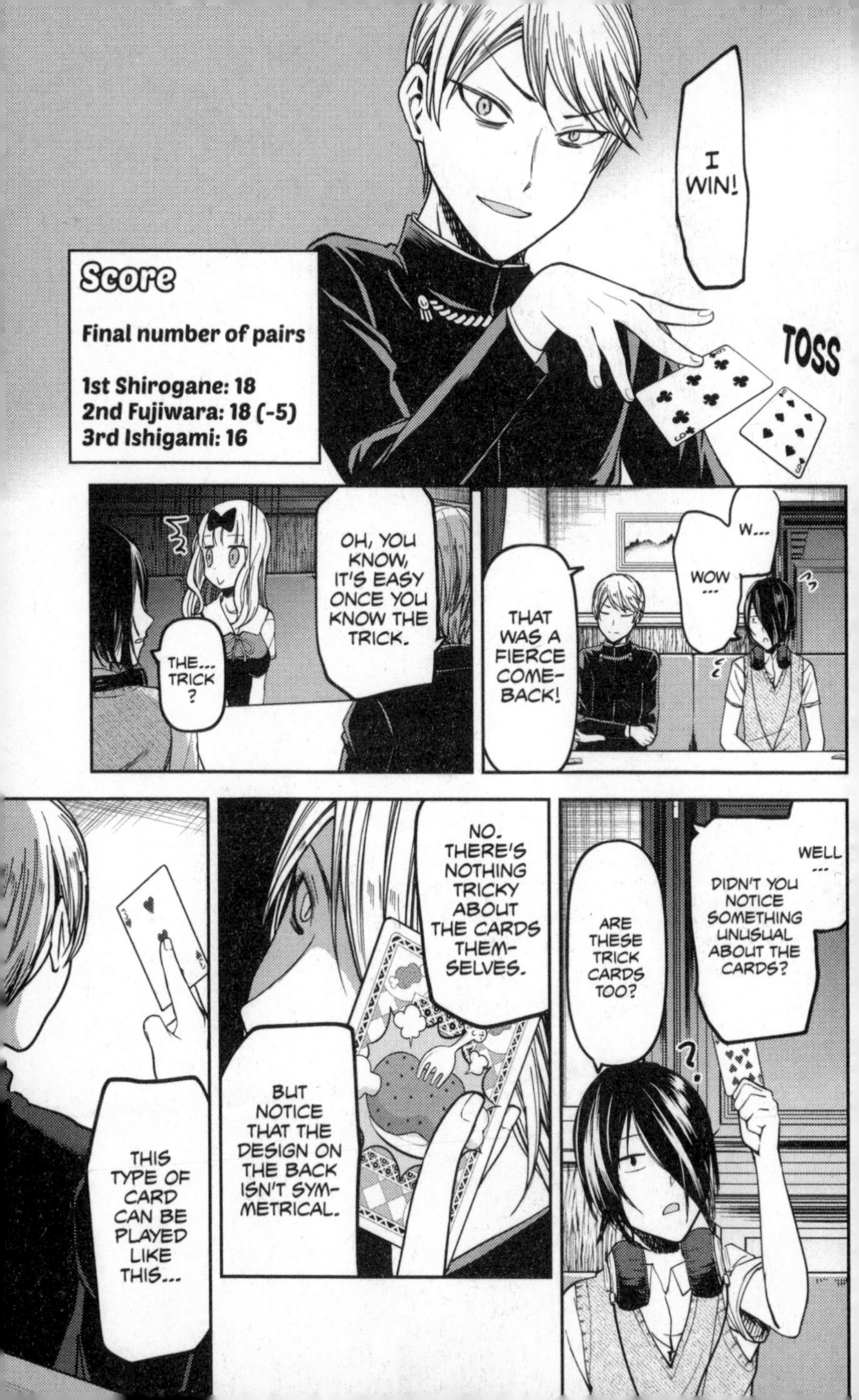
I WIN!
TOSS
Score
Final number of pairs
1st Shirogane: 18
2nd Fujiwara: 18 (-5)
3rd Ishigami: 16
W...
WOW...
THAT WAS A FIERCE COME-BACK!
OH, YOU KNOW, IT'S EASY ONCE YOU KNOW THE TRICK.
THE... TRICK?
WELL...
DIDN'T YOU NOTICE SOMETHING UNUSUAL ABOUT THE CARDS?
ARE THESE TRICK CARDS TOO?
NO. THERE'S NOTHING TRICKY ABOUT THE CARDS THEM-SELVES.
BUT NOTICE THAT THE DESIGN ON THE BACK ISN'T SYM-METRICAL.
THIS TYPE OF CARD CAN BE PLAYED LIKE THIS...

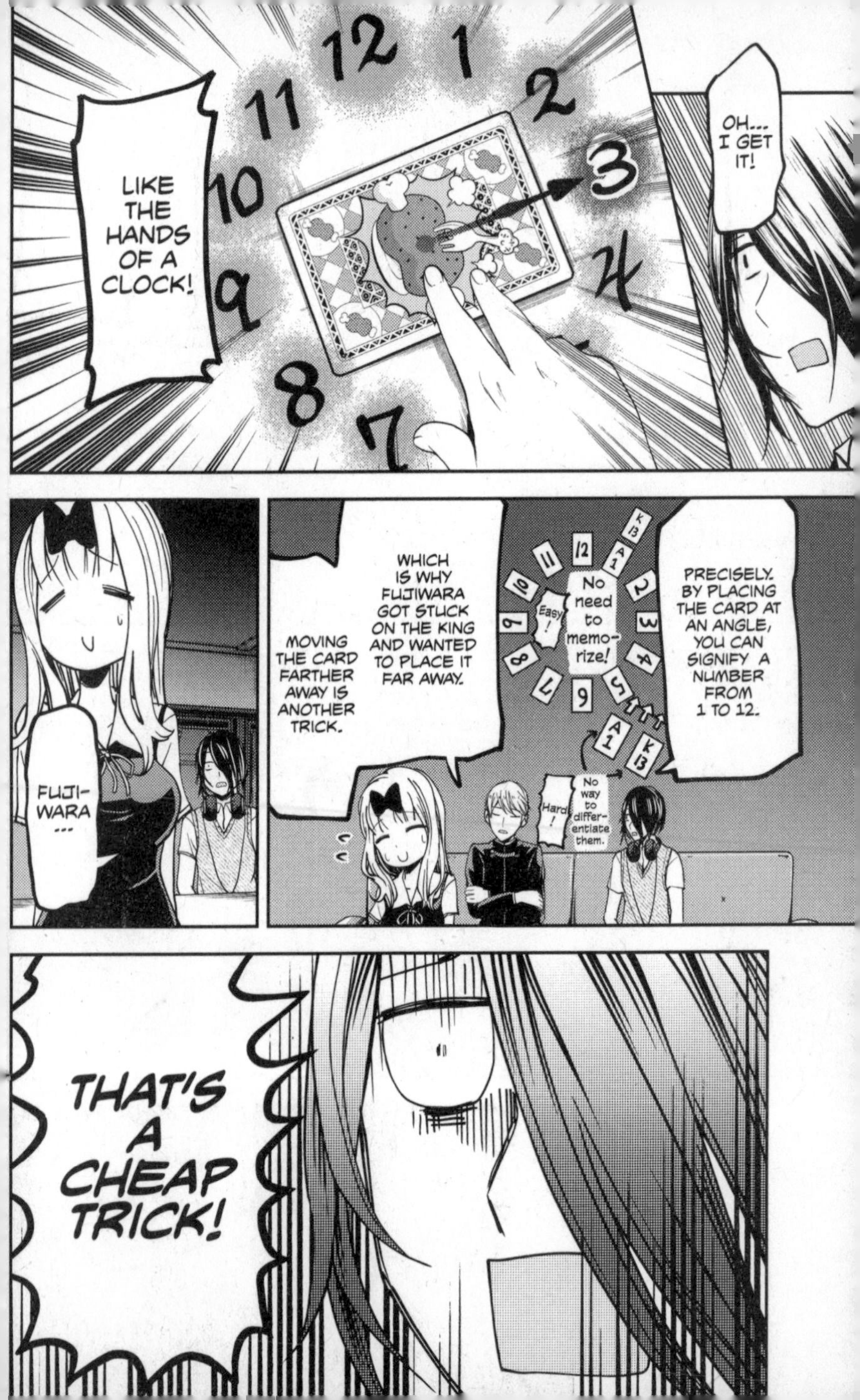
OH... I GET IT!
LIKE THE HANDS OF A CLOCK!
PRECISELY. BY PLACING THE CARD AT AN ANGLE, YOU CAN SIGNIFY A NUMBER FROM 1 TO 12.
No need to memo-rize!
Easy!
No way to differ-entiate them.
Hard!
WHICH IS WHY FUJIWARA GOT STUCK ON THE KING AND WANTED TO PLACE IT FAR AWAY.
MOVING THE CARD FARTHER AWAY IS ANOTHER TRICK.
FUJI-WARA ...
THAT'S A CHEAP TRICK!

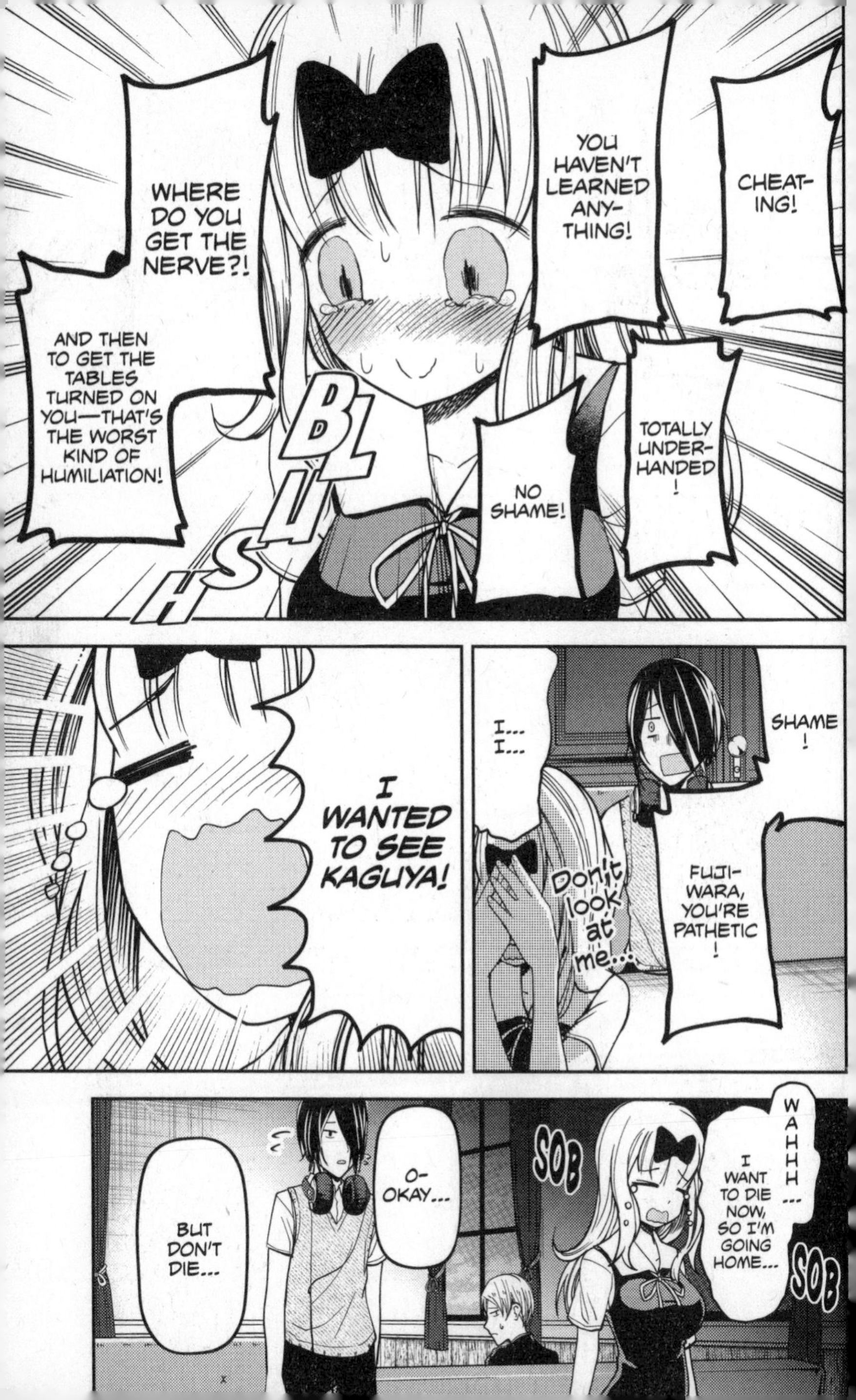
CHEAT-ING!
YOU HAVEN'T LEARNED ANY-THING!
WHERE DO YOU GET THE NERVE?!
TOTALLY UNDER-HANDED!
NO SHAME!
BLUSH
AND THEN TO GET THE TABLES TURNED ON YOU—THAT'S THE WORST KIND OF HUMILIATION!
SHAME!
I... I...
FUJI-WARA, YOU'RE PATHETIC!
Don't look at me...
I WANTED TO SEE KAGUYA!
WAHHH...
I WANT TO DIE NOW, SO I'M GOING HOME...
SOB
SOB
O-OKAY...
BUT DON'T DIE...

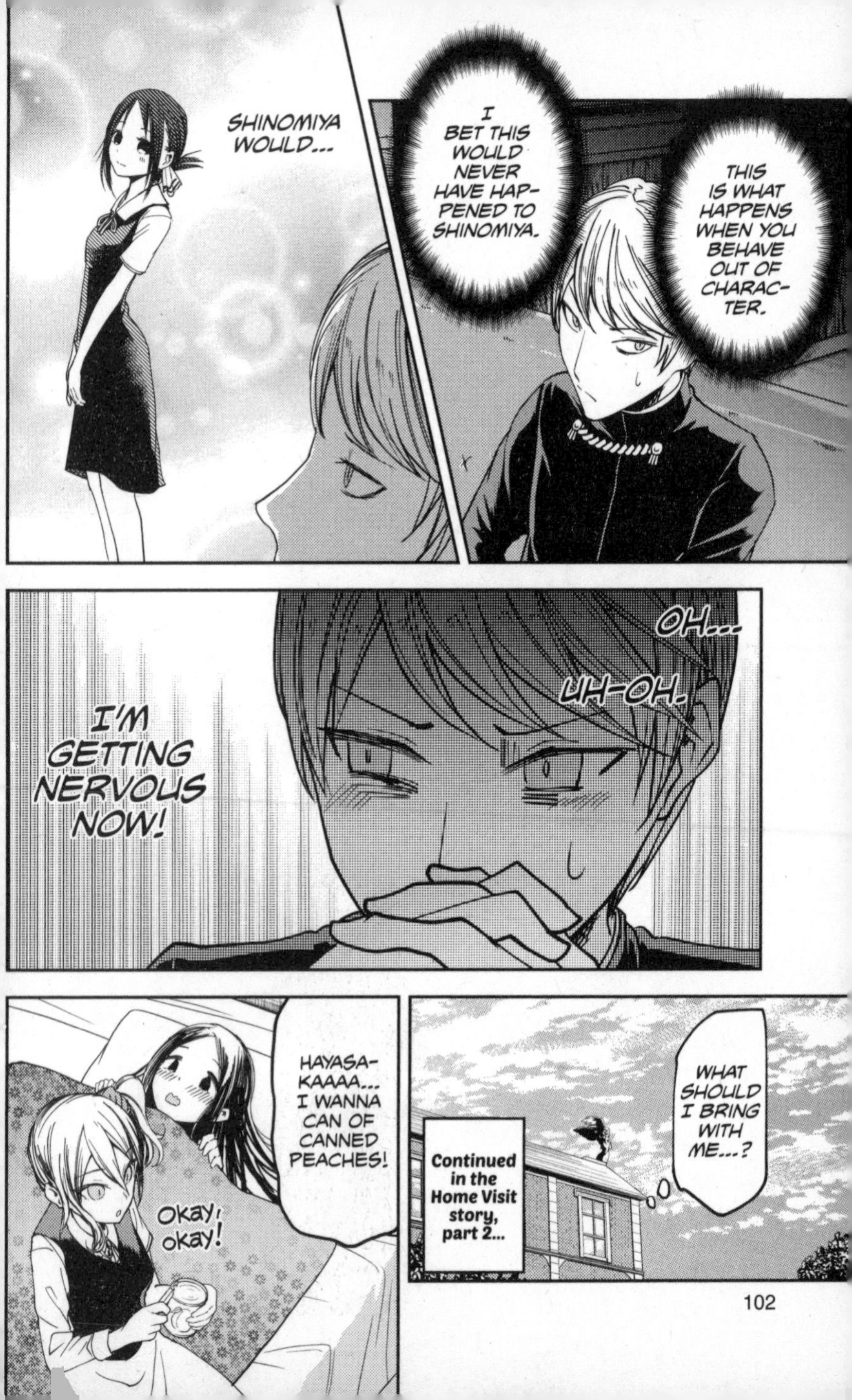
THIS IS WHAT HAPPENS WHEN YOU BEHAVE OUT OF CHARACTER.
I BET THIS WOULD NEVER HAVE HAPPENED TO SHINOMIYA.
SHINOMIYA WOULD...
OH...
UH-OH.
I'M GETTING NERVOUS NOW!
WHAT SHOULD I BRING WITH ME...?
Continued in the Home Visit story, part 2...
HAYASAKAAAA... I WANNA CAN OF CANNED PEACHES!
Okay! okay!

What do you bring as a gift to a rich person?

KAGUYA-SAMA
LOVE IS WAR

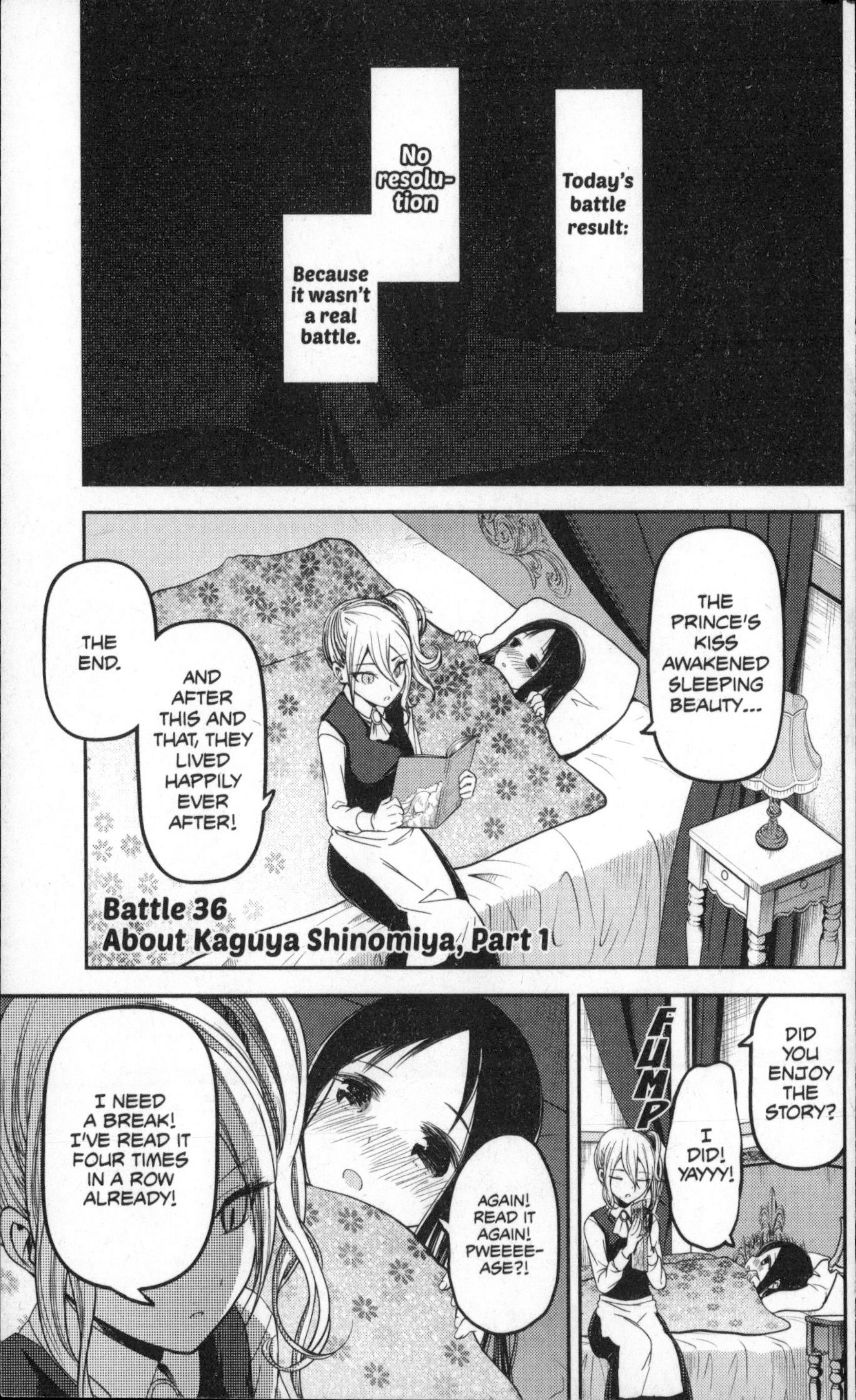
Today's battle result:
No resolution
Because it wasn't a real battle.
THE PRINCE'S KISS AWAKENED SLEEPING BEAUTY...
AND AFTER THIS AND THAT, THEY LIVED HAPPILY EVER AFTER!
THE END.
Battle 36
About Kaguya Shinomiya, Part 1
FUMP
DID YOU ENJOY THE STORY?
I DID! YAYYY!
AGAIN! READ IT AGAIN! PWEEEE-ASE?!
I NEED A BREAK! I'VE READ IT FOUR TIMES IN A ROW ALREADY!

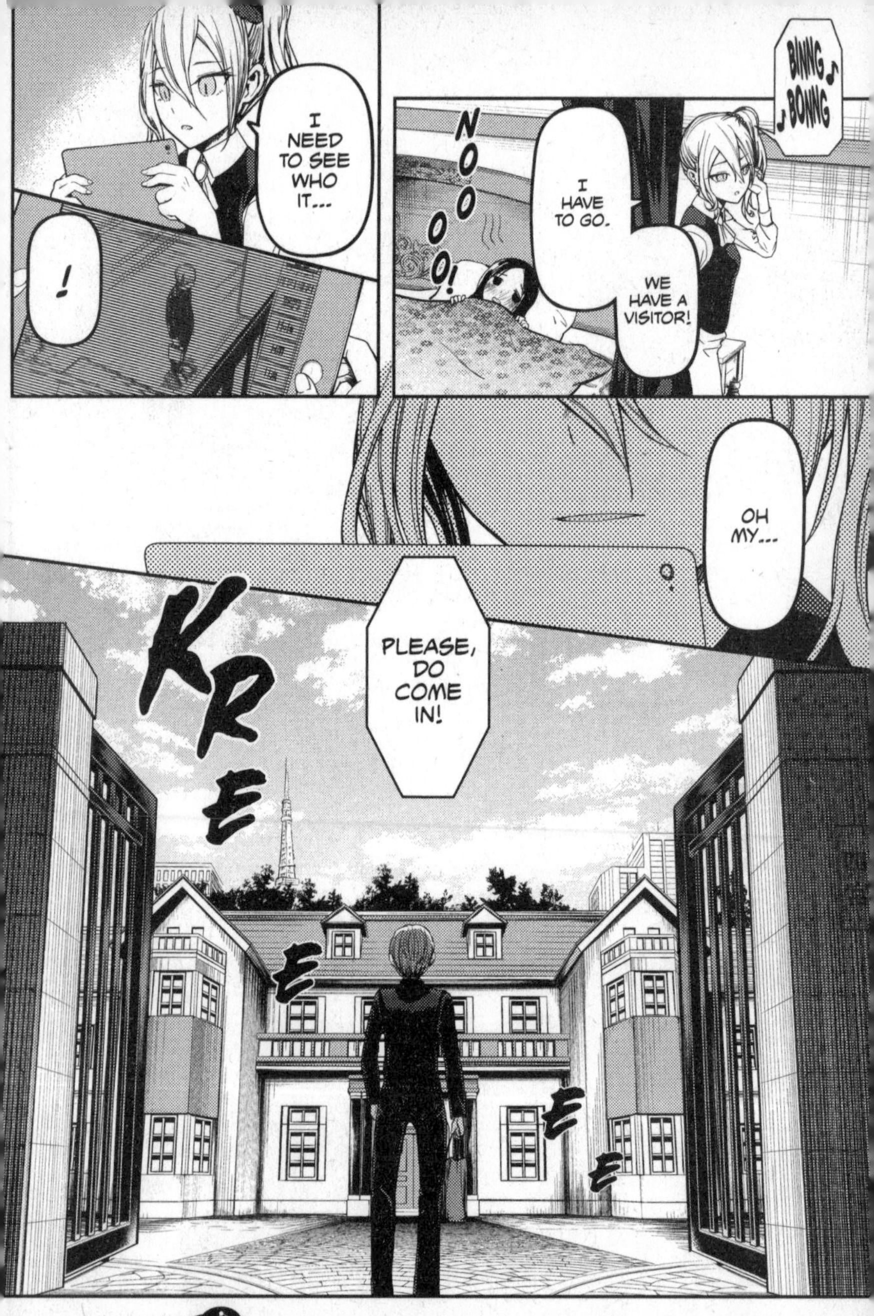
BINNG ♪ ♪ BONNG
I HAVE TO GO.
WE HAVE A VISITOR!
NOOOOO!
I NEED TO SEE WHO IT...
!
OH MY...
PLEASE, DO COME IN!
KREEEEE

Battle 36 About Kaguya Shinomiya, Part 1

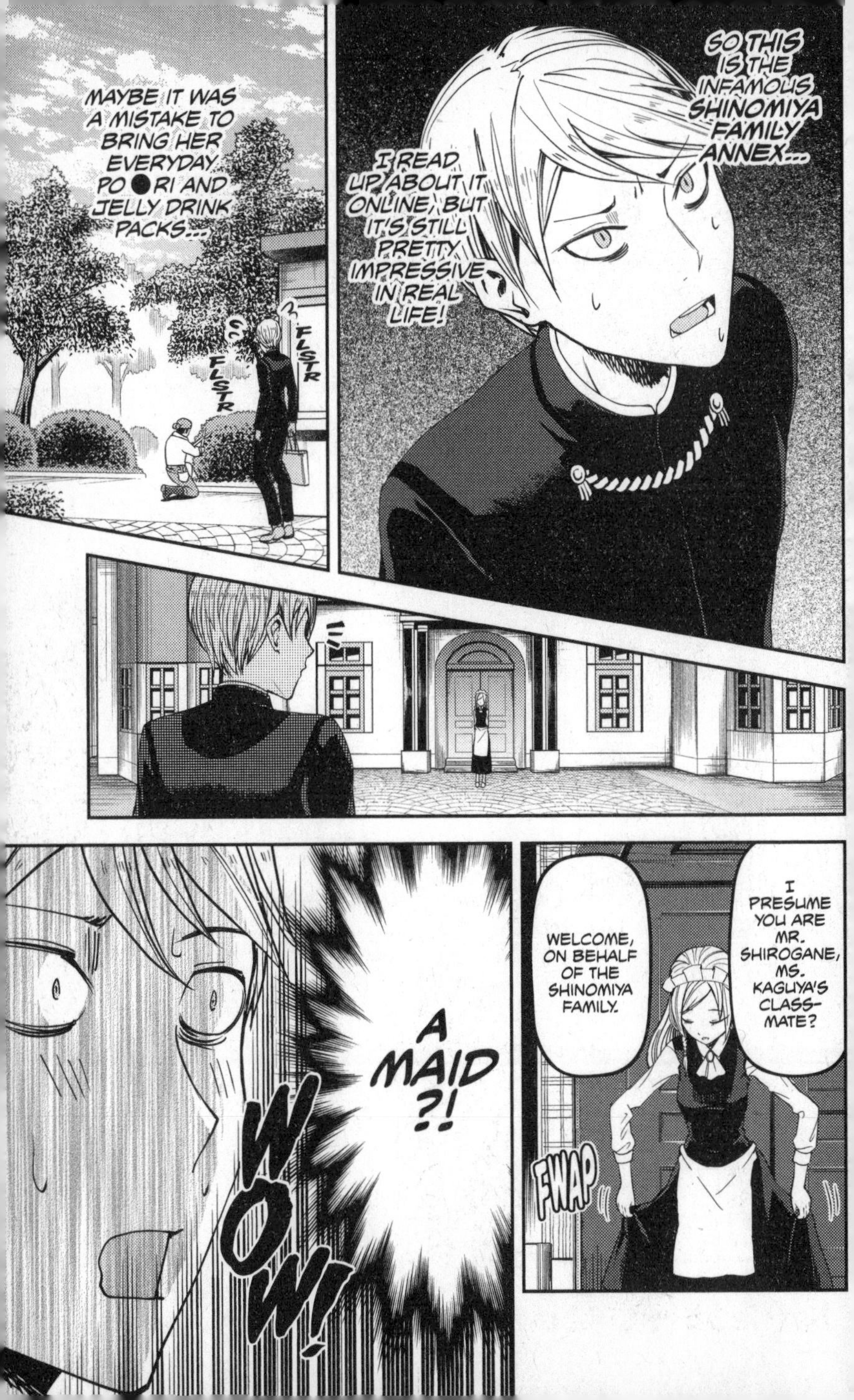
SO THIS IS THE INFAMOUS SHINOMIYA FAMILY ANNEX...
I READ UP ABOUT IT ONLINE, BUT IT'S STILL PRETTY IMPRESSIVE IN REAL LIFE!
MAYBE IT WAS A MISTAKE TO BRING HER EVERYDAY PO●RI AND JELLY DRINK PACKS...
FLSTR
FLSTR
I PRESUME YOU ARE MR. SHIROGANE, MS. KAGUYA'S CLASSMATE?
WELCOME, ON BEHALF OF THE SHINOMIYA FAMILY.
FWAP
A MAID?!
WOW!

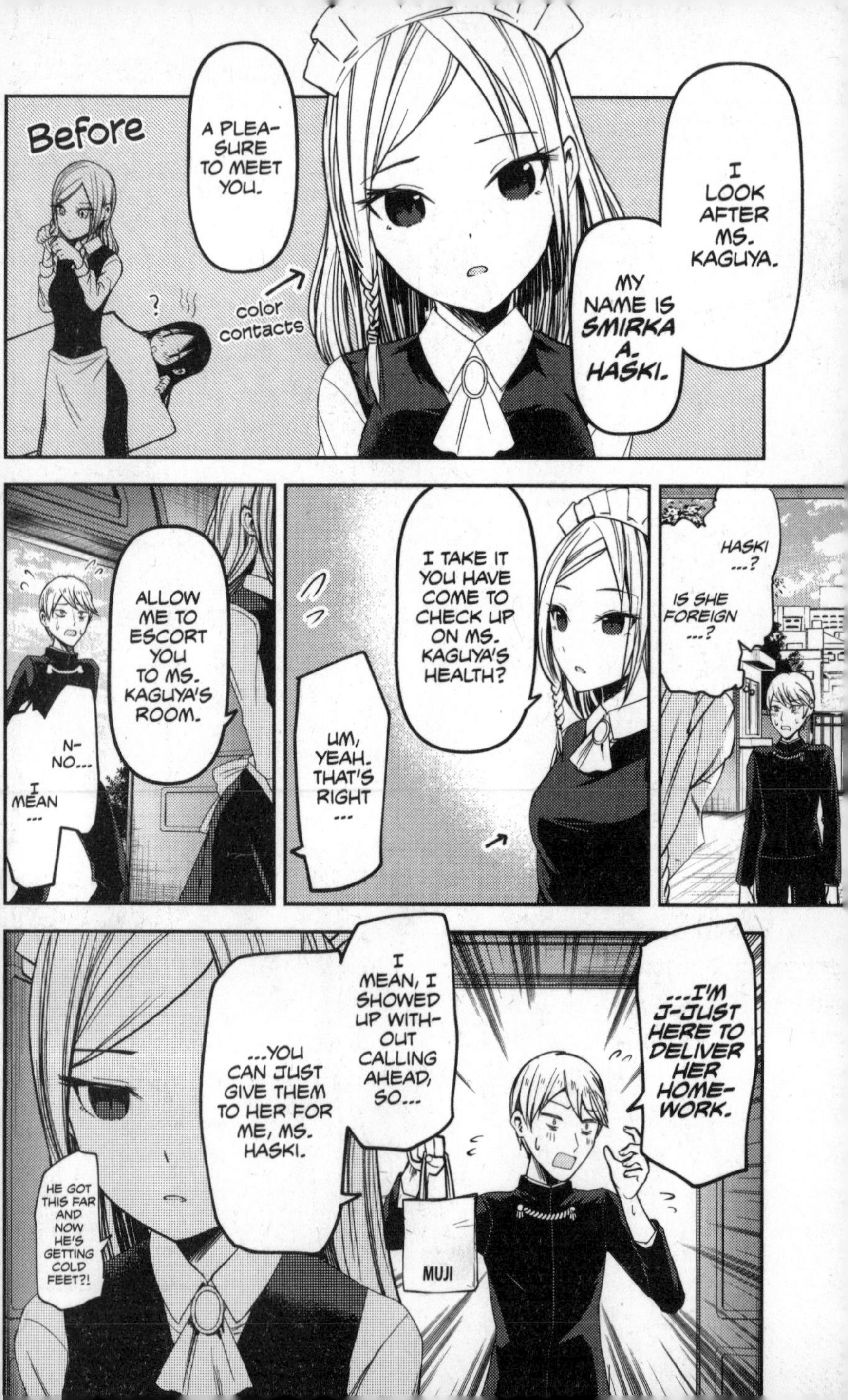
I LOOK AFTER MS. KAGUYA.
MY NAME IS SMIRKA A. HASKI.
A PLEASURE TO MEET YOU.
color contacts
Before
?
HASKI ...?
IS SHE FOREIGN ...?
I TAKE IT YOU HAVE COME TO CHECK UP ON MS. KAGUYA'S HEALTH?
UM, YEAH. THAT'S RIGHT ...
ALLOW ME TO ESCORT YOU TO MS. KAGUYA'S ROOM.
N-NO... I MEAN ...
...I'M J-JUST HERE TO DELIVER HER HOMEWORK.
I MEAN, I SHOWED UP WITHOUT CALLING AHEAD, SO...
...YOU CAN JUST GIVE THEM TO HER FOR ME, MS. HASKI.
HE GOT THIS FAR AND NOW HE'S GETTING COLD FEET?!
MUJI

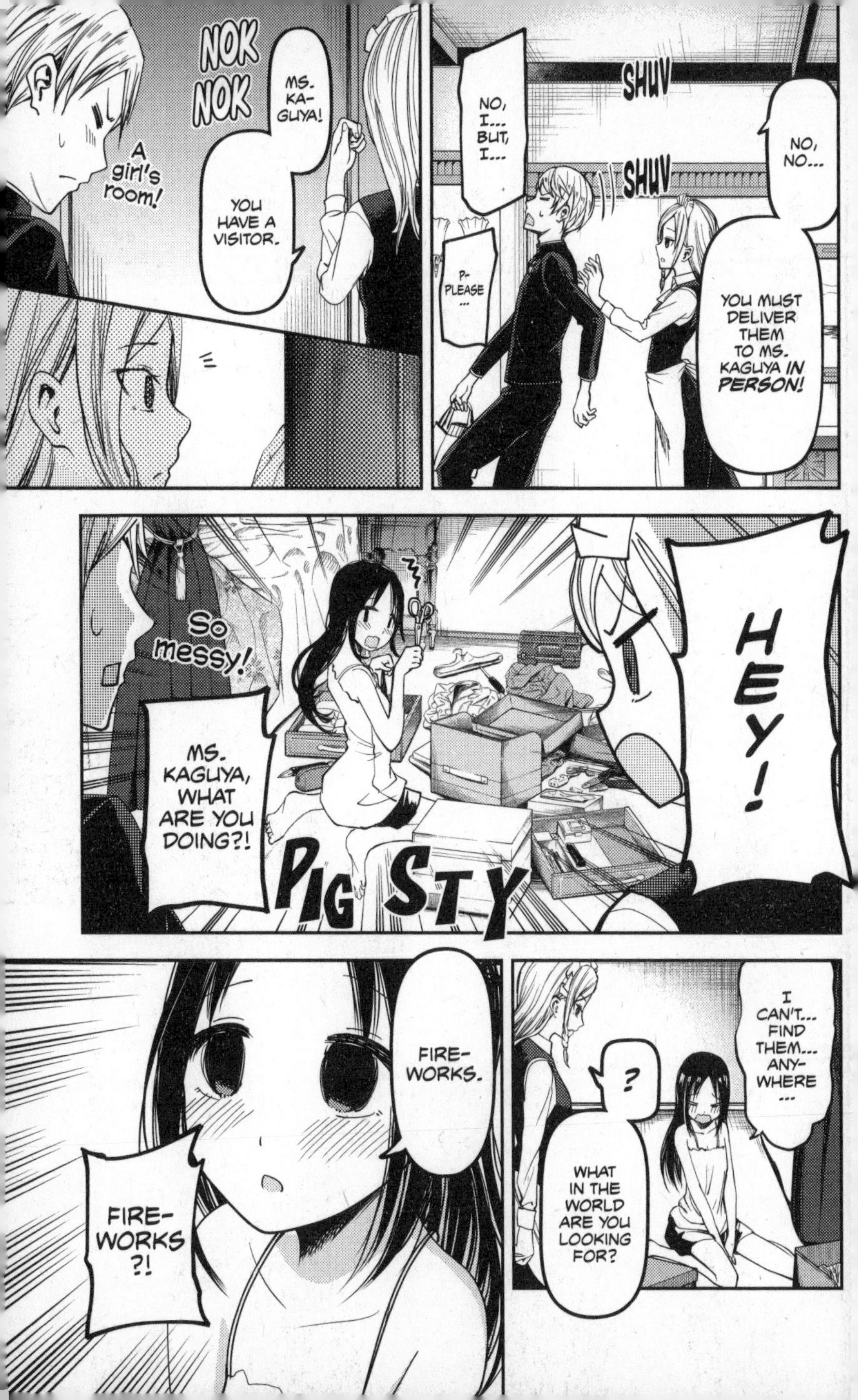
SHUV
SHUV
NO, NO...
YOU MUST DELIVER THEM TO MS. KAGUYA IN PERSON!
NO, I... BUT, I...
P-PLEASE...
NOK NOK
MS. KAGUYA!
YOU HAVE A VISITOR.
A girl's room!
HEY!
MS. KAGUYA, WHAT ARE YOU DOING?!
So messy!
PIG STY
I CAN'T... FIND THEM... ANYWHERE...
?
WHAT IN THE WORLD ARE YOU LOOKING FOR?
FIRE-WORKS.
FIRE-WORKS?!

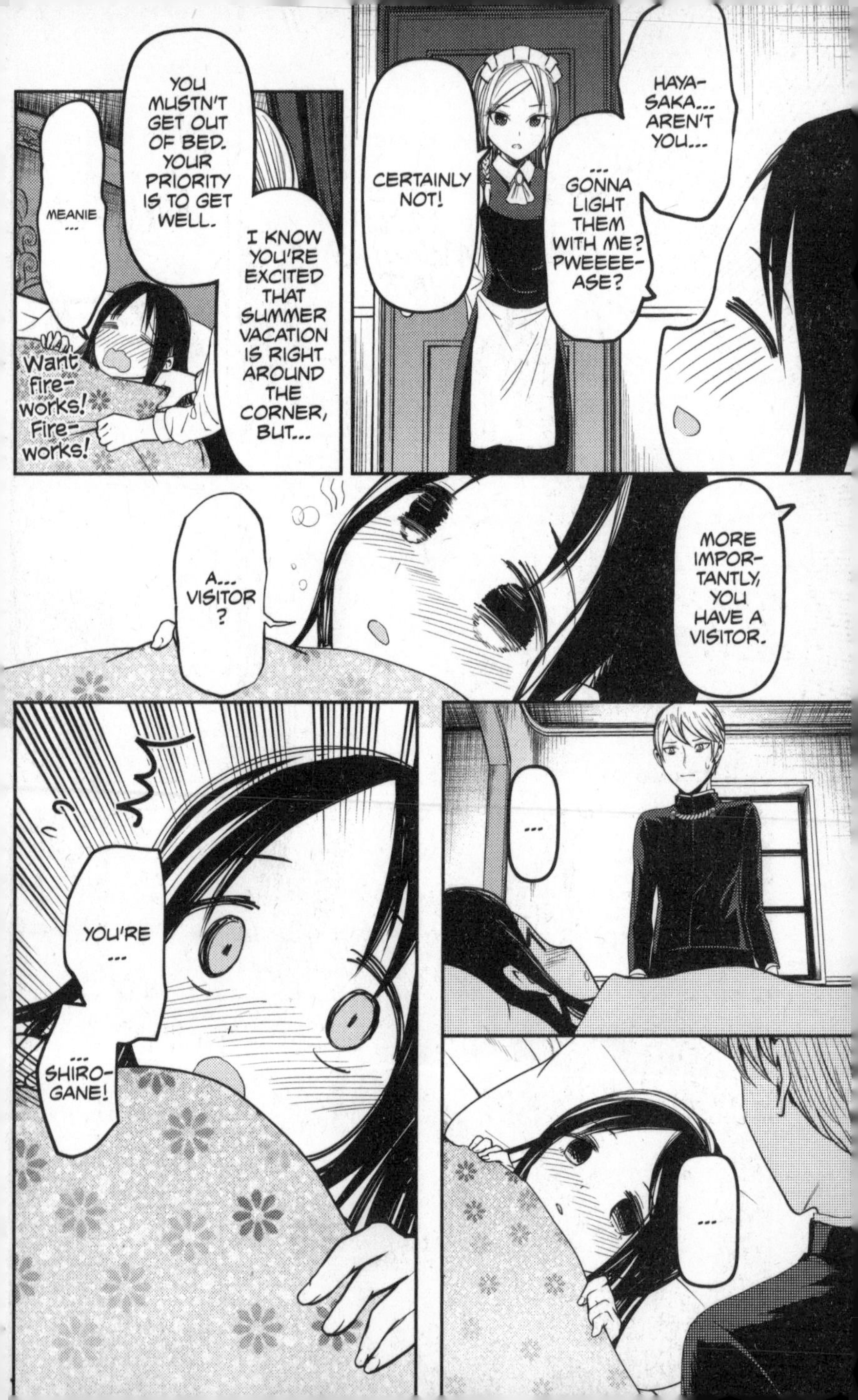
HAYA-SAKA... AREN'T YOU...
... GONNA LIGHT THEM WITH ME? PWEEEEE-ASE?
CERTAINLY NOT!
YOU MUSTN'T GET OUT OF BED. YOUR PRIORITY IS TO GET WELL.
I KNOW YOU'RE EXCITED THAT SUMMER VACATION IS RIGHT AROUND THE CORNER, BUT...
MEANIE ...
Want fire-works! Fire-works!
MORE IMPOR-TANTLY, YOU HAVE A VISITOR.
A... VISITOR ?
...
...
YOU'RE ...
... SHIRO-GANE!

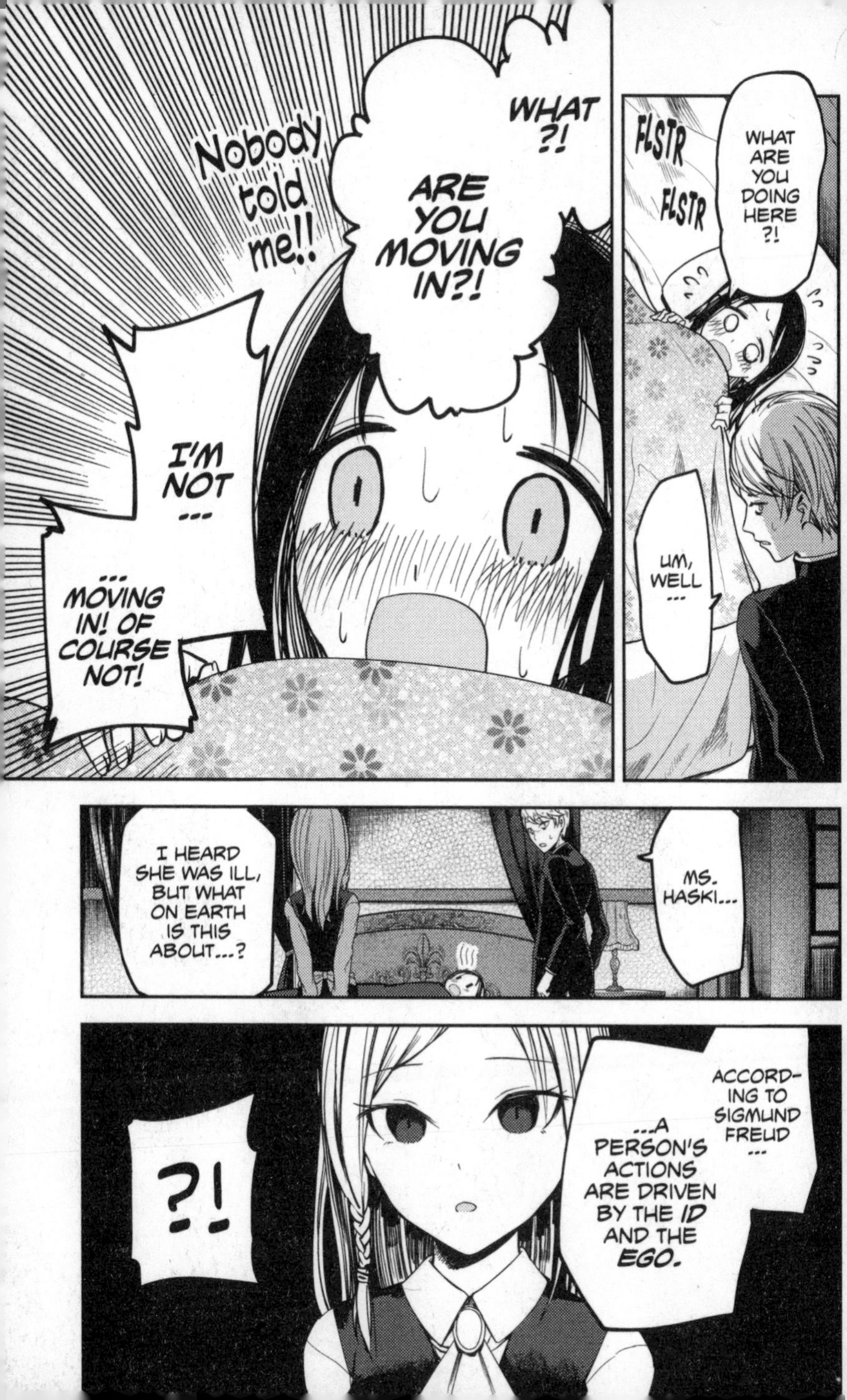
FLSTR
FLSTR
WHAT ARE YOU DOING HERE ?!
UM, WELL ---
WHAT ?!
ARE YOU MOVING IN?!
Nobody told me!!
I'M NOT ---
... MOVING IN! OF COURSE NOT!
MS. HASKI...
I HEARD SHE WAS ILL, BUT WHAT ON EARTH IS THIS ABOUT...?
ACCORDING TO SIGMUND FREUD ---
...A PERSON'S ACTIONS ARE DRIVEN BY THE ID AND THE EGO.
?!

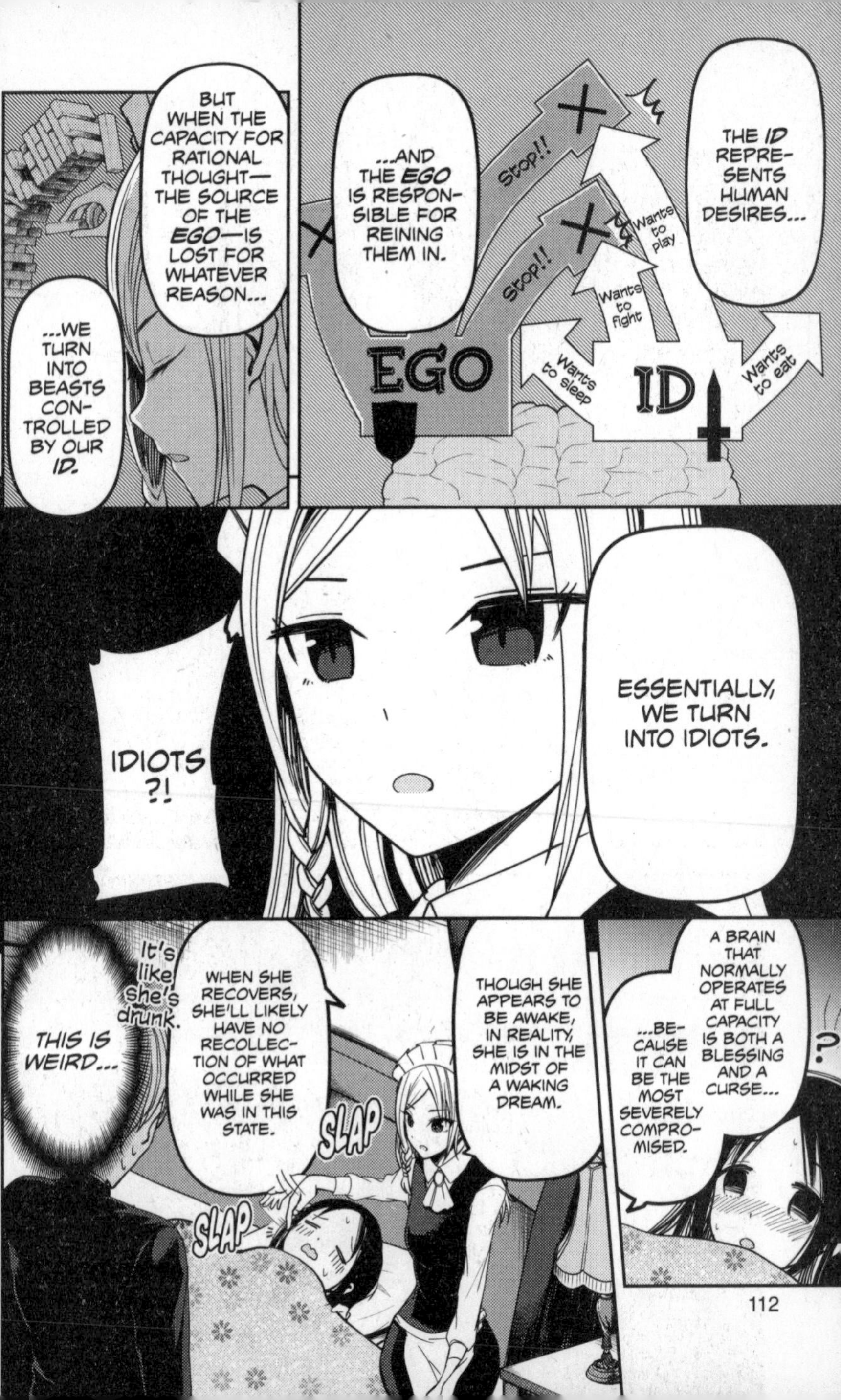
THE ID REPRESENTS HUMAN DESIRES...
...AND THE EGO IS RESPONSIBLE FOR REINING THEM IN.
Stop!!
Stop!!
Wants to play
Wants to fight
Wants to sleep
Wants to eat
EGO
ID
BUT WHEN THE CAPACITY FOR RATIONAL THOUGHT—THE SOURCE OF THE EGO—IS LOST FOR WHATEVER REASON...
...WE TURN INTO BEASTS CONTROLLED BY OUR ID.
ESSENTIALLY, WE TURN INTO IDIOTS.
IDIOTS?!
A BRAIN THAT NORMALLY OPERATES AT FULL CAPACITY IS BOTH A BLESSING AND A CURSE...
...BECAUSE IT CAN BE THE MOST SEVERELY COMPROMISED.
?
THOUGH SHE APPEARS TO BE AWAKE, IN REALITY, SHE IS IN THE MIDST OF A WAKING DREAM.
WHEN SHE RECOVERS, SHE'LL LIKELY HAVE NO RECOLLECTION OF WHAT OCCURRED WHILE SHE WAS IN THIS STATE.
SLAP
SLAP
It's like she's drunk.
THIS IS WEIRD...

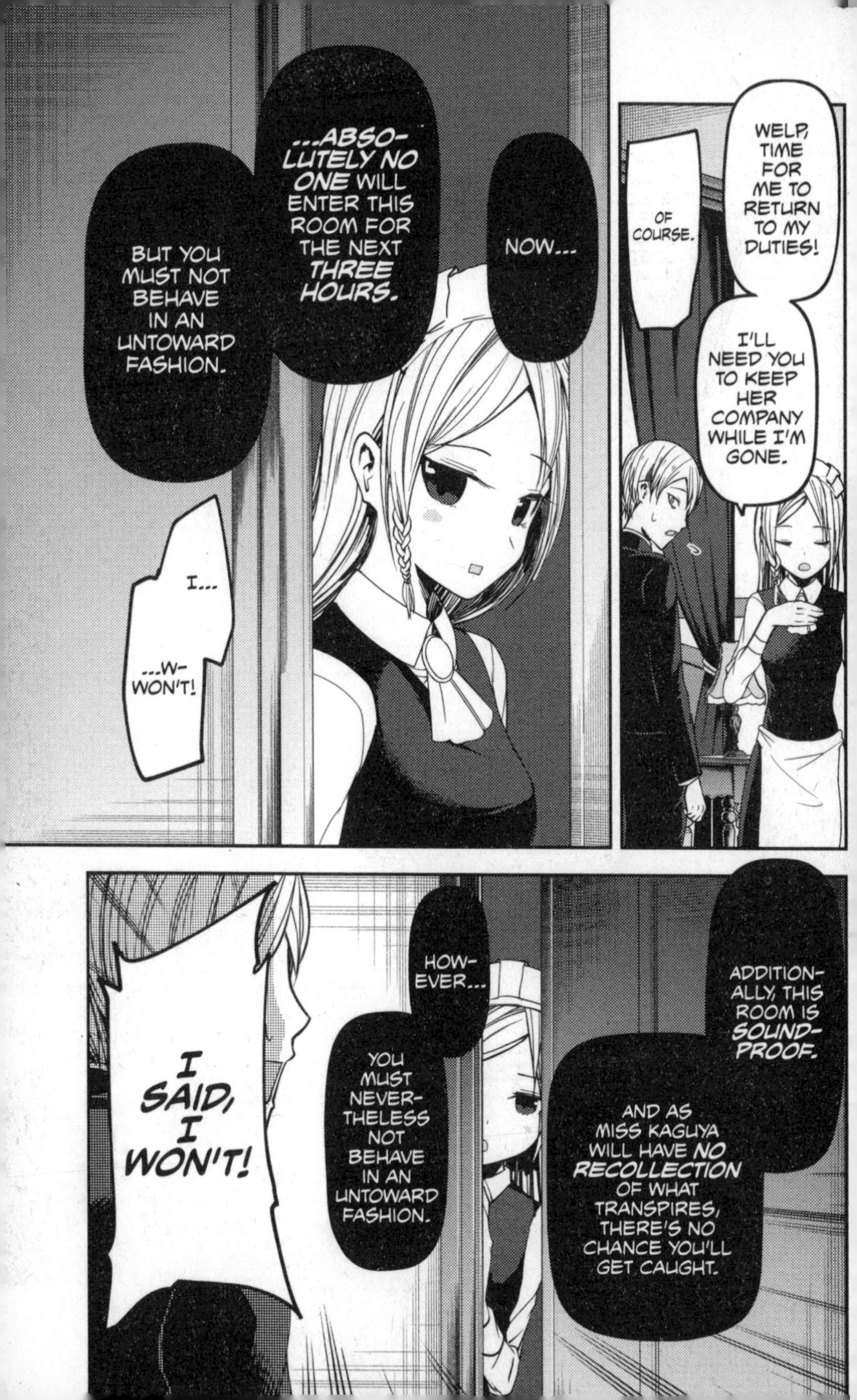
WELP, TIME FOR ME TO RETURN TO MY DUTIES!
I'LL NEED YOU TO KEEP HER COMPANY WHILE I'M GONE.
OF COURSE.
NOW...
...ABSOLUTELY NO ONE WILL ENTER THIS ROOM FOR THE NEXT THREE HOURS.
BUT YOU MUST NOT BEHAVE IN AN UNTOWARD FASHION.
I...
...W-WON'T!
ADDITIONALLY, THIS ROOM IS SOUNDPROOF.
AND AS MISS KAGUYA WILL HAVE NO RECOLLECTION OF WHAT TRANSPIRES, THERE'S NO CHANCE YOU'LL GET CAUGHT.
HOWEVER...
YOU MUST NEVERTHELESS NOT BEHAVE IN AN UNTOWARD FASHION.
I SAID, I WON'T!

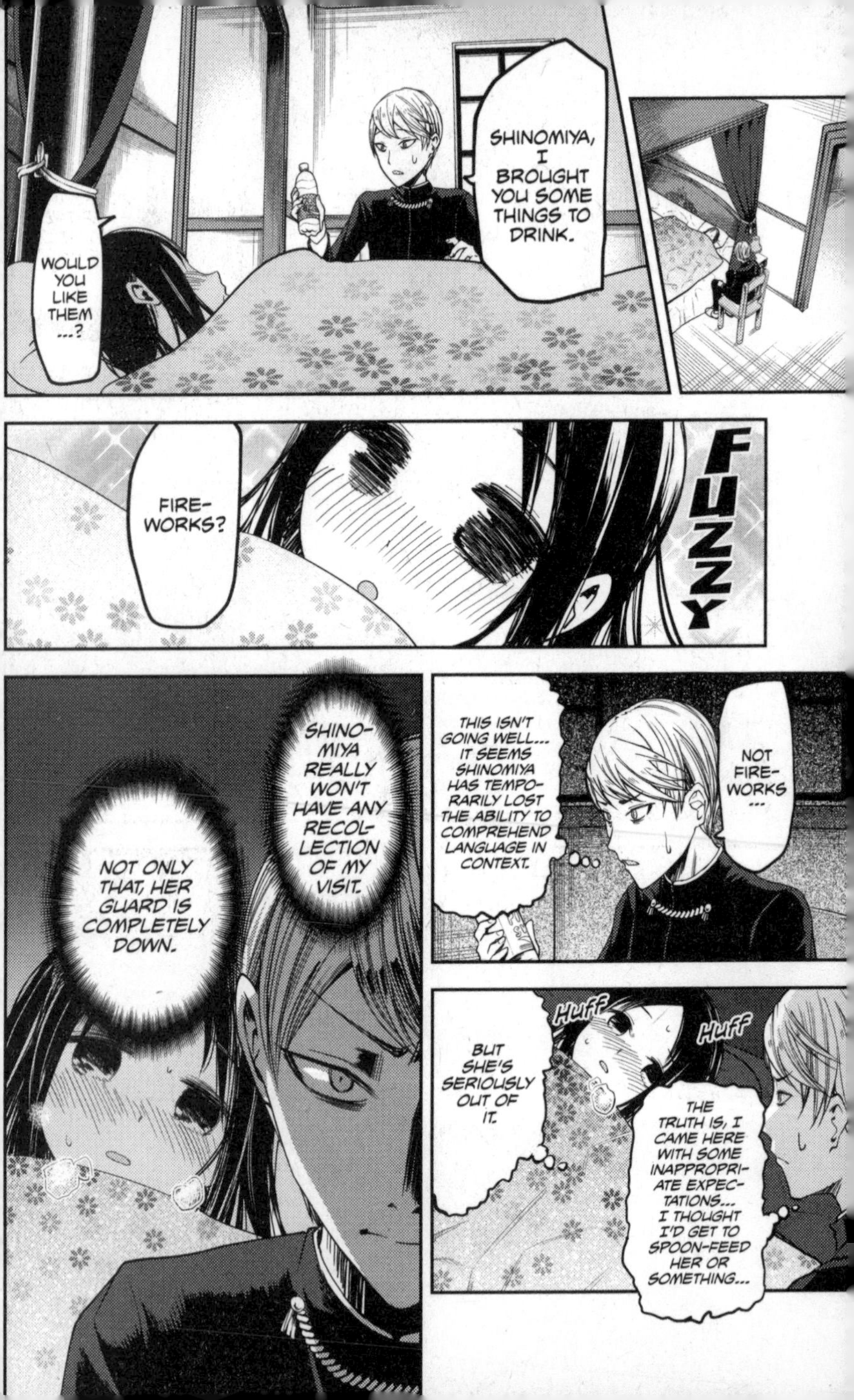
SHINOMIYA, I BROUGHT YOU SOME THINGS TO DRINK.
WOULD YOU LIKE THEM ...?
FUZZY
FIRE-WORKS?
NOT FIRE-WORKS ...
THIS ISN'T GOING WELL... IT SEEMS SHINOMIYA HAS TEMPORARILY LOST THE ABILITY TO COMPREHEND LANGUAGE IN CONTEXT.
Huff
Huff
THE TRUTH IS, I CAME HERE WITH SOME INAPPROPRIATE EXPECTATIONS... I THOUGHT I'D GET TO SPOON-FEED HER OR SOMETHING...
BUT SHE'S SERIOUSLY OUT OF IT.
SHINOMIYA REALLY WON'T HAVE ANY RECOLLECTION OF MY VISIT.
NOT ONLY THAT, HER GUARD IS COMPLETELY DOWN.

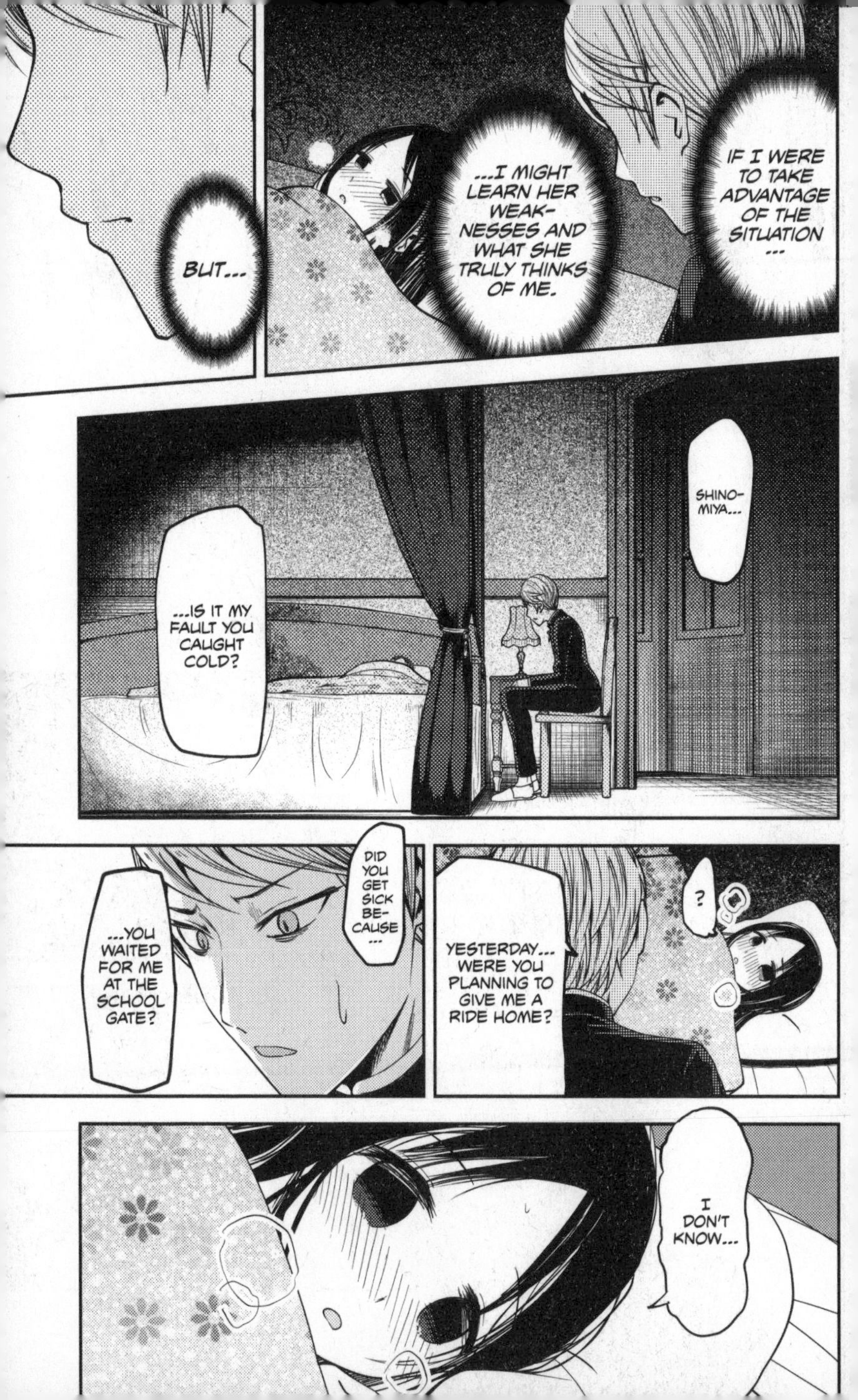
IF I WERE TO TAKE ADVANTAGE OF THE SITUATION...
...I MIGHT LEARN HER WEAK-NESSES AND WHAT SHE TRULY THINKS OF ME.
BUT...
SHINO-MIYA...
...IS IT MY FAULT YOU CAUGHT COLD?
?
YESTERDAY... WERE YOU PLANNING TO GIVE ME A RIDE HOME?
DID YOU GET SICK BE-CAUSE...
...YOU WAITED FOR ME AT THE SCHOOL GATE?
I DON'T KNOW...

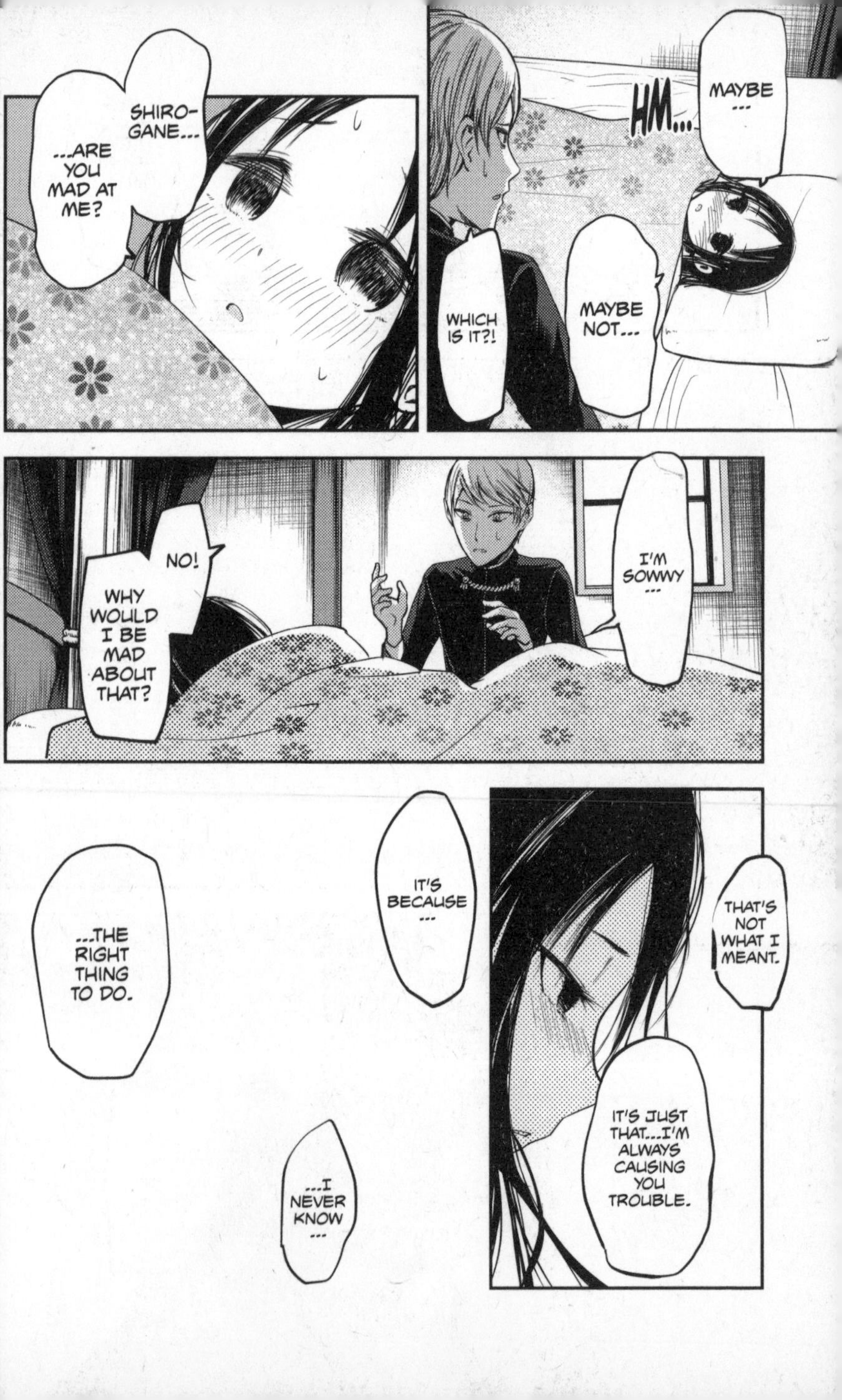
MAYBE ...
HM...
MAYBE NOT...
WHICH IS IT?!
SHIRO-GANE...
...ARE YOU MAD AT ME?
I'M SOWWY ...
NO!
WHY WOULD I BE MAD ABOUT THAT?
THAT'S NOT WHAT I MEANT.
IT'S JUST THAT...I'M ALWAYS CAUSING YOU TROUBLE.
IT'S BECAUSE ...
...I NEVER KNOW ...
...THE RIGHT THING TO DO.

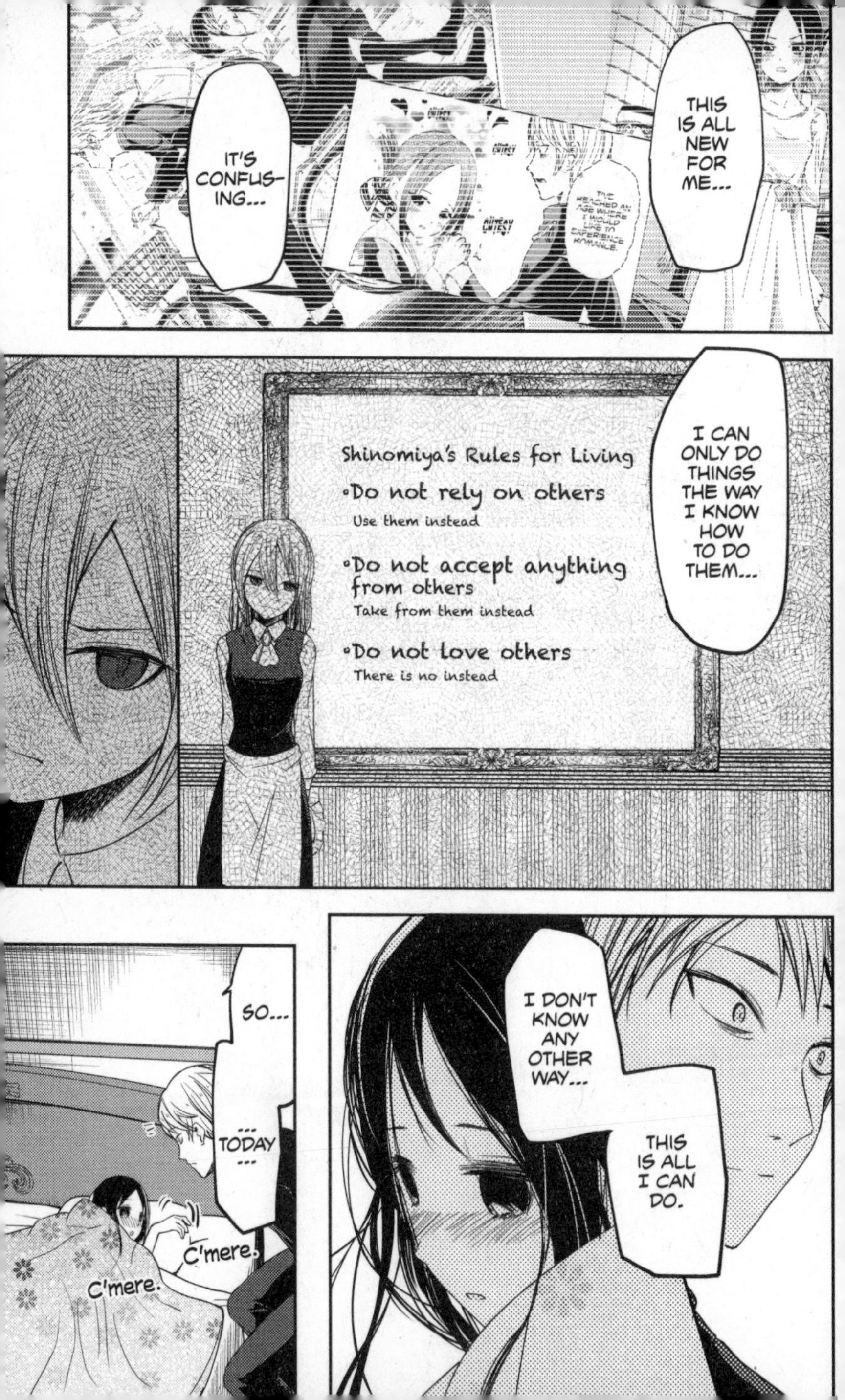
THIS IS ALL NEW FOR ME...
I'VE REACHED AN AGE WHERE I WOULD LIKE TO EXPERIENCE ROMANCE.
IT'S CONFUSING...
I CAN ONLY DO THINGS THE WAY I KNOW HOW TO DO THEM...
Shinomiya's Rules for Living
•Do not rely on others
Use them instead
•Do not accept anything from others
Take from them instead
•Do not love others
There is no instead
I DON'T KNOW ANY OTHER WAY...
THIS IS ALL I CAN DO.
SO...
...TODAY...
C'mere.
C'mere.

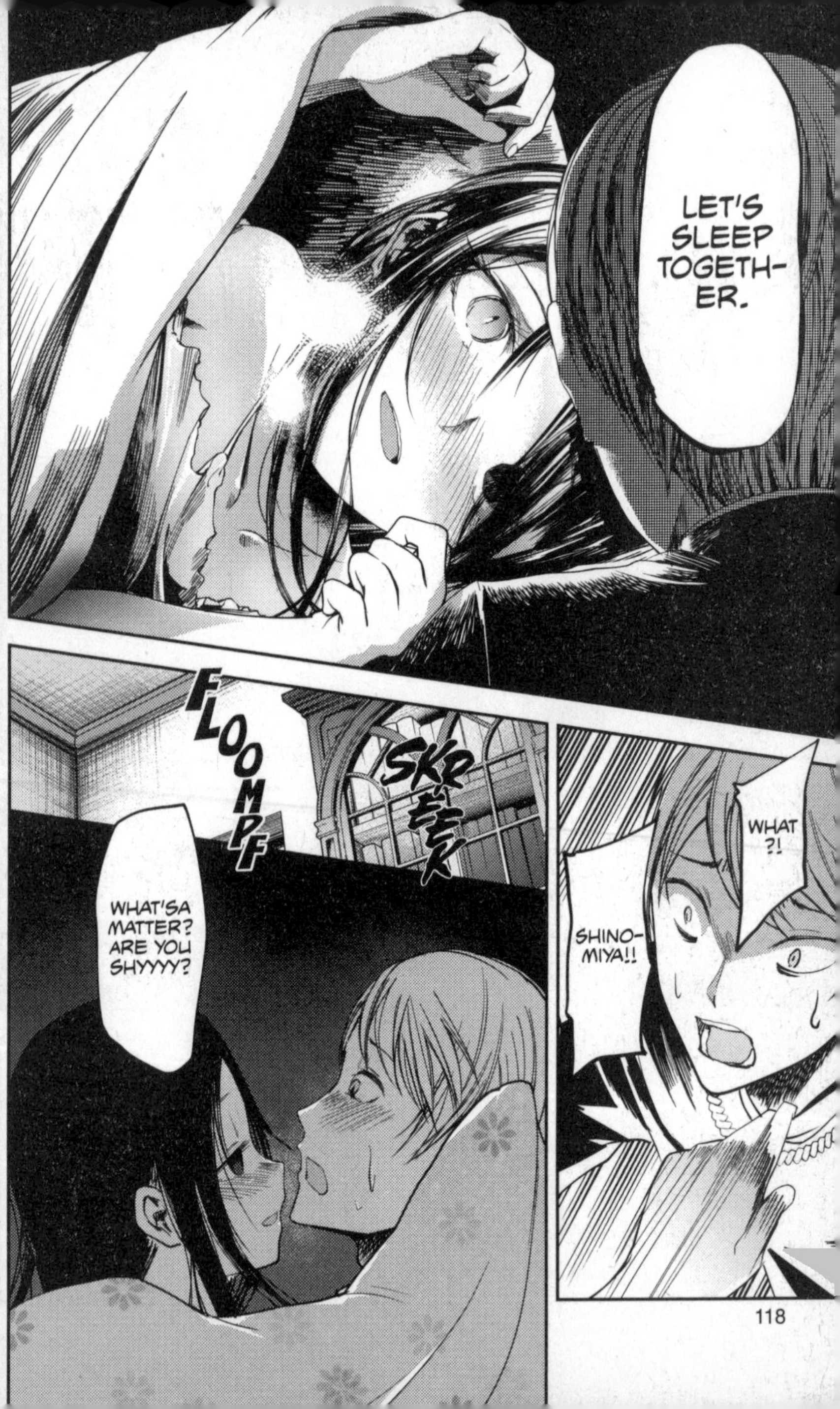
LET'S SLEEP TOGETH- ER.
WHAT ?!
SHINO- MIYA!!
FLOOMPF
SKREEEK
WHAT'SA MATTER? ARE YOU SHYYYY?

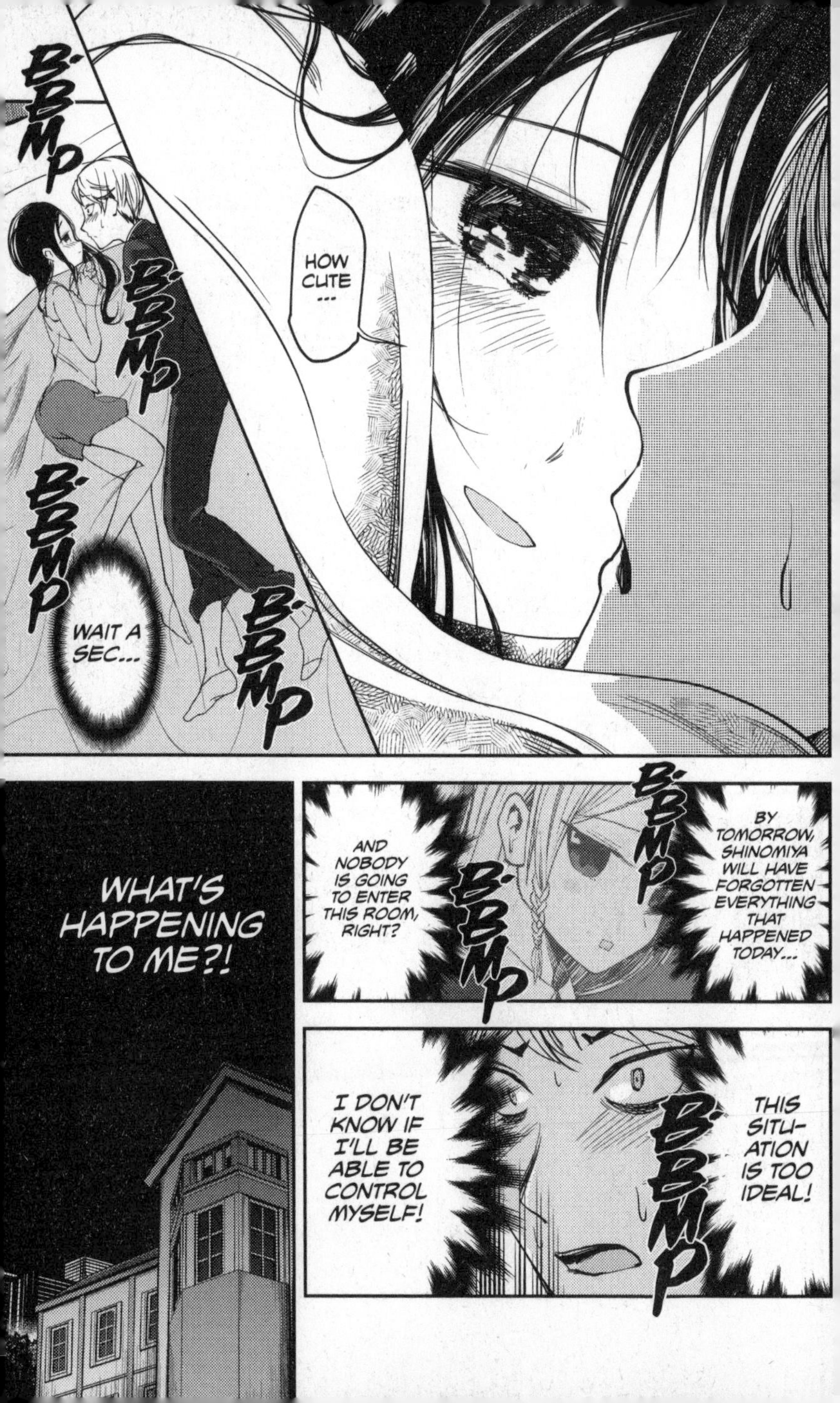
HOW CUTE ...
B-BMP
B-BMP
B-BMP
WAIT A SEC...
B-BMP
BY TOMORROW, SHINOMIYA WILL HAVE FORGOTTEN EVERYTHING THAT HAPPENED TODAY...
B-BMP
AND NOBODY IS GOING TO ENTER THIS ROOM, RIGHT?
B-BMP
THIS SITU-ATION IS TOO IDEAL!
B-BMP
I DON'T KNOW IF I'LL BE ABLE TO CONTROL MYSELF!
WHAT'S HAPPENING TO ME?!

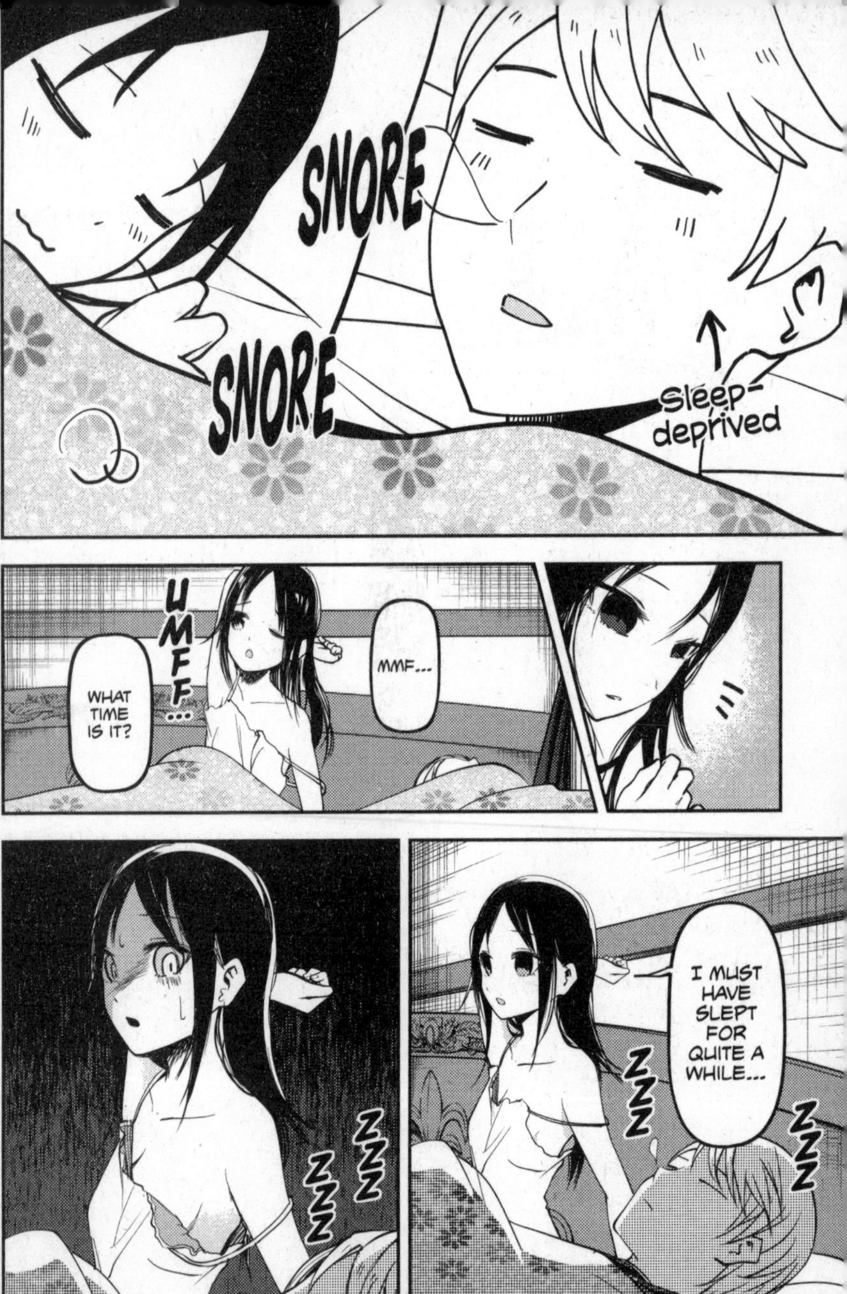
SNORE
SNORE
Sleep-deprived
MMF...
UMFF...
WHAT TIME IS IT?
I MUST HAVE SLEPT FOR QUITE A WHILE...
ZZZ
ZZZ
ZZZ
ZZZ

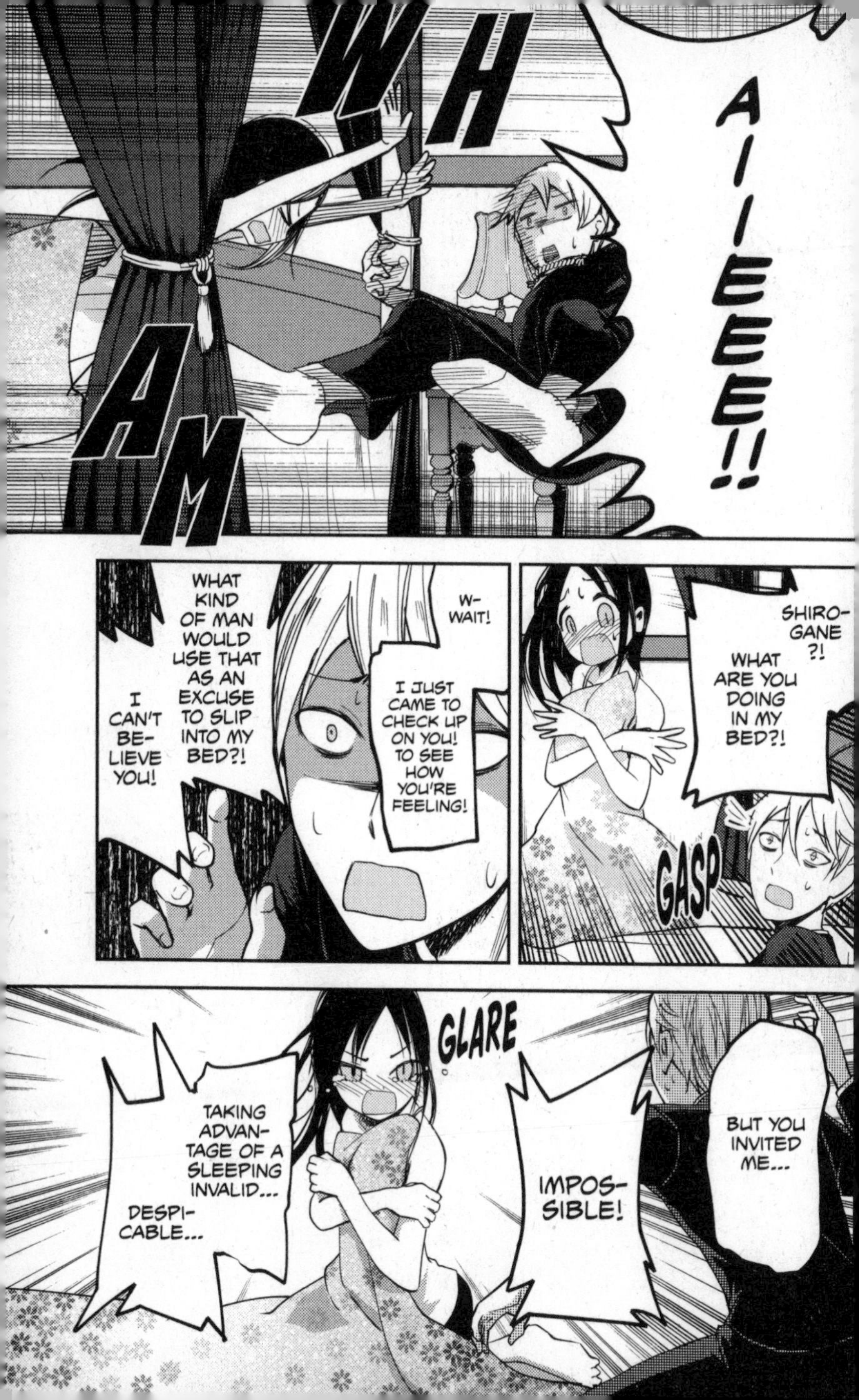
AIIEEE!!
WHAM
SHIROGANE?! WHAT ARE YOU DOING IN MY BED?!
GASP
W-WAIT!
I JUST CAME TO CHECK UP ON YOU! TO SEE HOW YOU'RE FEELING!
WHAT KIND OF MAN WOULD USE THAT AS AN EXCUSE TO SLIP INTO MY BED?!
I CAN'T BELIEVE YOU!
BUT YOU INVITED ME...
IMPOSSIBLE!
GLARE
TAKING ADVANTAGE OF A SLEEPING INVALID...
DESPICABLE...

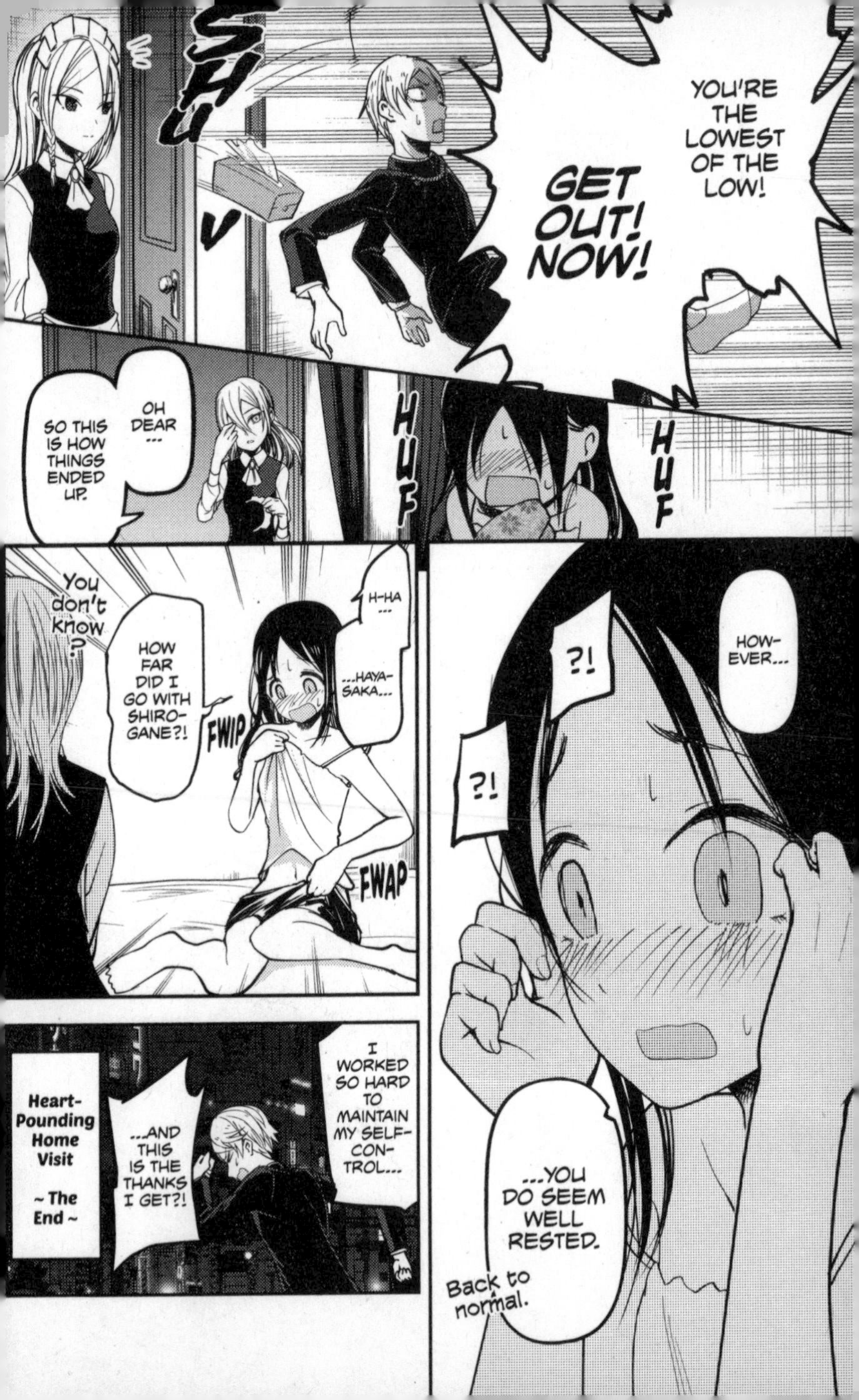
YOU'RE THE LOWEST OF THE LOW!
GET OUT! NOW!
SHU
V
HUF
HUF
HUF
HUF
OH DEAR...
SO THIS IS HOW THINGS ENDED UP.
HOW-EVER...
?!
?!
...YOU DO SEEM WELL RESTED.
Back to normal.
H-HA...
...HAYA-SAKA...
HOW FAR DID I GO WITH SHIRO-GANE?!
FWIP
FWAP
You don't know?
I WORKED SO HARD TO MAINTAIN MY SELF-CONTROL...
...AND THIS IS THE THANKS I GET?!
Heart-Pounding Home Visit
~ The End ~

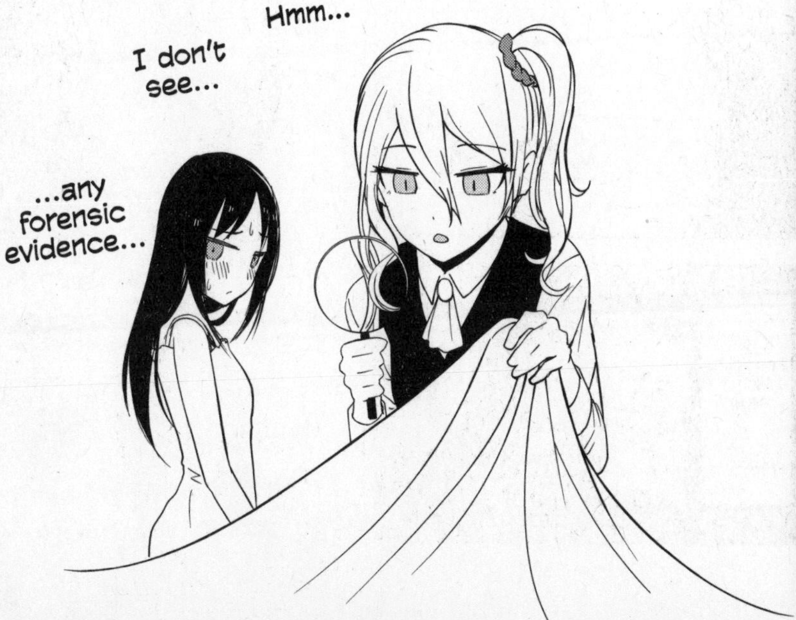
Hmm...
I don't see...
...any forensic evidence...

KAGUYA-SAMA

LOVE IS WAR

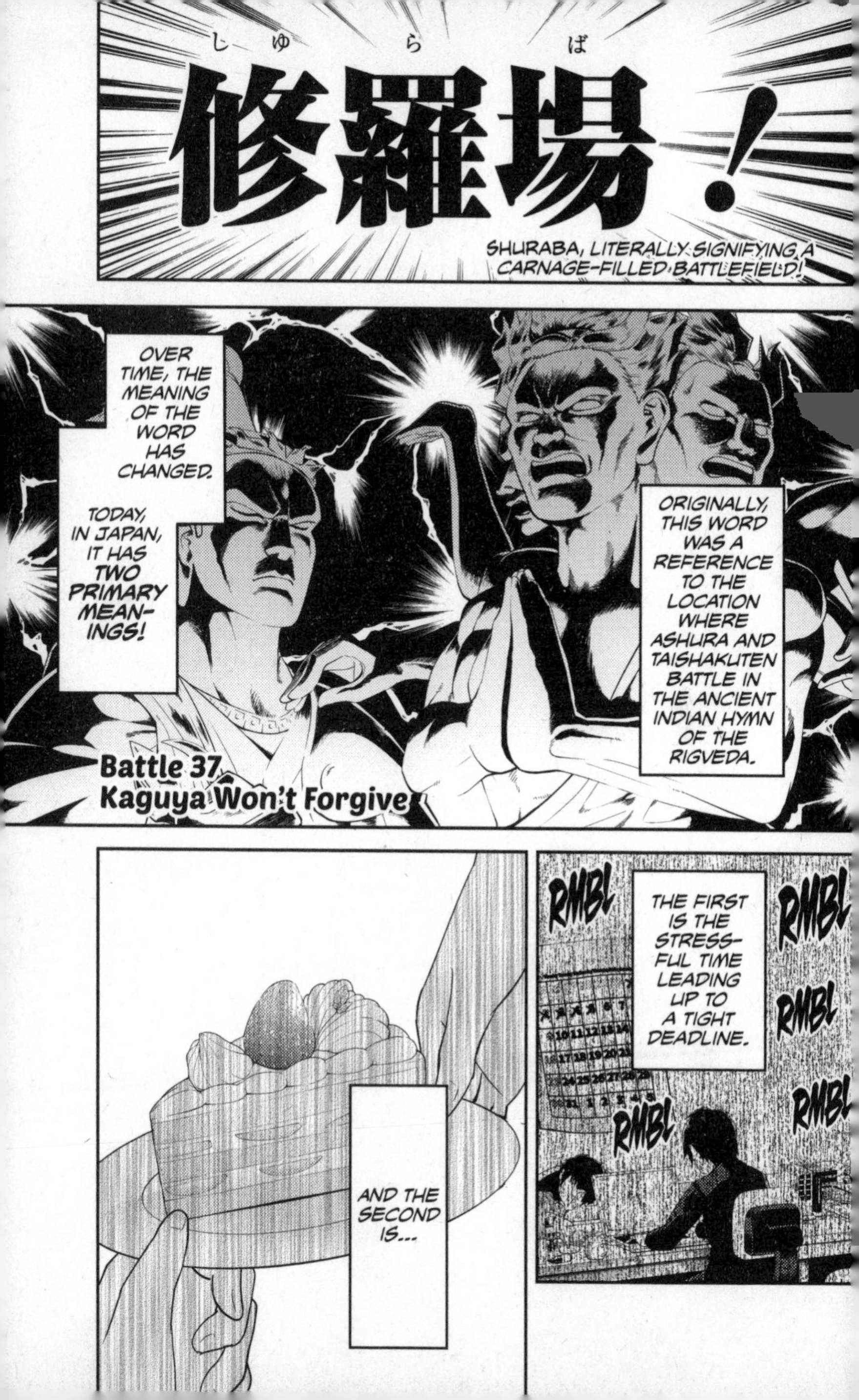
じゅらば
修羅場！
SHURABA, LITERALLY SIGNIFYING A CARNAGE-FILLED BATTLEFIELD!
ORIGINALLY, THIS WORD WAS A REFERENCE TO THE LOCATION WHERE ASHURA AND TAISHAKUTEN BATTLE IN THE ANCIENT INDIAN HYMN OF THE RIGVEDA.
OVER TIME, THE MEANING OF THE WORD HAS CHANGED.
TODAY, IN JAPAN, IT HAS TWO PRIMARY MEANINGS!
Battle 37
Kaguya Won't Forgive
RMBL
RMBL
THE FIRST IS THE STRESSFUL TIME LEADING UP TO A TIGHT DEADLINE.
RMBL
RMBL
RMBL
AND THE SECOND IS...

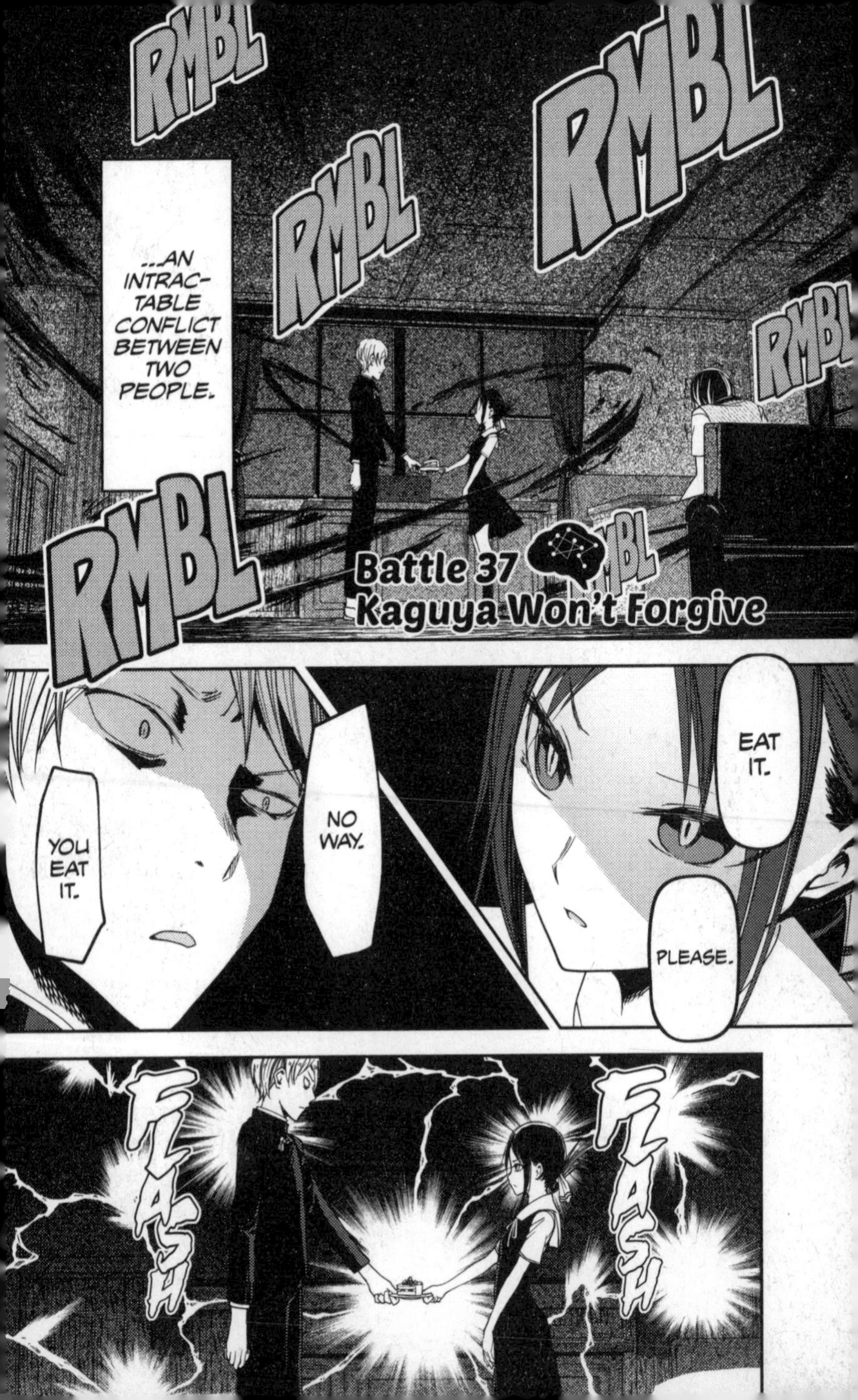
RMBL
RMBL
RMBL
RMBL
...AN INTRACTABLE CONFLICT BETWEEN TWO PEOPLE.
RMBL
RMBL
Battle 37 Kaguya Won't Forgive
EAT IT.
PLEASE.
NO WAY.
YOU EAT IT.
FLASH
FLASH

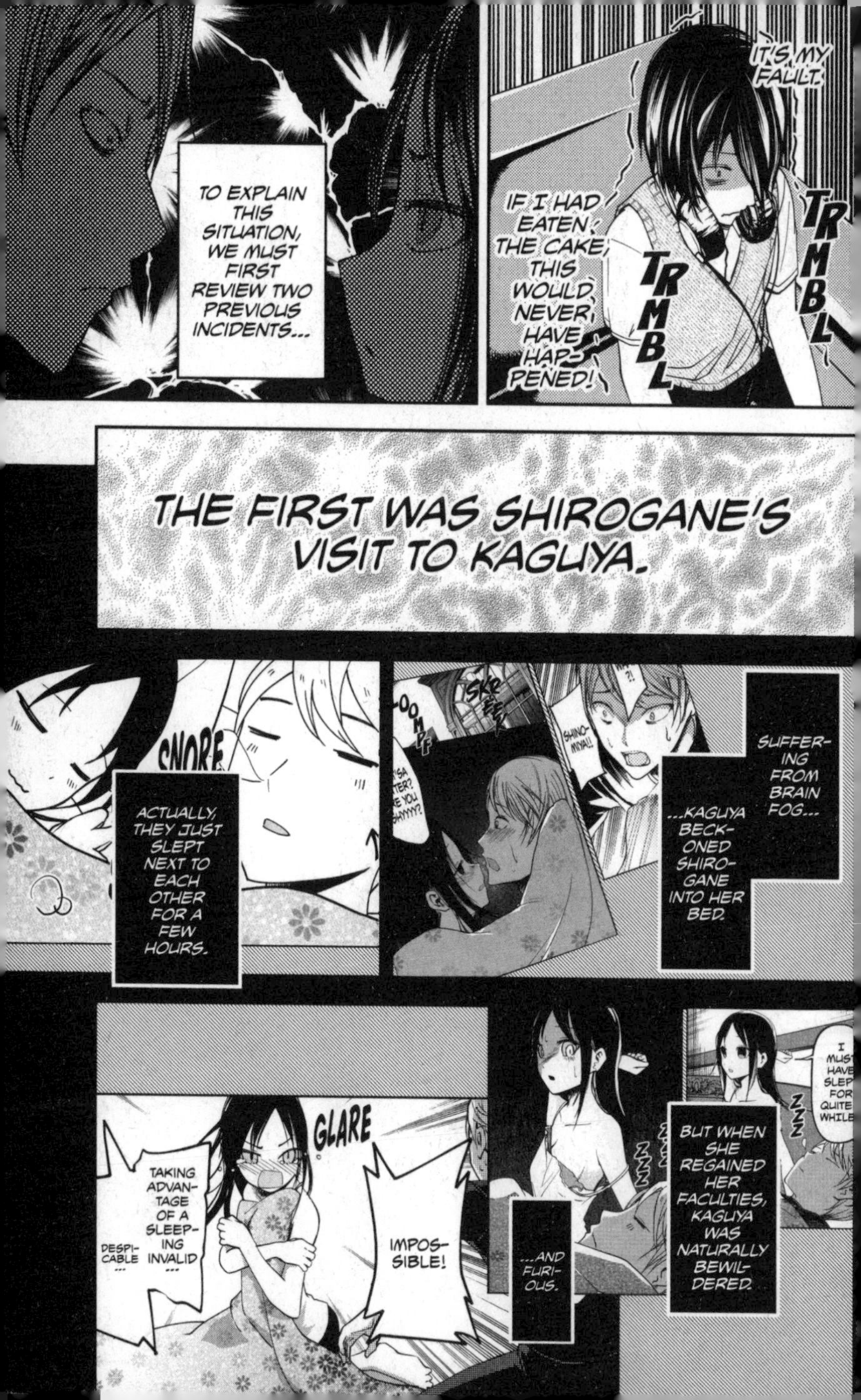
IT'S MY FAULT.
IF I HAD EATEN THE CAKE, THIS WOULD NEVER HAVE HAPPENED!
TRMBL
TRMBL
TO EXPLAIN THIS SITUATION, WE MUST FIRST REVIEW TWO PREVIOUS INCIDENTS...
THE FIRST WAS SHIROGANE'S VISIT TO KAGUYA.
SUFFERING FROM BRAIN FOG...
...KAGUYA BECKONED SHIROGANE INTO HER BED.
?!
SHINOMIYA!!
SKREEEK
OOMPF
SNORE
ACTUALLY, THEY JUST SLEPT NEXT TO EACH OTHER FOR A FEW HOURS.
ZZZ
BUT WHEN SHE REGAINED HER FACULTIES, KAGUYA WAS NATURALLY BEWILDERED.
ZZZ
...AND FURIOUS.
GLARE
IMPOSSIBLE!
TAKING ADVANTAGE OF A SLEEPING INVALID...
DESPICABLE...

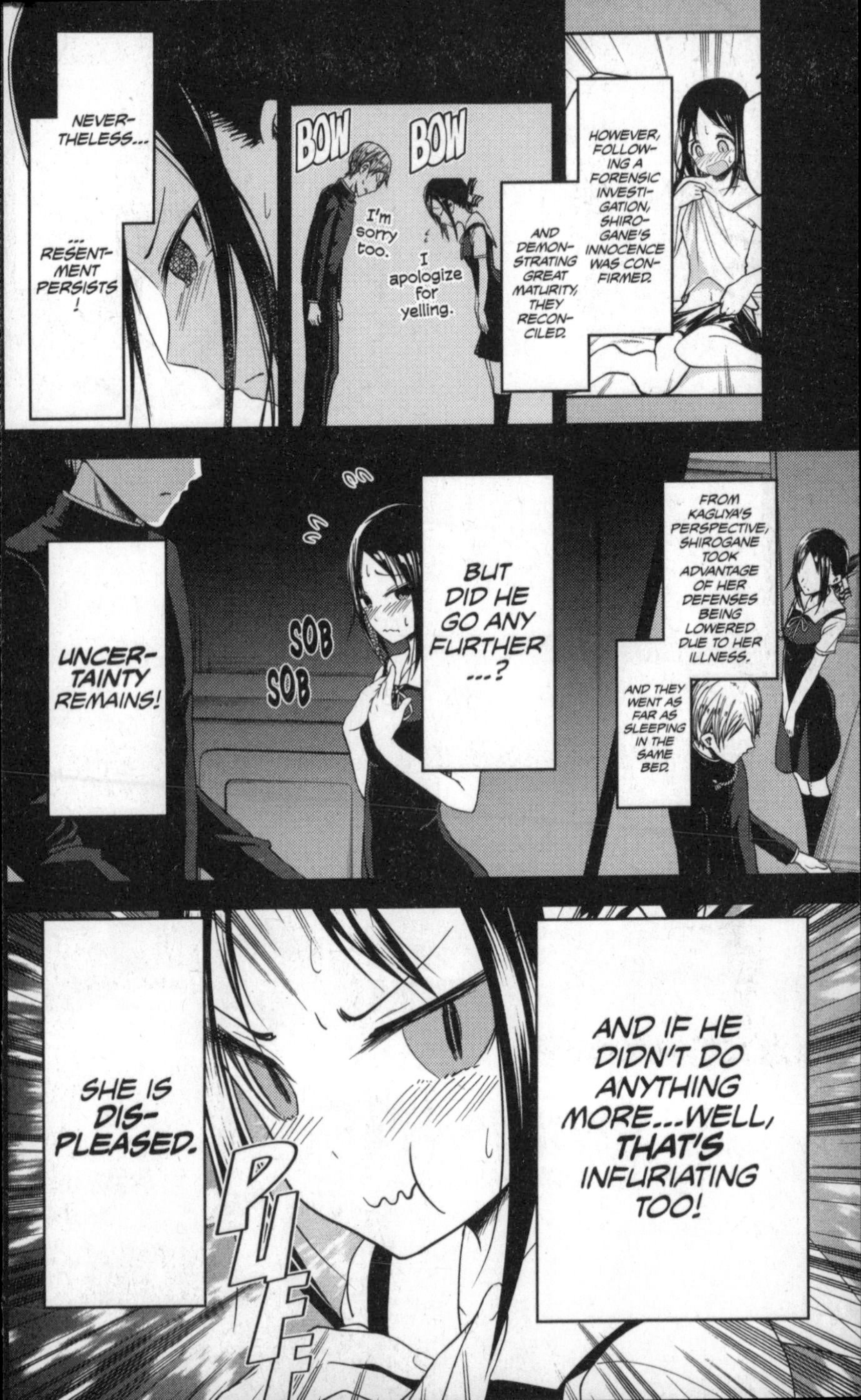
HOWEVER, FOLLOWING A FORENSIC INVESTIGATION, SHIROGANE'S INNOCENCE WAS CONFIRMED.
AND DEMONSTRATING GREAT MATURITY, THEY RECONCILED.
BOW
BOW
I apologize for yelling.
I'm sorry too.
NEVERTHELESS...
...RESENTMENT PERSISTS!
FROM KAGUYA'S PERSPECTIVE, SHIROGANE TOOK ADVANTAGE OF HER DEFENSES BEING LOWERED DUE TO HER ILLNESS.
AND THEY WENT AS FAR AS SLEEPING IN THE SAME BED.
BUT DID HE GO ANY FURTHER...?
SOB SOB
UNCERTAINTY REMAINS!
AND IF HE DIDN'T DO ANYTHING MORE...WELL, THAT'S INFURIATING TOO!
PUFF
SHE IS DISPLEASED.

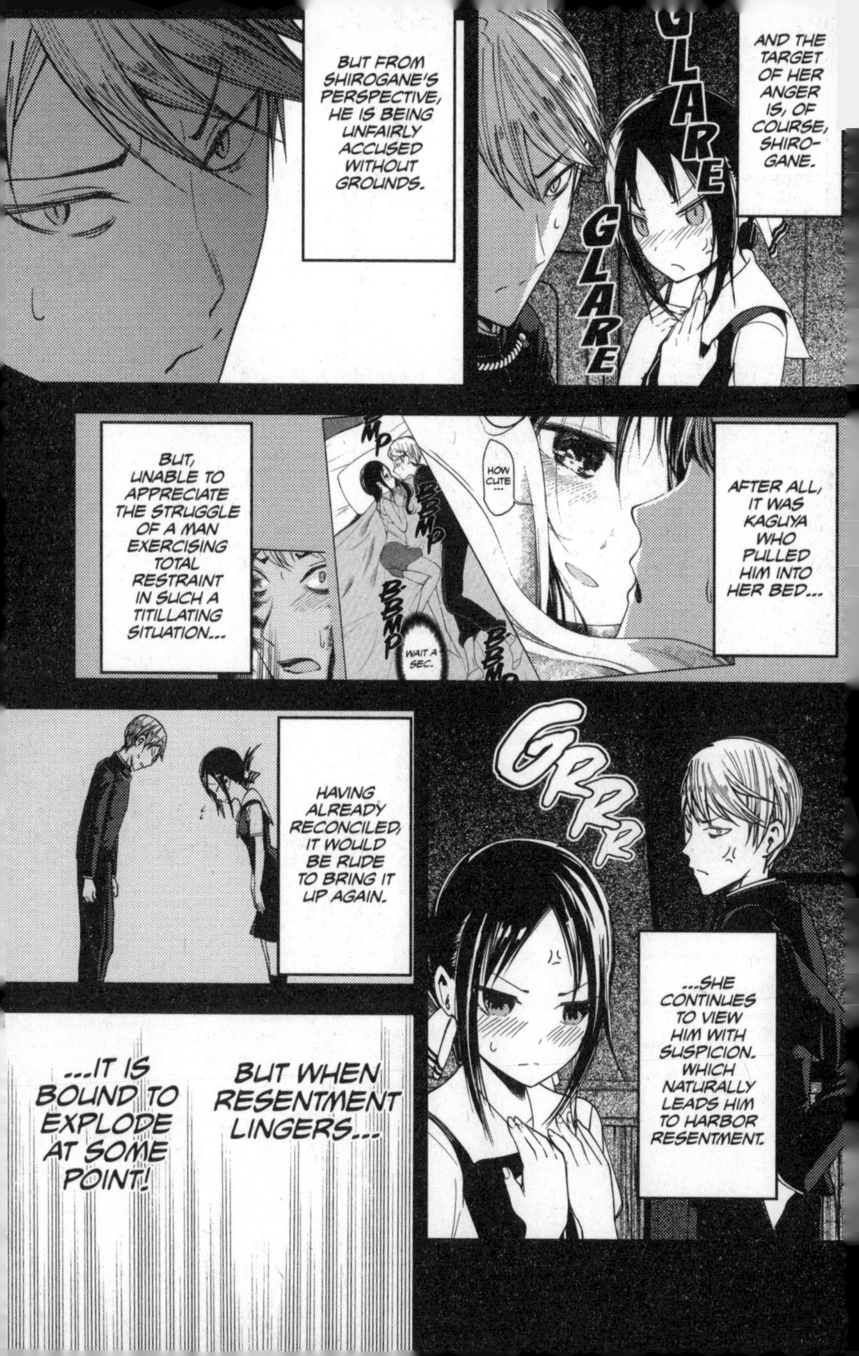
AND THE TARGET OF HER ANGER IS, OF COURSE, SHIRO-GANE.
GLARE
GLARE
BUT FROM SHIROGANE'S PERSPECTIVE, HE IS BEING UNFAIRLY ACCUSED WITHOUT GROUNDS.
AFTER ALL, IT WAS KAGUYA WHO PULLED HIM INTO HER BED...
HOW CUTE...
WAIT A SEC.
BUT, UNABLE TO APPRECIATE THE STRUGGLE OF A MAN EXERCISING TOTAL RESTRAINT IN SUCH A TITILLATING SITUATION...
GRRR
...SHE CONTINUES TO VIEW HIM WITH SUSPICION. WHICH NATURALLY LEADS HIM TO HARBOR RESENTMENT.
HAVING ALREADY RECONCILED, IT WOULD BE RUDE TO BRING IT UP AGAIN.
BUT WHEN RESENTMENT LINGERS...
...IT IS BOUND TO EXPLODE AT SOME POINT!

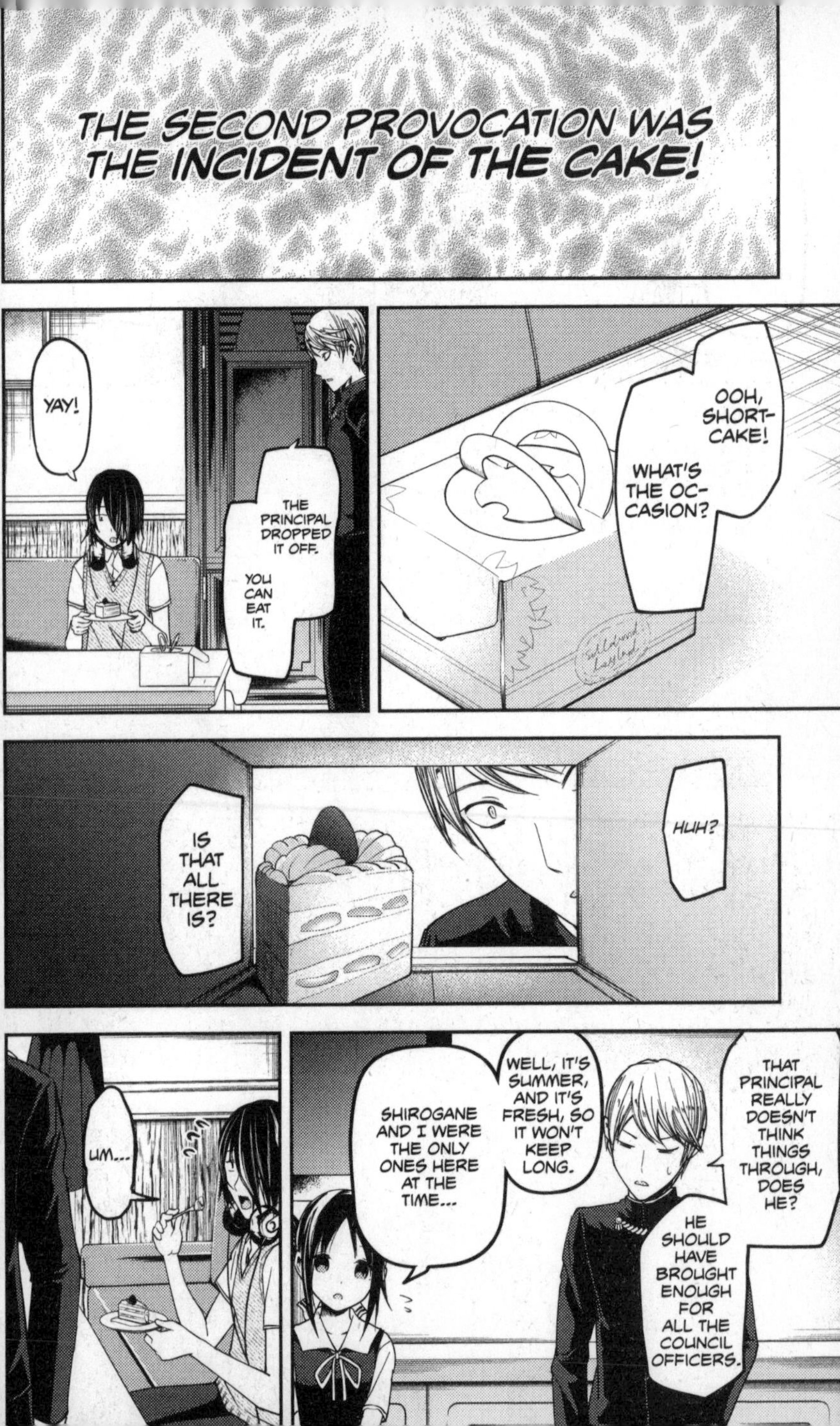
THE SECOND PROVOCATION WAS THE INCIDENT OF THE CAKE!
OOH, SHORTCAKE!
WHAT'S THE OCCASION?
THE PRINCIPAL DROPPED IT OFF.
YOU CAN EAT IT.
YAY!
HUH?
IS THAT ALL THERE IS?
THAT PRINCIPAL REALLY DOESN'T THINK THINGS THROUGH, DOES HE?
HE SHOULD HAVE BROUGHT ENOUGH FOR ALL THE COUNCIL OFFICERS.
WELL, IT'S SUMMER, AND IT'S FRESH, SO IT WON'T KEEP LONG.
SHIROGANE AND I WERE THE ONLY ONES HERE AT THE TIME...
UM...

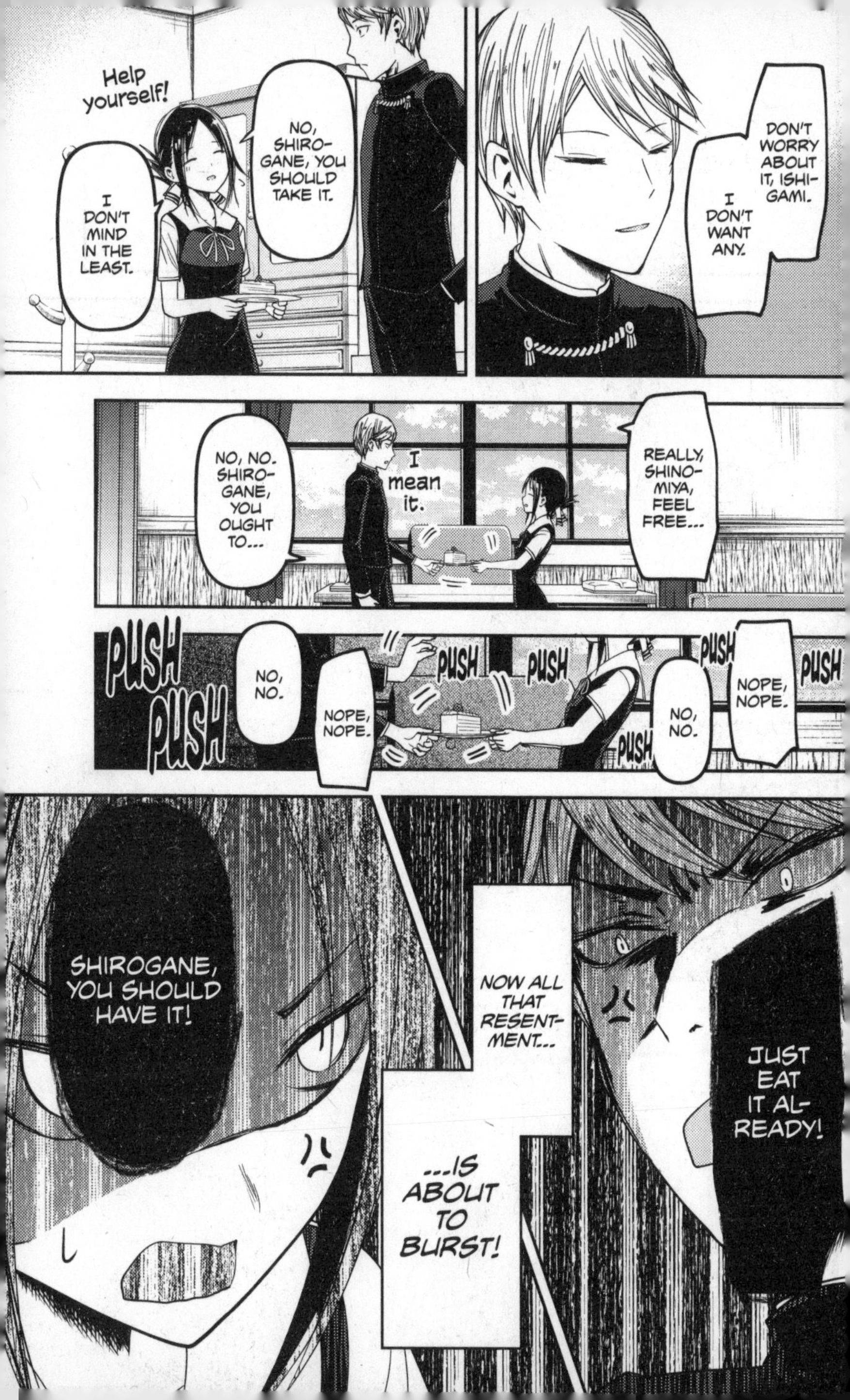
DON'T WORRY ABOUT IT, ISHIGAMI.
I DON'T WANT ANY.
NO, SHIROGANE, YOU SHOULD TAKE IT.
Help yourself!
I DON'T MIND IN THE LEAST.
REALLY, SHINOMIYA, FEEL FREE...
I mean it.
NO, NO. SHIROGANE, YOU OUGHT TO...
PUSH
NOPE, NOPE.
PUSH
NO, NO.
PUSH
PUSH
PUSH
NOPE, NOPE.
NO, NO.
PUSH PUSH
JUST EAT IT ALREADY!
NOW ALL THAT RESENTMENT...
...IS ABOUT TO BURST!
SHIROGANE, YOU SHOULD HAVE IT!

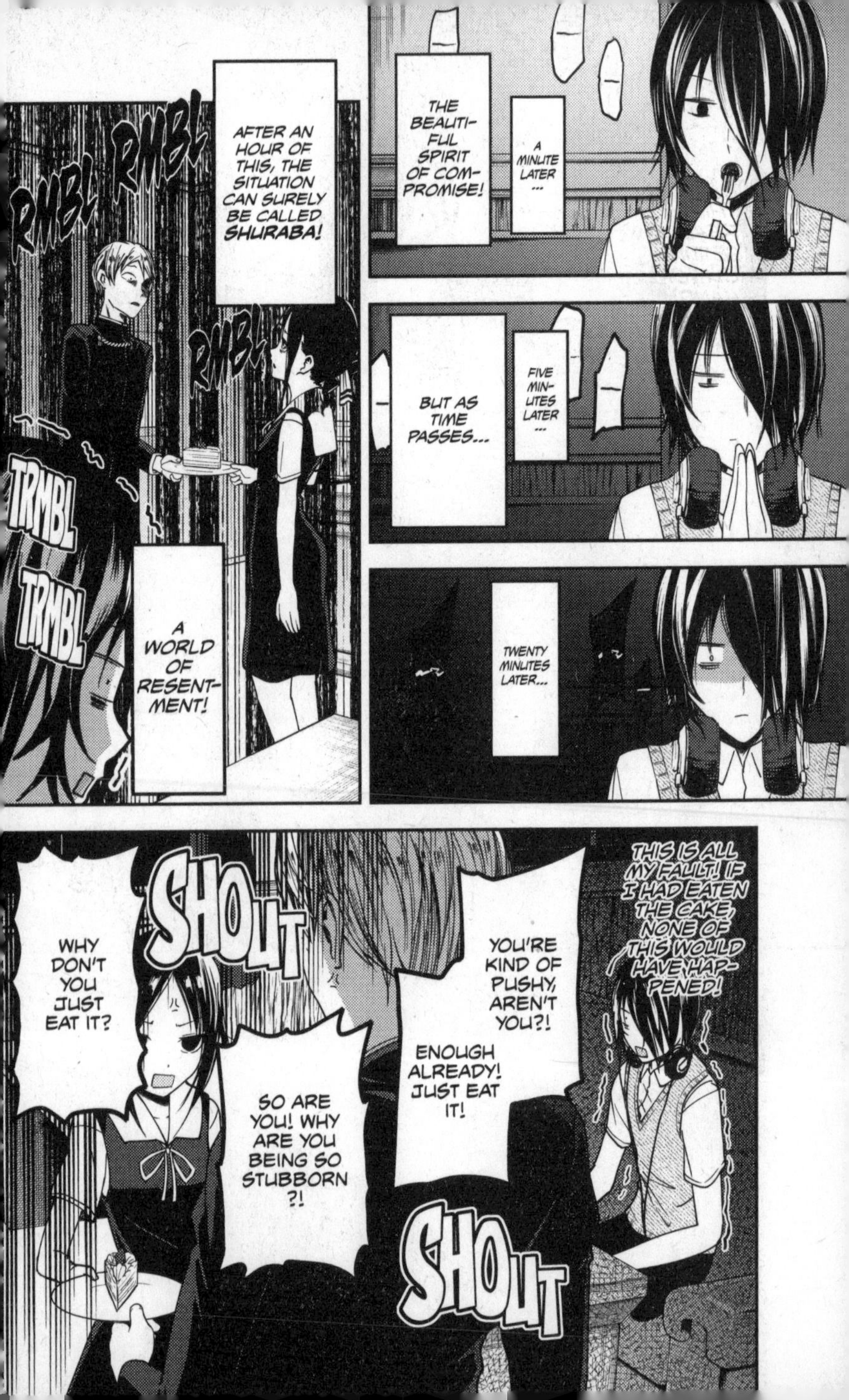
A MINUTE LATER...
THE BEAUTIFUL SPIRIT OF COMPROMISE!
FIVE MINUTES LATER...
BUT AS TIME PASSES...
TWENTY MINUTES LATER...
RMBL RMBL
AFTER AN HOUR OF THIS, THE SITUATION CAN SURELY BE CALLED SHURABA!
RMBL
TRMBL
TRMBL
A WORLD OF RESENTMENT!
THIS IS ALL MY FAULT! IF I HAD EATEN THE CAKE, NONE OF THIS WOULD HAVE HAPPENED!
YOU'RE KIND OF PUSHY, AREN'T YOU?!
SHOUT
WHY DON'T YOU JUST EAT IT?
ENOUGH ALREADY! JUST EAT IT!
SO ARE YOU! WHY ARE YOU BEING SO STUBBORN?!
SHOUT

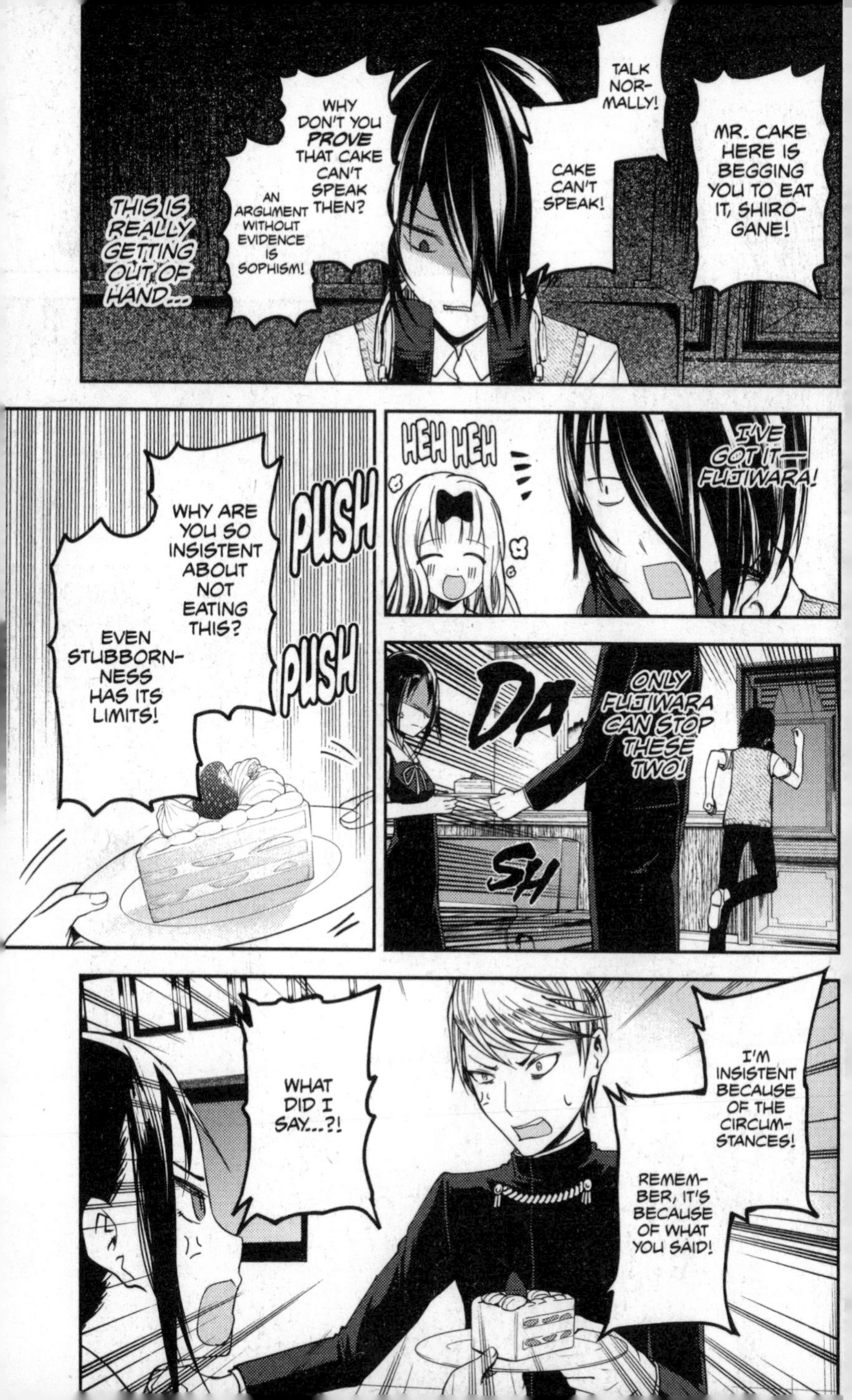
MR. CAKE HERE IS BEGGING YOU TO EAT IT, SHIROGANE!
TALK NOR-MALLY!
CAKE CAN'T SPEAK!
WHY DON'T YOU *PROVE* THAT CAKE CAN'T SPEAK THEN?
AN ARGUMENT WITHOUT EVIDENCE IS SOPHISM!
THIS IS REALLY GETTING OUT OF HAND...
I'VE GOT IT— FUJIWARA!
HEH HEH
ONLY FUJIWARA CAN STOP THESE TWO!
DA
SH
PUSH
PUSH
WHY ARE YOU SO INSISTENT ABOUT NOT EATING THIS?
EVEN STUBBORN-NESS HAS ITS LIMITS!
I'M INSISTENT BECAUSE OF THE CIRCUM-STANCES!
REMEM-BER, IT'S BECAUSE OF WHAT YOU SAID!
WHAT DID I SAY...?!

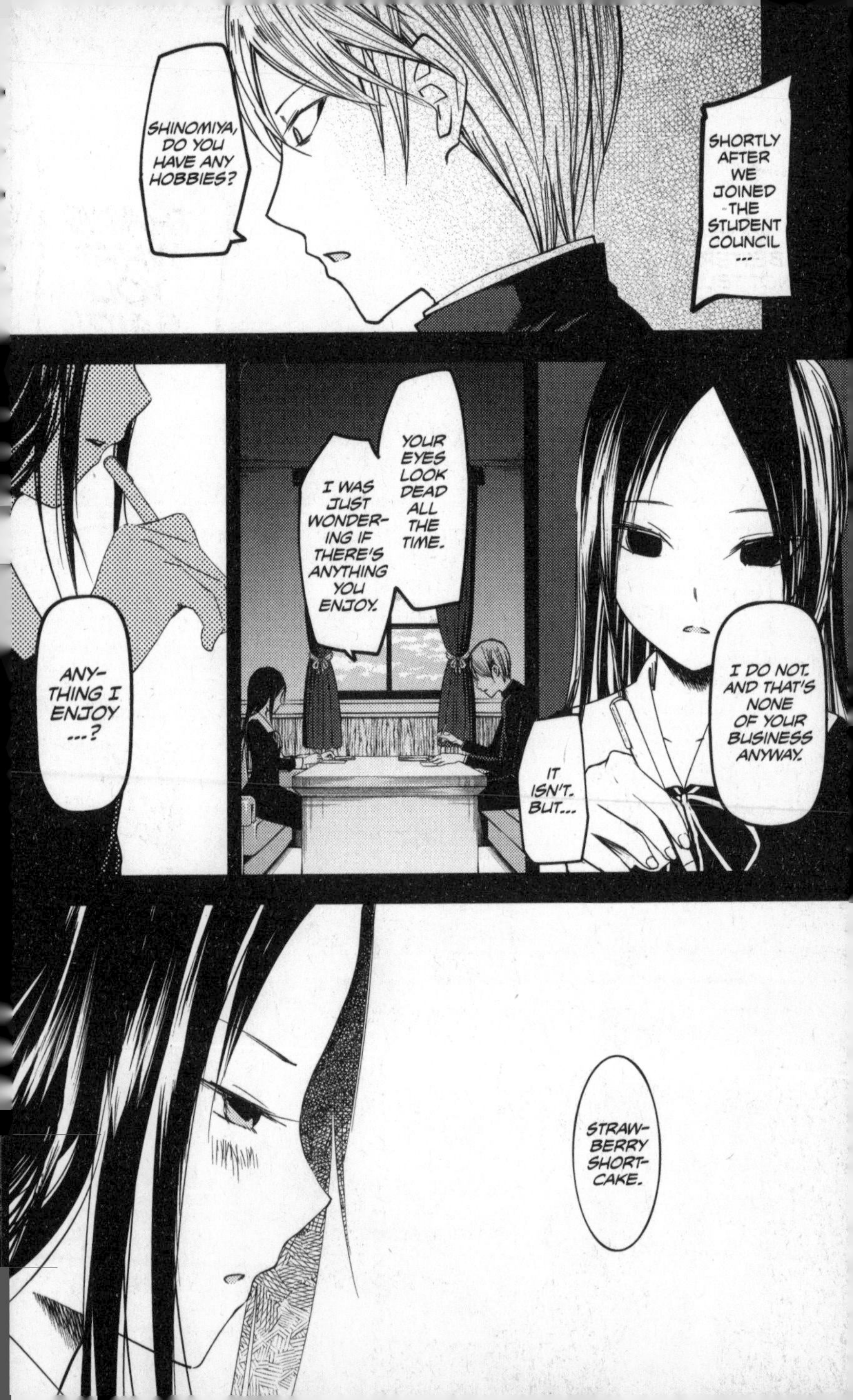
SHORTLY AFTER WE JOINED THE STUDENT COUNCIL...
SHINOMIYA, DO YOU HAVE ANY HOBBIES?
I DO NOT. AND THAT'S NONE OF YOUR BUSINESS ANYWAY.
IT ISN'T. BUT...
YOUR EYES LOOK DEAD ALL THE TIME.
I WAS JUST WONDERING IF THERE'S ANYTHING YOU ENJOY.
ANYTHING I ENJOY...?
STRAWBERRY SHORTCAKE.

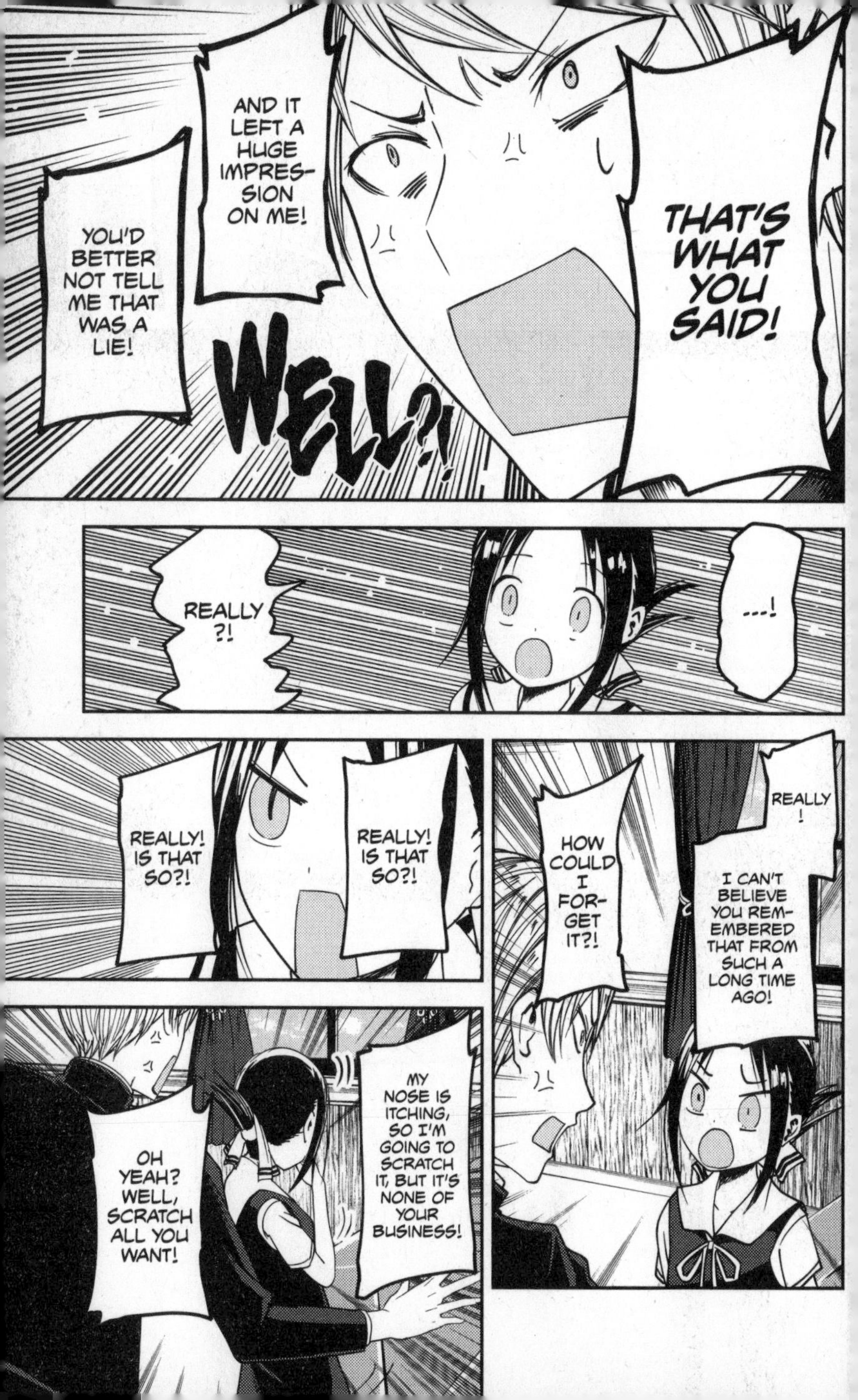
THAT'S WHAT YOU SAID!
AND IT LEFT A HUGE IMPRESSION ON ME!
YOU'D BETTER NOT TELL ME THAT WAS A LIE!
WELL?!
---!
REALLY ?!
REALLY !
I CAN'T BELIEVE YOU REMEMBERED THAT FROM SUCH A LONG TIME AGO!
HOW COULD I FORGET IT?!
REALLY! IS THAT SO?!
REALLY! IS THAT SO?!
MY NOSE IS ITCHING, SO I'M GOING TO SCRATCH IT, BUT IT'S NONE OF YOUR BUSINESS!
OH YEAH? WELL, SCRATCH ALL YOU WANT!

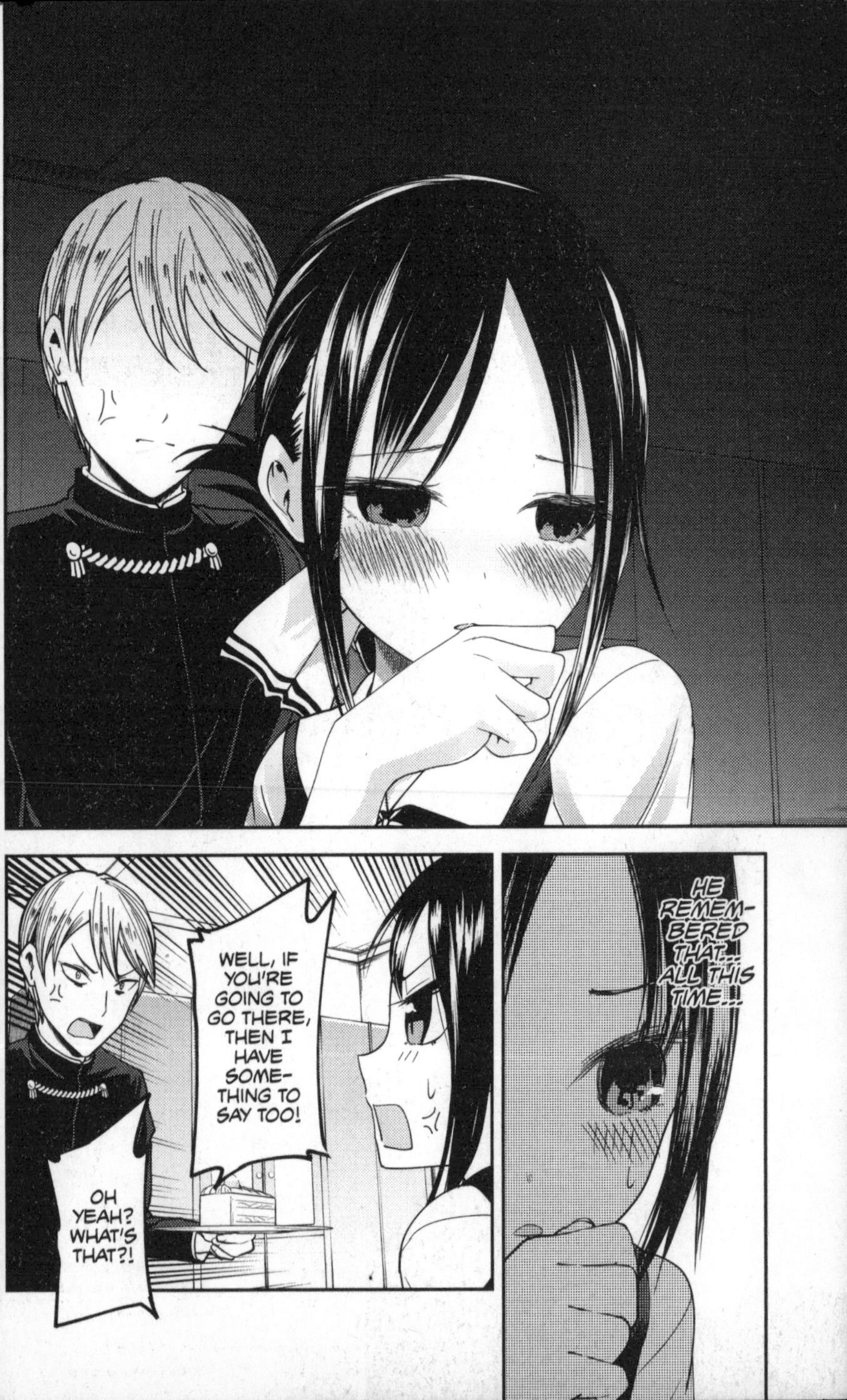
HE REMEMBERED THAT... ALL THIS TIME...!
WELL, IF YOU'RE GOING TO GO THERE, THEN I HAVE SOMETHING TO SAY TOO!
OH YEAH? WHAT'S THAT?!

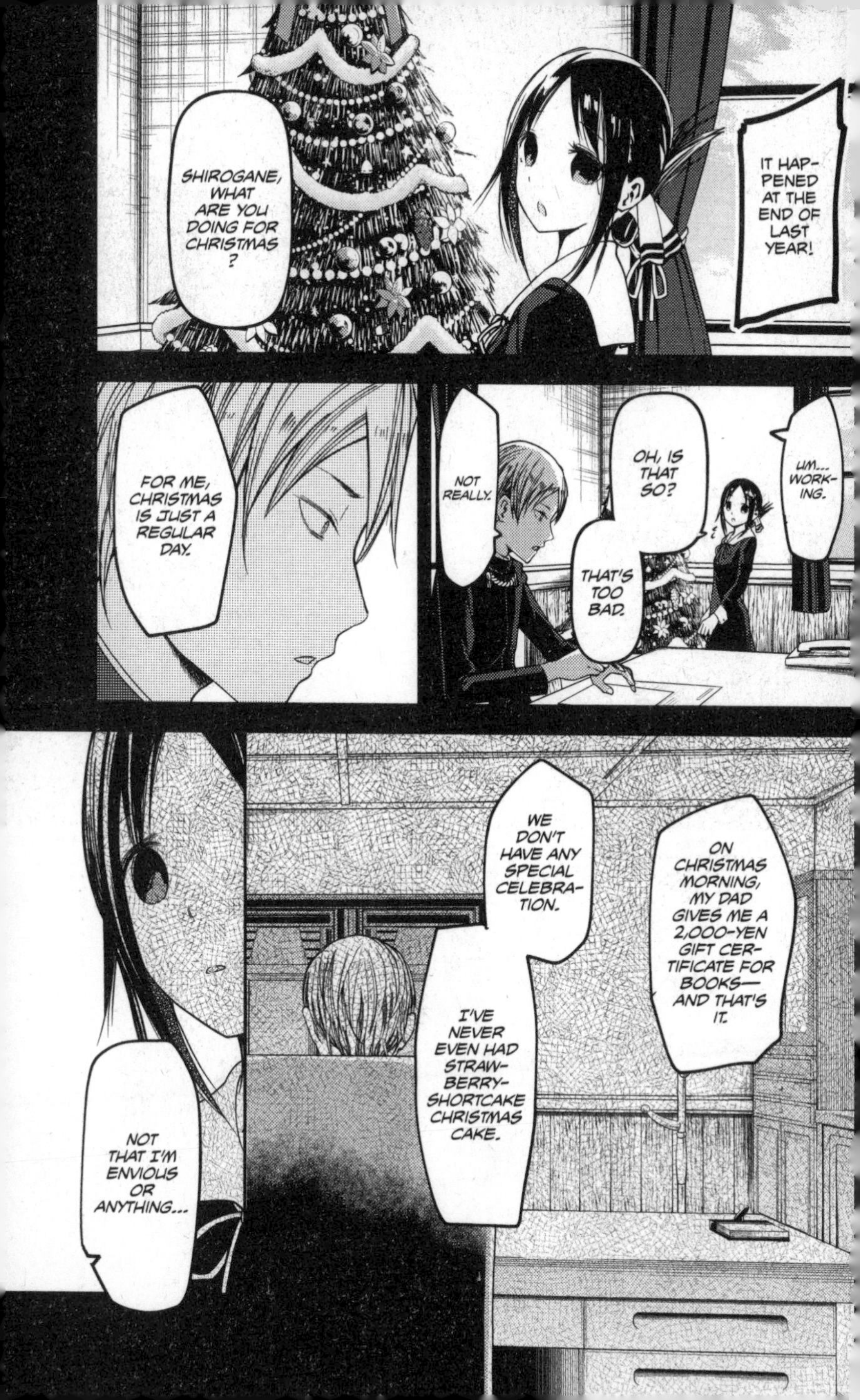
IT HAPPENED AT THE END OF LAST YEAR!
SHIROGANE, WHAT ARE YOU DOING FOR CHRISTMAS?
UM... WORKING.
OH, IS THAT SO?
THAT'S TOO BAD.
NOT REALLY.
FOR ME, CHRISTMAS IS JUST A REGULAR DAY.
ON CHRISTMAS MORNING, MY DAD GIVES ME A 2,000-YEN GIFT CERTIFICATE FOR BOOKS—AND THAT'S IT.
WE DON'T HAVE ANY SPECIAL CELEBRATION.
I'VE NEVER EVEN HAD STRAWBERRY-SHORTCAKE CHRISTMAS CAKE.
NOT THAT I'M ENVIOUS OR ANYTHING...

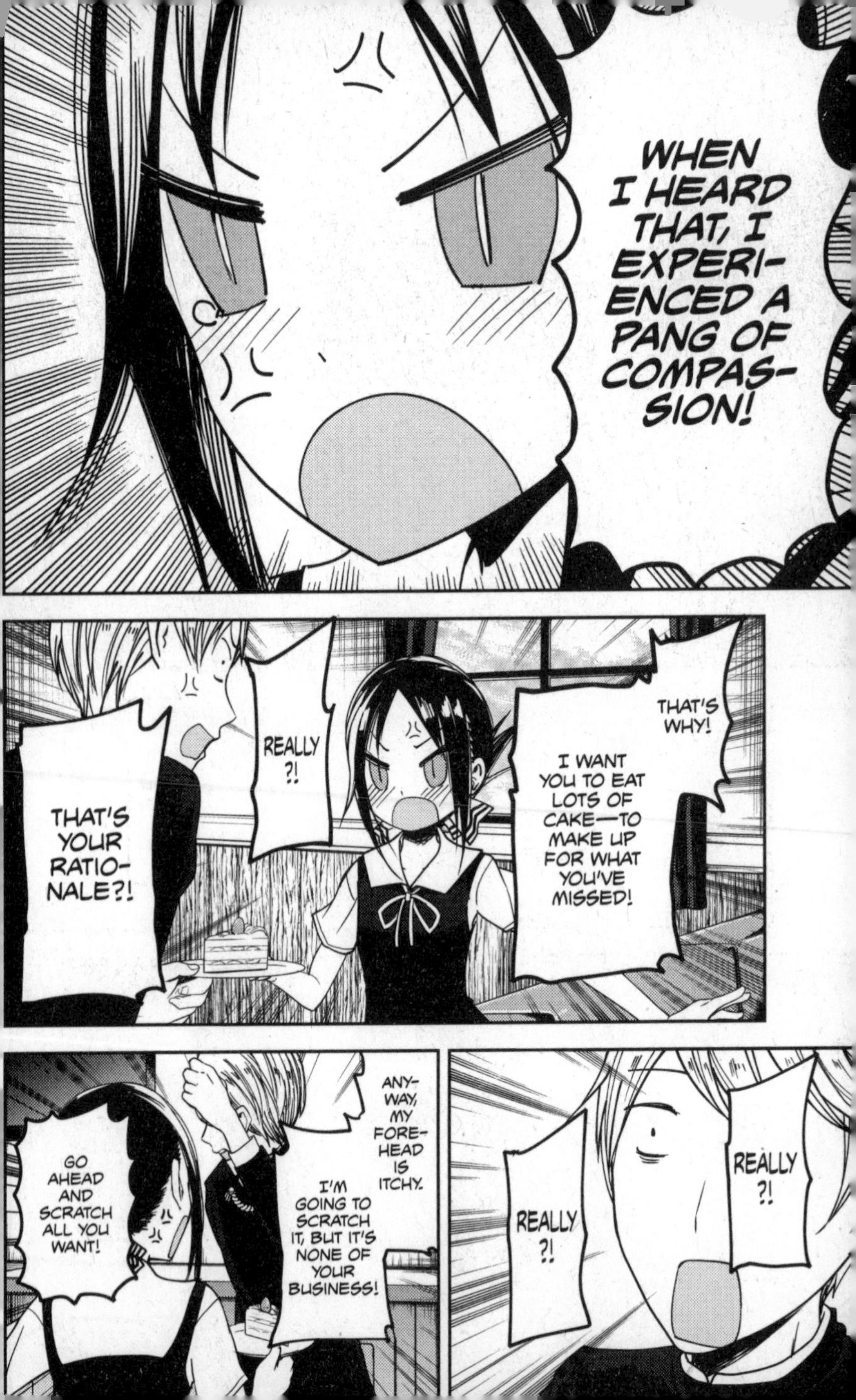

WHEN I HEARD THAT, I EXPERIENCED A PANG OF COMPASSION!
THAT'S WHY!
I WANT YOU TO EAT LOTS OF CAKE—TO MAKE UP FOR WHAT YOU'VE MISSED!
REALLY ?!
THAT'S YOUR RATIONALE?!
REALLY ?!
REALLY ?!
ANYWAY, MY FOREHEAD IS ITCHY.
I'M GOING TO SCRATCH IT, BUT IT'S NONE OF YOUR BUSINESS!
GO AHEAD AND SCRATCH ALL YOU WANT!

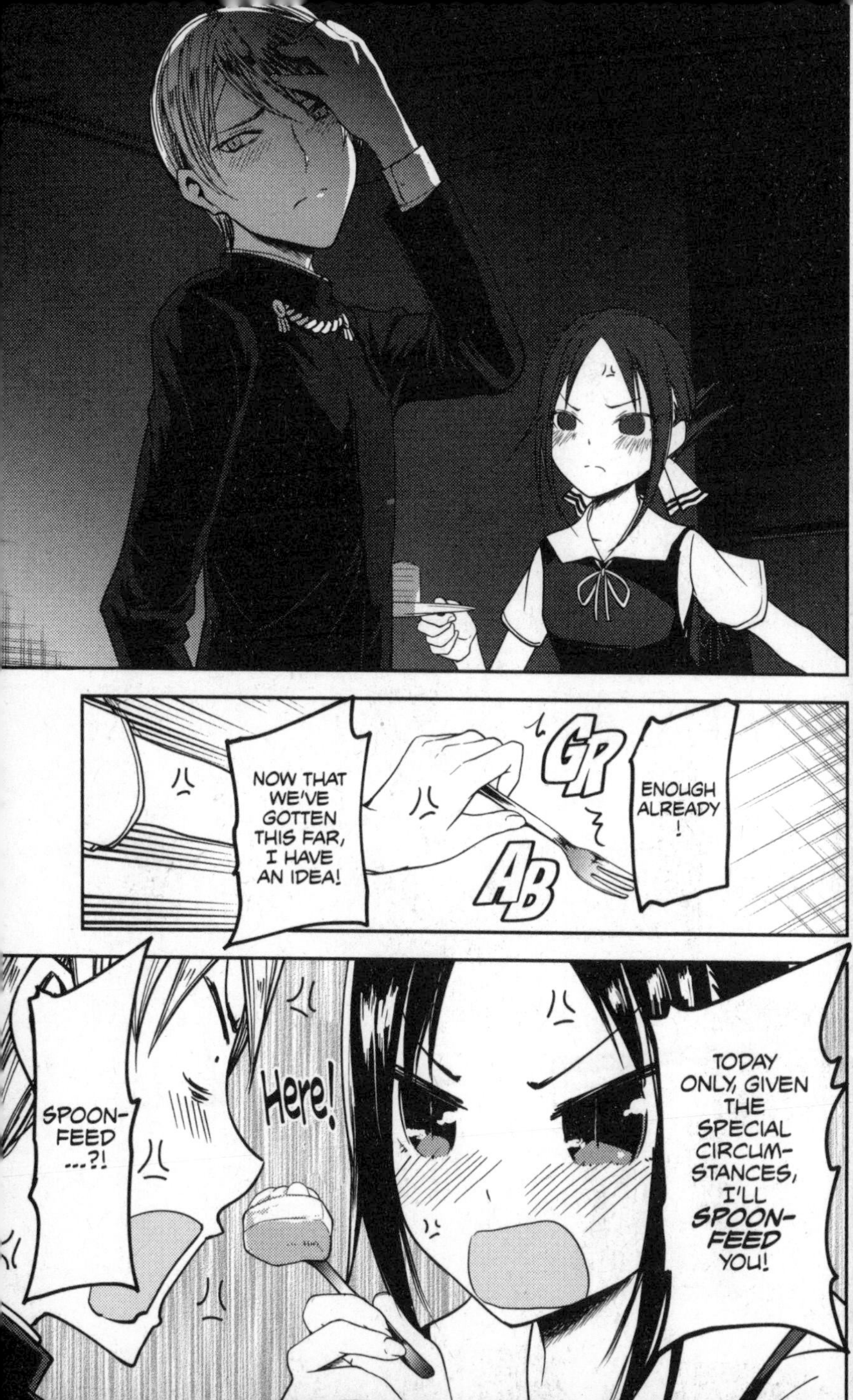
ENOUGH ALREADY!
GRAB
NOW THAT WE'VE GOTTEN THIS FAR, I HAVE AN IDEA!
TODAY ONLY, GIVEN THE SPECIAL CIRCUMSTANCES, I'LL SPOON-FEED YOU!
Here!
SPOON-FEED...?!

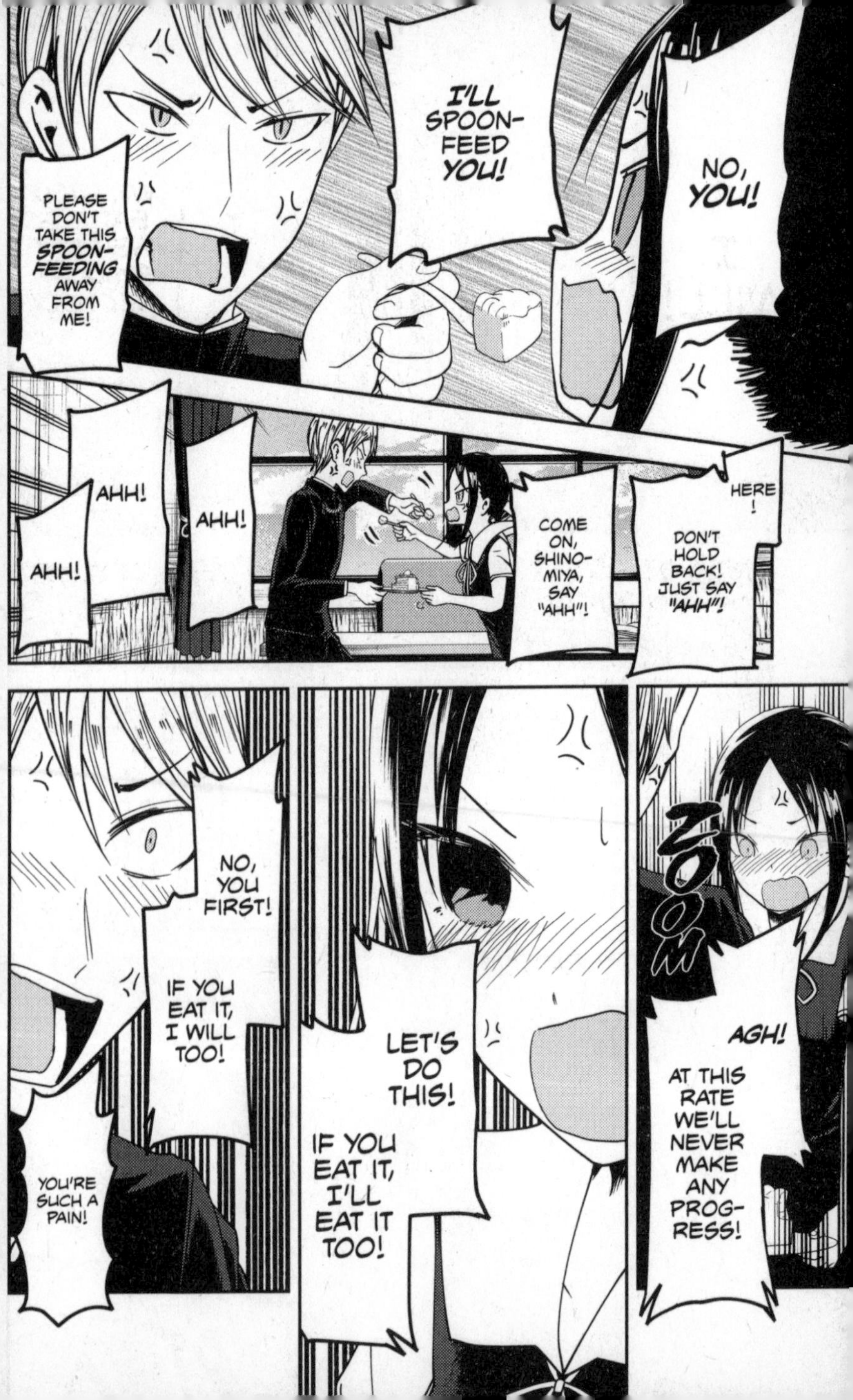
NO, YOU!
I'LL SPOON-FEED YOU!
PLEASE DON'T TAKE THIS SPOON-FEEDING AWAY FROM ME!
HERE!
DON'T HOLD BACK! JUST SAY "AHH"!
COME ON, SHINOMIYA, SAY "AHH"!
AHH!
AHH!
AHH!
ZOOM
AGH!
AT THIS RATE WE'LL NEVER MAKE ANY PROGRESS!
LET'S DO THIS!
IF YOU EAT IT, I'LL EAT IT TOO!
NO, YOU FIRST!
IF YOU EAT IT, I WILL TOO!
YOU'RE SUCH A PAIN!

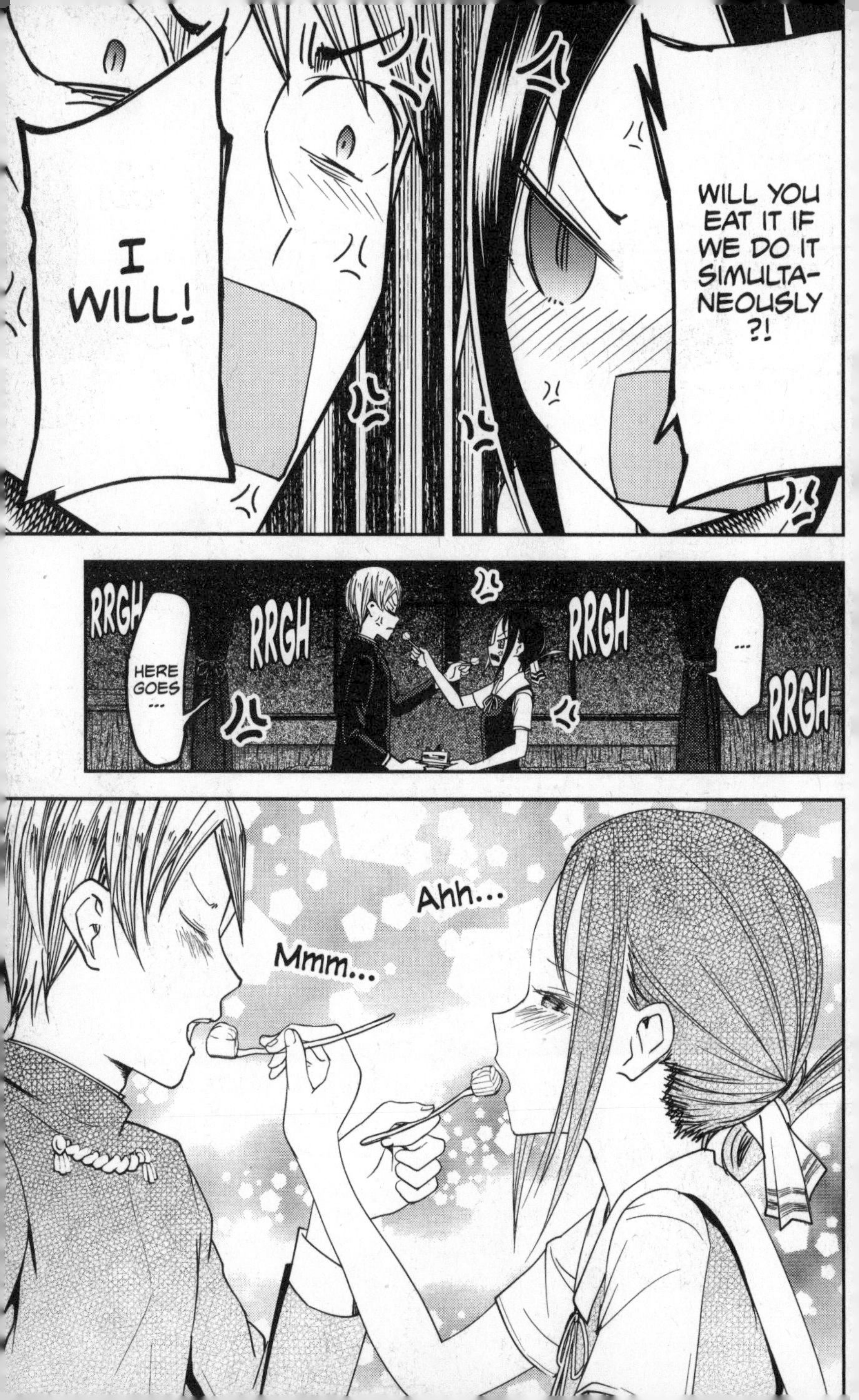
WILL YOU EAT IT IF WE DO IT SIMULTANEOUSLY?!
I WILL!
...
RRGH
RRGH
RRGH
HERE GOES...
RRGH
Ahh...
Mmm...

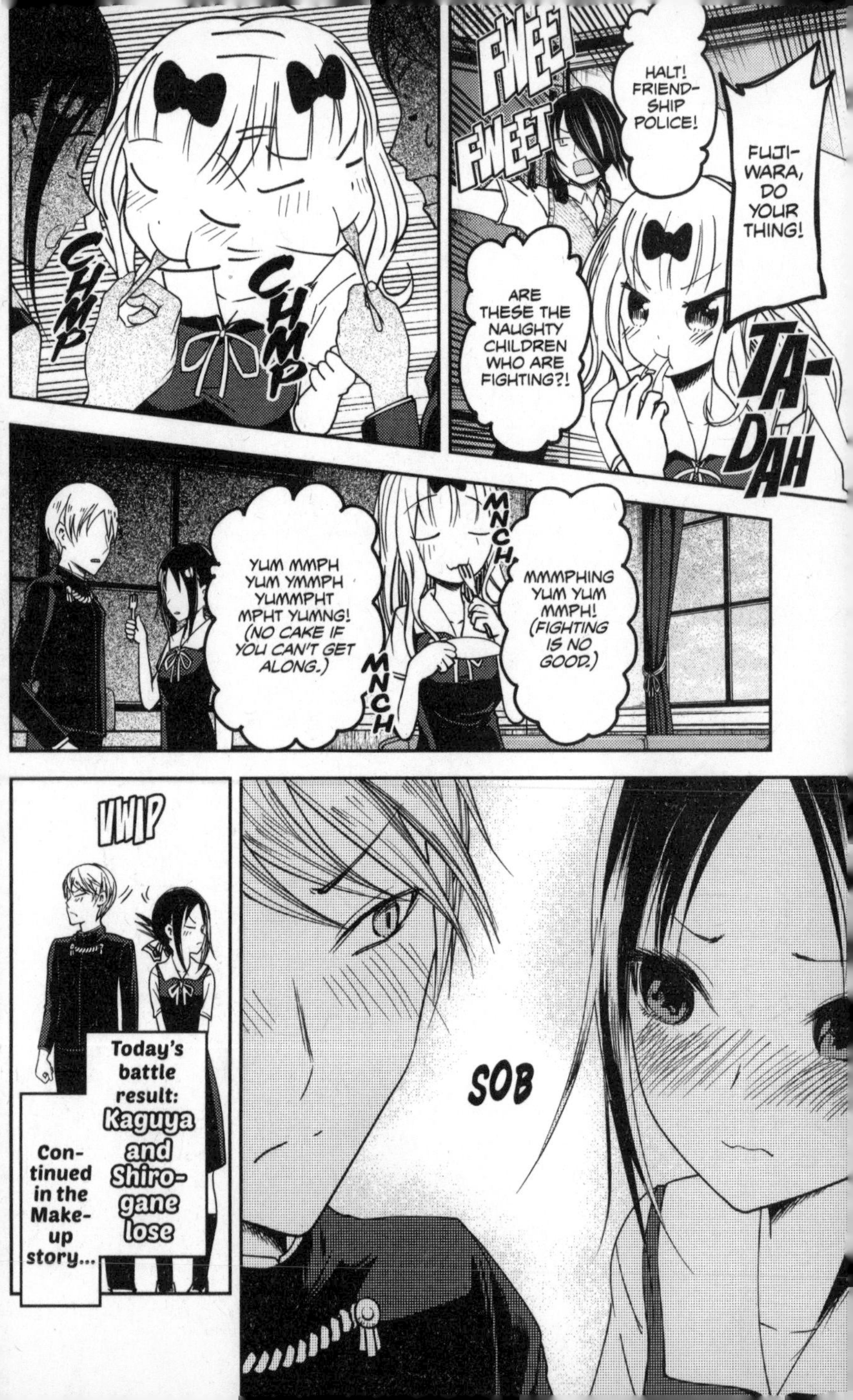
FNEET
FNEET
HALT! FRIEND-SHIP POLICE!
FUJI-WARA, DO YOUR THING!
ARE THESE THE NAUGHTY CHILDREN WHO ARE FIGHTING?!
TA-DAH
CHMP
CHMP
MNCH
MMMPHING YUM YUM MMPH! (FIGHTING IS NO GOOD.)
YUM MMPH YUM YMMPH YUMMPHT MPHT YUMNG! (NO CAKE IF YOU CAN'T GET ALONG.)
MNCH
SOB
VWIP
Today's battle result: Kaguya and Shiro-gane lose
Con-tinued in the Make-up story...

Mm...

Ç'est bon!

WAR
CRIMINAL

KAGUYA-SAMA
LOVE IS WAR

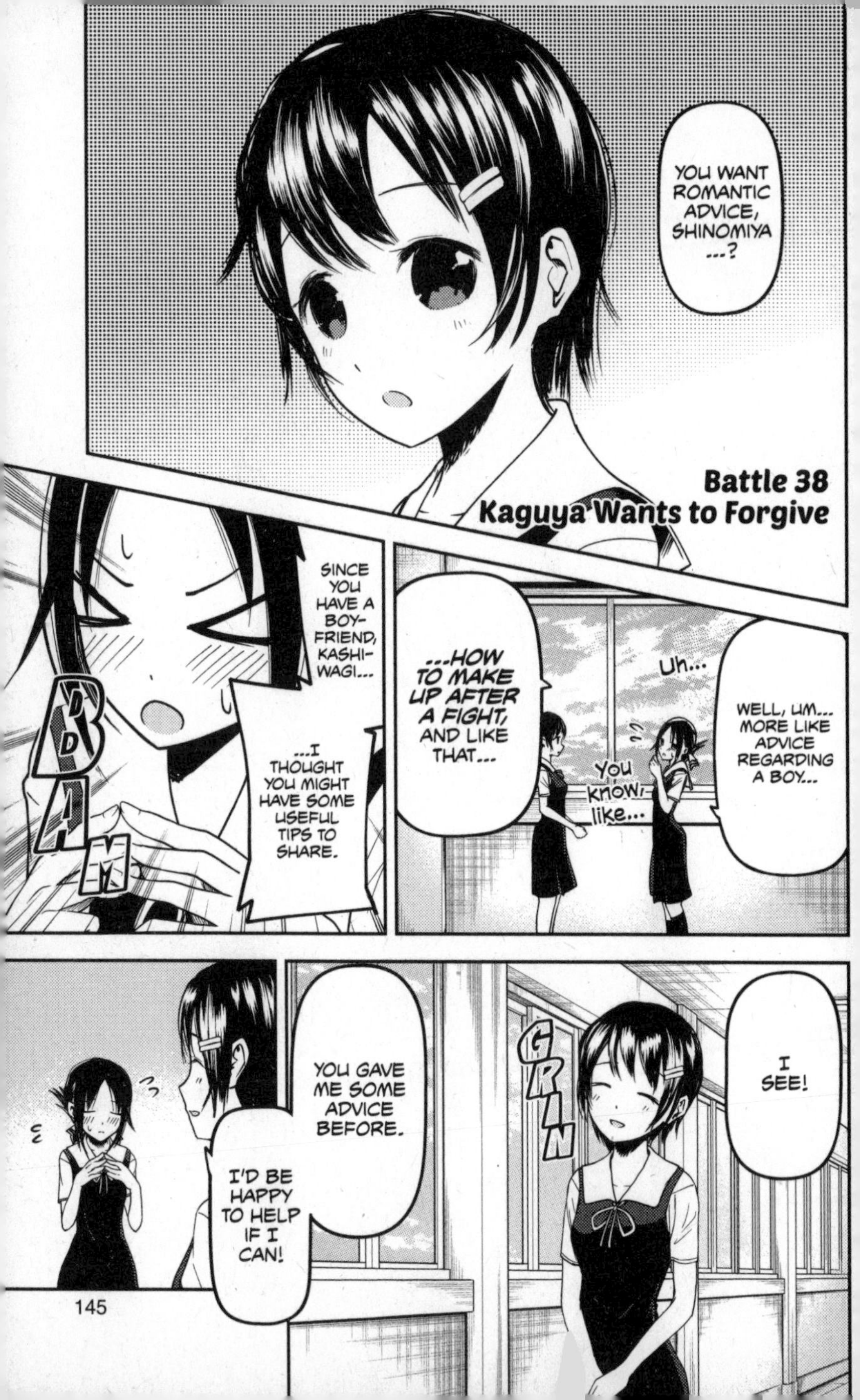
YOU WANT ROMANTIC ADVICE, SHINOMIYA...?
Battle 38
Kaguya Wants to Forgive
WELL, UM... MORE LIKE ADVICE REGARDING A BOY...
Uh...
You know, like...
...HOW TO MAKE UP AFTER A FIGHT, AND LIKE THAT...
SINCE YOU HAVE A BOY-FRIEND, KASHI-WAGI...
...I THOUGHT YOU MIGHT HAVE SOME USEFUL TIPS TO SHARE.
BAM
I SEE!
GRIN
YOU GAVE ME SOME ADVICE BEFORE.
I'D BE HAPPY TO HELP IF I CAN!

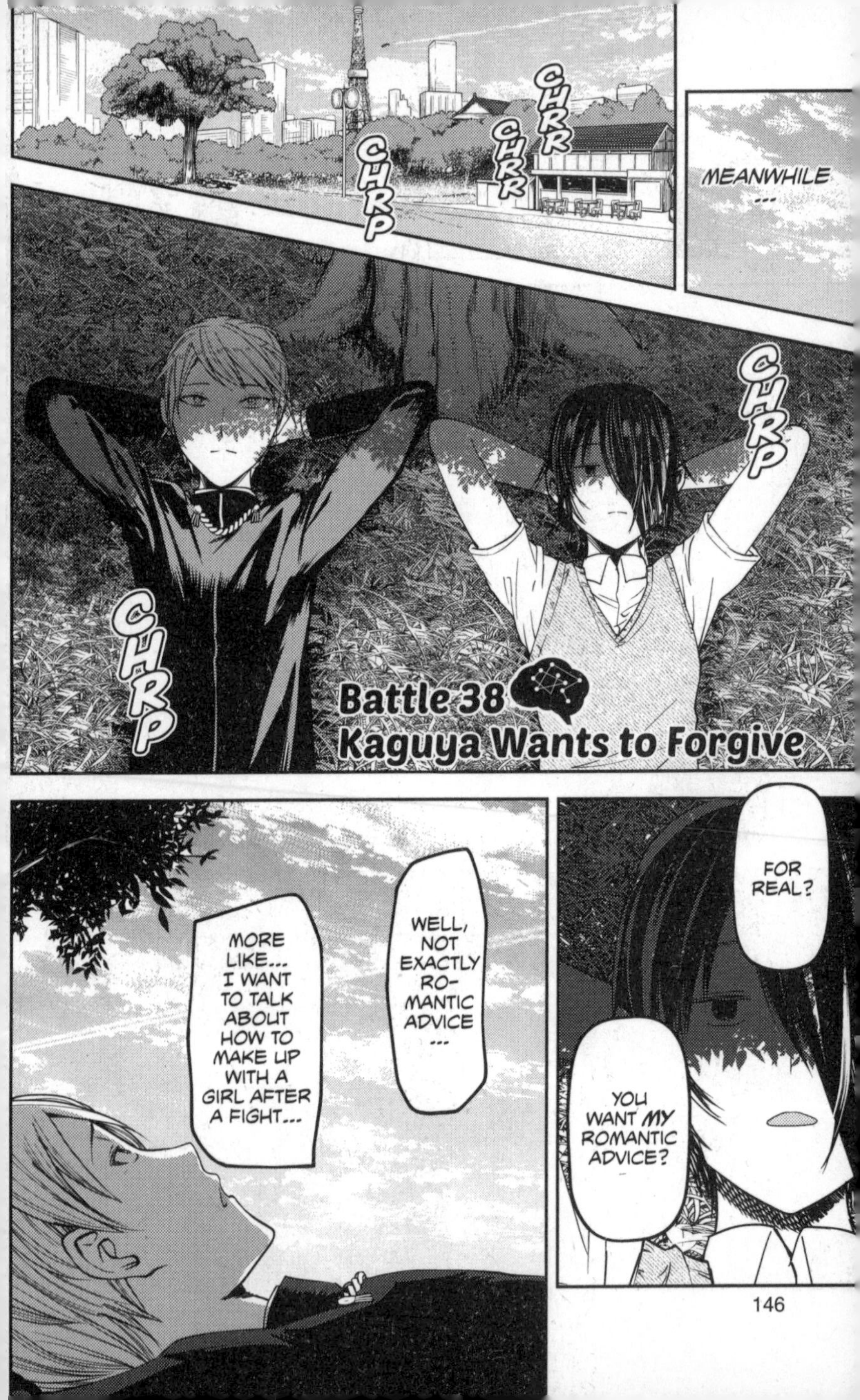

MEANWHILE...
CHRR
CHRR
CHRP
CHRP
CHRP
Battle 38
Kaguya Wants to Forgive
FOR REAL?
YOU WANT *MY* ROMANTIC ADVICE?
WELL, NOT EXACTLY RO-MANTIC ADVICE...
MORE LIKE... I WANT TO TALK ABOUT HOW TO MAKE UP WITH A GIRL AFTER A FIGHT...

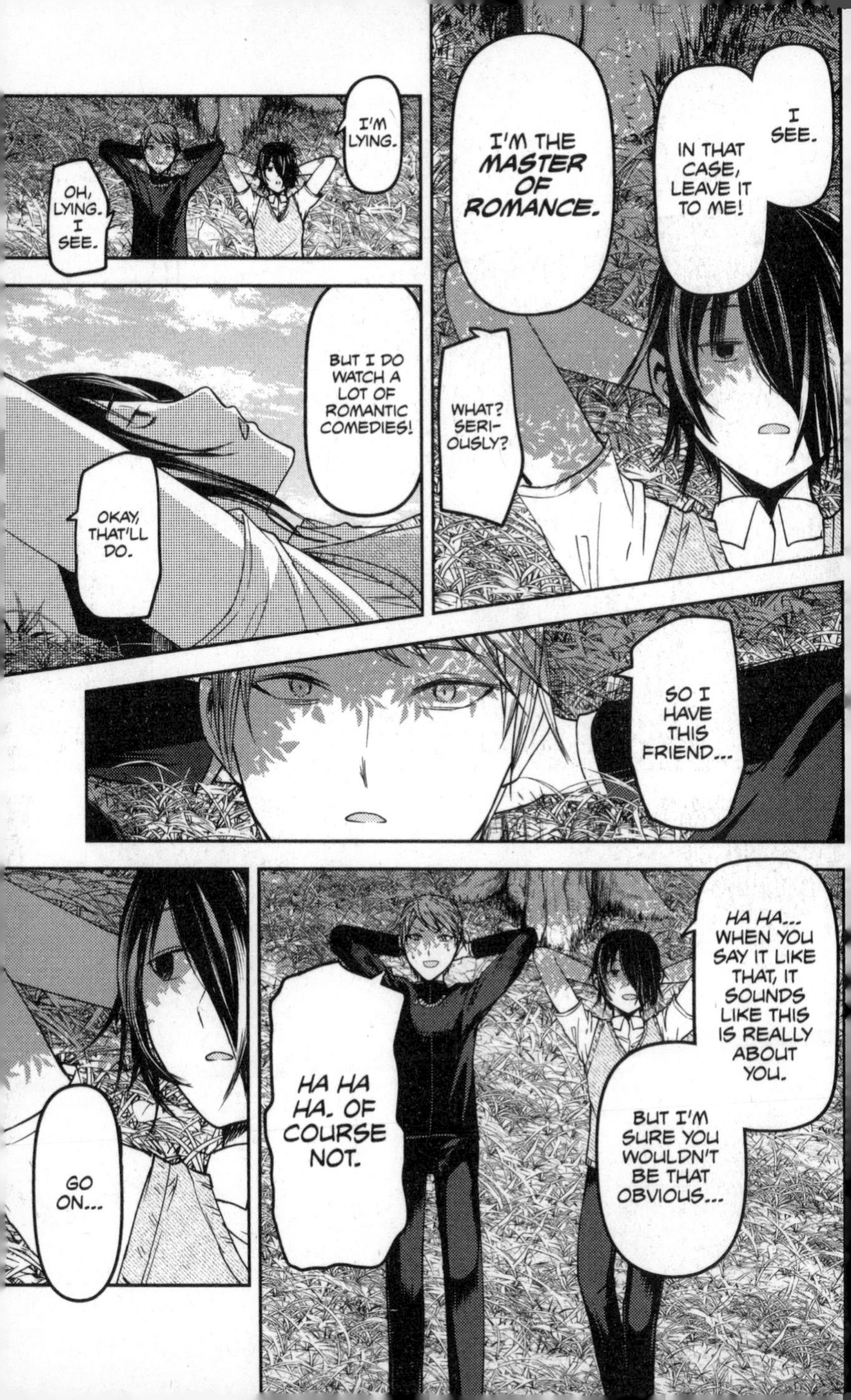
I SEE.
IN THAT CASE, LEAVE IT TO ME!
I'M THE *MASTER OF ROMANCE.*
I'M LYING.
OH, LYING. I SEE.
BUT I DO WATCH A LOT OF ROMANTIC COMEDIES!
WHAT? SERIOUSLY?
OKAY, THAT'LL DO.
SO I HAVE THIS FRIEND...
HA HA... WHEN YOU SAY IT LIKE THAT, IT SOUNDS LIKE THIS IS REALLY ABOUT YOU.
BUT I'M SURE YOU WOULDN'T BE THAT OBVIOUS...
HA HA HA. OF COURSE NOT.
GO ON...

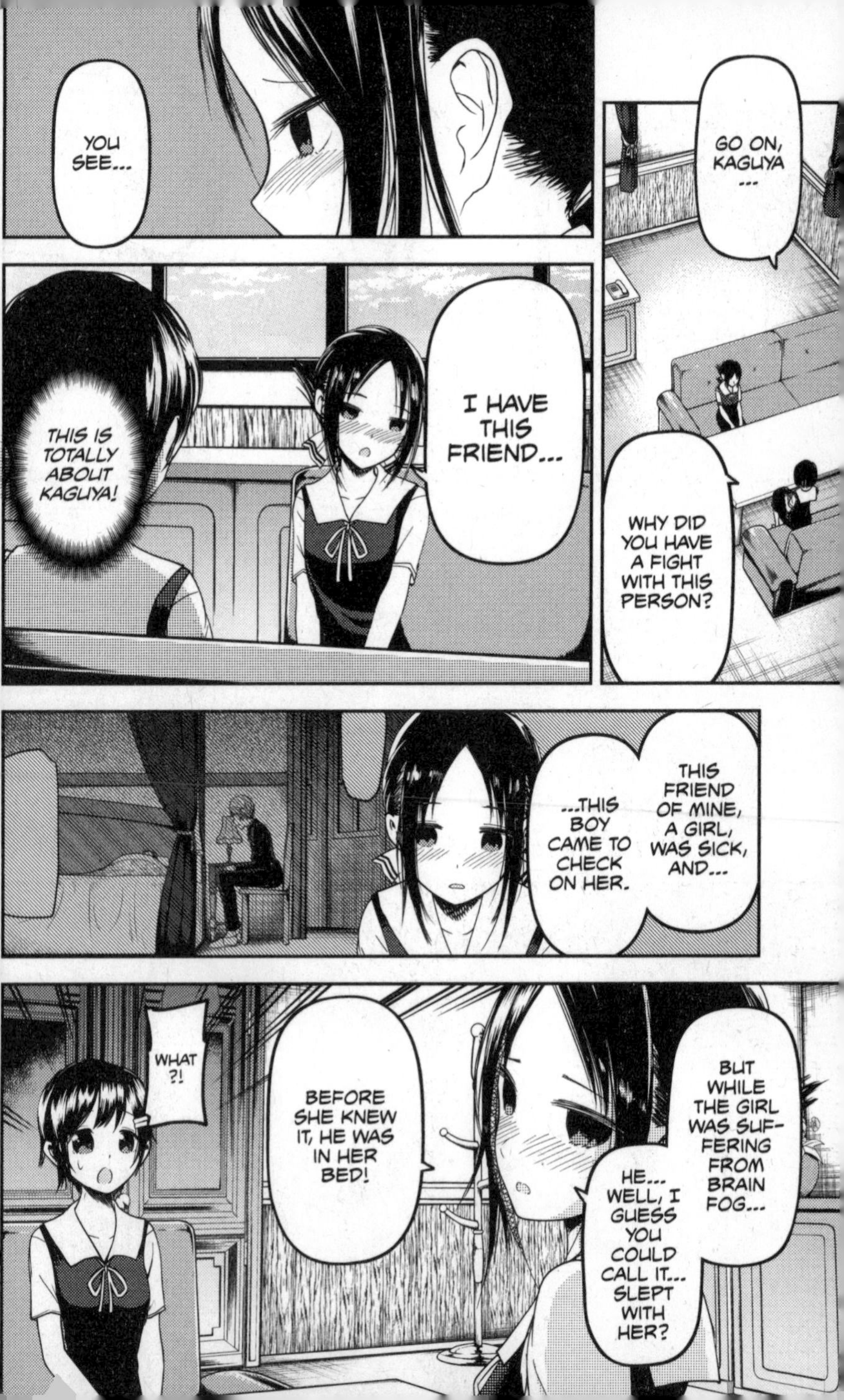
GO ON, KAGUYA ...
WHY DID YOU HAVE A FIGHT WITH THIS PERSON?
YOU SEE...
I HAVE THIS FRIEND...
THIS IS TOTALLY ABOUT KAGUYA!
THIS FRIEND OF MINE, A GIRL, WAS SICK, AND...
...THIS BOY CAME TO CHECK ON HER.
BUT WHILE THE GIRL WAS SUFFERING FROM BRAIN FOG...
HE... WELL, I GUESS YOU COULD CALL IT... SLEPT WITH HER?
BEFORE SHE KNEW IT, HE WAS IN HER BED!
WHAT ?!

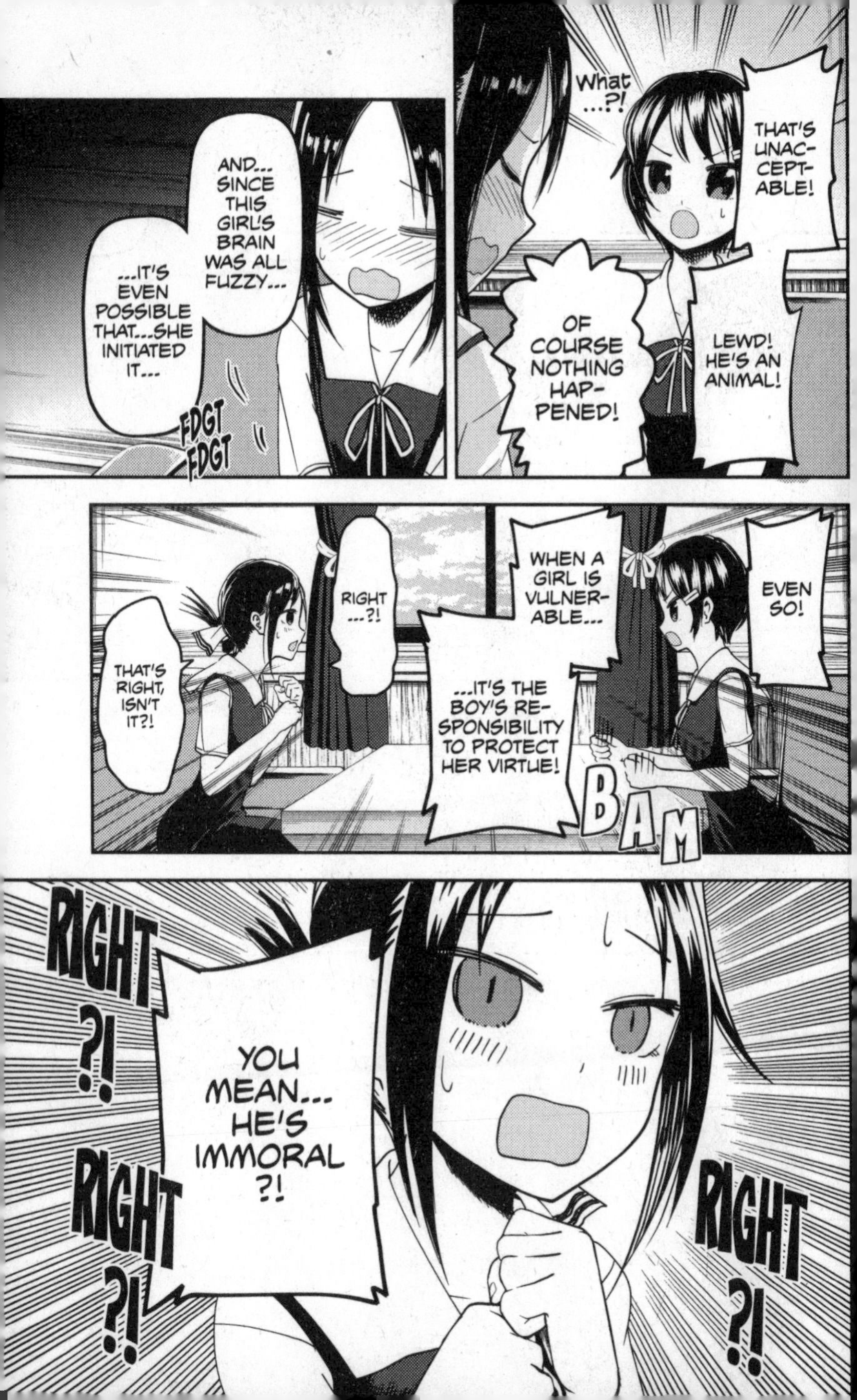
What ...?!
THAT'S UNACCEPTABLE!
LEWD! HE'S AN ANIMAL!
OF COURSE NOTHING HAPPENED!
AND... SINCE THIS GIRL'S BRAIN WAS ALL FUZZY...
...IT'S EVEN POSSIBLE THAT...SHE INITIATED IT...
FDGT FDGT
EVEN SO!
WHEN A GIRL IS VULNERABLE...
...IT'S THE BOY'S RESPONSIBILITY TO PROTECT HER VIRTUE!
BAM
RIGHT ...?!
THAT'S RIGHT, ISN'T IT?!
RIGHT ?!
YOU MEAN... HE'S IMMORAL ?!
RIGHT ?!
RIGHT ?!

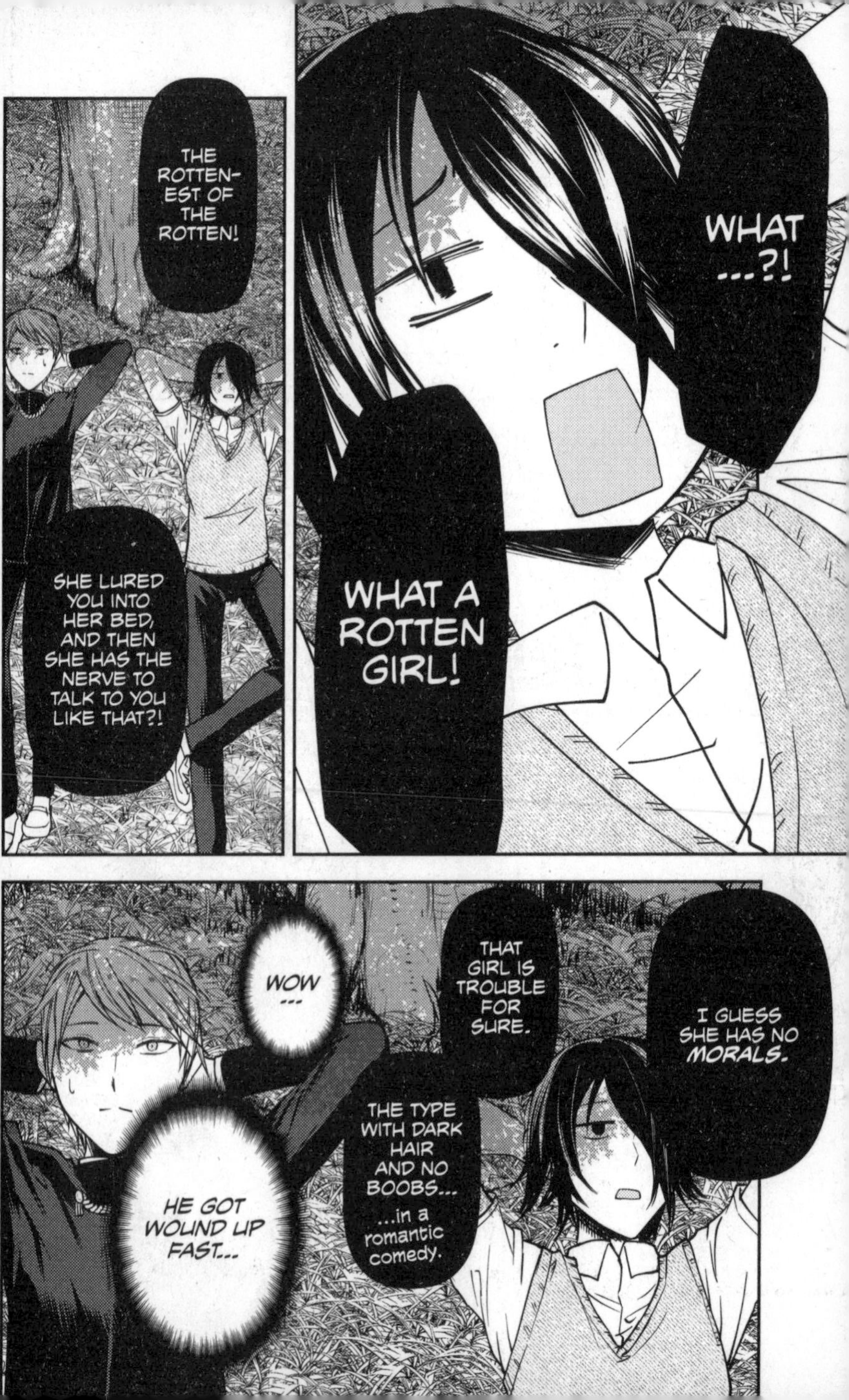
WHAT ...?!
WHAT A ROTTEN GIRL!
THE ROTTEN-EST OF THE ROTTEN!
SHE LURED YOU INTO HER BED, AND THEN SHE HAS THE NERVE TO TALK TO YOU LIKE THAT?!
I GUESS SHE HAS NO *MORALS.*
THAT GIRL IS TROUBLE FOR SURE.
THE TYPE WITH DARK HAIR AND NO BOOBS...
...in a romantic comedy.
WOW...
HE GOT WOUND UP FAST...

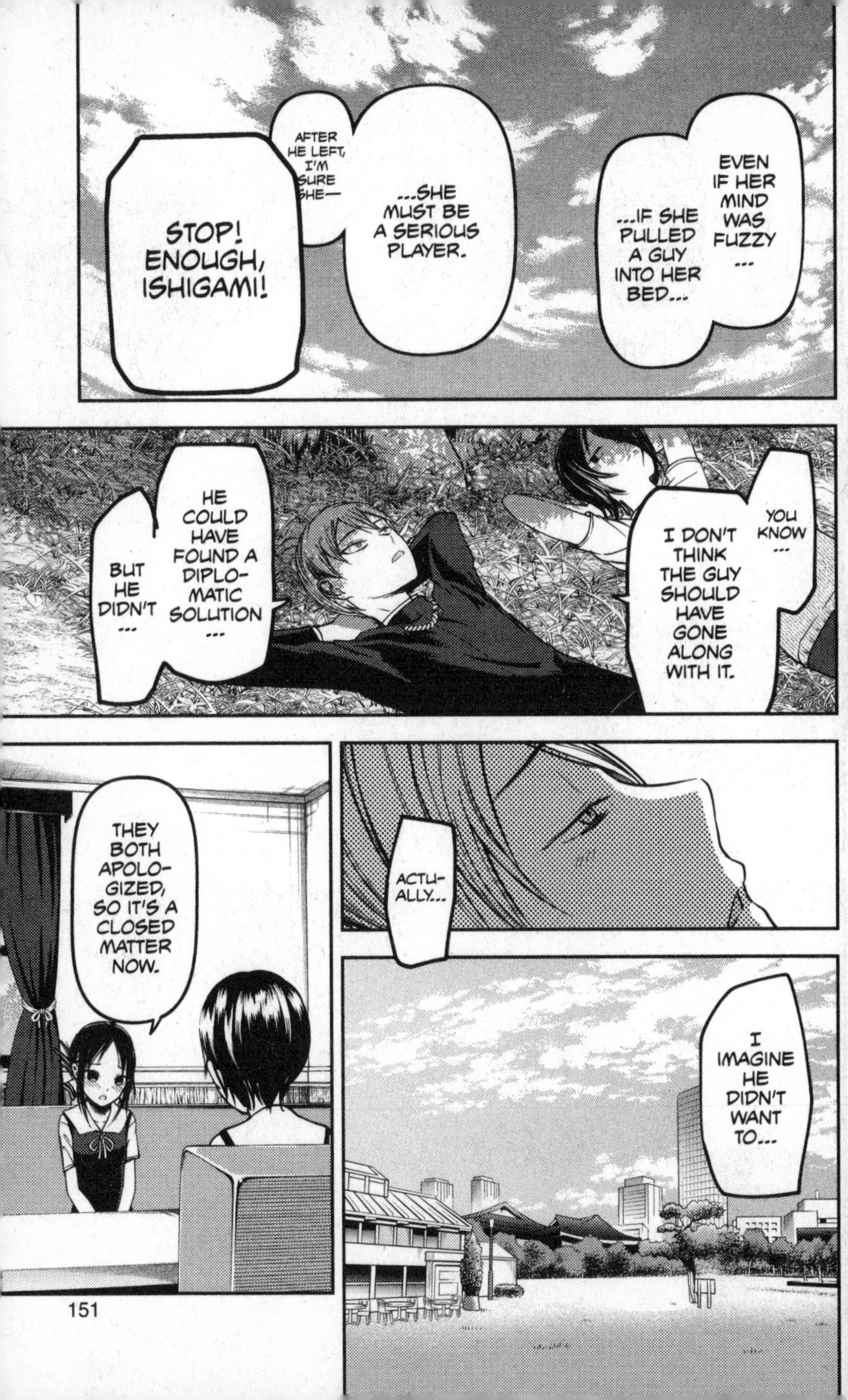
EVEN IF HER MIND WAS FUZZY...
...IF SHE PULLED A GUY INTO HER BED...
...SHE MUST BE A SERIOUS PLAYER.
AFTER HE LEFT, I'M SURE SHE—
STOP! ENOUGH, ISHIGAMI!
YOU KNOW...
I DON'T THINK THE GUY SHOULD HAVE GONE ALONG WITH IT.
HE COULD HAVE FOUND A DIPLOMATIC SOLUTION...
BUT HE DIDN'T...
ACTUALLY...
I IMAGINE HE DIDN'T WANT TO...
THEY BOTH APOLOGIZED, SO IT'S A CLOSED MATTER NOW.

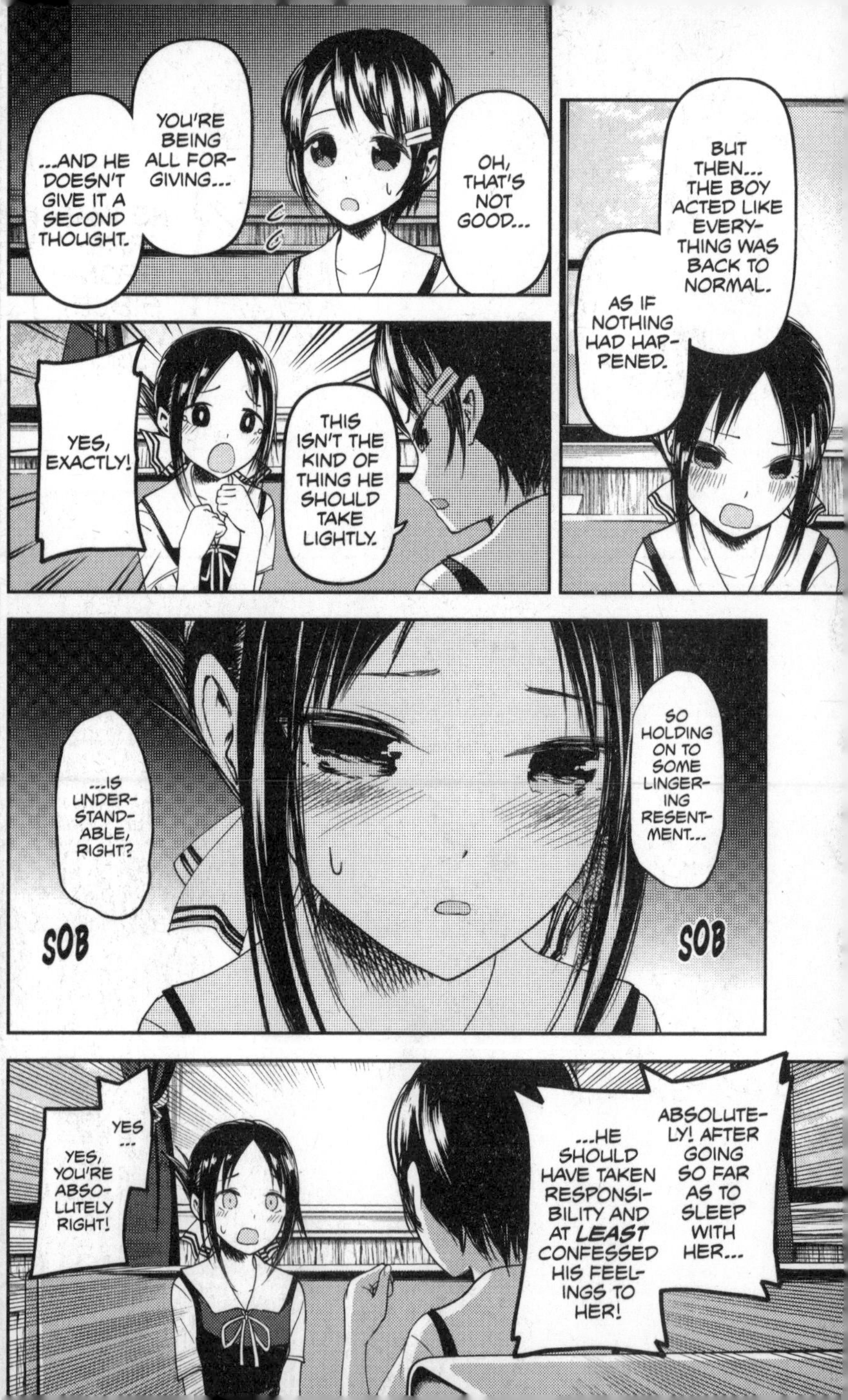
BUT THEN... THE BOY ACTED LIKE EVERYTHING WAS BACK TO NORMAL.
AS IF NOTHING HAD HAPPENED.
OH, THAT'S NOT GOOD...
YOU'RE BEING ALL FORGIVING...
...AND HE DOESN'T GIVE IT A SECOND THOUGHT.
THIS ISN'T THE KIND OF THING HE SHOULD TAKE LIGHTLY.
YES, EXACTLY!
SO HOLDING ON TO SOME LINGERING RESENTMENT...
SOB
...IS UNDERSTANDABLE, RIGHT?
SOB
ABSOLUTELY! AFTER GOING SO FAR AS TO SLEEP WITH HER...
...HE SHOULD HAVE TAKEN RESPONSIBILITY AND AT *LEAST* CONFESSED HIS FEELINGS TO HER!
YES... YES, YOU'RE ABSOLUTELY RIGHT!

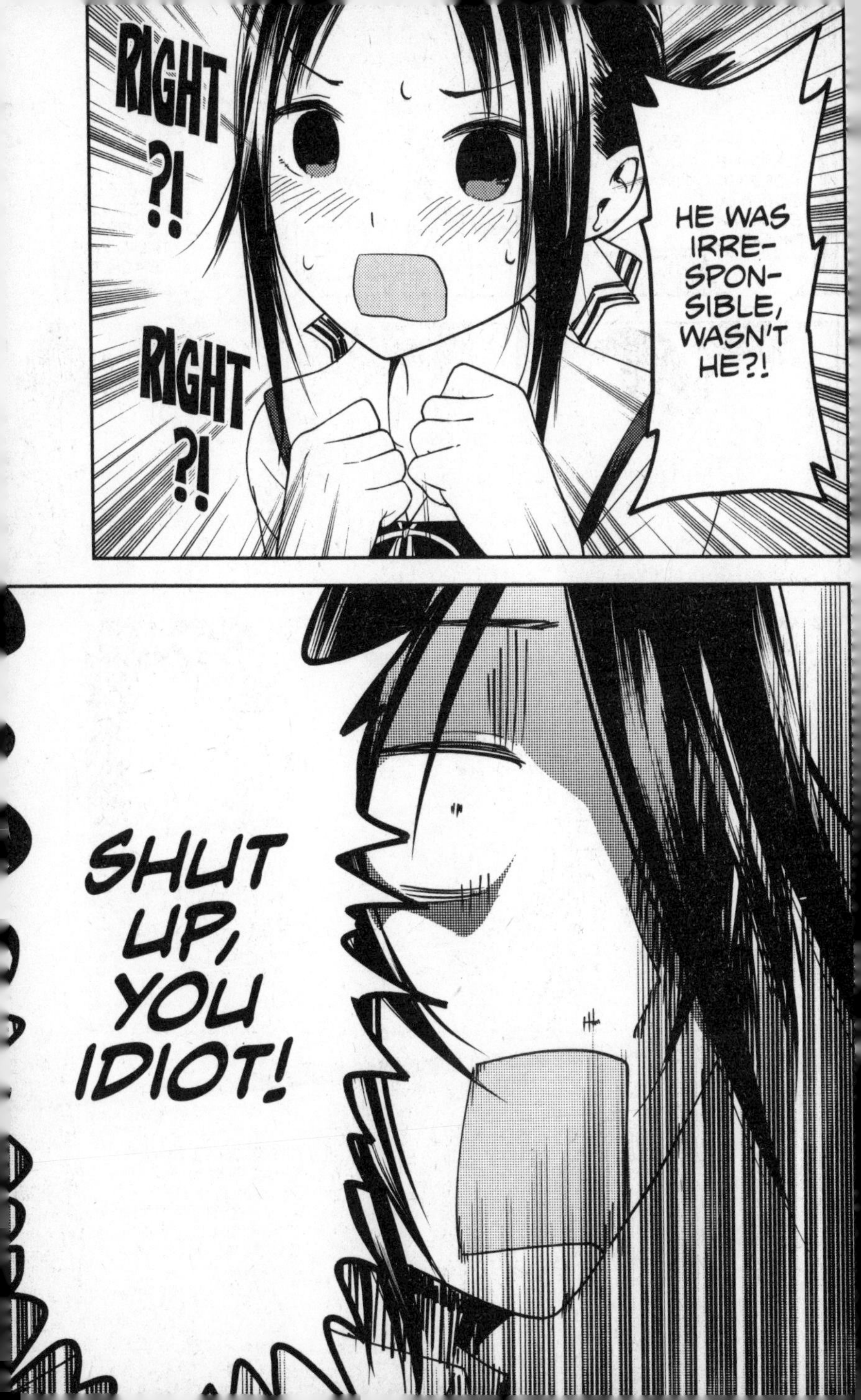
HE WAS IRRE-SPON-SIBLE, WASN'T HE?!
RIGHT ?!
RIGHT ?!
SHUT UP, YOU IDIOT!

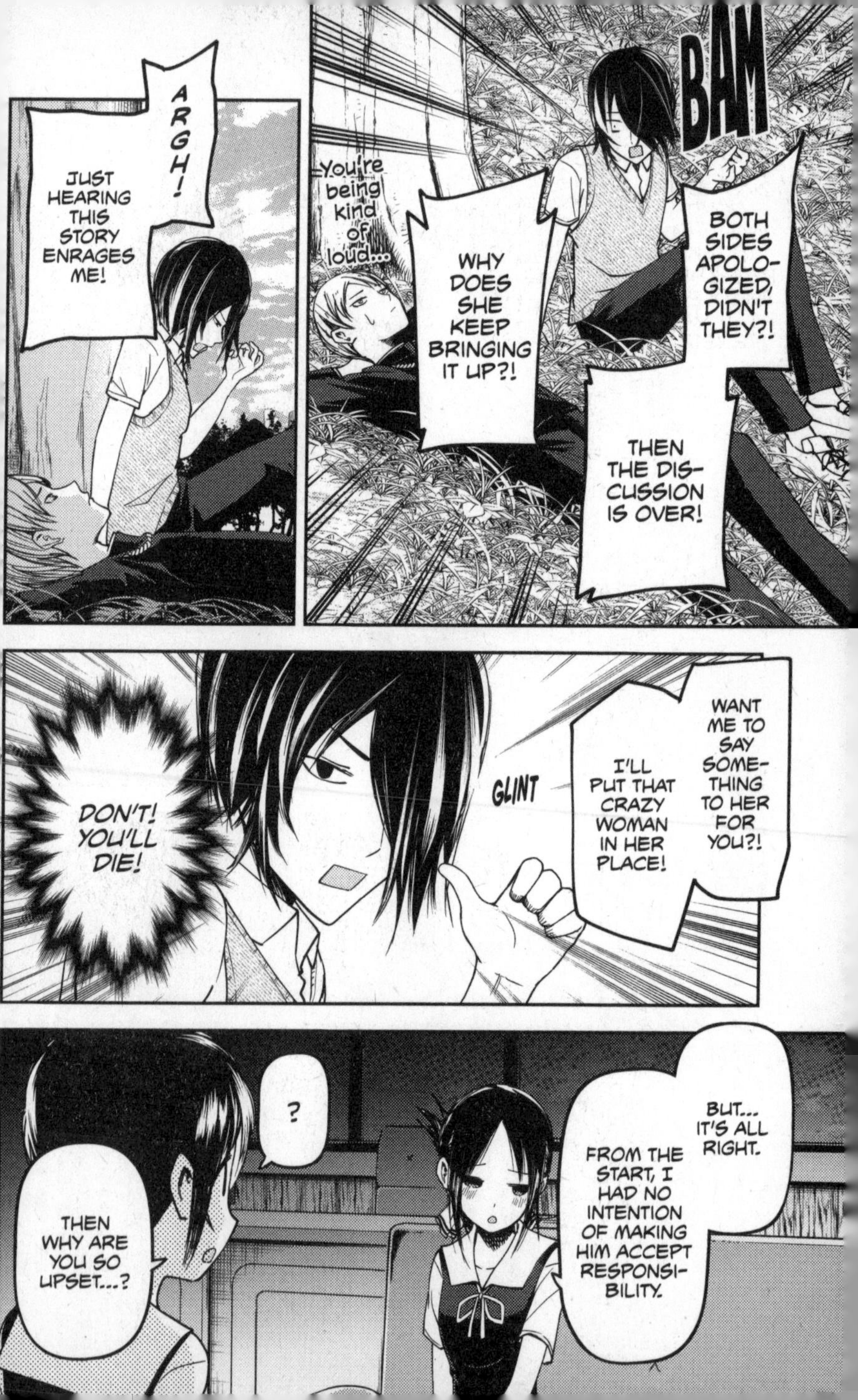
BAM
BOTH SIDES APOLOGIZED, DIDN'T THEY?!
THEN THE DISCUSSION IS OVER!
WHY DOES SHE KEEP BRINGING IT UP?!
You're being kind of loud...
ARGH!
JUST HEARING THIS STORY ENRAGES ME!
WANT ME TO SAY SOMETHING TO HER FOR YOU?!
I'LL PUT THAT CRAZY WOMAN IN HER PLACE!
GLINT
DON'T! YOU'LL DIE!
BUT... IT'S ALL RIGHT.
FROM THE START, I HAD NO INTENTION OF MAKING HIM ACCEPT RESPONSIBILITY.
?
THEN WHY ARE YOU SO UPSET...?

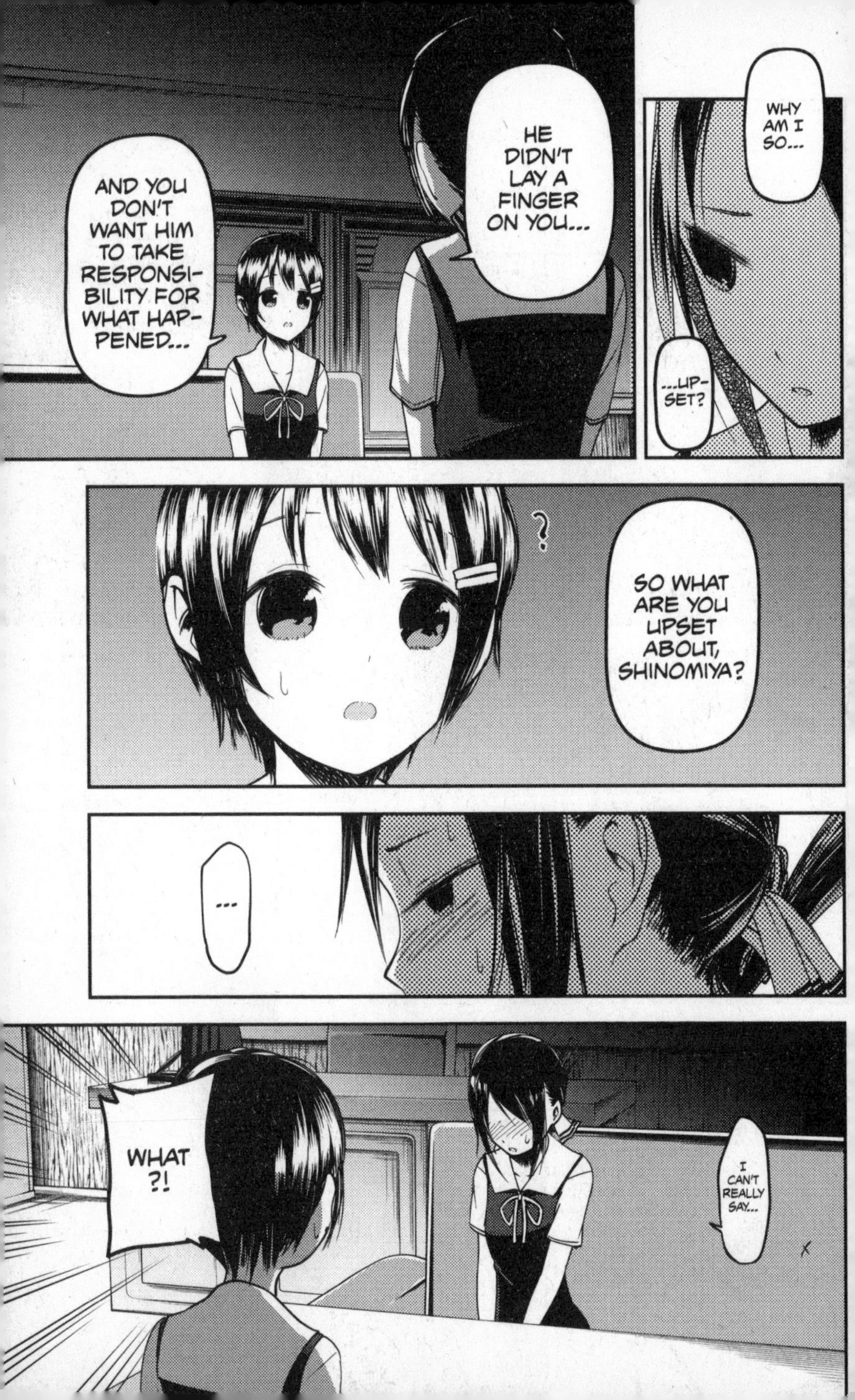
WHY AM I SO...
...UP-SET?
HE DIDN'T LAY A FINGER ON YOU...
AND YOU DON'T WANT HIM TO TAKE RESPONSI-BILITY FOR WHAT HAP-PENED...
?
SO WHAT ARE YOU UPSET ABOUT, SHINOMIYA?
...
I CAN'T REALLY SAY...
WHAT ?!

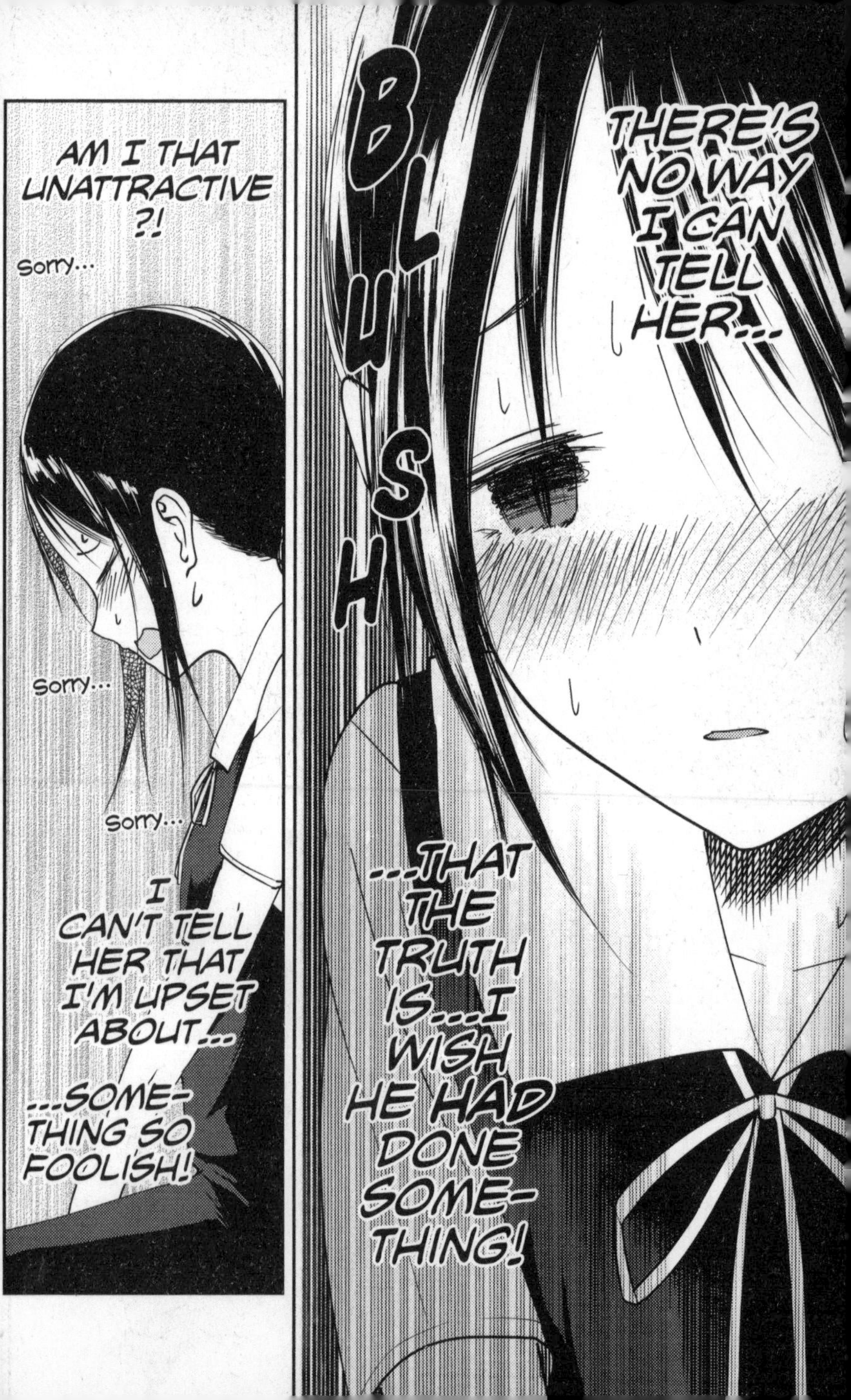
BLUSH
THERE IS NO WAY I CAN TELL HER...
...THAT THE TRUTH IS... I WISH HE HAD DONE SOME-THING!
AM I THAT UNATTRACTIVE ?!
Sorry...
Sorry...
Sorry...
I CAN'T TELL HER THAT I'M UPSET ABOUT...
...SOME-THING SO FOOLISH!

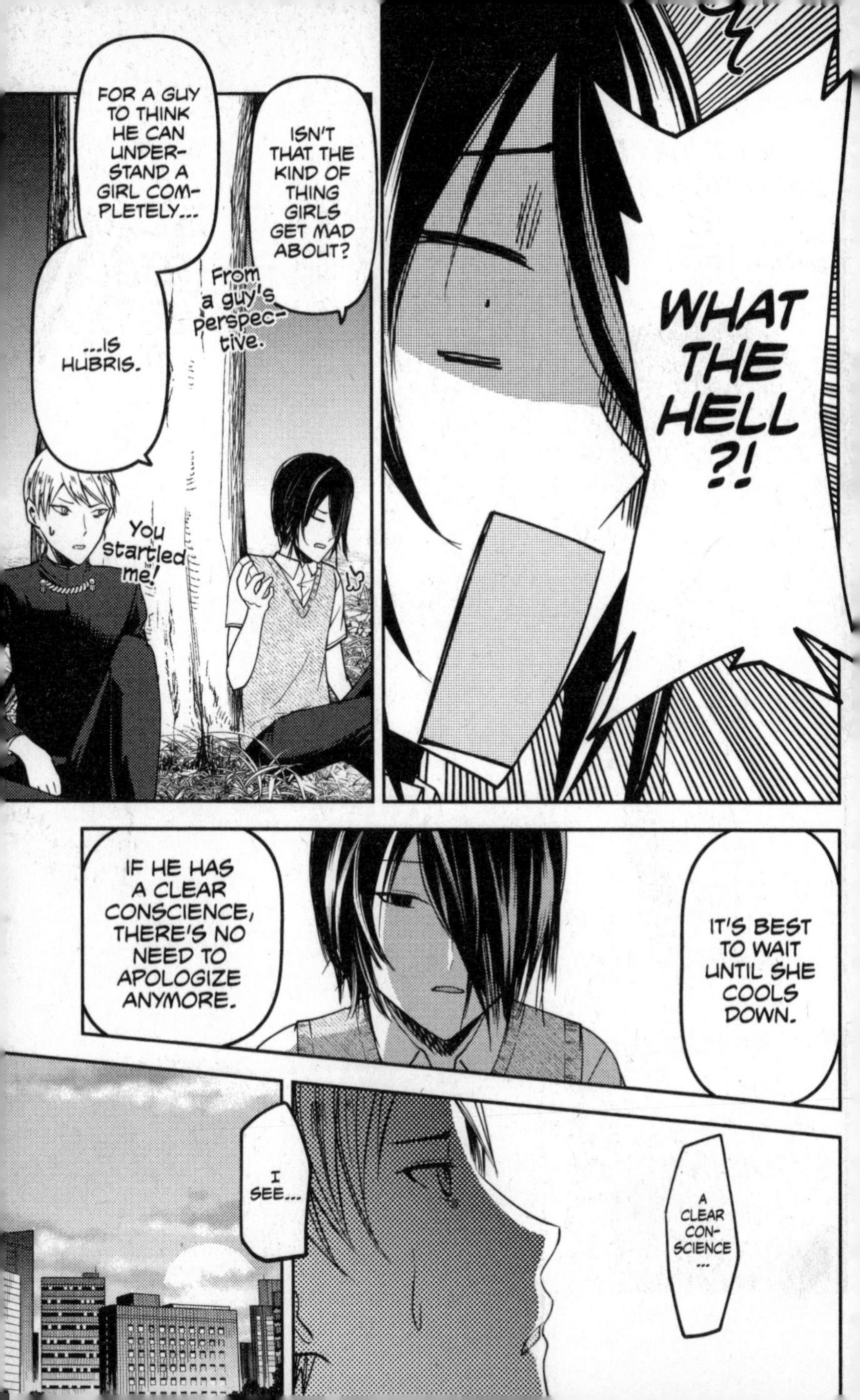
WHAT THE HELL ?!
ISN'T THAT THE KIND OF THING GIRLS GET MAD ABOUT?
From a guy's perspective.
FOR A GUY TO THINK HE CAN UNDERSTAND A GIRL COMPLETELY...
...IS HUBRIS.
You startled me!
IT'S BEST TO WAIT UNTIL SHE COOLS DOWN.
IF HE HAS A CLEAR CONSCIENCE, THERE'S NO NEED TO APOLOGIZE ANYMORE.
A CLEAR CONSCIENCE...
I SEE...

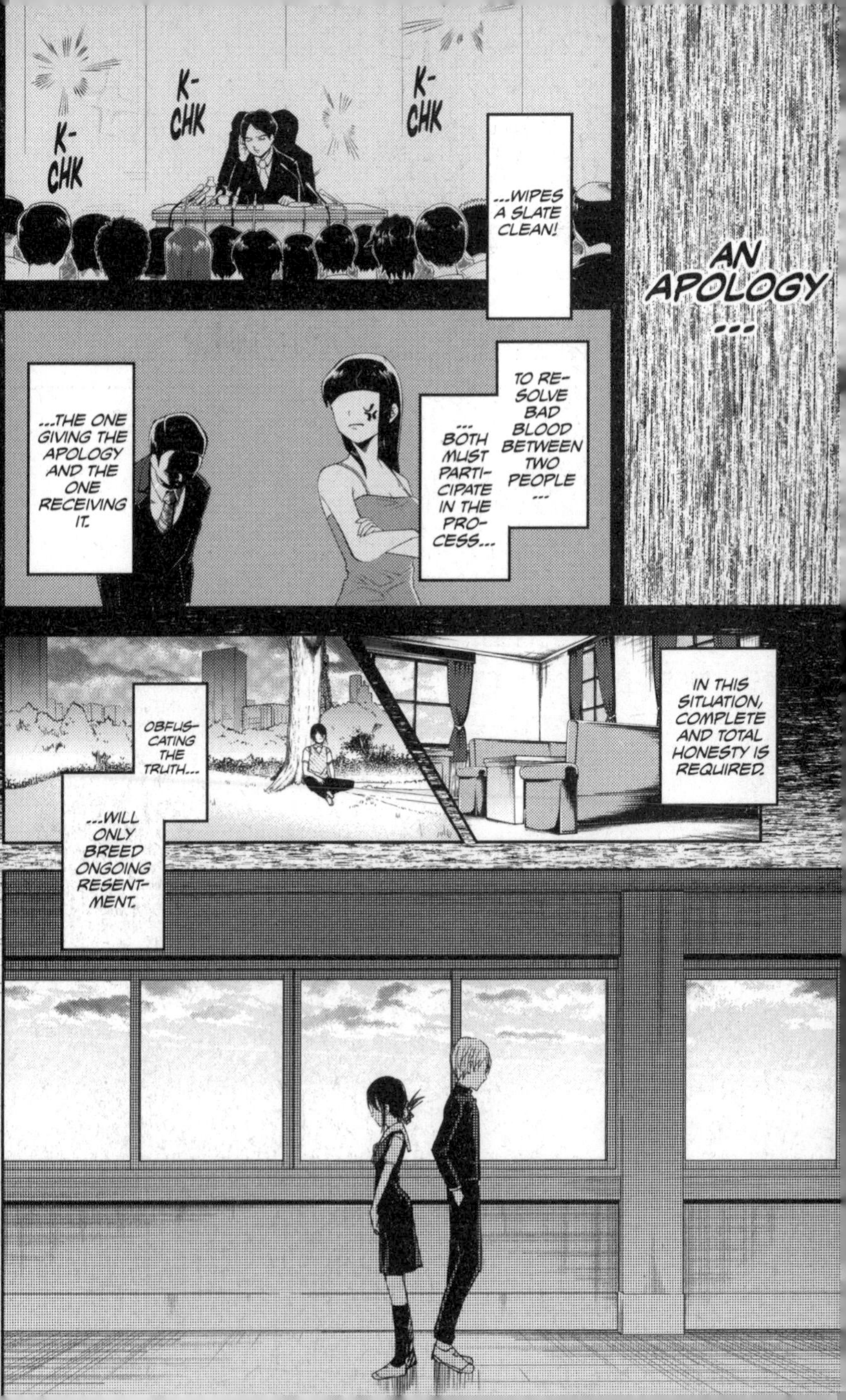
AN APOLOGY...
...WIPES A SLATE CLEAN!
K-CHK
K-CHK
K-CHK
TO RE-SOLVE BAD BLOOD BETWEEN TWO PEOPLE...
...BOTH MUST PARTI-CIPATE IN THE PRO-CESS...
...THE ONE GIVING THE APOLOGY AND THE ONE RECEIVING IT.
IN THIS SITUATION, COMPLETE AND TOTAL HONESTY IS REQUIRED.
OBFUS-CATING THE TRUTH...
...WILL ONLY BREED ONGOING RESENT-MENT.

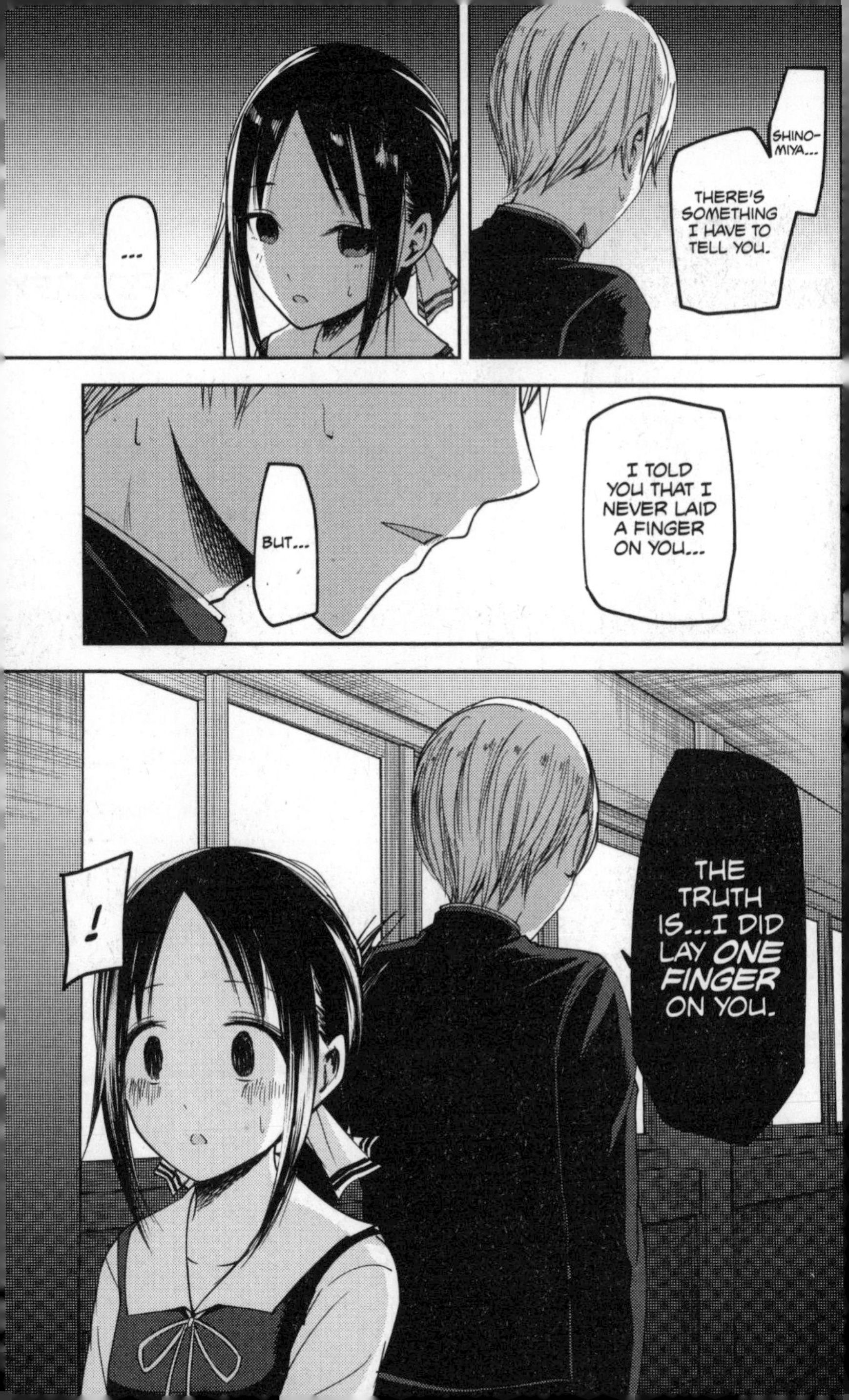
SHINO-MIYA...
THERE'S SOMETHING I HAVE TO TELL YOU.
...
I TOLD YOU THAT I NEVER LAID A FINGER ON YOU...
BUT...
THE TRUTH IS...I DID LAY *ONE FINGER* ON YOU.
!

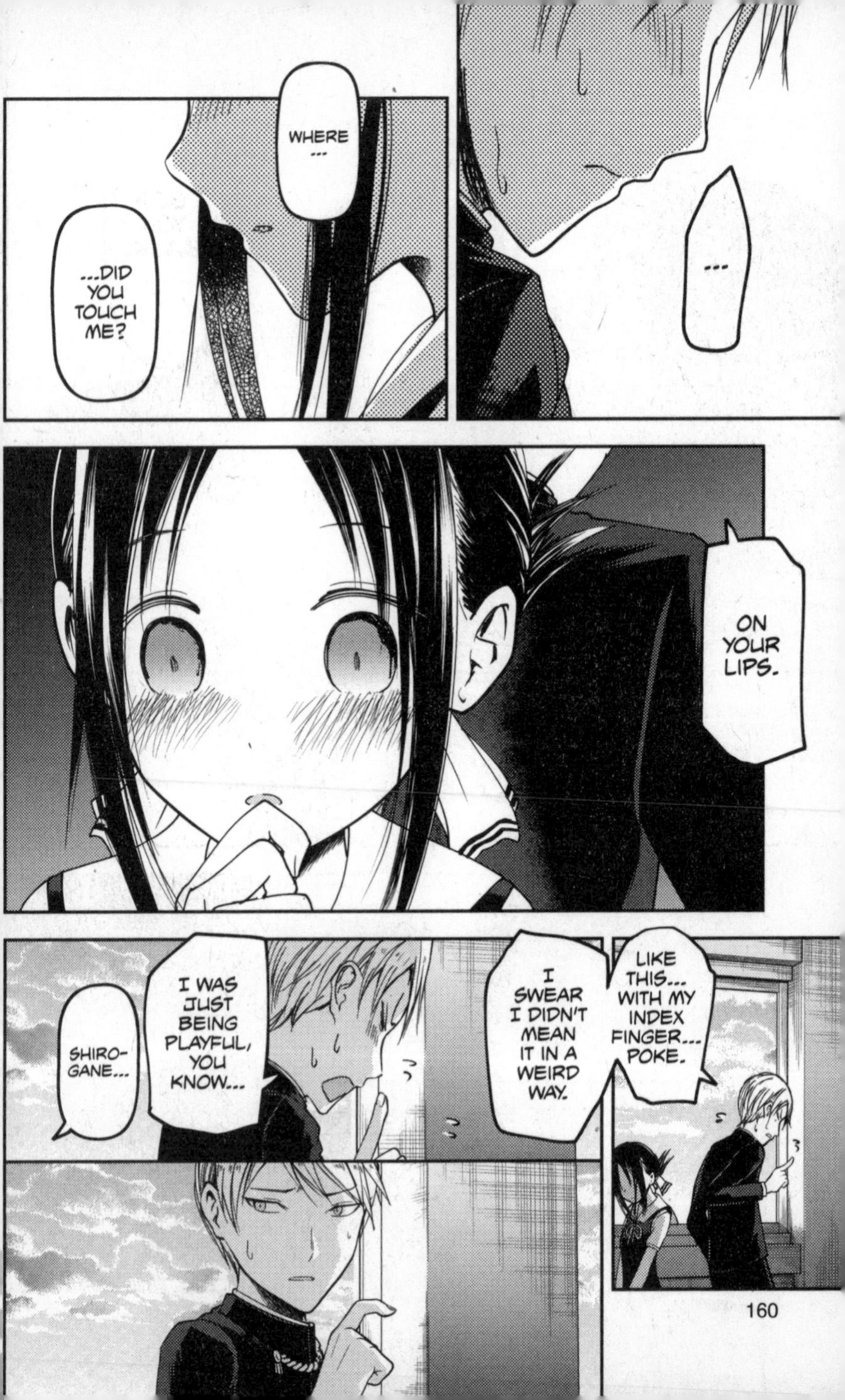
...
WHERE ...
...DID YOU TOUCH ME?
ON YOUR LIPS.
LIKE THIS... WITH MY INDEX FINGER... POKE.
I SWEAR I DIDN'T MEAN IT IN A WEIRD WAY.
I WAS JUST BEING PLAYFUL, YOU KNOW...
SHIRO-GANE...

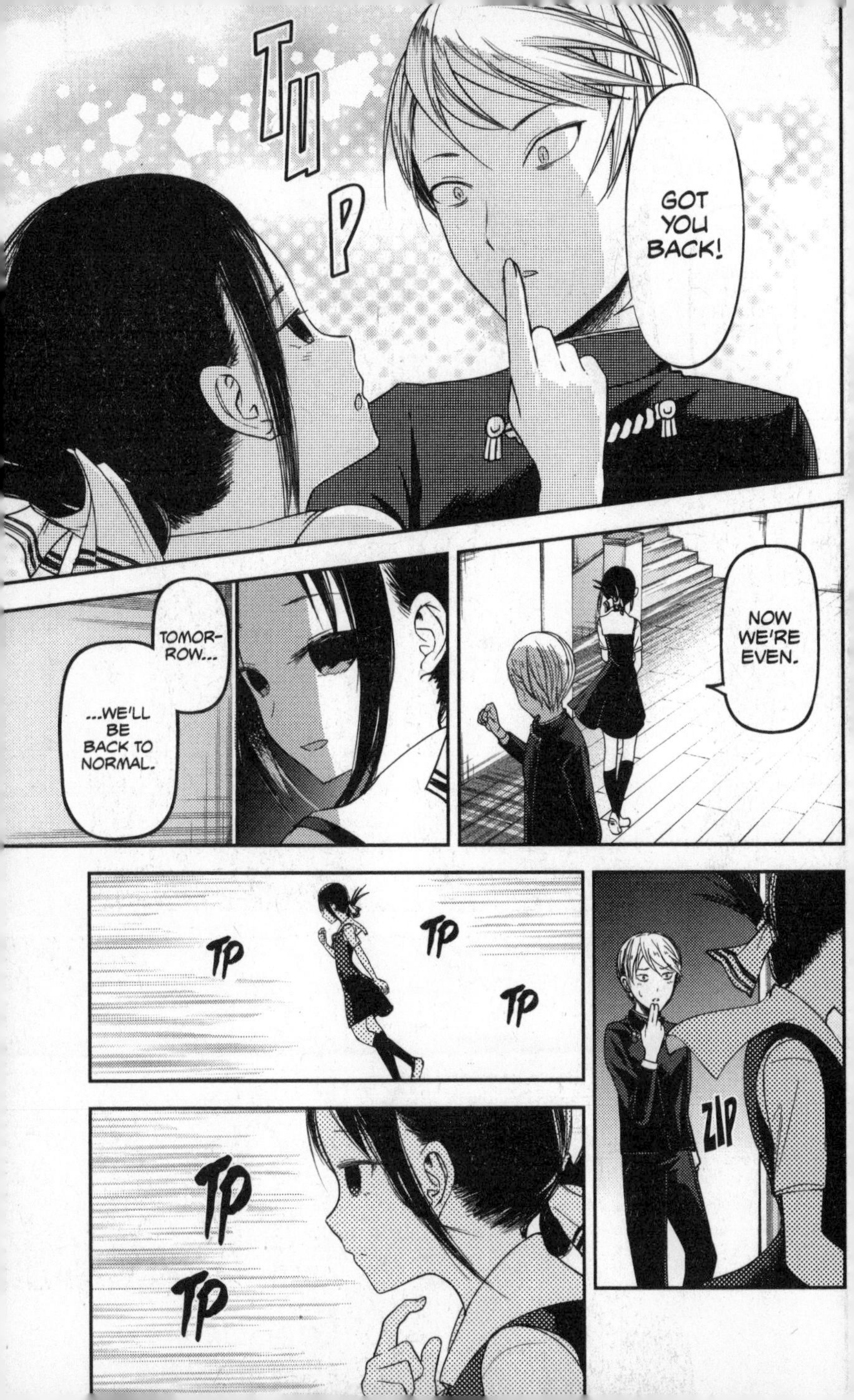
GOT YOU BACK!
TUP
NOW WE'RE EVEN.
TOMORROW...
...WE'LL BE BACK TO NORMAL.
ZIP
TP
TP
TP
TP
TP

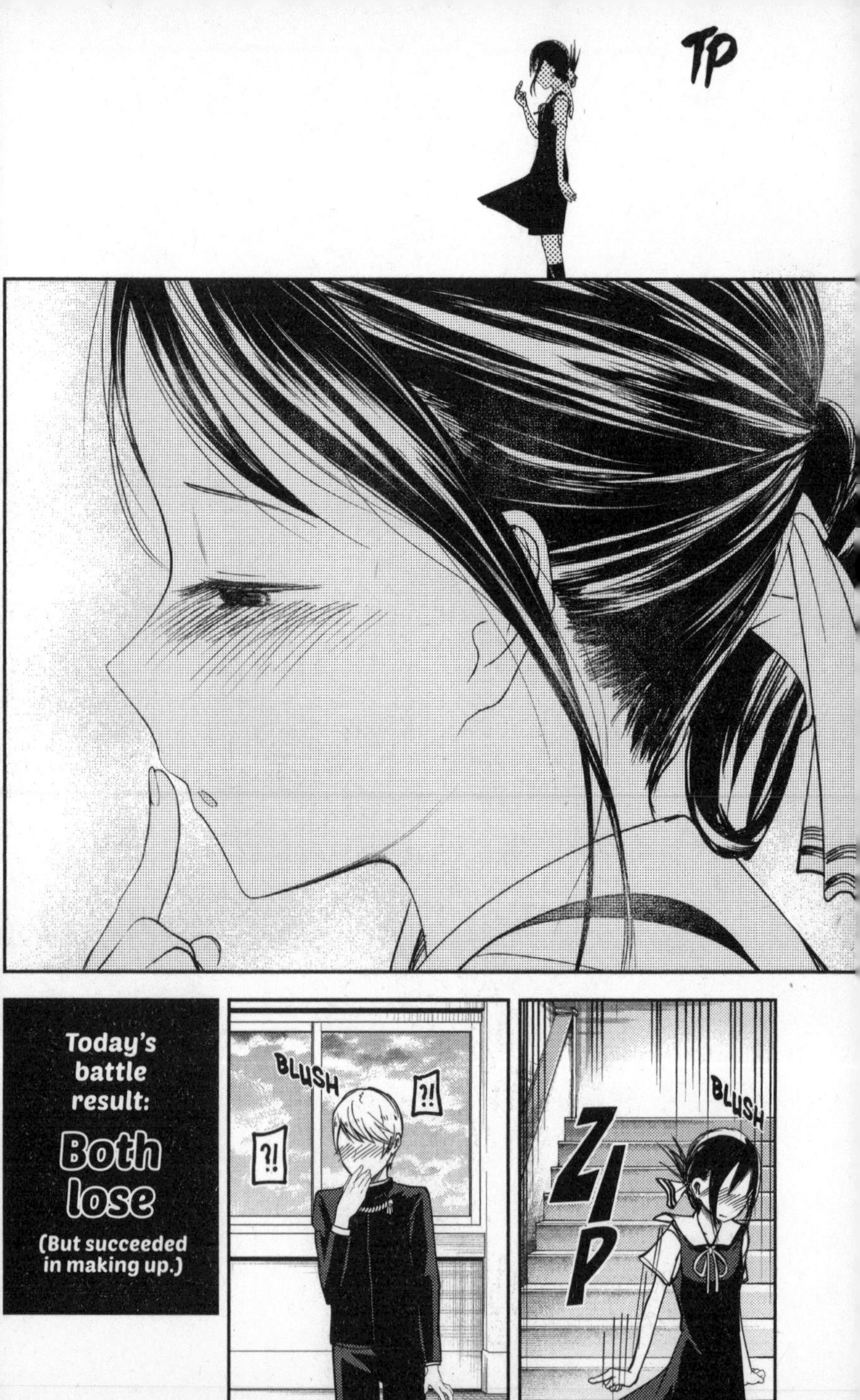
TP
ZIP
BLUSH
BLUSH
?!
?!
Today's battle result:
Both lose
(But succeeded in making up.)

GOT YOU BACK!

NOW WE'RE EVEN.

So quick...

A BYSTANDER

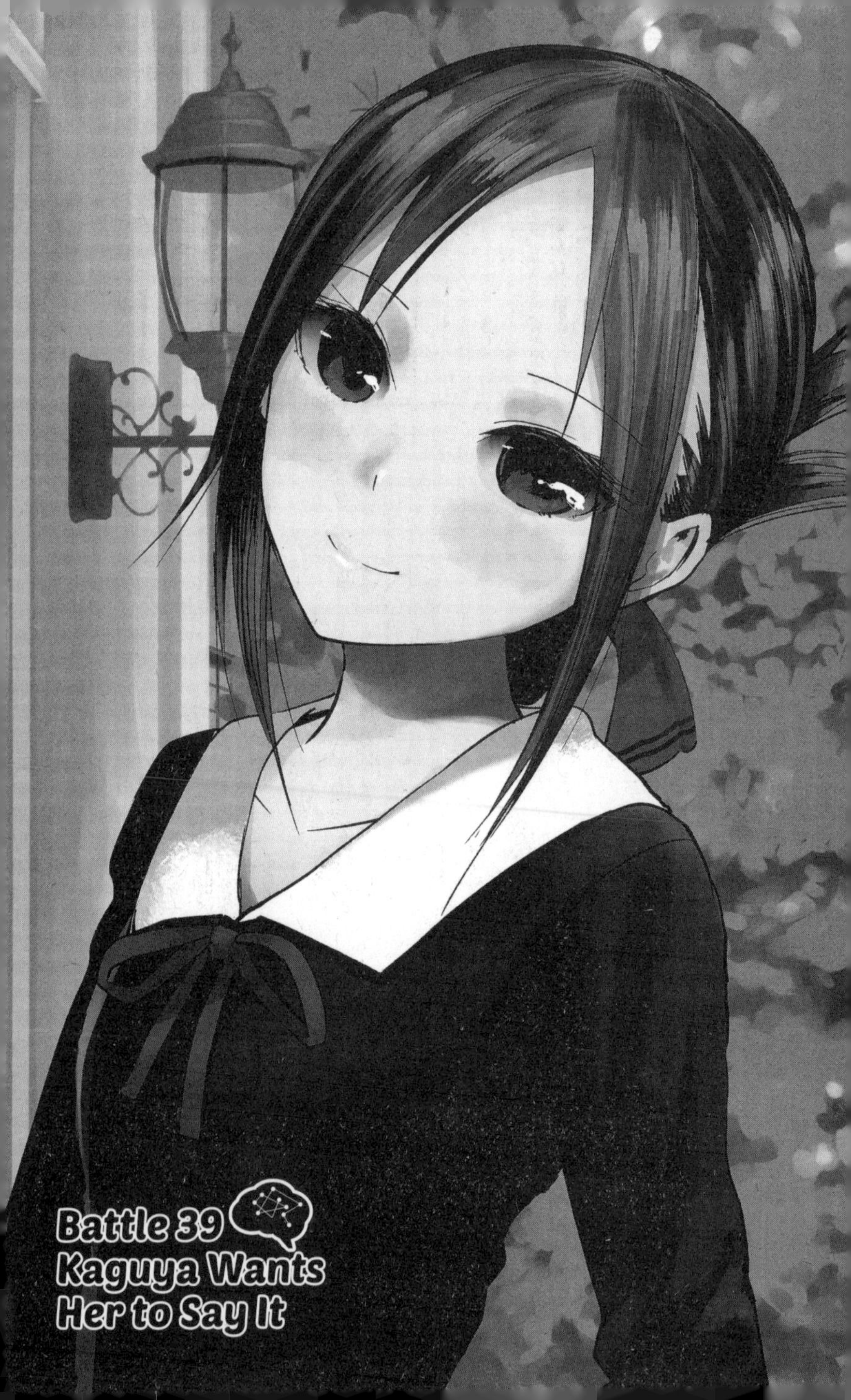

Battle 39 Kaguya Wants Her to Say It

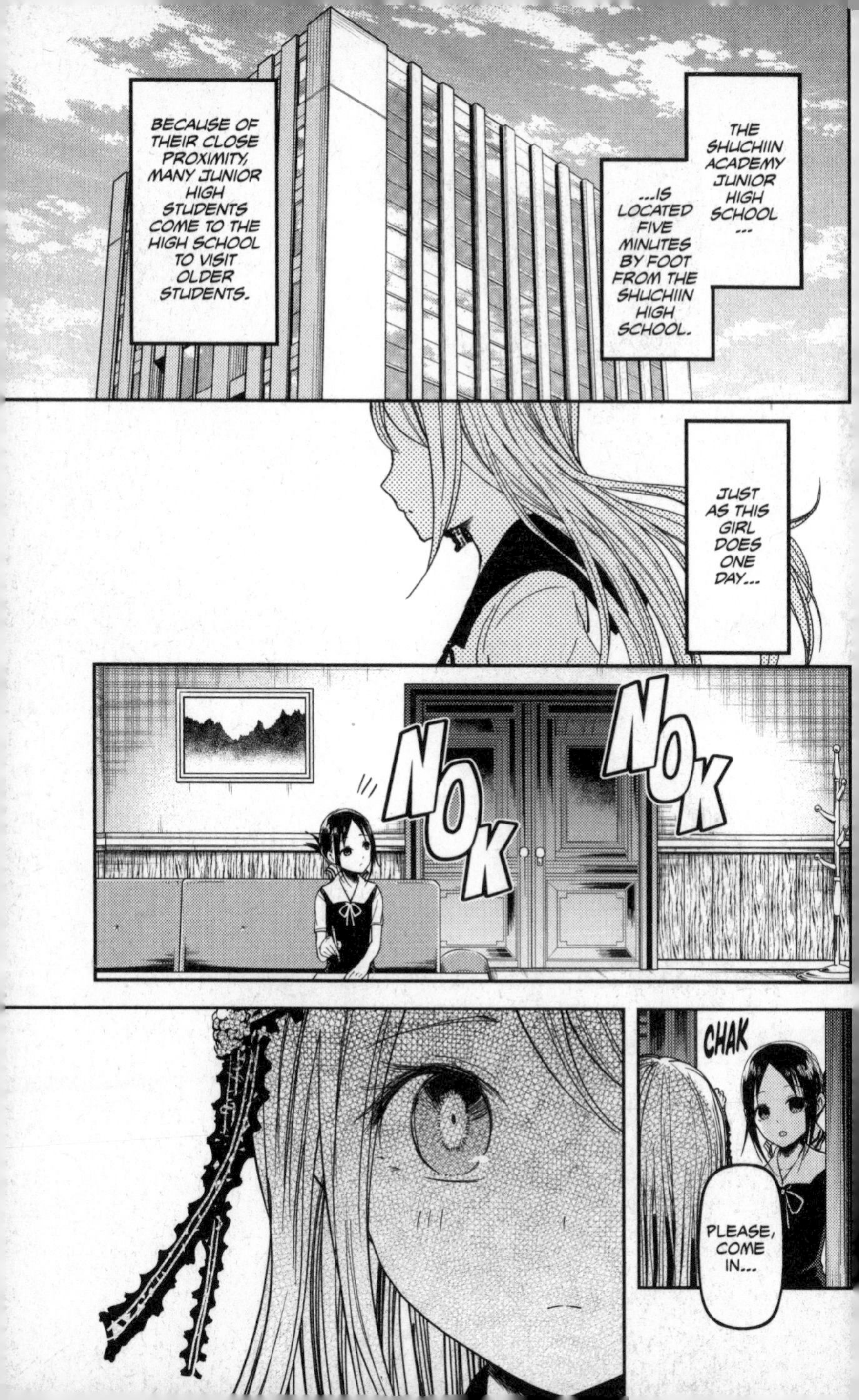
THE SHUCHIIN ACADEMY JUNIOR HIGH SCHOOL...
...IS LOCATED FIVE MINUTES BY FOOT FROM THE SHUCHIIN HIGH SCHOOL.
BECAUSE OF THEIR CLOSE PROXIMITY, MANY JUNIOR HIGH STUDENTS COME TO THE HIGH SCHOOL TO VISIT OLDER STUDENTS.
JUST AS THIS GIRL DOES ONE DAY...
NOK
NOK
CHAK
PLEASE, COME IN...

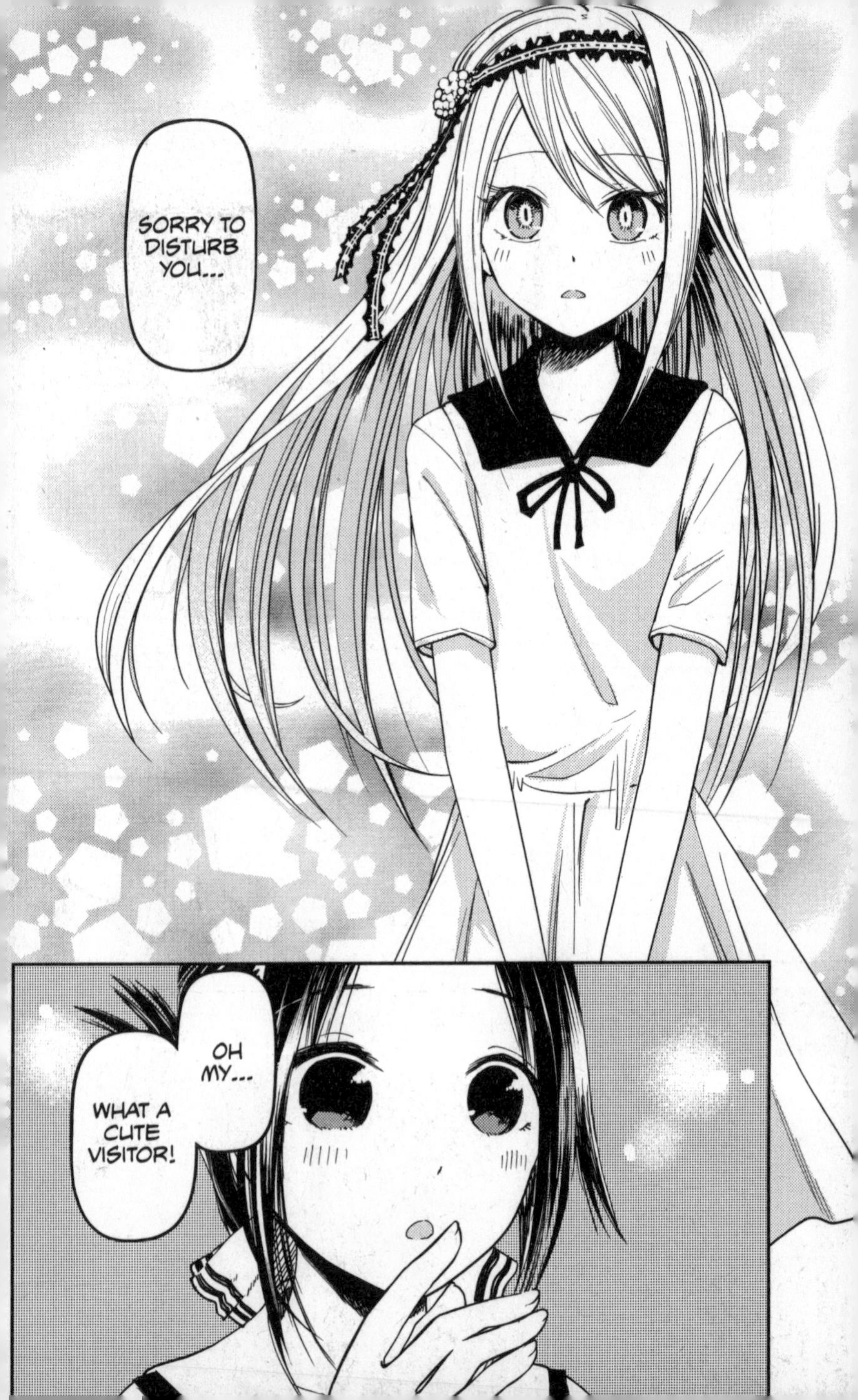
SORRY TO DISTURB YOU...
OH MY...
WHAT A CUTE VISITOR!

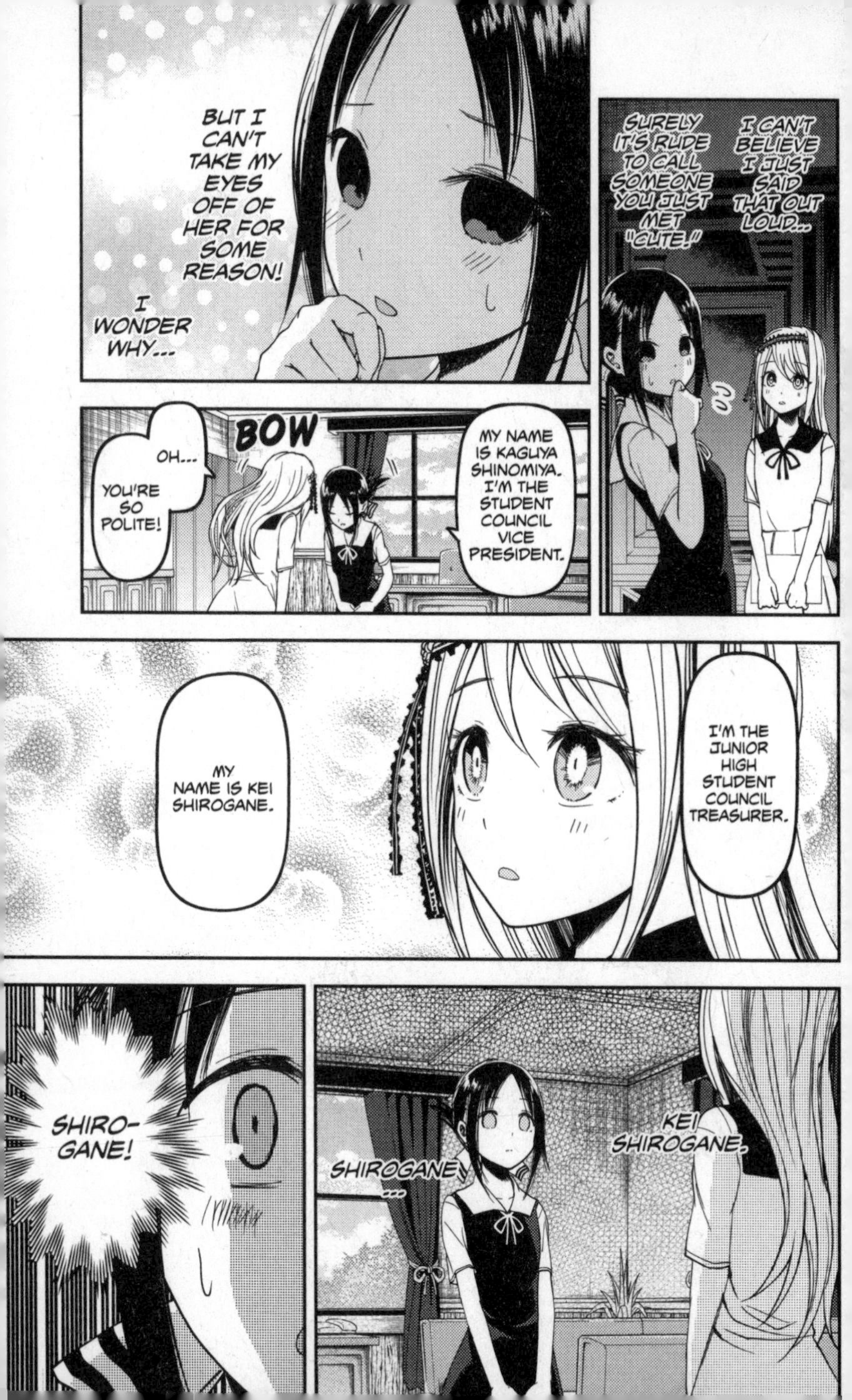
I CAN'T BELIEVE I JUST SAID THAT OUT LOUD...
SURELY IT'S RUDE TO CALL SOMEONE YOU JUST MET "CUTE."
BUT I CAN'T TAKE MY EYES OFF OF HER FOR SOME REASON!
I WONDER WHY...
MY NAME IS KAGUYA SHINOMIYA. I'M THE STUDENT COUNCIL VICE PRESIDENT.
BOW
OH...
YOU'RE SO POLITE!
I'M THE JUNIOR HIGH STUDENT COUNCIL TREASURER.
MY NAME IS KEI SHIROGANE.
KEI SHIROGANE.
SHIROGANE...
SHIRO-GANE!

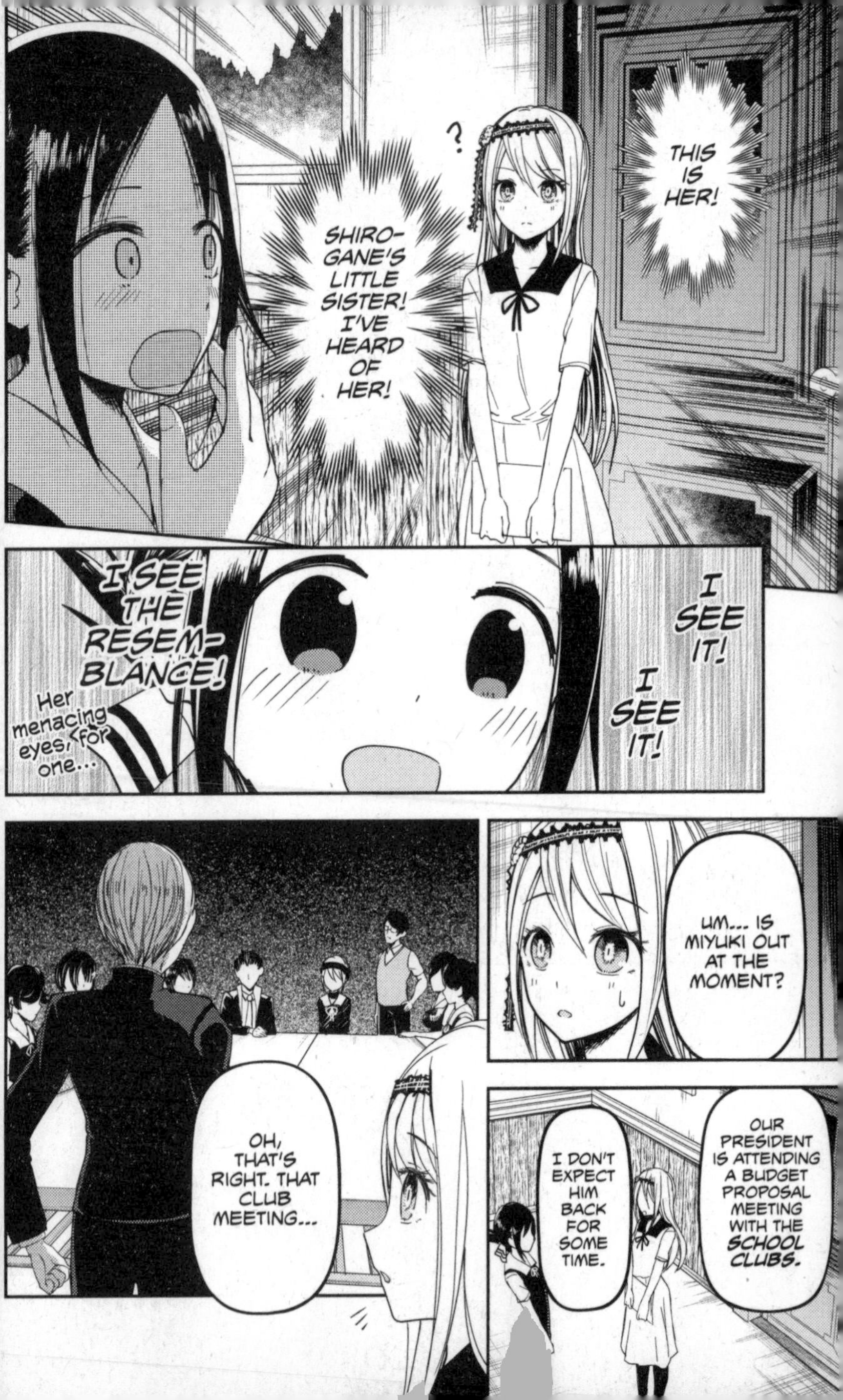
THIS IS HER!
?
SHIRO-GANE'S LITTLE SISTER! I'VE HEARD OF HER!
I SEE IT!
I SEE IT!
I SEE THE RESEM-BLANCE!
Her menacing eyes, for one...
UM... IS MIYUKI OUT AT THE MOMENT?
OUR PRESIDENT IS ATTENDING A BUDGET PROPOSAL MEETING WITH THE SCHOOL CLUBS.
I DON'T EXPECT HIM BACK FOR SOME TIME.
OH, THAT'S RIGHT. THAT CLUB MEETING...

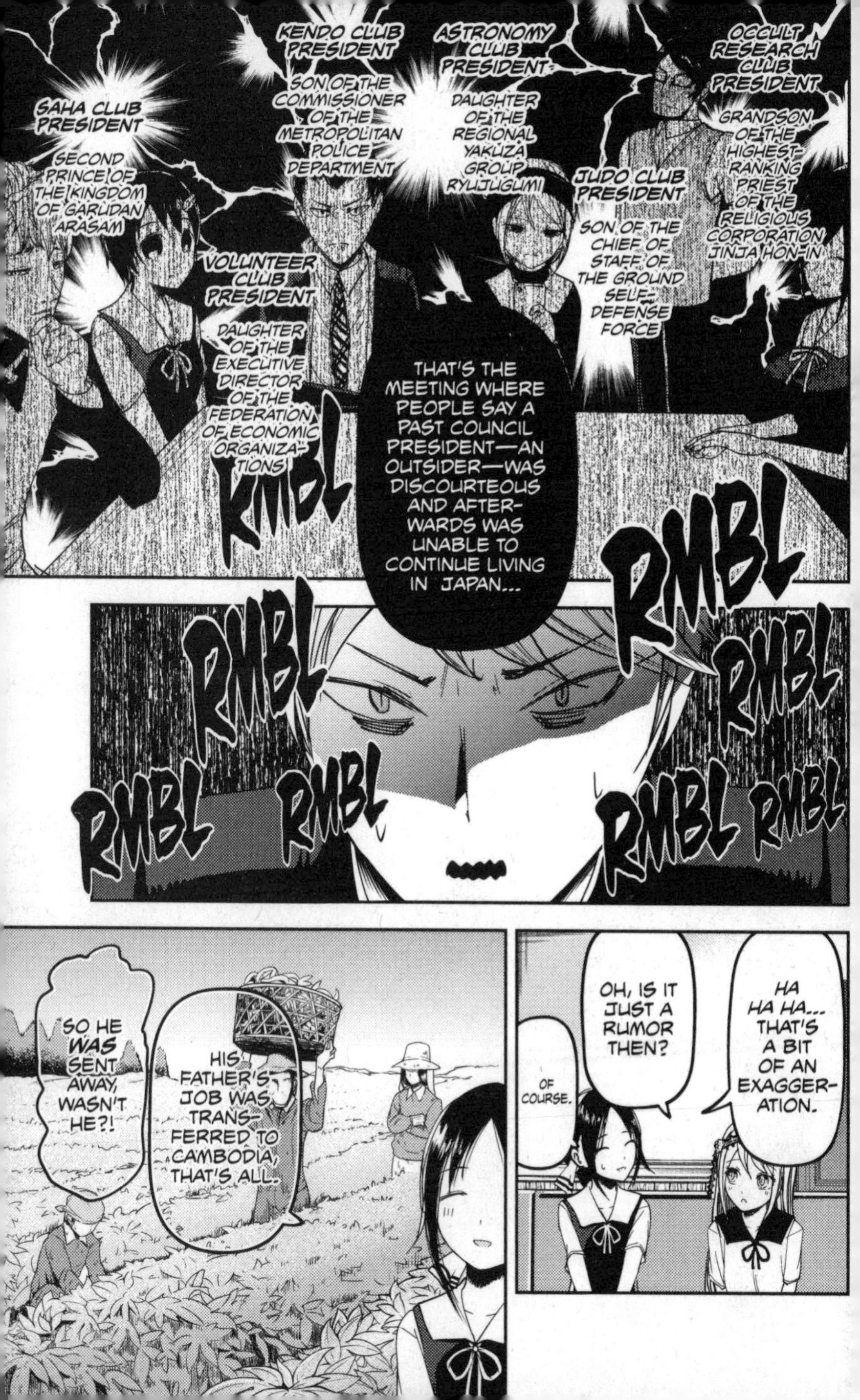
OCCULT RESEARCH CLUB PRESIDENT
GRANDSON OF THE HIGHEST-RANKING PRIEST OF THE RELIGIOUS CORPORATION JINJA HON-IN
ASTRONOMY CLUB PRESIDENT
DAUGHTER OF THE REGIONAL YAKUZA GROUP RYUJUGUMI
KENDO CLUB PRESIDENT
SON OF THE COMMISSIONER OF THE METROPOLITAN POLICE DEPARTMENT
JUDO CLUB PRESIDENT
SON OF THE CHIEF OF STAFF OF THE GROUND SELF-DEFENSE FORCE
SAHA CLUB PRESIDENT
SECOND PRINCE OF THE KINGDOM OF GARUDAN ARASAM
VOLUNTEER CLUB PRESIDENT
DAUGHTER OF THE EXECUTIVE DIRECTOR OF THE FEDERATION OF ECONOMIC ORGANIZATIONS
THAT'S THE MEETING WHERE PEOPLE SAY A PAST COUNCIL PRESIDENT—AN OUTSIDER—WAS DISCOURTEOUS AND AFTERWARDS WAS UNABLE TO CONTINUE LIVING IN JAPAN...
RMBL
RMBL
RMBL
RMBL
RMBL
RMBL
RMBL
RMBL
RMBL
HA HA HA... THAT'S A BIT OF AN EXAGGERATION.
OH, IS IT JUST A RUMOR THEN?
OF COURSE.
HIS FATHER'S JOB WAS TRANSFERRED TO CAMBODIA, THAT'S ALL.
SO HE WAS SENT AWAY, WASN'T HE?!

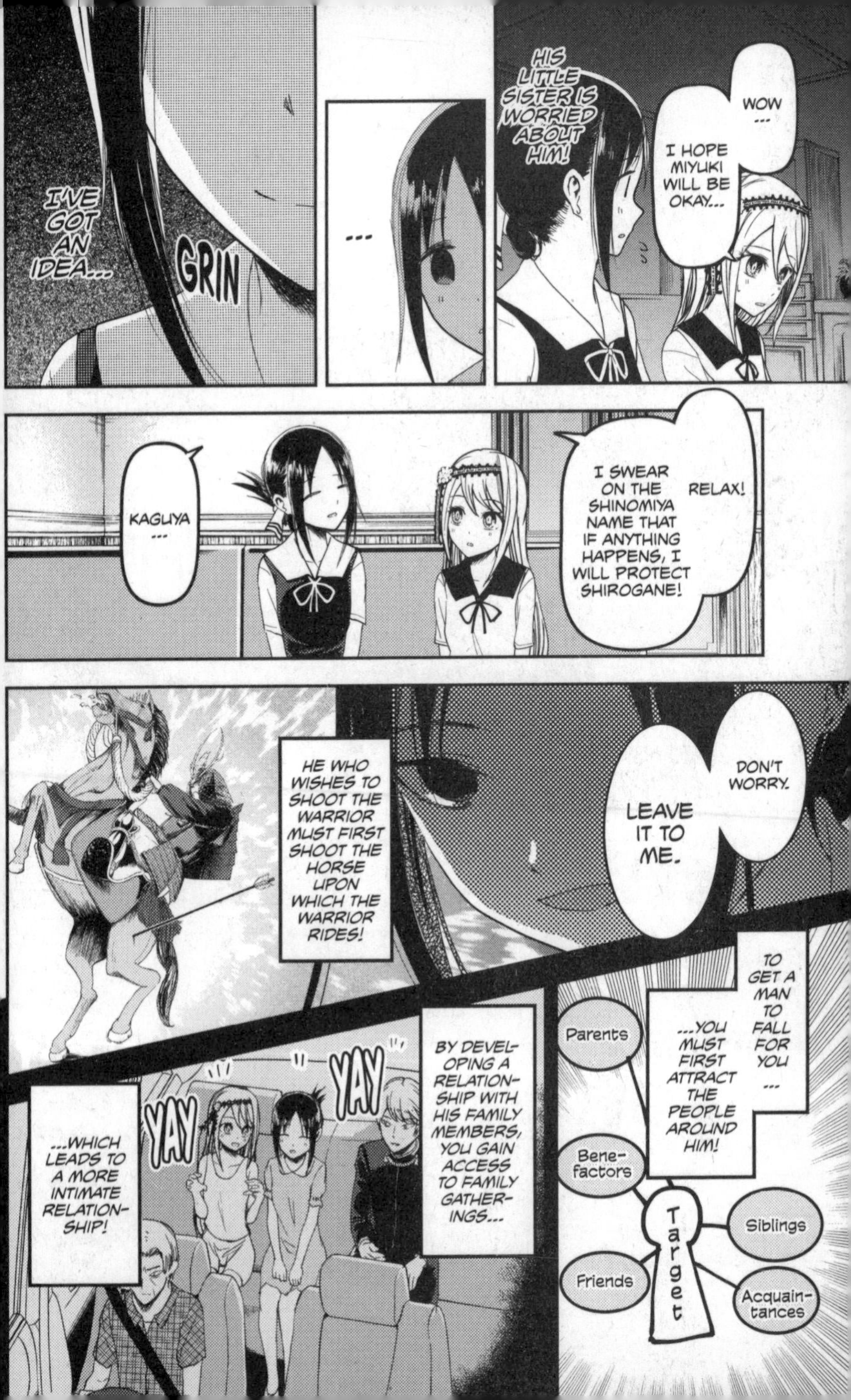
WOW...
I HOPE MIYUKI WILL BE OKAY...
HIS LITTLE SISTER IS WORRIED ABOUT HIM!
...
I'VE GOT AN IDEA...
GRIN
RELAX!
I SWEAR ON THE SHINOMIYA NAME THAT IF ANYTHING HAPPENS, I WILL PROTECT SHIROGANE!
KAGUYA...
DON'T WORRY.
LEAVE IT TO ME.
HE WHO WISHES TO SHOOT THE WARRIOR MUST FIRST SHOOT THE HORSE UPON WHICH THE WARRIOR RIDES!
TO GET A MAN TO FALL FOR YOU...
...YOU MUST FIRST ATTRACT THE PEOPLE AROUND HIM!
Parents
Bene-factors
Target
Siblings
Friends
Acquain-tances
BY DEVEL-OPING A RELATION-SHIP WITH HIS FAMILY MEMBERS, YOU GAIN ACCESS TO FAMILY GATHER-INGS...
YAY
YAY
...WHICH LEADS TO A MORE INTIMATE RELATION-SHIP!

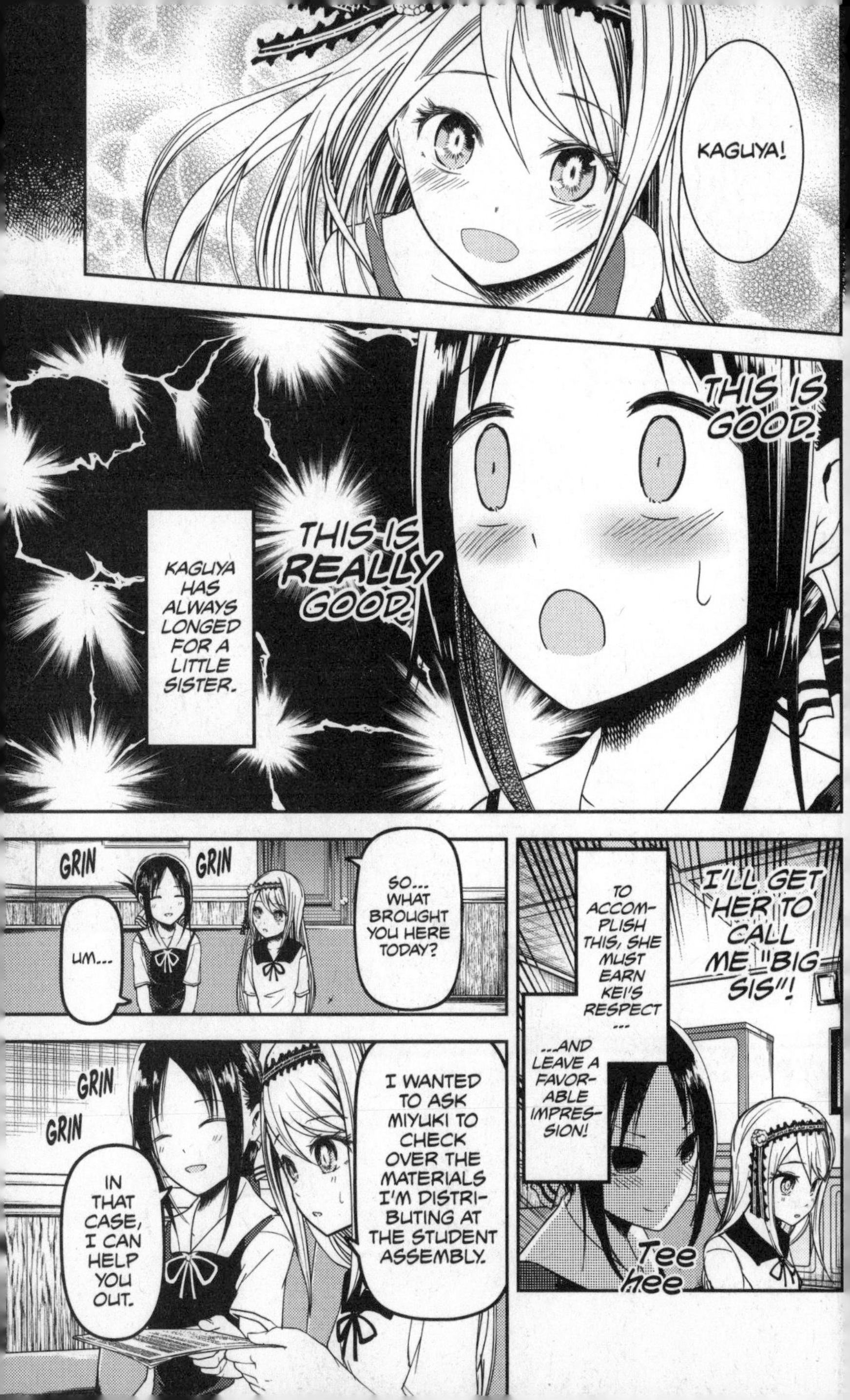
KAGUYA!
THIS IS GOOD.
THIS IS REALLY GOOD.
KAGUYA HAS ALWAYS LONGED FOR A LITTLE SISTER.
I'LL GET HER TO CALL ME "BIG SIS"!
TO ACCOMPLISH THIS, SHE MUST EARN KEI'S RESPECT...
...AND LEAVE A FAVORABLE IMPRESSION!
Tee hee
SO... WHAT BROUGHT YOU HERE TODAY?
GRIN
GRIN
UM...
I WANTED TO ASK MIYUKI TO CHECK OVER THE MATERIALS I'M DISTRIBUTING AT THE STUDENT ASSEMBLY.
GRIN
GRIN
IN THAT CASE, I CAN HELP YOU OUT.

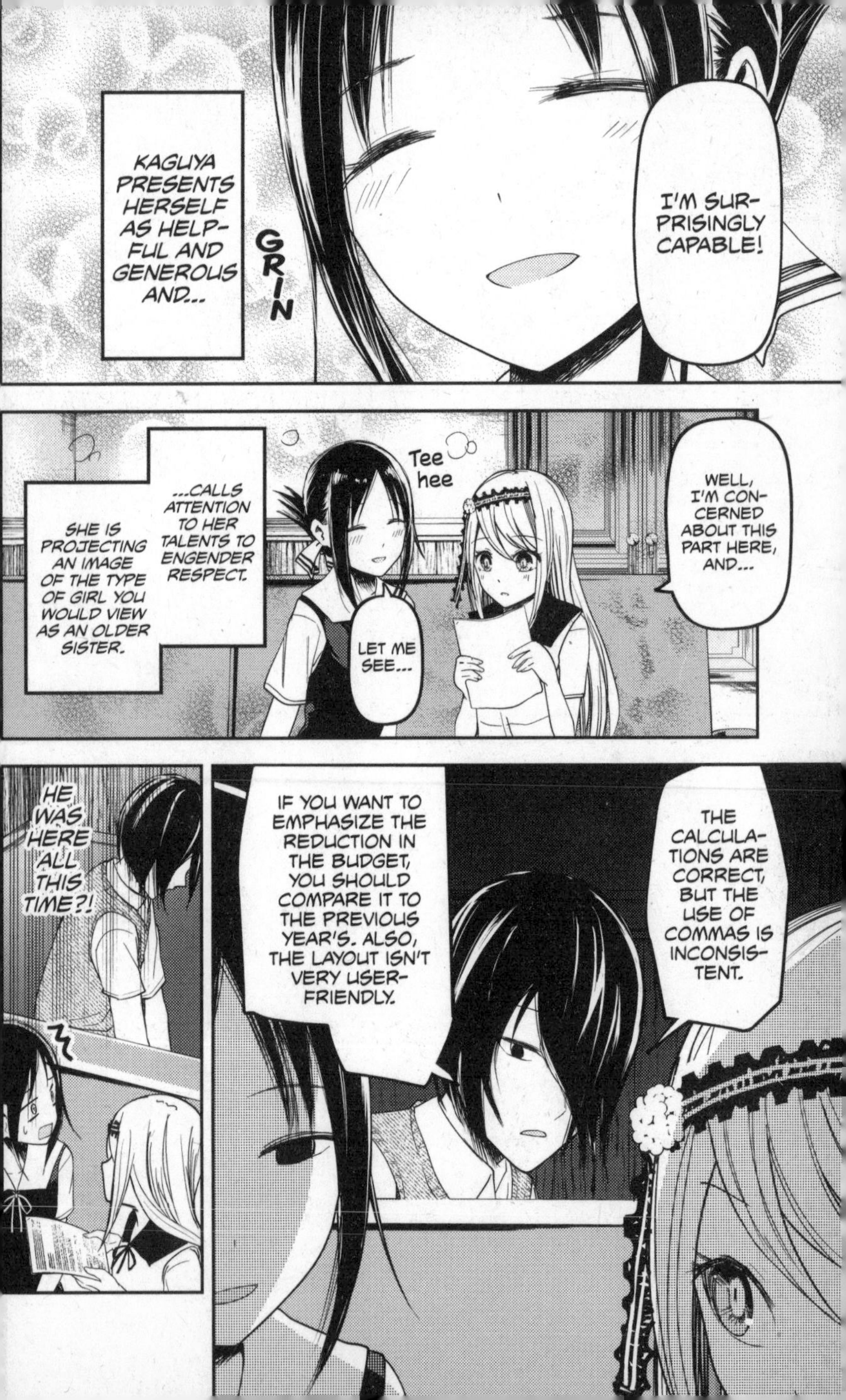
I'M SURPRISINGLY CAPABLE!
GRIN
KAGUYA PRESENTS HERSELF AS HELPFUL AND GENEROUS AND...
WELL, I'M CONCERNED ABOUT THIS PART HERE, AND...
Tee hee
LET ME SEE...
...CALLS ATTENTION TO HER TALENTS TO ENGENDER RESPECT.
SHE IS PROJECTING AN IMAGE OF THE TYPE OF GIRL YOU WOULD VIEW AS AN OLDER SISTER.
THE CALCULATIONS ARE CORRECT, BUT THE USE OF COMMAS IS INCONSISTENT.
IF YOU WANT TO EMPHASIZE THE REDUCTION IN THE BUDGET, YOU SHOULD COMPARE IT TO THE PREVIOUS YEAR'S. ALSO, THE LAYOUT ISN'T VERY USER-FRIENDLY.
HE WAS HERE ALL THIS TIME?!

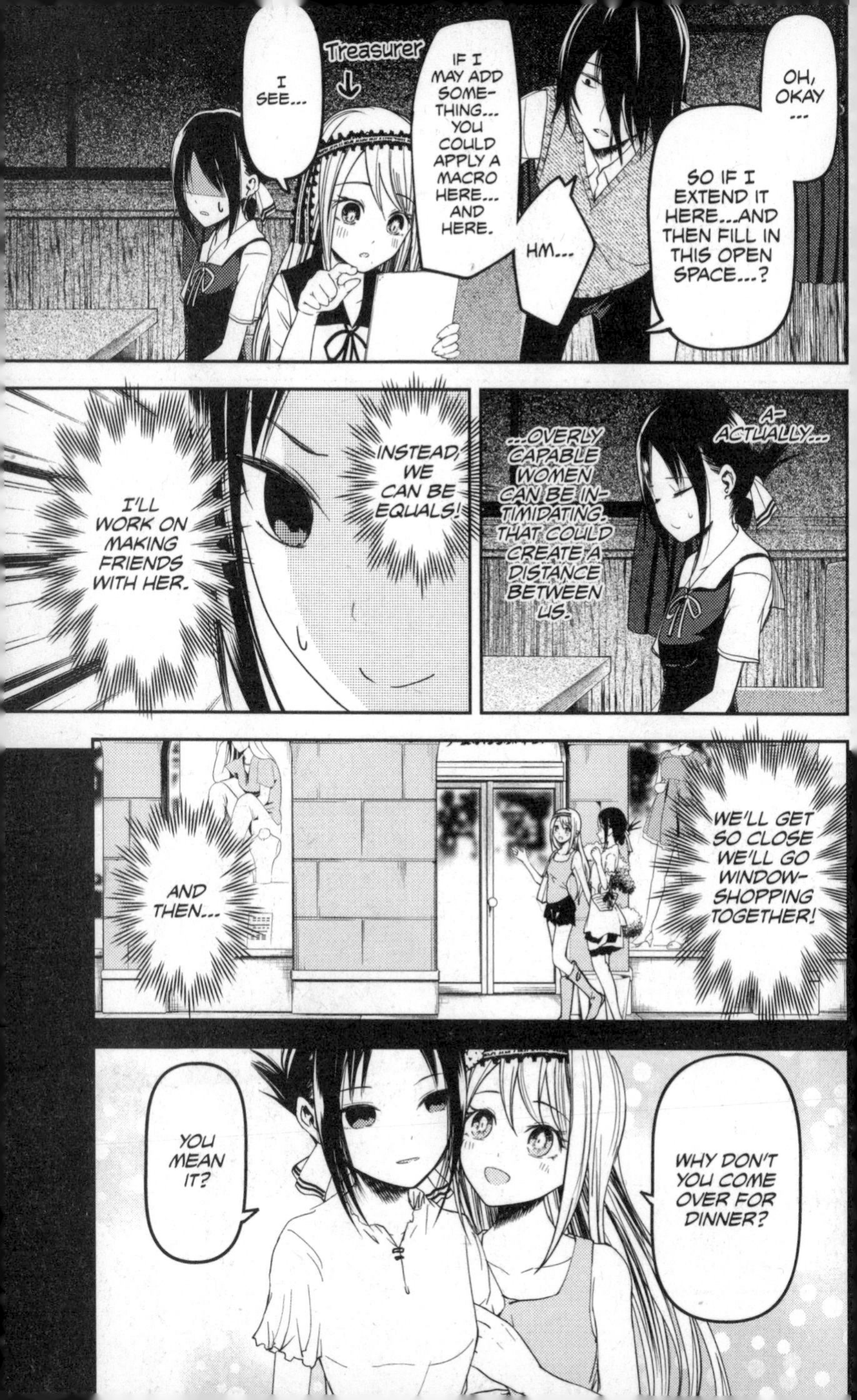
OH, OKAY ...
SO IF I EXTEND IT HERE...AND THEN FILL IN THIS OPEN SPACE...?
HM...
IF I MAY ADD SOMETHING... YOU COULD APPLY A MACRO HERE... AND HERE.
Treasurer
I SEE...
A-ACTUALLY...
...OVERLY CAPABLE WOMEN CAN BE INTIMIDATING. THAT COULD CREATE A DISTANCE BETWEEN US.
INSTEAD, WE CAN BE EQUALS!
I'LL WORK ON MAKING FRIENDS WITH HER.
WE'LL GET SO CLOSE WE'LL GO WINDOW-SHOPPING TOGETHER!
AND THEN...
WHY DON'T YOU COME OVER FOR DINNER?
YOU MEAN IT?

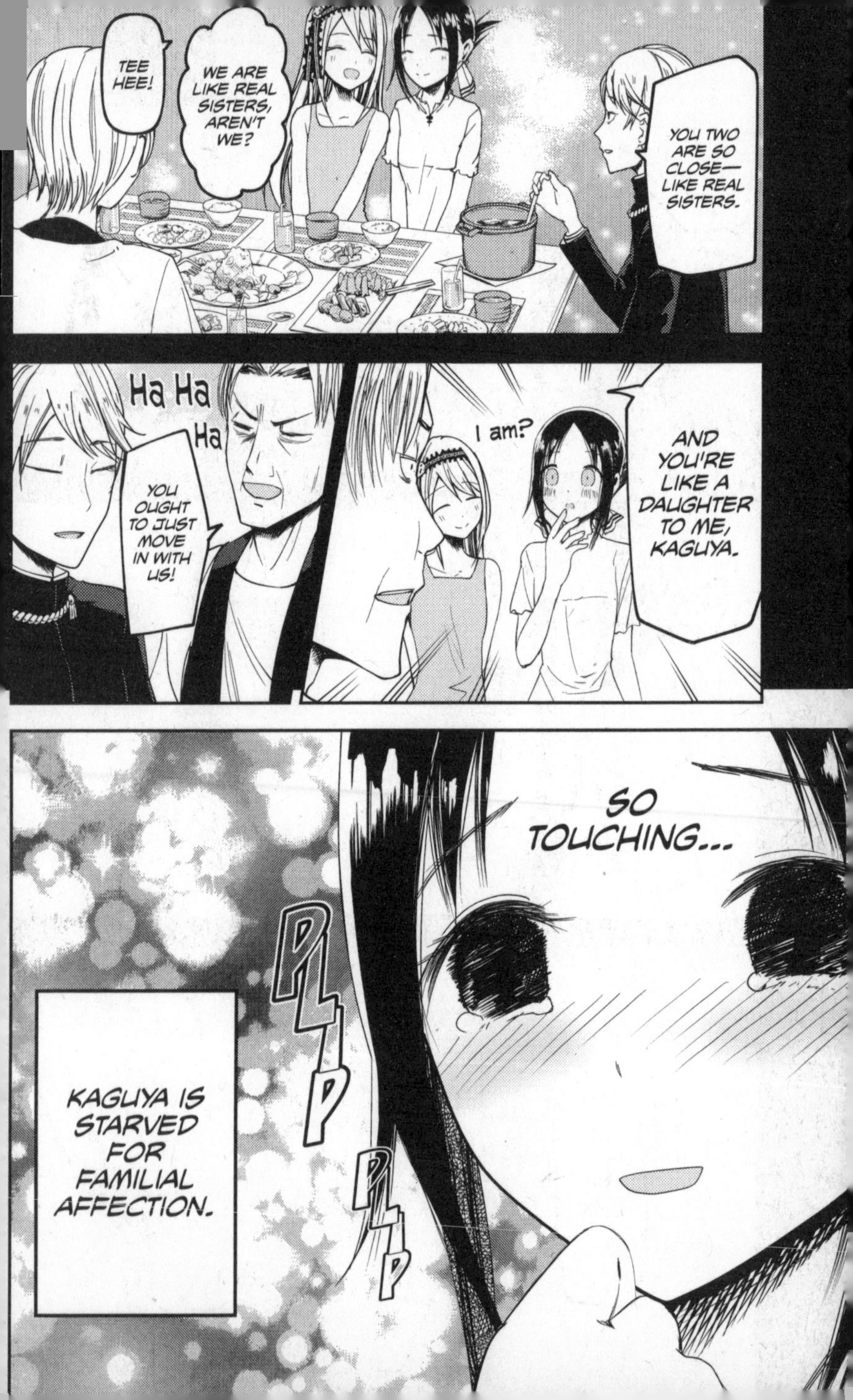
YOU TWO ARE SO CLOSE— LIKE REAL SISTERS.
WE ARE LIKE REAL SISTERS, AREN'T WE?
TEE HEE!
AND YOU'RE LIKE A DAUGHTER TO ME, KAGUYA.
I am?
Ha Ha Ha
YOU OUGHT TO JUST MOVE IN WITH US!
SO TOUCHING...
PLIP
PLIP
KAGUYA IS STARVED FOR FAMILIAL AFFECTION.

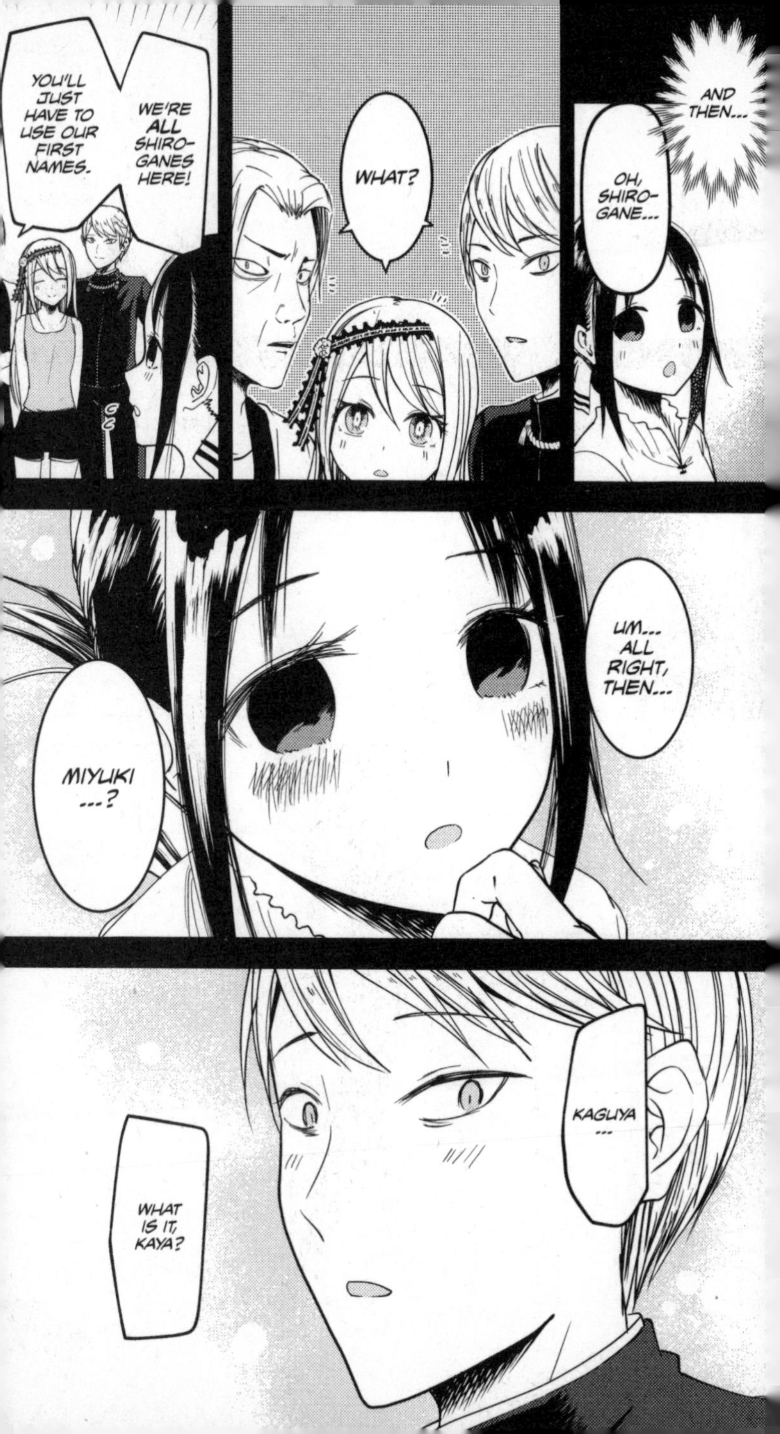
AND THEN...
OH, SHIRO-GANE...
WHAT?
WE'RE ALL SHIRO-GANES HERE!
YOU'LL JUST HAVE TO USE OUR FIRST NAMES.
UM... ALL RIGHT, THEN...
MIYUKI...?
KAGUYA...
WHAT IS IT, KAYA?

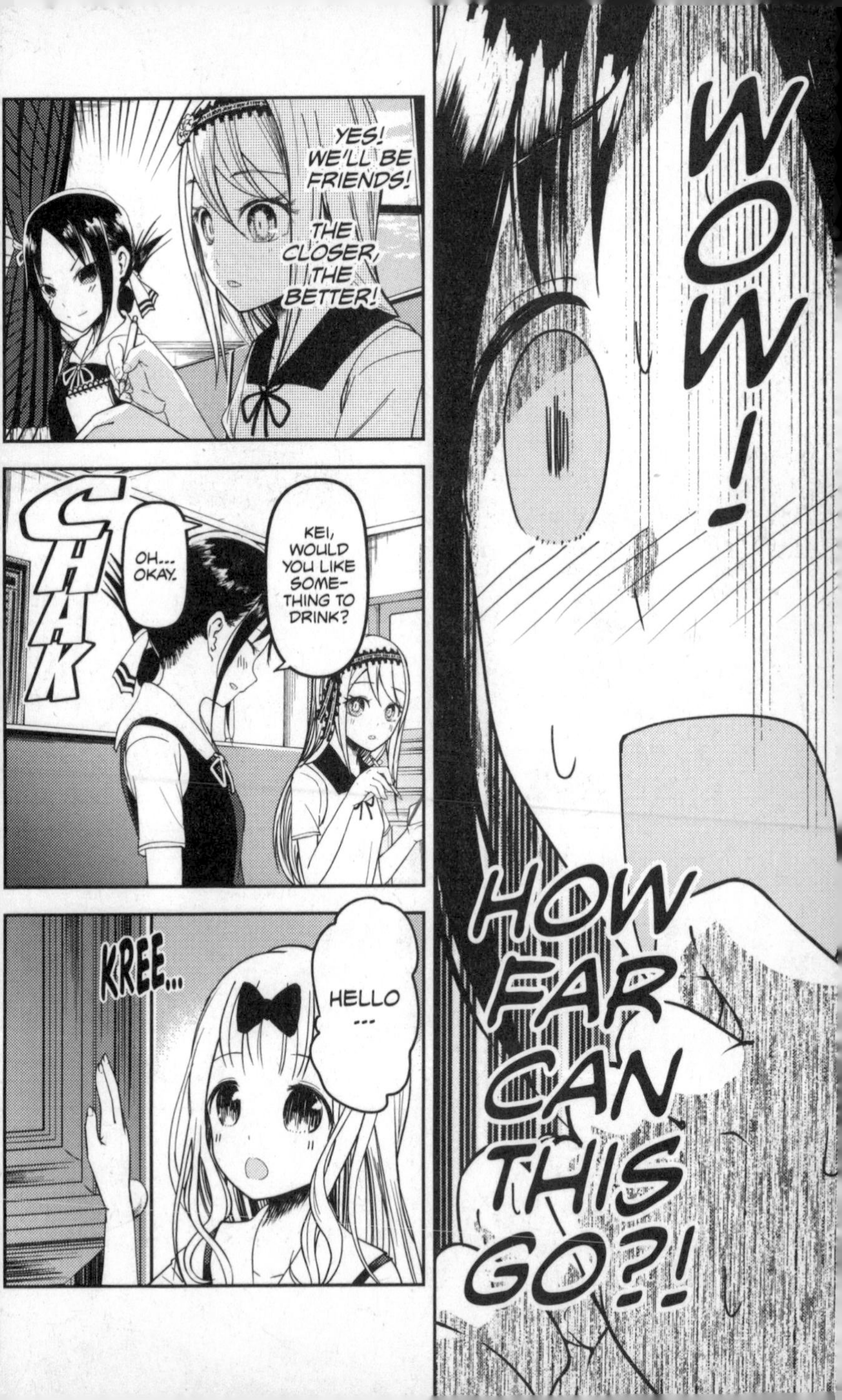
WOW!
HOW FAR CAN THIS GO?!
YES! WE'LL BE FRIENDS!
THE CLOSER, THE BETTER!
KEI, WOULD YOU LIKE SOME-THING TO DRINK?
OH... OKAY.
CHAK
HELLO ...
KREE...

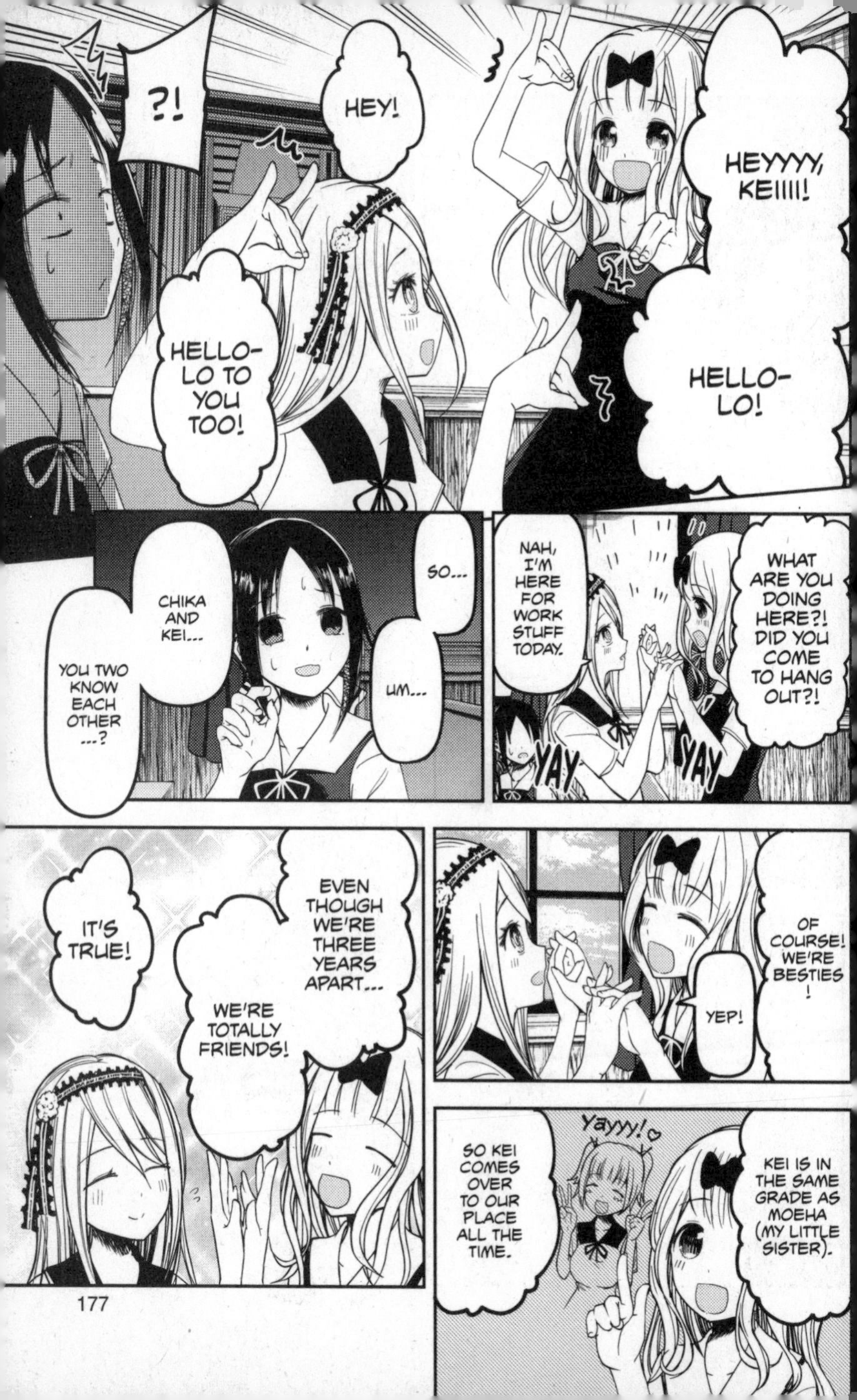
HEYYYY, KEI!!!!!
HEY!
?!
HELLO-LO!
HELLO-LO TO YOU TOO!
WHAT ARE YOU DOING HERE?! DID YOU COME TO HANG OUT?!
NAH, I'M HERE FOR WORK STUFF TODAY.
YAY
YAY
SO...
UM...
CHIKA AND KEI...
YOU TWO KNOW EACH OTHER ...?
OF COURSE! WE'RE BESTIES!
YEP!
KEI IS IN THE SAME GRADE AS MOEHA (MY LITTLE SISTER).
Yayyy!♡
SO KEI COMES OVER TO OUR PLACE ALL THE TIME.
EVEN THOUGH WE'RE THREE YEARS APART...
WE'RE TOTALLY FRIENDS!
IT'S TRUE!

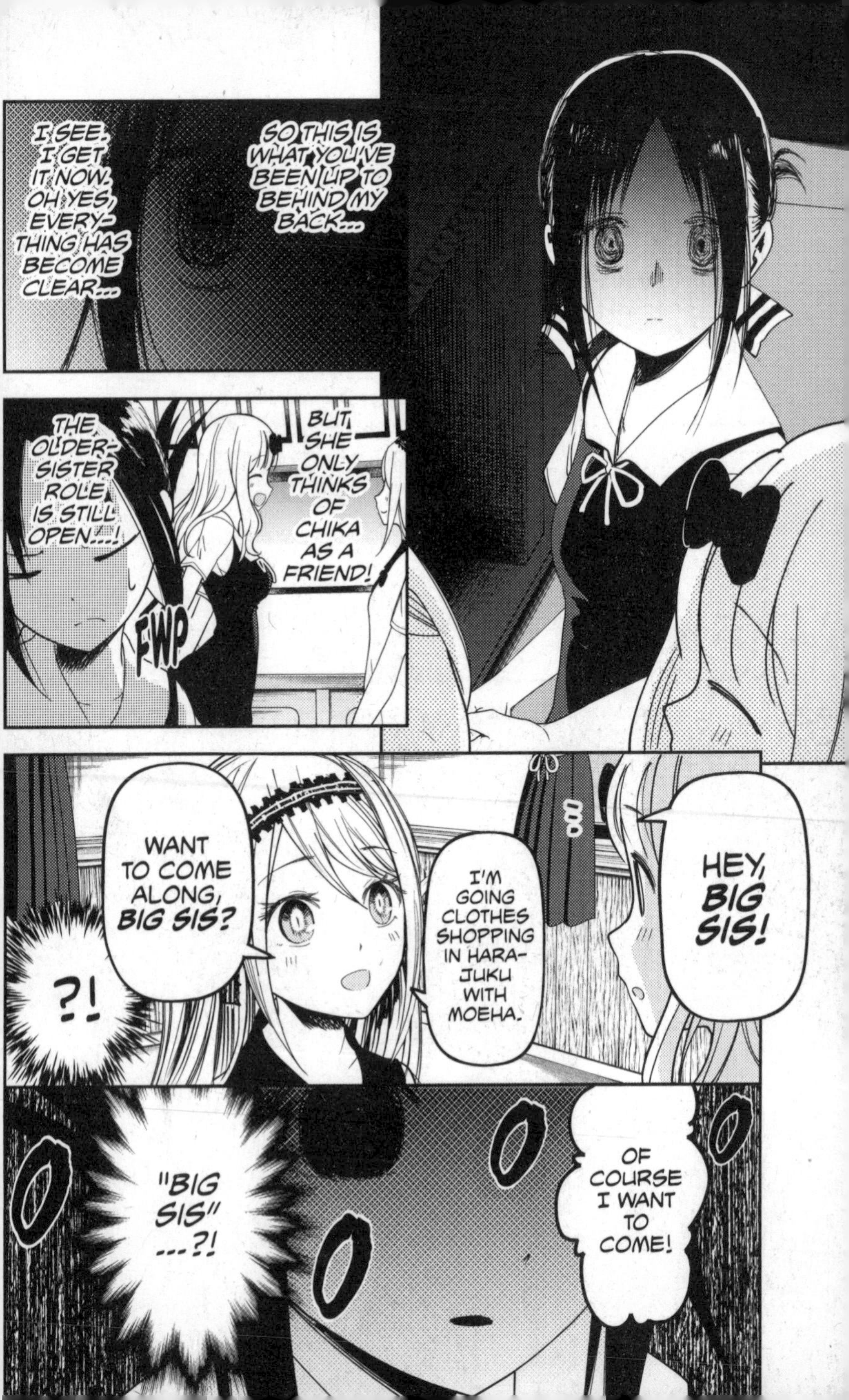
SO THIS IS WHAT YOU'VE BEEN UP TO BEHIND MY BACK...
I SEE. I GET IT NOW. OH YES, EVERYTHING HAS BECOME CLEAR...
BUT SHE ONLY THINKS OF CHIKA AS A FRIEND!
THE OLDER-SISTER ROLE IS STILL OPEN...!
FWP
HEY, BIG SIS!
I'M GOING CLOTHES SHOPPING IN HARAJUKU WITH MOEHA.
WANT TO COME ALONG, BIG SIS?
?!
OF COURSE I WANT TO COME!
"BIG SIS"...?!

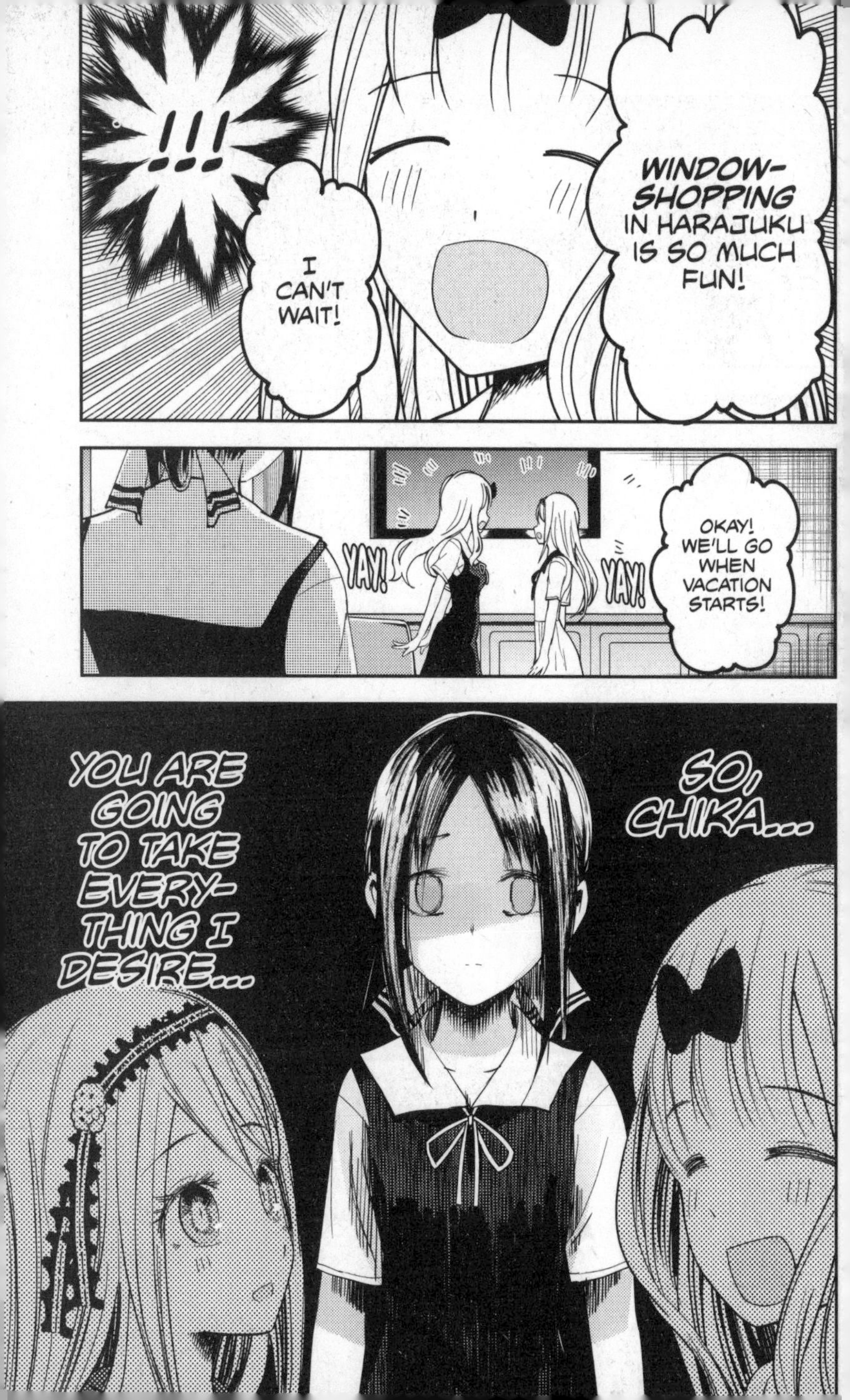
WINDOW-SHOPPING IN HARAJUKU IS SO MUCH FUN!
I CAN'T WAIT!
!!!
OKAY! WE'LL GO WHEN VACATION STARTS!
YAY!
YAY!
SO, CHIKA...
YOU ARE GOING TO TAKE EVERY-THING I DESIRE...

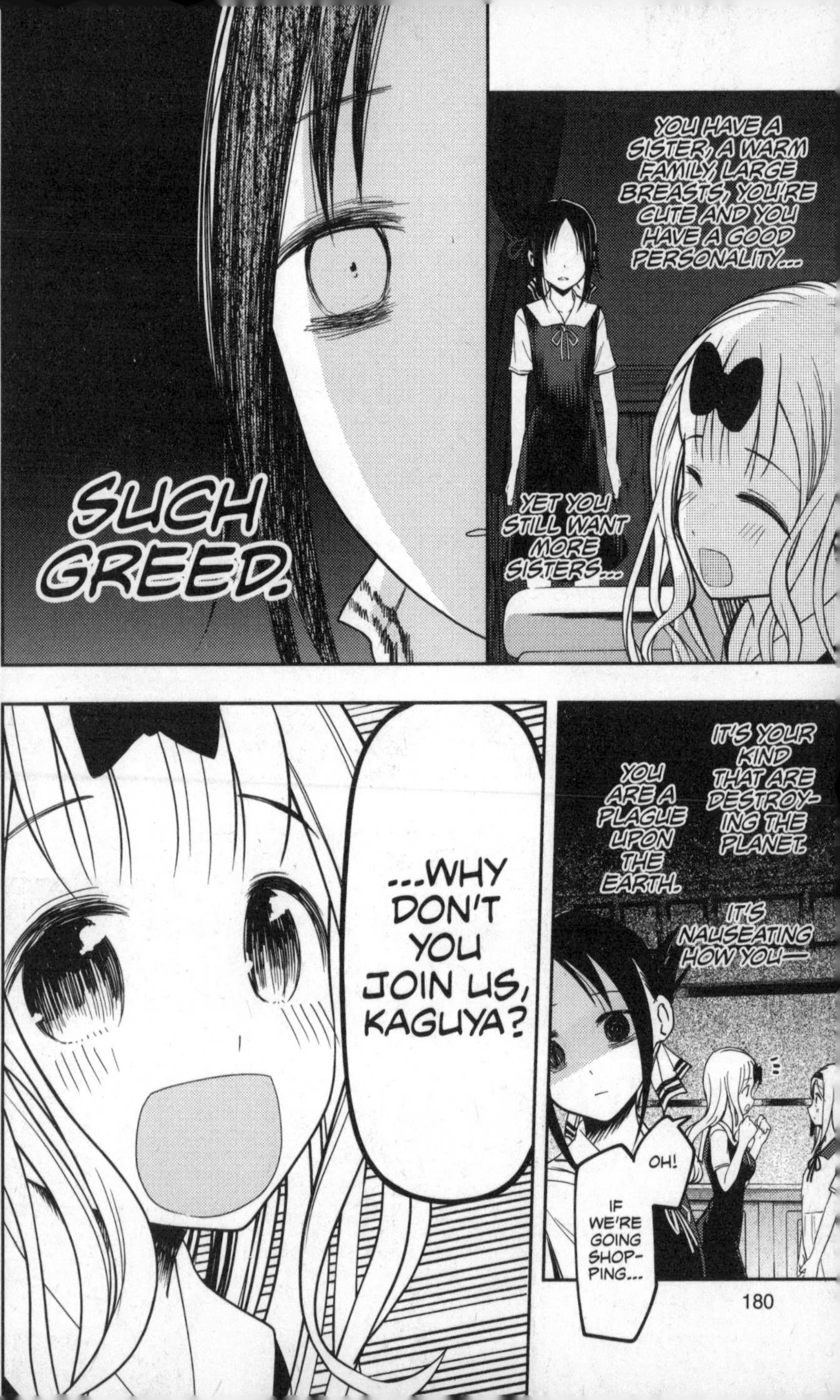
YOU HAVE A SISTER, A WARM FAMILY, LARGE BREASTS, YOU'RE CUTE AND YOU HAVE A GOOD PERSONALITY...
YET YOU STILL WANT MORE SISTERS...
SUCH GREED.
IT'S YOUR KIND THAT ARE DESTROY-ING THE PLANET.
YOU ARE A PLAGUE UPON THE EARTH.
IT'S NAUSEATING HOW YOU—
OH!
IF WE'RE GOING SHOP-PING...
...WHY DON'T YOU JOIN US, KAGUYA?

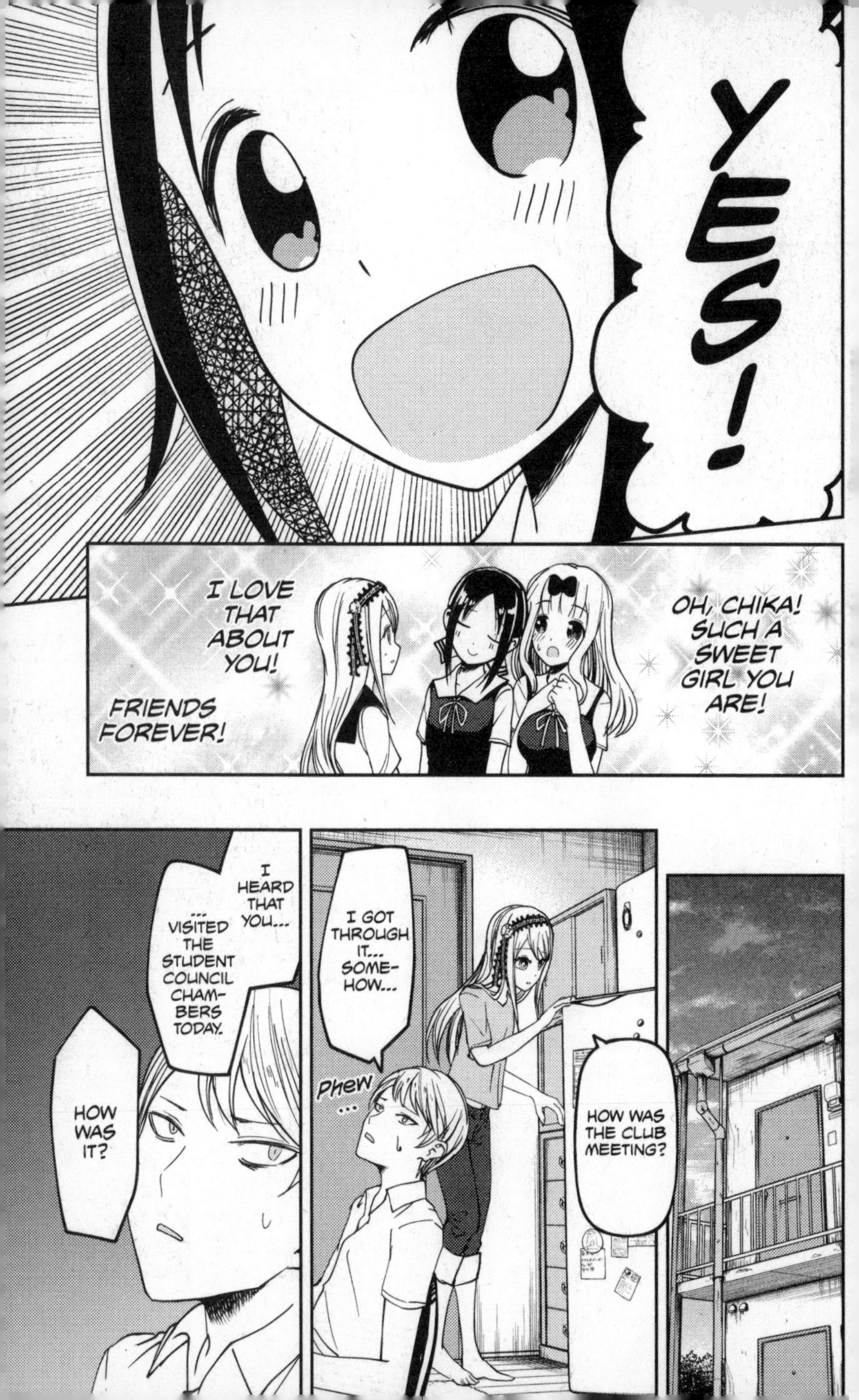
YES!
OH, CHIKA! SUCH A SWEET GIRL YOU ARE!
I LOVE THAT ABOUT YOU!
FRIENDS FOREVER!
HOW WAS THE CLUB MEETING?
I GOT THROUGH IT... SOMEHOW...
Phew...
I HEARD THAT YOU...
...VISITED THE STUDENT COUNCIL CHAMBERS TODAY.
HOW WAS IT?

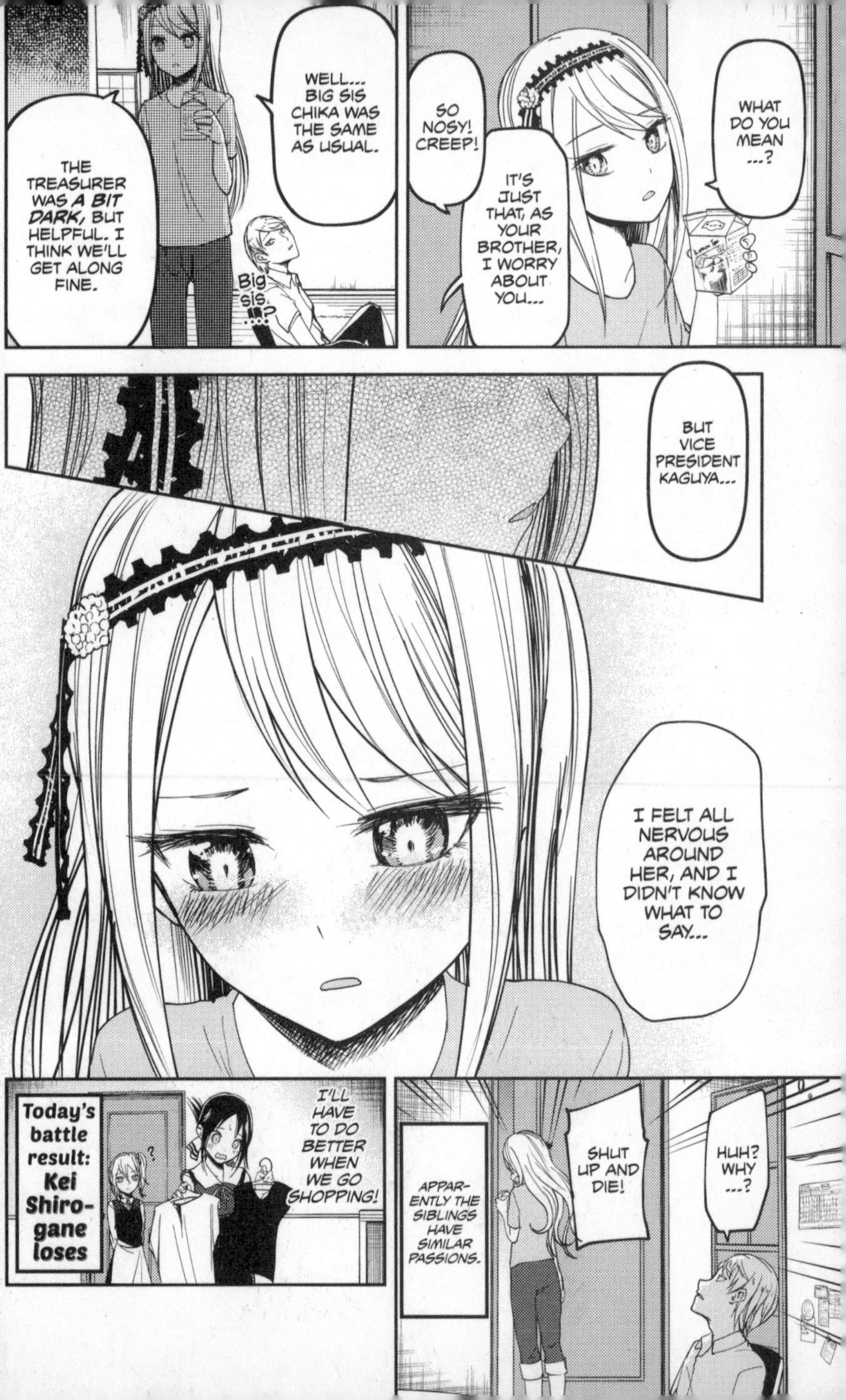
WHAT DO YOU MEAN ...?
IT'S JUST THAT, AS YOUR BROTHER, I WORRY ABOUT YOU...
SO NOSY! CREEP!
WELL... BIG SIS CHIKA WAS THE SAME AS USUAL.
THE TREASURER WAS A BIT DARK, BUT HELPFUL. I THINK WE'LL GET ALONG FINE.
Big sis...?
BUT VICE PRESIDENT KAGUYA...
I FELT ALL NERVOUS AROUND HER, AND I DIDN'T KNOW WHAT TO SAY...
HUH? WHY ...?
SHUT UP AND DIE!
APPARENTLY THE SIBLINGS HAVE SIMILAR PASSIONS.
I'LL HAVE TO DO BETTER WHEN WE GO SHOPPING!
Today's battle result: Kei Shirogane loses

Toyomi, oldest

Chika, middle

Moeha, youngest

KAGUYA-SAMA
LOVE IS WAR

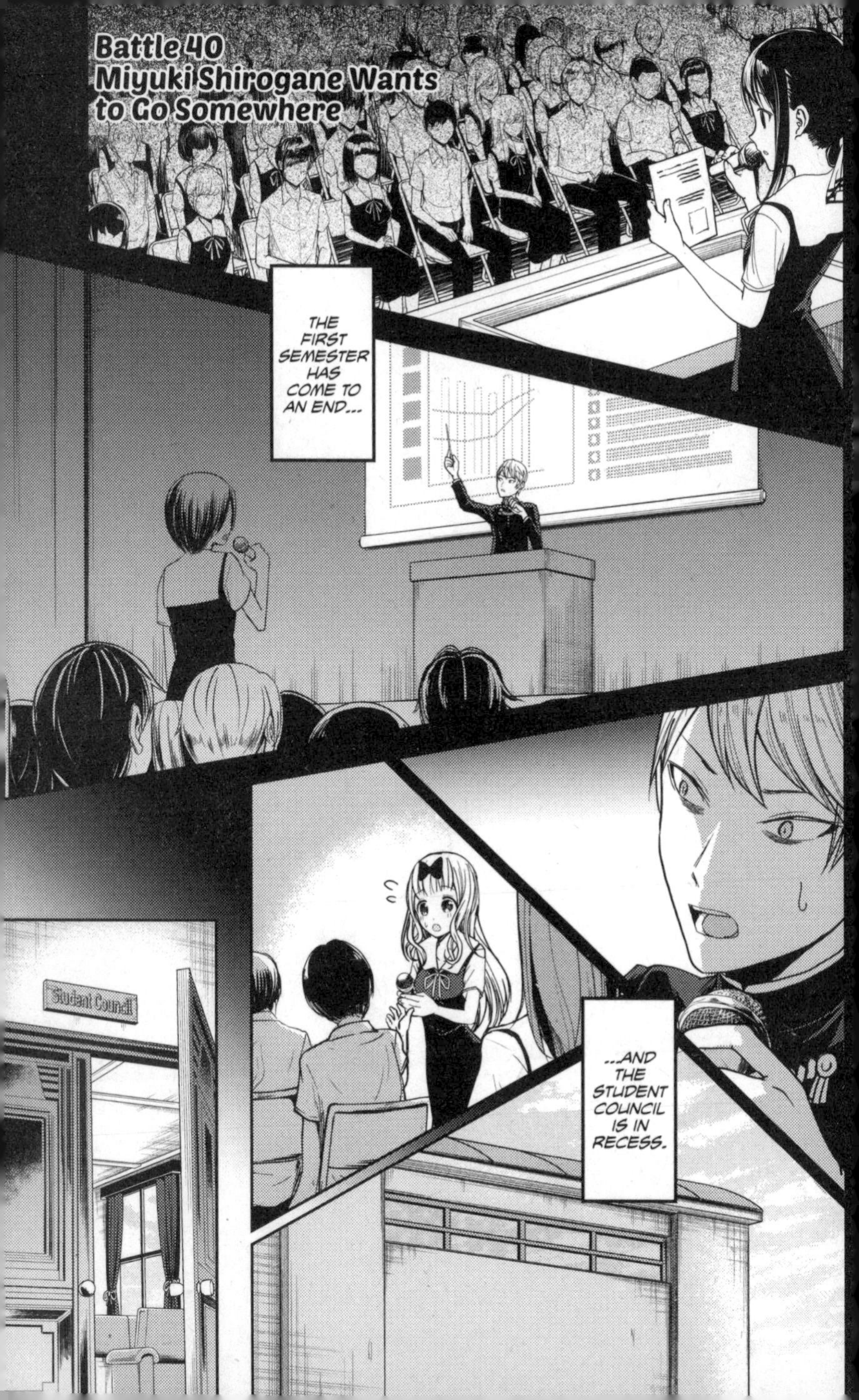
Battle 40
Miyuki Shirogane Wants to Go Somewhere
THE FIRST SEMESTER HAS COME TO AN END...
...AND THE STUDENT COUNCIL IS IN RECESS.
Student Council

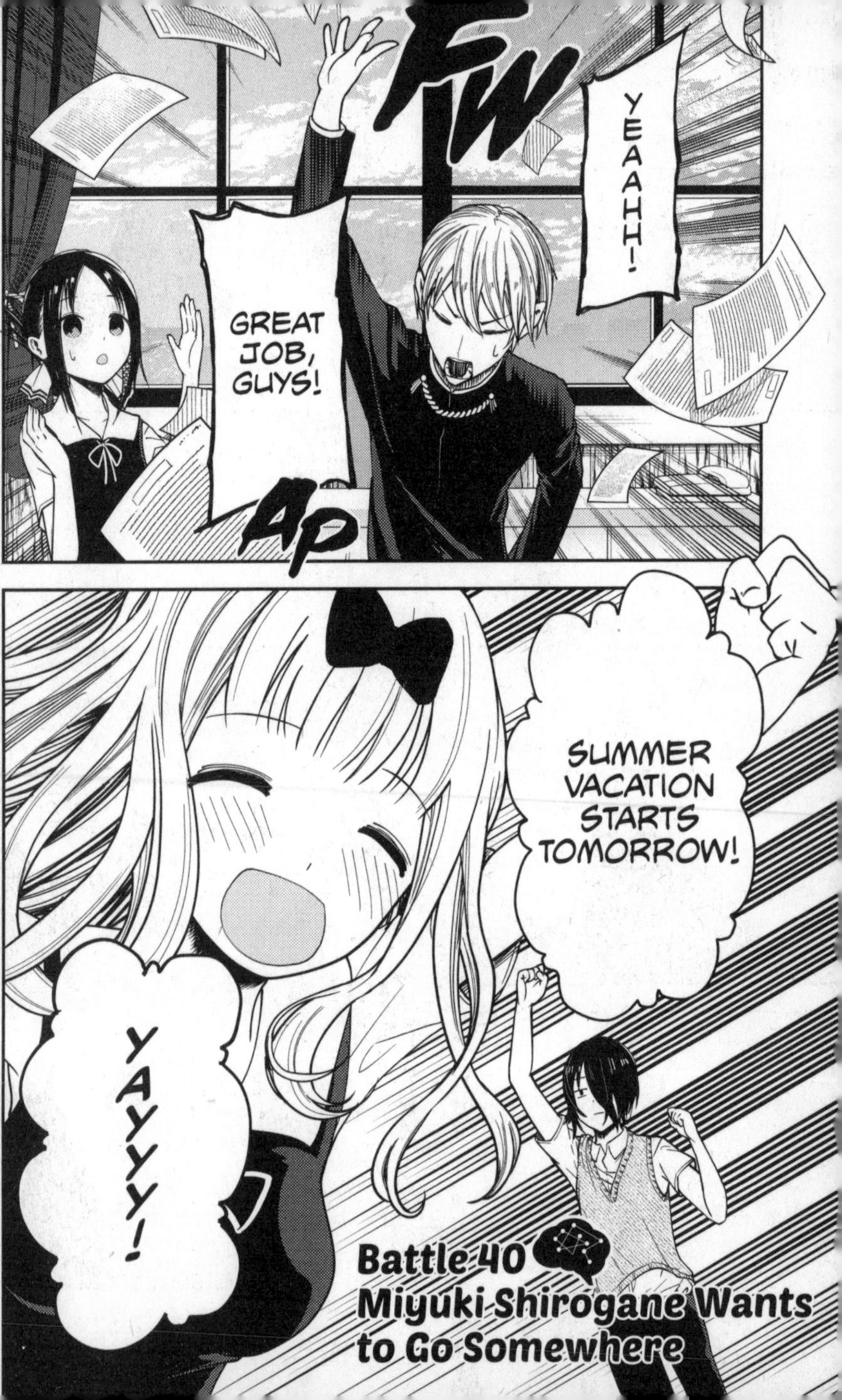
YEAAHH!
FW
GREAT JOB, GUYS!
AP
SUMMER VACATION STARTS TOMORROW!
YAYYY!

Battle 40 Miyuki Shirogane Wants to Go Somewhere

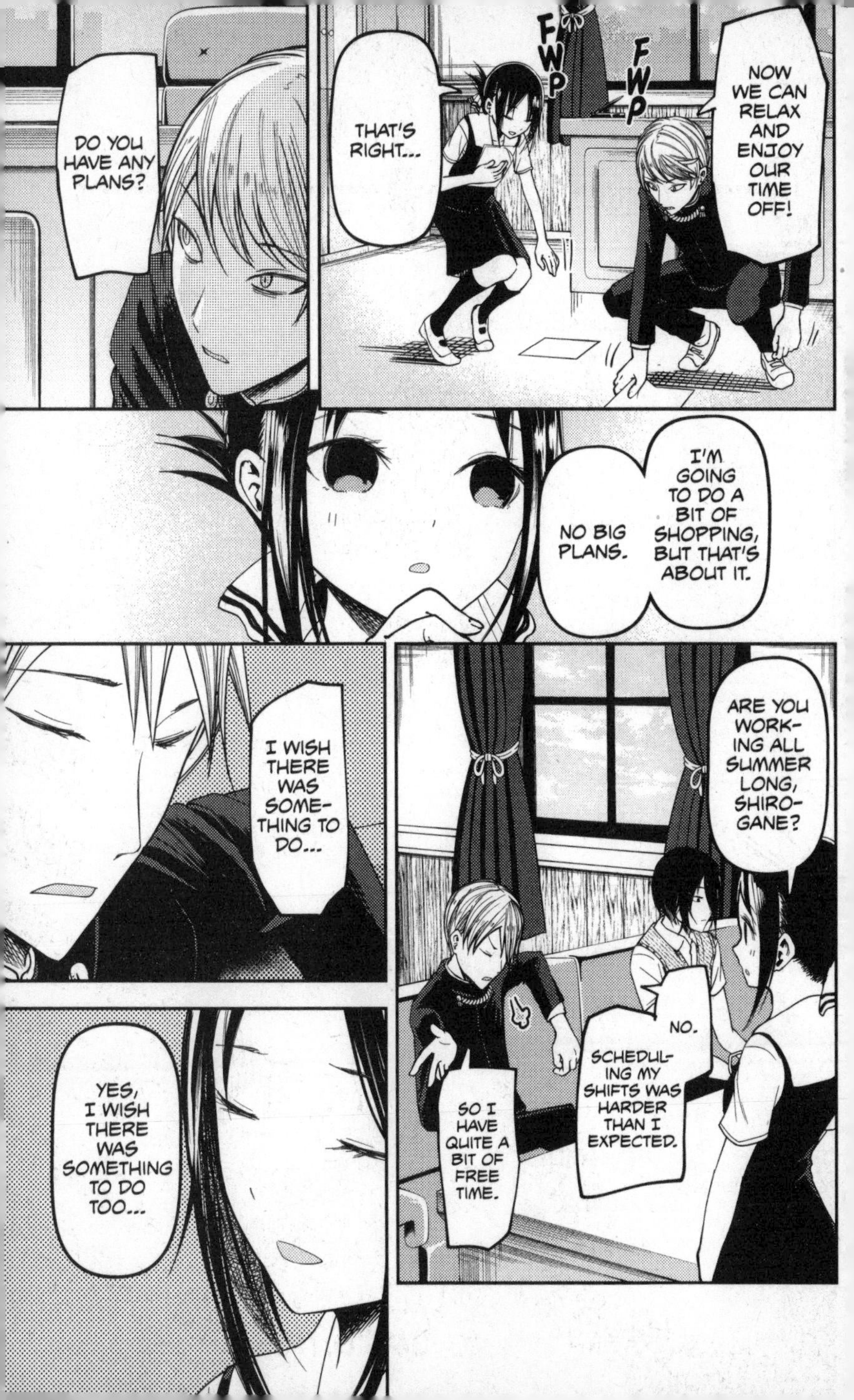
NOW WE CAN RELAX AND ENJOY OUR TIME OFF!
FWP
FWP
THAT'S RIGHT...
DO YOU HAVE ANY PLANS?
I'M GOING TO DO A BIT OF SHOPPING, BUT THAT'S ABOUT IT.
NO BIG PLANS.
ARE YOU WORKING ALL SUMMER LONG, SHIROGANE?
NO.
SCHEDULING MY SHIFTS WAS HARDER THAN I EXPECTED.
SO I HAVE QUITE A BIT OF FREE TIME.
I WISH THERE WAS SOMETHING TO DO...
YES, I WISH THERE WAS SOMETHING TO DO TOO...

SUMMER PLANS!

THAT'S THE OPPOSITE OF WHAT YOU JUST SAID!

LET'S GO TO THE MOUNTAINS!

THE BEACH WILL BE CROWDED, WE'LL GET SWEATY AND THERE'LL BE SHARKS.

ALTHOUGH DISCUSSED AT LENGTH IN THE STUDENT COUNCIL CHAMBERS...

THIS SUMMER, LET'S GO ON A STUDENT COUNCIL TRIP TOGETHER!

I VOTE FOR THE OCEAN!

NOW YOU TOO?!

LET'S GO TO THE OCEAN!

THE MOUNTAINS WILL BE RAINY AND FULL OF BUGS!

...THE TRAVEL DEBATE WAS LEFT UNRESOLVED!

From volume 1, chapter 7

MANY EVENTS TAKE PLACE OVER SUMMER VACATION...

August

Monday	Tuesday	Wednesday	Thursday
1	2	3	4
8	9	10	

ALL IS ABOUT TO BE DETERMINED!

WILL THEIR PLAN TO GO ON A COUNCIL TRIP EVAPORATE OR COME TO FRUITION?

Hm...

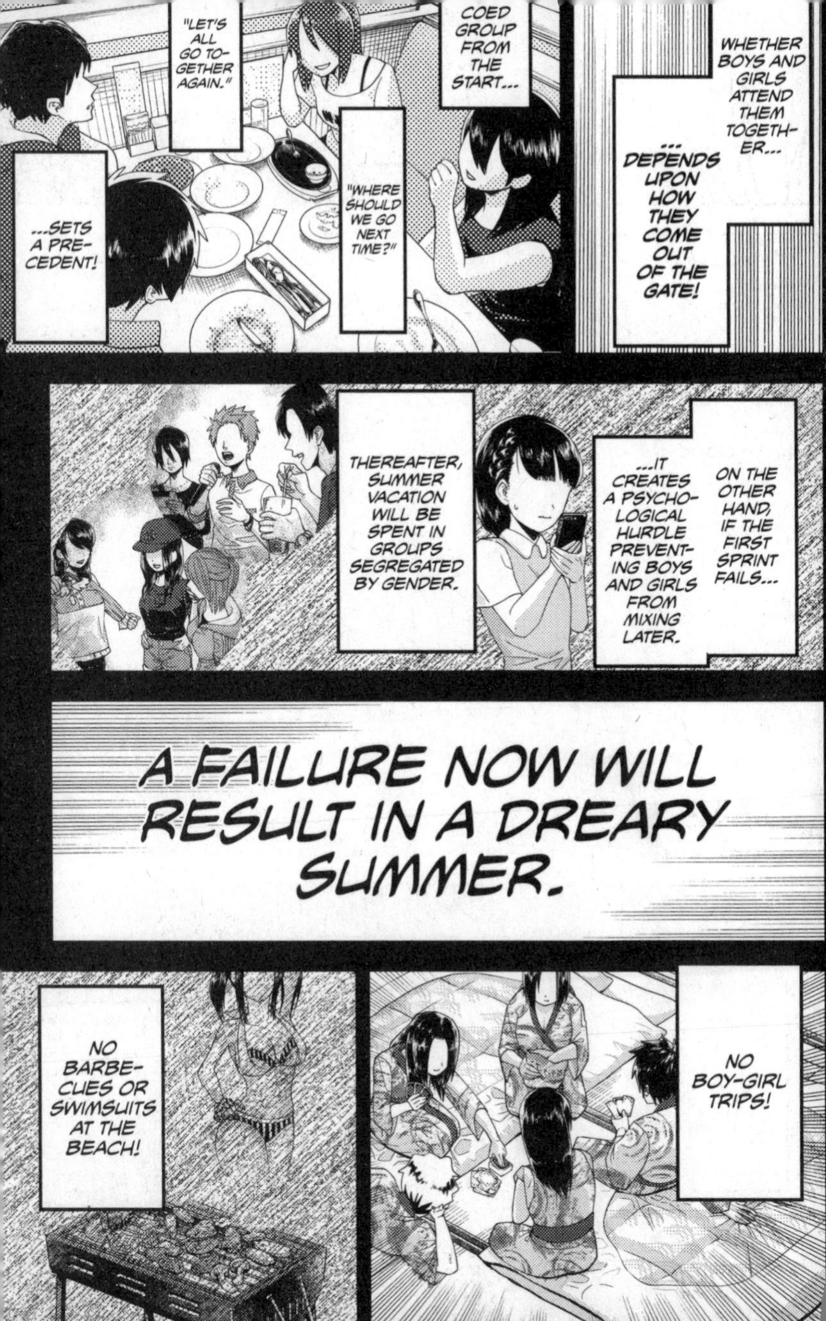
WHETHER BOYS AND GIRLS ATTEND THEM TOGETHER...
...DEPENDS UPON HOW THEY COME OUT OF THE GATE!
COED GROUP FROM THE START...
"LET'S ALL GO TOGETHER AGAIN."
"WHERE SHOULD WE GO NEXT TIME?"
...SETS A PRECEDENT!
ON THE OTHER HAND, IF THE FIRST SPRINT FAILS...
...IT CREATES A PSYCHOLOGICAL HURDLE PREVENTING BOYS AND GIRLS FROM MIXING LATER.
THEREAFTER, SUMMER VACATION WILL BE SPENT IN GROUPS SEGREGATED BY GENDER.
A FAILURE NOW WILL RESULT IN A DREARY SUMMER.
NO BOY-GIRL TRIPS!
NO BARBECUES OR SWIMSUITS AT THE BEACH!

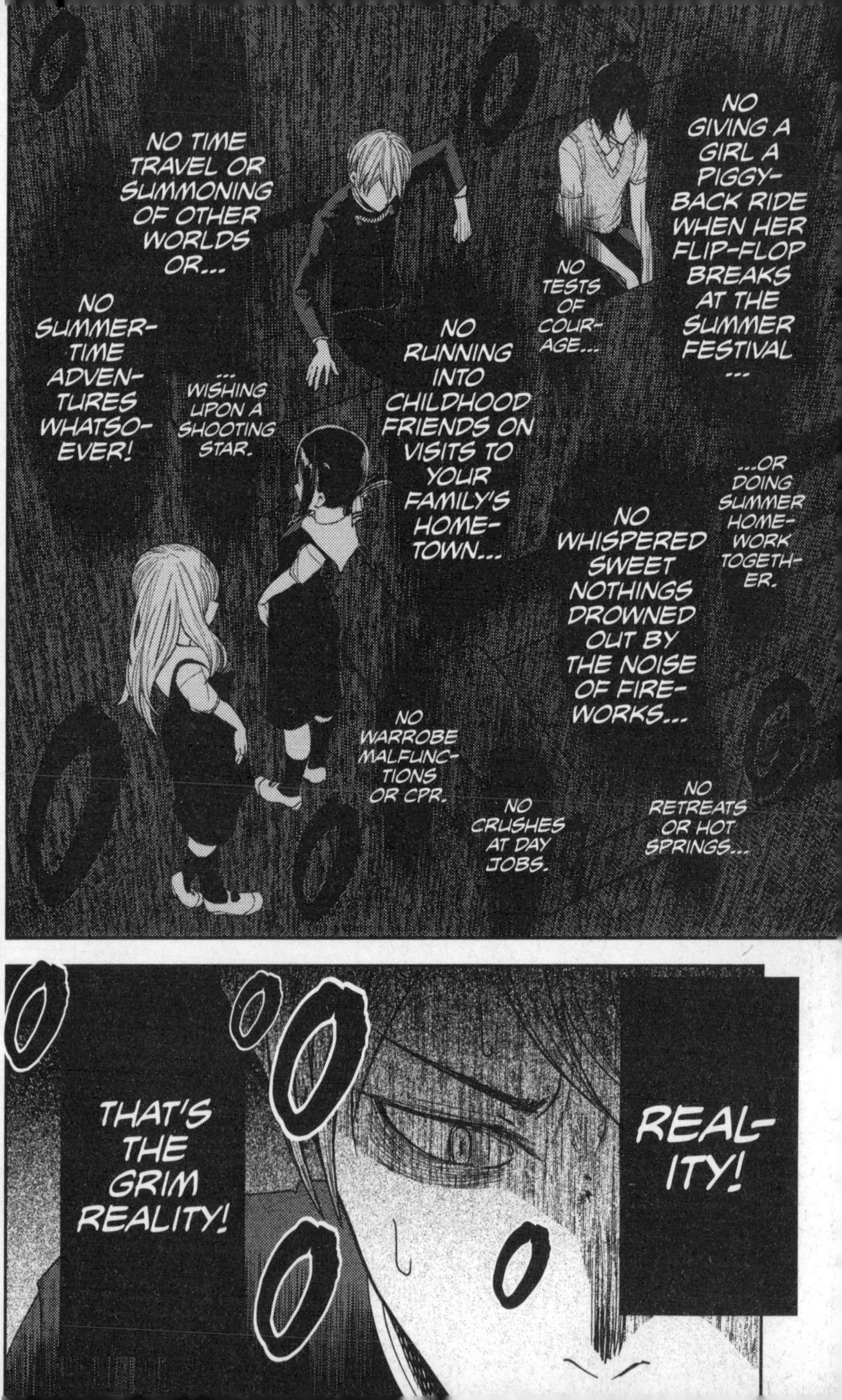

NO GIVING A GIRL A PIGGY-BACK RIDE WHEN HER FLIP-FLOP BREAKS AT THE SUMMER FESTIVAL ---
NO TESTS OF COURAGE...
NO TIME TRAVEL OR SUMMONING OF OTHER WORLDS OR...
NO RUNNING INTO CHILDHOOD FRIENDS ON VISITS TO YOUR FAMILY'S HOMETOWN...
...WISHING UPON A SHOOTING STAR.
NO SUMMERTIME ADVENTURES WHATSOEVER!
...OR DOING SUMMER HOMEWORK TOGETHER.
NO WHISPERED SWEET NOTHINGS DROWNED OUT BY THE NOISE OF FIREWORKS...
NO WARROBE MALFUNCTIONS OR CPR.
NO RETREATS OR HOT SPRINGS...
NO CRUSHES AT DAY JOBS.
REALITY!
THAT'S THE GRIM REALITY!

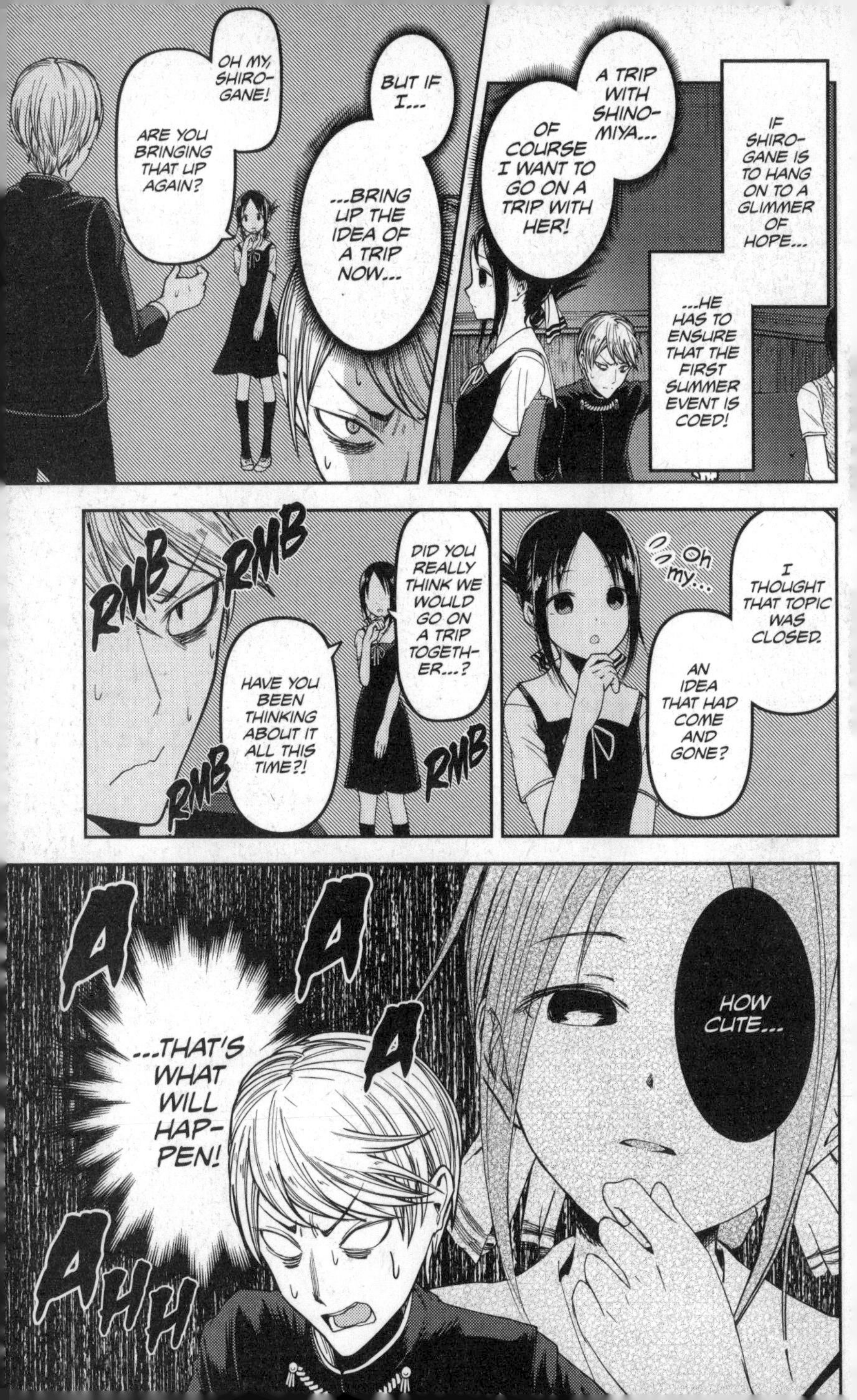
IF SHIROGANE IS TO HANG ON TO A GLIMMER OF HOPE...
...HE HAS TO ENSURE THAT THE FIRST SUMMER EVENT IS COED!
A TRIP WITH SHINOMIYA...
OF COURSE I WANT TO GO ON A TRIP WITH HER!
BUT IF I...
...BRING UP THE IDEA OF A TRIP NOW...
OH MY, SHIROGANE!
ARE YOU BRINGING THAT UP AGAIN?
Oh my...
I THOUGHT THAT TOPIC WAS CLOSED.
AN IDEA THAT HAD COME AND GONE?
DID YOU REALLY THINK WE WOULD GO ON A TRIP TOGETHER...?
HAVE YOU BEEN THINKING ABOUT IT ALL THIS TIME?!
RMB RMB RMB RMB
HOW CUTE...
...THAT'S WHAT WILL HAPPEN!
A A A AHH

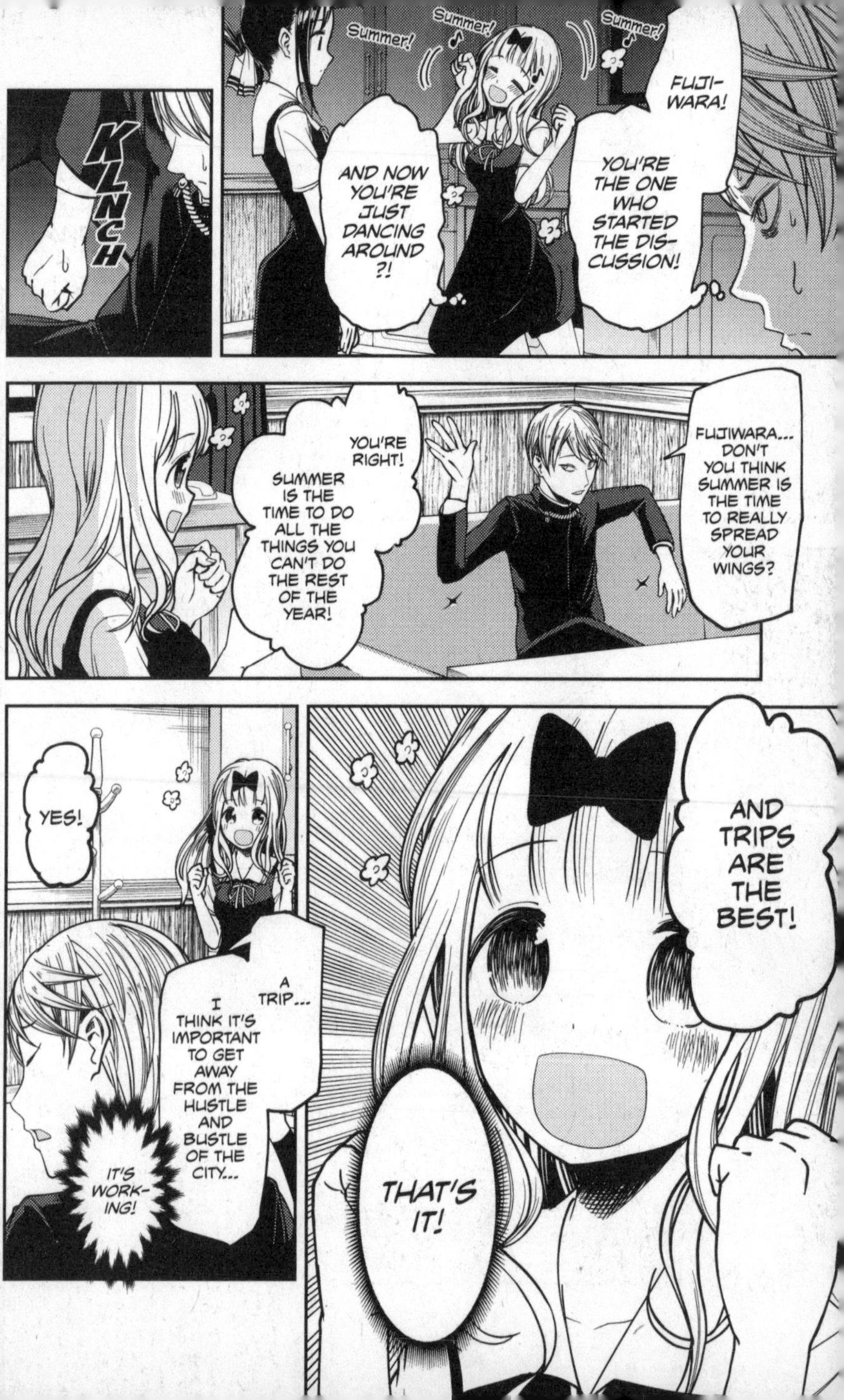
Summer!
Summer!
Summer!
FUJI-WARA!
YOU'RE THE ONE WHO STARTED THE DIS-CUSSION!
AND NOW YOU'RE JUST DANCING AROUND?!
KLNCH
FUJIWARA... DON'T YOU THINK SUMMER IS THE TIME TO REALLY SPREAD YOUR WINGS?
YOU'RE RIGHT!
SUMMER IS THE TIME TO DO ALL THE THINGS YOU CAN'T DO THE REST OF THE YEAR!
AND TRIPS ARE THE BEST!
THAT'S IT!
YES!
A TRIP...
I THINK IT'S IMPORTANT TO GET AWAY FROM THE HUSTLE AND BUSTLE OF THE CITY...
IT'S WORKING!

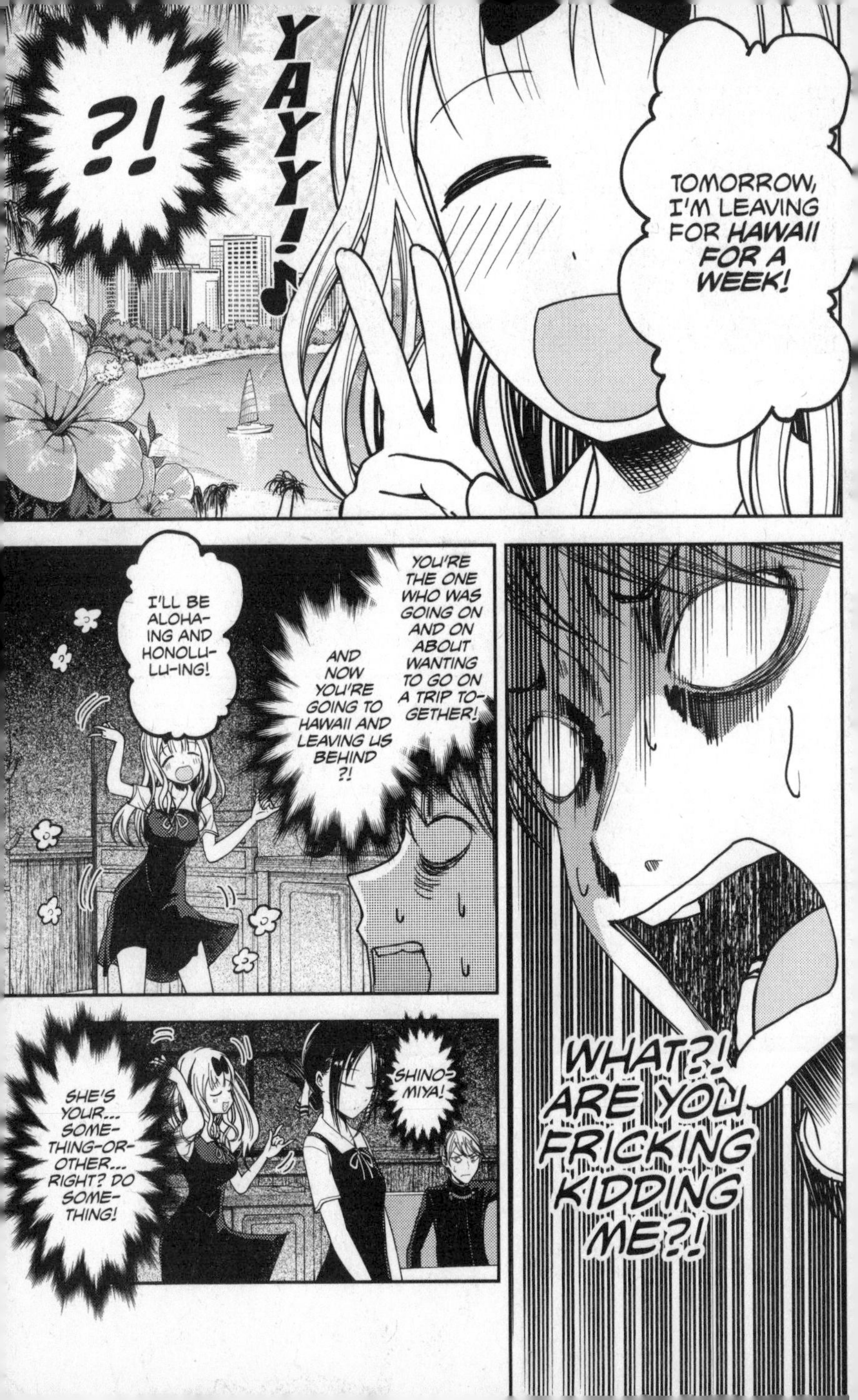
TOMORROW, I'M LEAVING FOR *HAWAII FOR A WEEK!*
YAYY!♪
?!
WHAT?! ARE YOU FRICKING KIDDING ME?!
YOU'RE THE ONE WHO WAS GOING ON AND ON ABOUT WANTING TO GO ON A TRIP TO-GETHER!
AND NOW YOU'RE GOING TO HAWAII AND LEAVING US BEHIND?!
I'LL BE ALOHA-ING AND HONOLU-LU-ING!
SHINO-MIYA!
SHE'S YOUR... SOME-THING-OR-OTHER... RIGHT? DO SOME-THING!

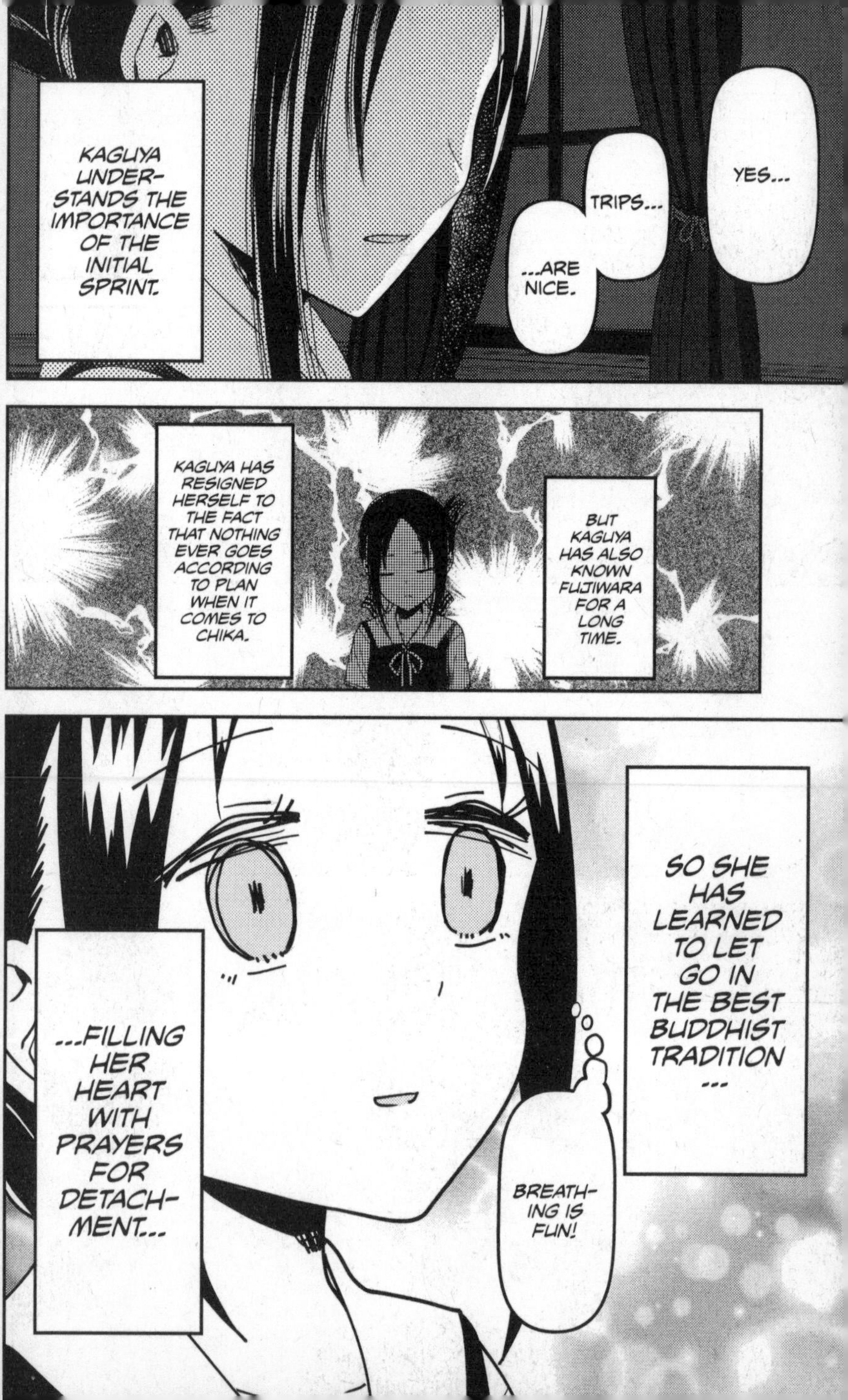
YES...
TRIPS...
...ARE NICE.
KAGUYA UNDERSTANDS THE IMPORTANCE OF THE INITIAL SPRINT.
BUT KAGUYA HAS ALSO KNOWN FUJIWARA FOR A LONG TIME.
KAGUYA HAS RESIGNED HERSELF TO THE FACT THAT NOTHING EVER GOES ACCORDING TO PLAN WHEN IT COMES TO CHIKA.
SO SHE HAS LEARNED TO LET GO IN THE BEST BUDDHIST TRADITION...
BREATHING IS FUN!
...FILLING HER HEART WITH PRAYERS FOR DETACHMENT...

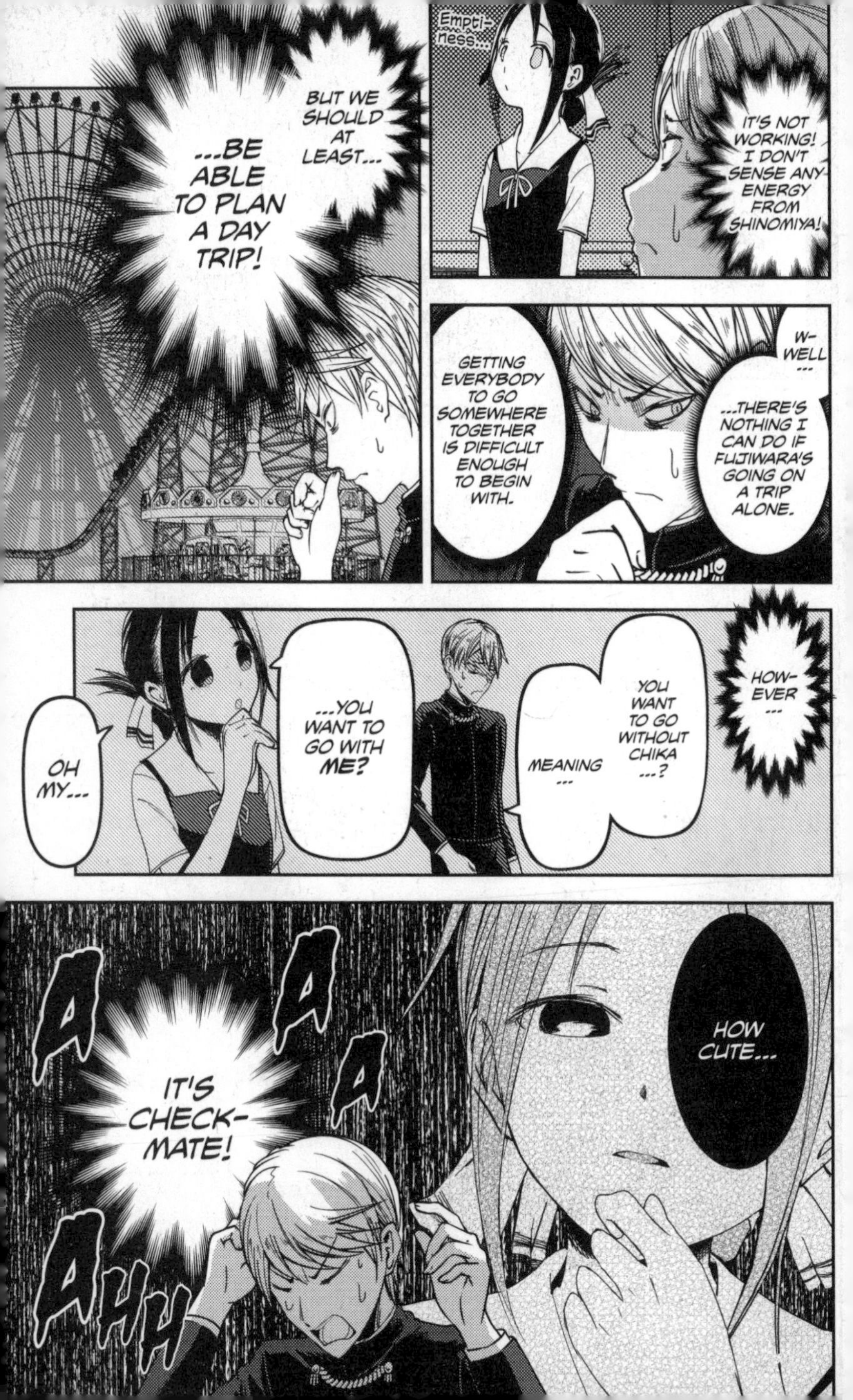
IT'S NOT WORKING! I DON'T SENSE ANY-ENERGY FROM SHINOMIYA!
Empti-ness...
W-WELL...
...THERE'S NOTHING I CAN DO IF FUJIWARA'S GOING ON A TRIP ALONE.
GETTING EVERYBODY TO GO SOMEWHERE TOGETHER IS DIFFICULT ENOUGH TO BEGIN WITH.
BUT WE SHOULD AT LEAST...
...BE ABLE TO PLAN A DAY TRIP!
HOW-EVER...
YOU WANT TO GO WITHOUT CHIKA...?
MEANING...
...YOU WANT TO GO WITH ME?
OH MY...
HOW CUTE...
AAA
IT'S CHECK-MATE!
AHH

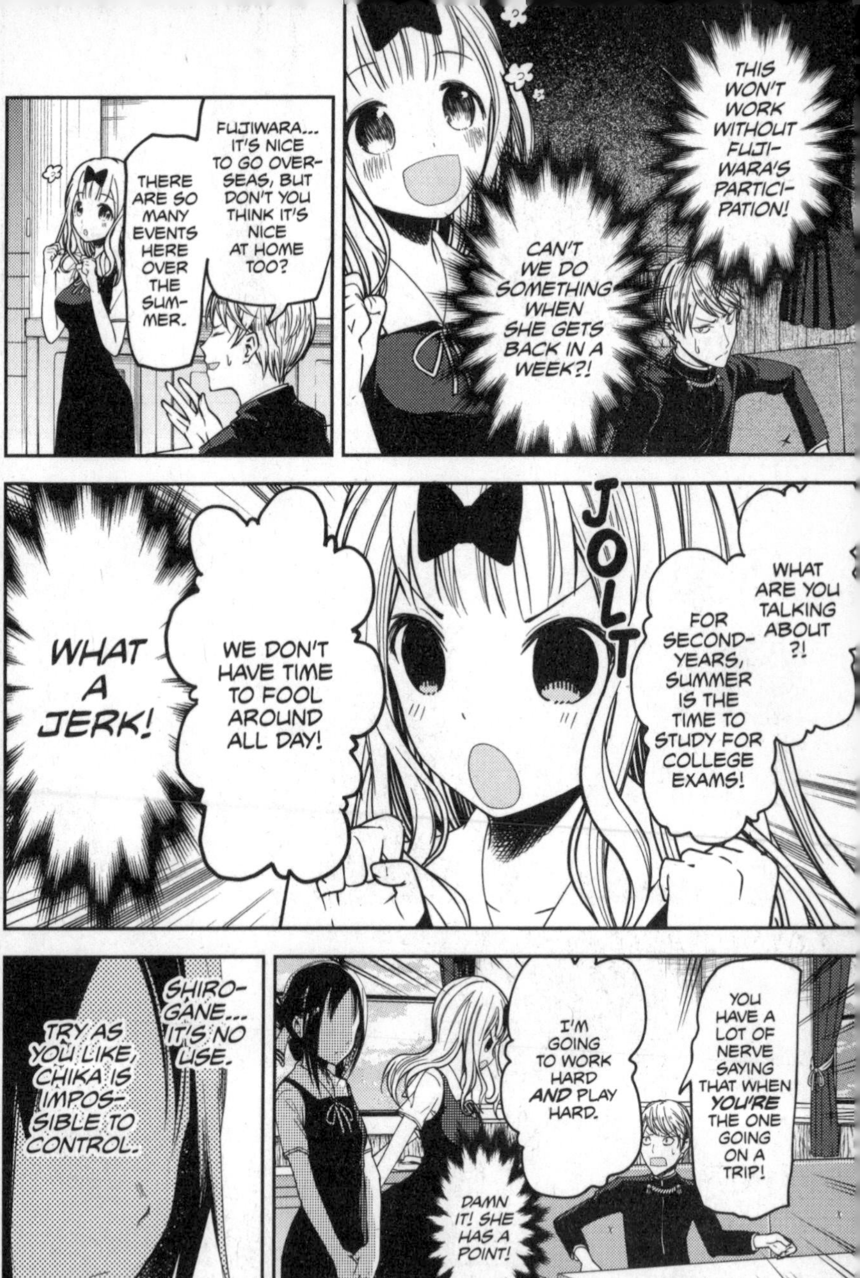
THIS WON'T WORK WITHOUT FUJIWARA'S PARTICIPATION!
CAN'T WE DO SOMETHING WHEN SHE GETS BACK IN A WEEK?!
FUJIWARA... IT'S NICE TO GO OVERSEAS, BUT DON'T YOU THINK IT'S NICE AT HOME TOO?
THERE ARE SO MANY EVENTS HERE OVER THE SUMMER.
JOLT
WHAT ARE YOU TALKING ABOUT?!
FOR SECOND-YEARS, SUMMER IS THE TIME TO STUDY FOR COLLEGE EXAMS!
WE DON'T HAVE TIME TO FOOL AROUND ALL DAY!
WHAT A JERK!
YOU HAVE A LOT OF NERVE SAYING THAT WHEN *YOU'RE* THE ONE GOING ON A TRIP!
I'M GOING TO WORK HARD *AND* PLAY HARD.
DAMN IT! SHE HAS A POINT!
SHIROGANE... IT'S NO USE.
TRY AS YOU LIKE, CHIKA IS IMPOSSIBLE TO CONTROL.

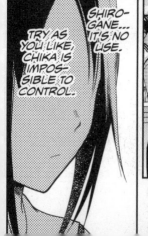

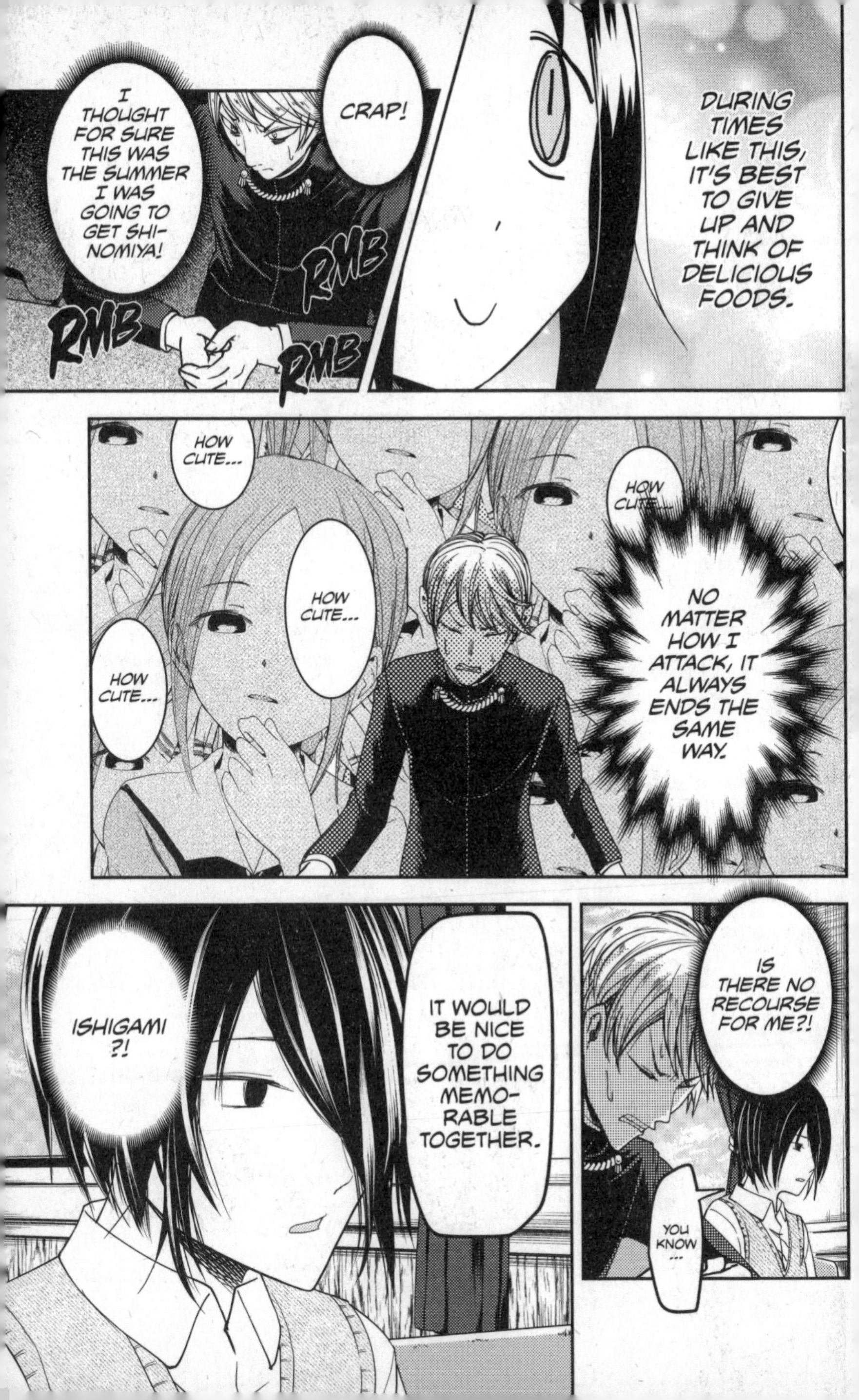
DURING TIMES LIKE THIS, IT'S BEST TO GIVE UP AND THINK OF DELICIOUS FOODS.
CRAP!
I THOUGHT FOR SURE THIS WAS THE SUMMER I WAS GOING TO GET SHI-NOMIYA!
RMB
RMB
RMB
HOW CUTE...
NO MATTER HOW I ATTACK, IT ALWAYS ENDS THE SAME WAY.
HOW CUTE...
HOW CUTE...
HOW CUTE...
IS THERE NO RECOURSE FOR ME?!
YOU KNOW...
IT WOULD BE NICE TO DO SOMETHING MEMO-RABLE TOGETHER.
ISHIGAMI?!

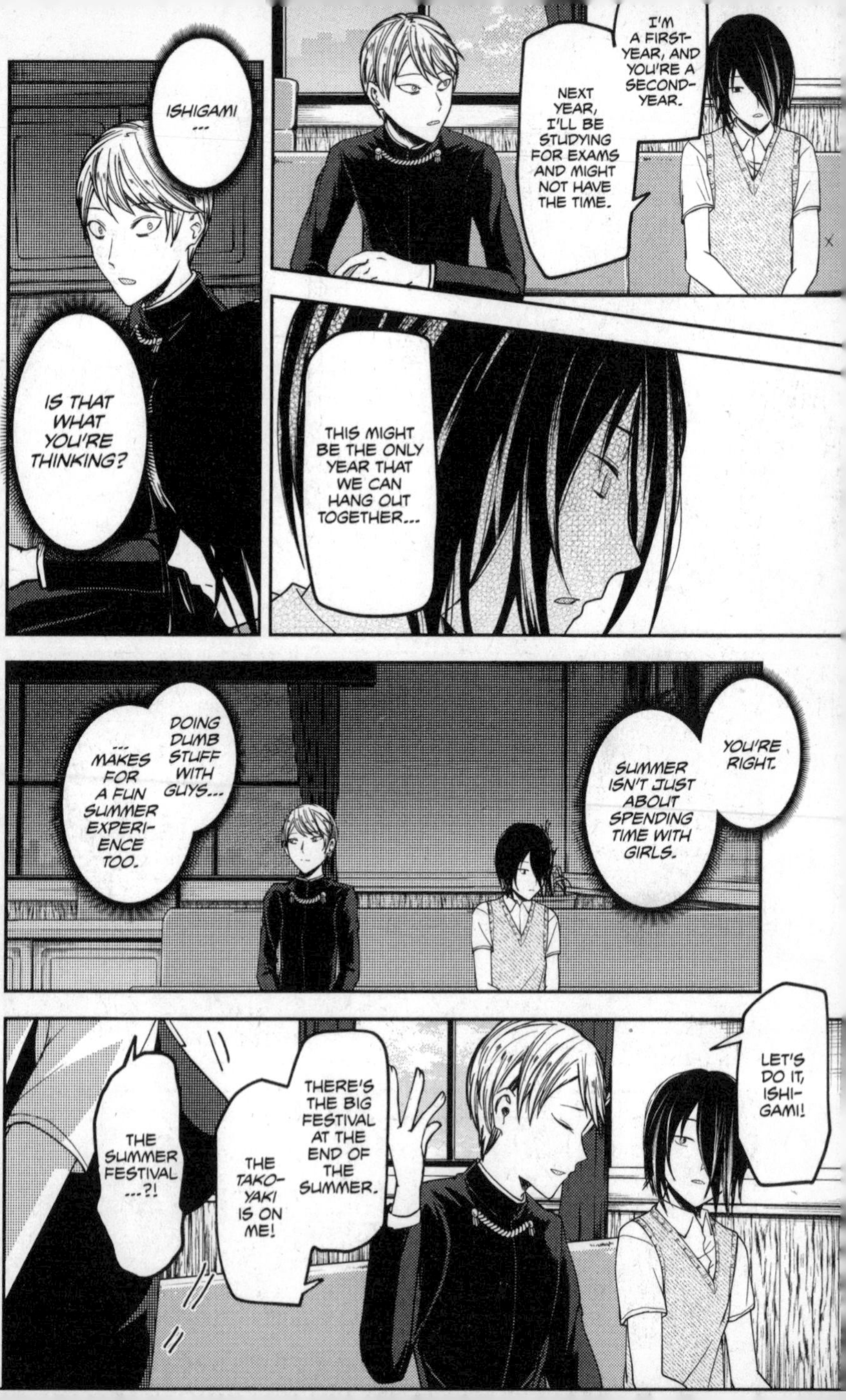
I'M A FIRST-YEAR, AND YOU'RE A SECOND-YEAR.
NEXT YEAR, I'LL BE STUDYING FOR EXAMS AND MIGHT NOT HAVE THE TIME.
THIS MIGHT BE THE ONLY YEAR THAT WE CAN HANG OUT TOGETHER...
ISHIGAMI...
IS THAT WHAT YOU'RE THINKING?
YOU'RE RIGHT.
SUMMER ISN'T JUST ABOUT SPENDING TIME WITH GIRLS.
DOING DUMB STUFF WITH GUYS...
...MAKES FOR A FUN SUMMER EXPERIENCE TOO.
LET'S DO IT, ISHIGAMI!
THERE'S THE BIG FESTIVAL AT THE END OF THE SUMMER.
THE TAKO-YAKI IS ON ME!
THE SUMMER FESTIVAL...?!

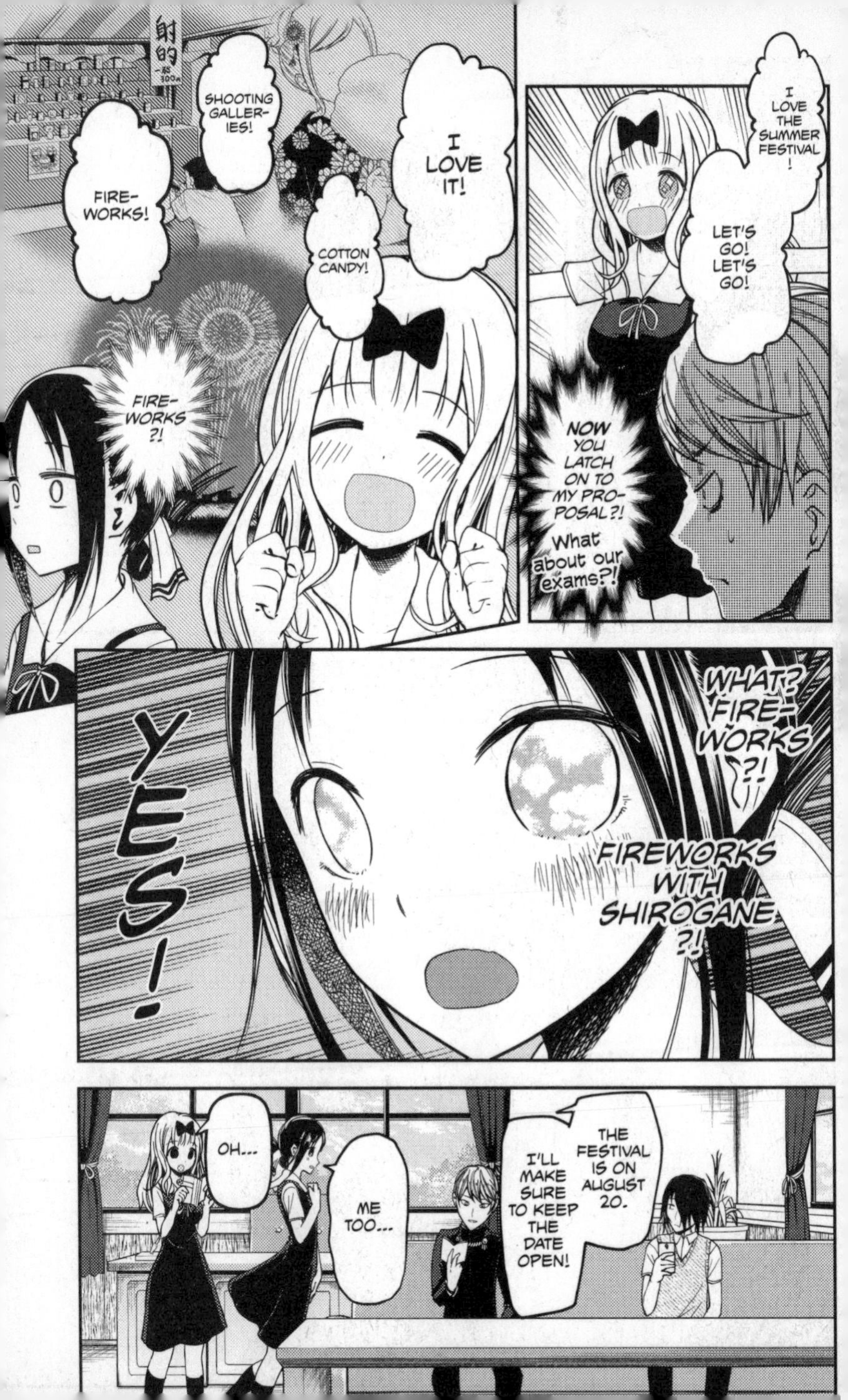
I LOVE THE SUMMER FESTIVAL!
LET'S GO! LET'S GO!
NOW YOU LATCH ON TO MY PROPOSAL?!
What about our exams?!
I LOVE IT!
SHOOTING GALLERIES!
COTTON CANDY!
FIREWORKS!
FIREWORKS?!
WHAT? FIREWORKS?!
FIREWORKS WITH SHIROGANE?!
YES!
THE FESTIVAL IS ON AUGUST 20.
I'LL MAKE SURE TO KEEP THE DATE OPEN!
ME TOO...
OH...

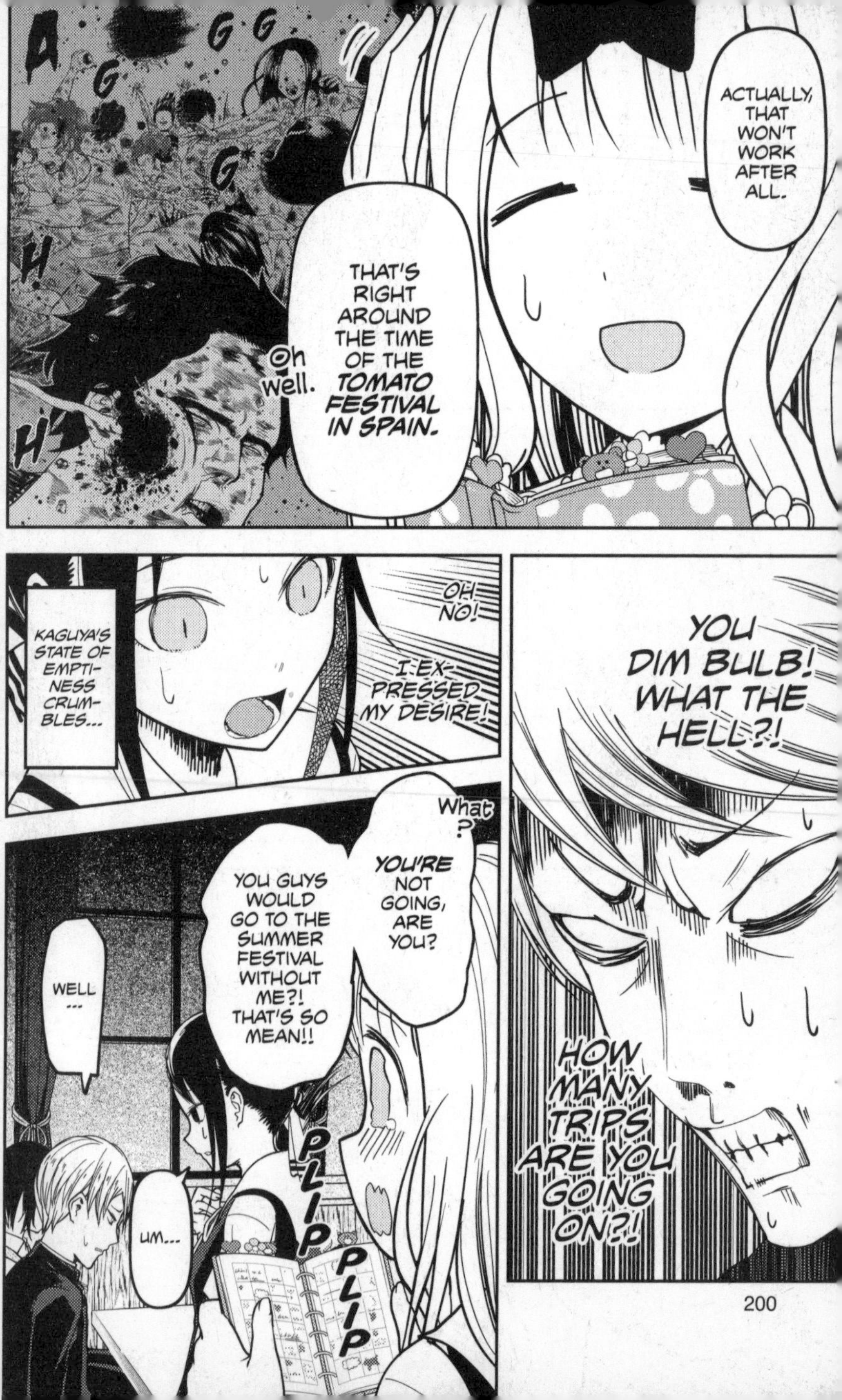
ACTUALLY, THAT WON'T WORK AFTER ALL.
THAT'S RIGHT AROUND THE TIME OF THE *TOMATO FESTIVAL IN SPAIN.*
Oh well.
AGGGGHH
YOU DIM BULB! WHAT THE HELL?!
HOW MANY TRIPS ARE YOU GOING ON?!
OH NO!
I EXPRESSED MY DESIRE!
KAGUYA'S STATE OF EMPTINESS CRUMBLES...
What?
YOU'RE NOT GOING, ARE YOU?
YOU GUYS WOULD GO TO THE SUMMER FESTIVAL WITHOUT ME?! THAT'S SO MEAN!!
WELL...
UM...
PLIP PLIP PLIP

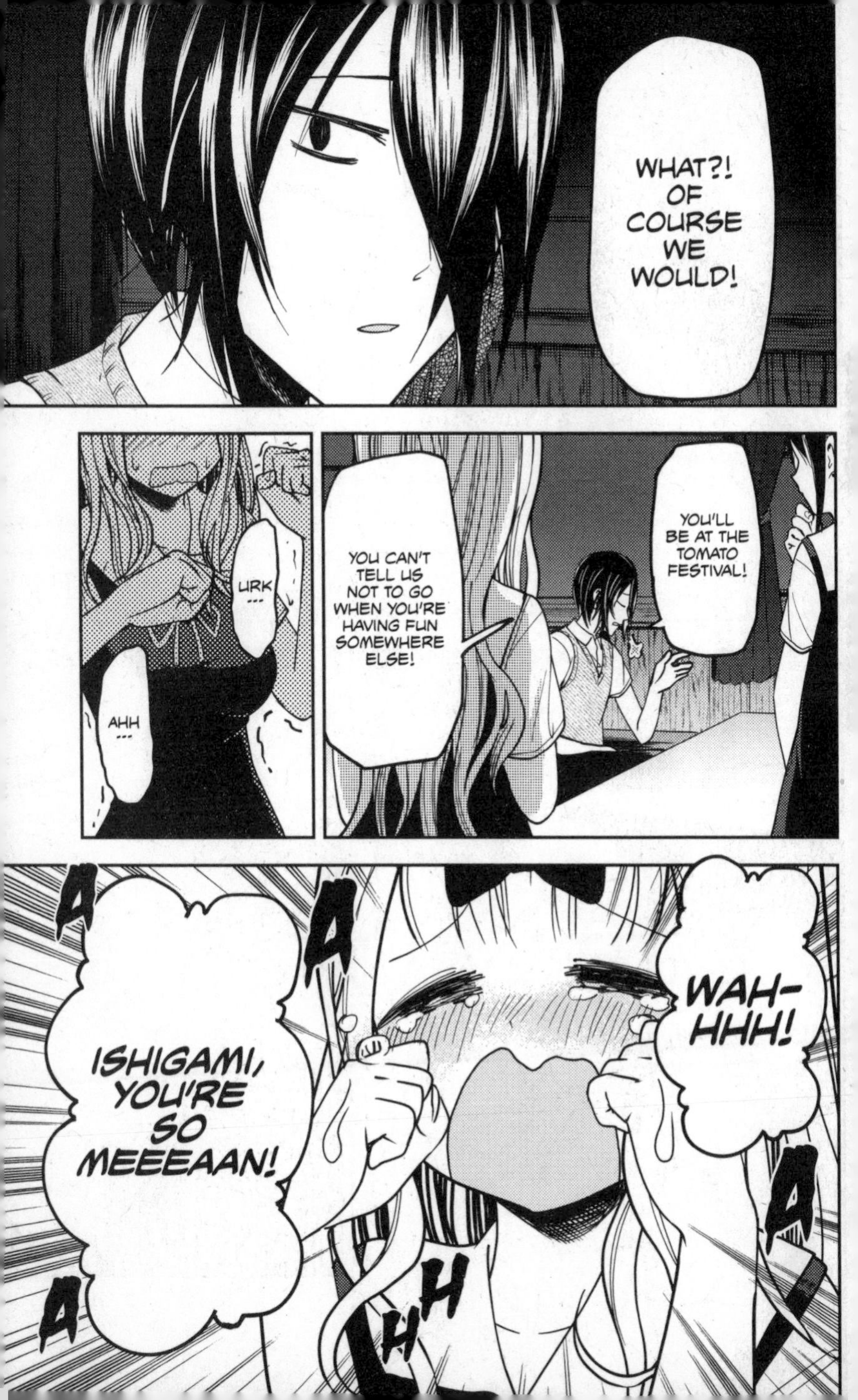
WHAT?! OF COURSE WE WOULD!
YOU'LL BE AT THE TOMATO FESTIVAL!
YOU CAN'T TELL US NOT TO GO WHEN YOU'RE HAVING FUN SOMEWHERE ELSE!
URK---
AHH---
WAH-HHH!
ISHIGAMI, YOU'RE SO MEEEEAAN!

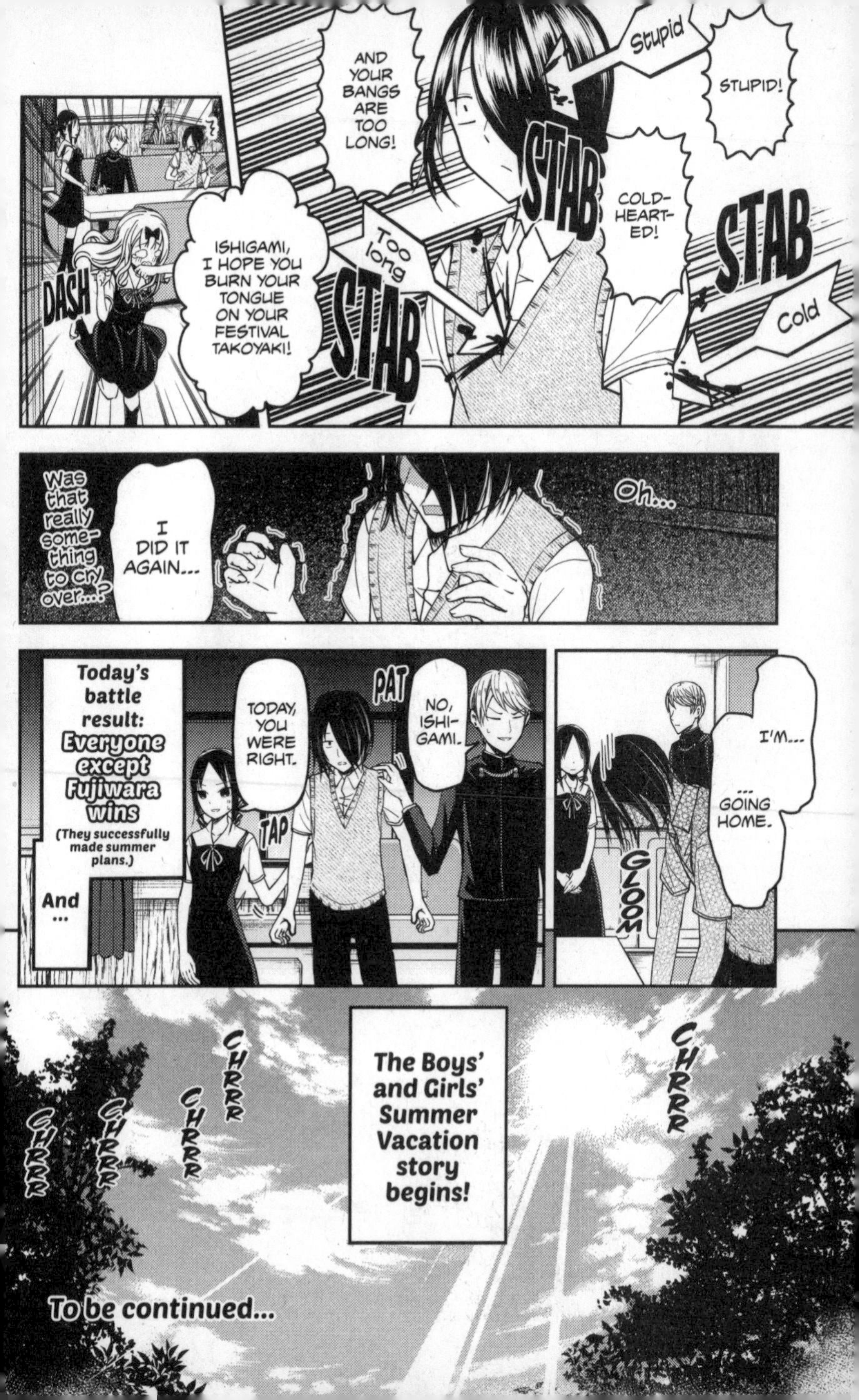
STUPID!
Stupid
STAB
COLD-HEARTED!
STAB
Cold
AND YOUR BANGS ARE TOO LONG!
Too long
STAB
ISHIGAMI, I HOPE YOU BURN YOUR TONGUE ON YOUR FESTIVAL TAKOYAKI!
DASH
Oh...
I DID IT AGAIN...
Was that really something to cry over...?
I'M...
...GOING HOME.
GLOOM
NO, ISHIGAMI.
PAT
TODAY, YOU WERE RIGHT.
TAP
Today's battle result: Everyone except Fujiwara wins
(They successfully made summer plans.)
And...
CHRRR
CHRRR
CHRRR
CHRRR
CHRRR
The Boys' and Girls' Summer Vacation story begins!
To be continued...

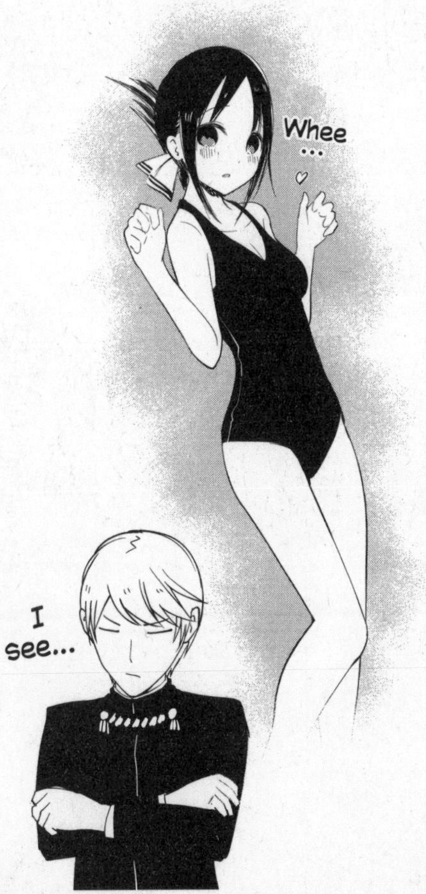
Whee...
I see...

Q&A!

A look back at the first semester!

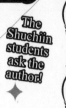

The Shuchiin students ask the author!

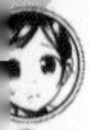

Q

Shirogane is a bit off. How has he made it this far?

A

He's a hard worker and somehow overcomes every challenge.

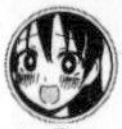

Q

You say that Kaguya only utilizes 60 percent of her ability, but she seems quite upset about losing to Fujiwara. Why?

A

At the end of the day, Fujiwara is a fierce opponent, so Kaguya competes seriously with her. Kaguya doesn't like losing when she has given something her all.

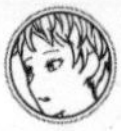

Q

What is Kaguya's cup size?

A

I'm not sure exactly, but it is a bit exaggerated for the manga.

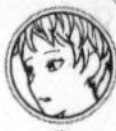

Q

Kaguya's sexual education is limited, so why did she say that males are creatures driven by the lower half of their bodies?

A

She gets that kind of information from either Hayasaka or Fujiwara.

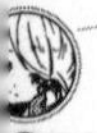

Q

Is Ishigami aware of what's going on between Kaguya and Shirogane?

A

He was suspicious at first, but then Kaguya denied it, and because he's afraid of her, he tries not to think about it.

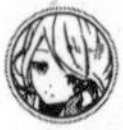

Q

What is Ishigami listening to on his headphones?

A

Probably anime soundtracks.

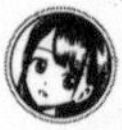

Q

Is Fujiwara's ribbon getting bigger?

A

Her extreme black ribbon varies in size depending on the humidity that day.

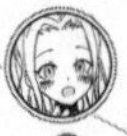

Q

Can high school students really become certified chick sexers?

A

This story assumes an alternate history in which the Taketori Monogatari might be real. It branches out from there beginning around the ninth century. In this alternate reality, the four major Japanese conglomerates are different, and they were never dismantled. Aside from that, there are many areas where reality and fiction are mixed together. Thus, in this world, a high school student can obtain a certification for chick sexing.

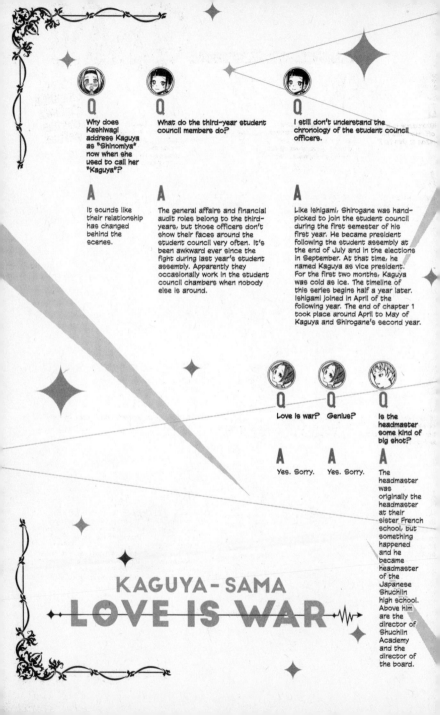

Q

Why does Kashiwagi address Kaguya as "Shinomiya" now when she used to call her "Kaguya"?

A

It sounds like their relationship has changed behind the scenes.

Q

What do the third-year student council members do?

A

The general affairs and financial audit roles belong to the third-years, but those officers don't show their faces around the student council very often. It's been awkward ever since the fight during last year's student assembly. Apparently they occasionally work in the student council chambers when nobody else is around.

Q

I still don't understand the chronology of the student council officers.

A

Like Ishigami, Shirogane was hand-picked to join the student council during the first semester of his first year. He became president following the student assembly at the end of July and in the elections in September. At that time, he named Kaguya as vice president. For the first two months, Kaguya was cold as ice. The timeline of this series begins half a year later. Ishigami joined in April of the following year. The end of chapter 1 took place around April to May of Kaguya and Shirogane's second year.

Q

Love is war?

A

Yes. Sorry.

Q

Genius?

A

Yes. Sorry.

Q

Is the headmaster some kind of big shot?

A

The headmaster was originally the headmaster at their sister French school, but something happened and he became headmaster of the Japanese Shuchiin high school. Above him are the director of Shuchiin Academy and the director of the board.

KAGUYA-SAMA
LOVE IS WAR

> BY NATURE, HUMANS ARE DRIVEN BY REASON OR EMOTION. LOVE ENTAILS BOTH.

AKA AKASAKA

Aka Akasaka got his start as an assistant to Jinsei Kataoka and Kazuma Kondou, the creators of *Deadman Wonderland*. His first serialized manga was an adaptation of the light novel series *Sayonara Piano Sonata*, published by Kadokawa in 2011. *Kaguya-sama: Love Is War* began serialization in *Miracle Jump* in 2015 but was later moved to *Weekly Young Jump* in 2016 due to its popularity.

The Student Council Presents

A TSUKKOMI CONTEST

Explanation

IN JAPANESE *MANZAI* COMEDY DUOS, ONE CHARACTER IS THE *BOKE* (FOOL) AND THE OTHER IS THE *TSUKKOMI* (STRAIGHT MAN). THE BOKE SAYS SILLY THINGS AND MAKES TERRIBLE JOKES. TSUKKOMI TRY TO KEEP THEIR COOL BUT SOON LOSE CONTROL AND BLOW UP OVER THE ABSURDITY OF THE BOKE'S STATEMENTS.

CHIKA HAS JUST READ ALOUD A MANZAI BOKE VERSION OF THE FAMILIAR JAPANESE FOLKTALE "MOMOTARO."

HOW MUCH OF A TSUKKOMI ARE *YOU*? YOUR RANK IS DETERMINED BY THE NUMBER OF CALLOUTS YOU MAKE!

GET READY TO TSUKKOMI!

Long, long ago, in a faraway land, lived Momotaro and an old man. The old man went to the river to wash clothes.

The old woman went to the mountain to wash clothes.

Suddenly, a peach floated up to her from the ocean. It went *splish, splash, sis boom bah.*

The old woman brought the peach to her ex-husband, the old man, and returned to her studio apartment where her girlfriend and adopted son awaited her.

When the old man used a paring knife to cut the peach in two, out came an embryo. The old man and Momotaro were overjoyed, as they had no children.

The old man named the embryo Momotaro, or "Peach Boy."

Momotaro grew quickly, and one day he announced, "I shall go to defeat the *oni.*"

And so, Momotaro headed out to Oni Island.

Along the way, he met a dog, a monkey and some *kibi dango* dumplings. All were on the verge of starvation.

Momotaro fed a pheasant from Momotaro to the monkey and his gang, and with great reluctance, they joined Momotaro on his journey.

Soon they arrived at Oni Island. The dog sniffed out the location of the hidden treasure, the monkey snuck into a building duct and successfully disarmed the security system, and the kibi dango allowed themselves to be eaten and then destroyed the oni from the inside.

Momotaro and the dog and the monkey took the treasure and returned home.

The old man, Momotaro and Momotaro lived happily ever after. The end.

Momo

4 KAGUYA-SAMA LOVE IS WAR

Examples

Long, long ago, in a faraway land, lived Momotaro *Momotaro's there from the start?!* and an old man. The old man went to the river to wash clothes.

The old woman went to the mountain *Mountains are for gathering wood!* to wash clothes. *Why aren't they washing their clothes together?!*

Suddenly, a peach floated up to her from the ocean. *Upstream?!* It went *splish, splash, sis boom bah.* *Percussion sound effects?!*

The old woman brought the peach to her ex-husband *Complicated relationship!*, the old man, and returned to her studio apartment *Is this set in the modern day?!* where her girlfriend *Wait—what?!* and adopted son awaited her.

When the old man used a paring knife *Fancy!* to cut the peach in two, out came an embryo. *That's crazy!* The old man and Momotaro were overjoyed, as they had no children. *Oh, their relationship is modern too!*

The old man named the embryo Momotaro, or "Peach Boy." *Two Momotaros?!*

Momotaro grew quickly *Fast-paced story!*, and one day he announced, "I shall go to defeat the *oni.*" *So brave!*

And so, Momotaro headed out to Oni Island. *Which Momotaro?! It's confusing!*

Along the way, he met a dog, a monkey and some *kibi dango* dumplings. *Kibi dango?!* All were on the verge of starvation. *Why the extreme motivation?!*

Momotaro fed a pheasant *This should be the kibi dango!* from Momotaro *Confusing!* to the monkey and his gang, and with great reluctance *Oh no!*, they joined Momotaro on his journey.

Soon they arrived at Oni Island. The dog sniffed out the location of the hidden treasure *Talented!*, the monkey snuck into a building duct and successfully disarmed the security system *Talented!*, and the kibi dango allowed themselves to be eaten and then destroyed the oni from the inside. *Kibi dango…?!*

Momotaro and the dog and the monkey took the treasure and returned home. *Kibi dango?!!*

The old man, Momotaro and Momotaro *Still confusing!* lived happily ever after. The end. *KIBI DANGO???!!!*

Results!

How much of a tsukkomi are you?

★ Less than 10: Kaguya Level

You lack common sense. You seem incapable of understanding what's correct and what is not. You should go out into the world and let yourself be contaminated.

★ 10 to 14: Chika Level

You are able to identify general abnormalities and things that are completely off. However, at times you might lack the critical ability to deflect and simply react. Take care to read every situation thoroughly.

★ 15 to 19: Ishigami Level

Although you are able to see things clearly, you have difficulty being a tsukkomi due to your cowardice. Don't run. Stand your ground and fight.

★ 20 to 26: Miyuki Level

Although your tsukkomi character is rather high, you possess characteristics that are open to being attacked by tsukkomi. Work on taking a more objective view and calling out your own failings.

★ 27 or more: Ai Level

You are a cold-blooded tsukkomi machine. With this level of tsukkomi skill, you are often designated as the one to put the brakes on others. This is a stressful way to live. Take a chill pill.

KAGUYA-SAMA
LOVE IS WAR

SHONEN JUMP MANGA EDITION

4

STORY AND ART BY
AKA AKASAKA

Translation/Emi Louie-Nishikawa
English Adaptation/Annette Roman
Touch-Up Art & Lettering/Stephen Dutro
Cover & Interior Design/Izumi Evers
Editor/Annette Roman

KAGUYA-SAMA WA KOKURASETAI~TENSAITACHI NO REN'AI ZUNO SEN~
© 2015 by Aka Akasaka
All rights reserved.
First published in Japan in 2015 by SHUEISHA Inc., Tokyo.
English translation rights arranged by SHUEISHA Inc.

Printed in Canada
Published by VIZ Media, LLC
P.O. Box 77010
San Francisco, CA 94107

10 9 8 7 6 5 4 3 2 1
First printing, September 2018

viz.com

shonenjump.com

COMING NEXT VOLUME

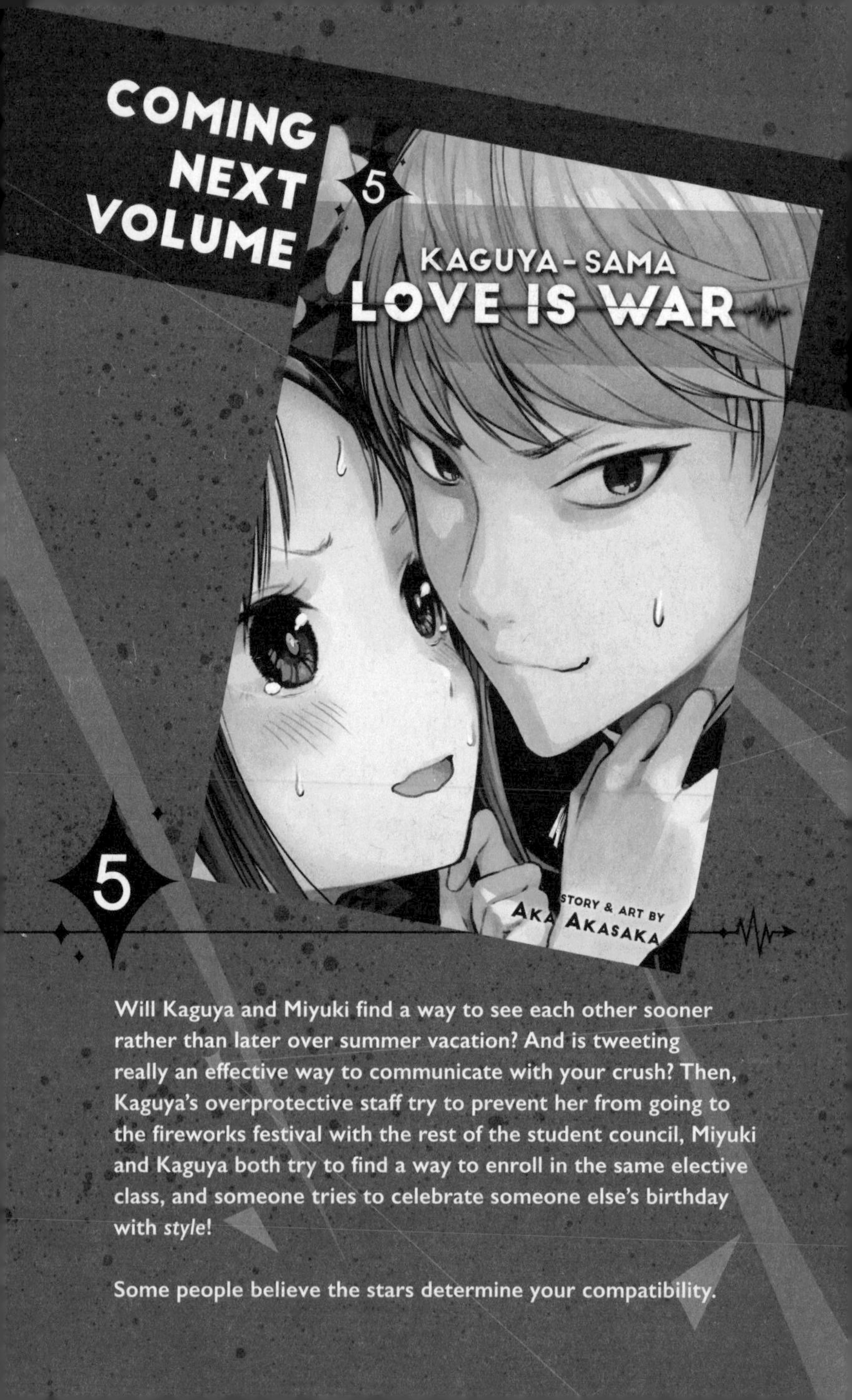
5
KAGUYA-SAMA
LOVE IS WAR
STORY & ART BY
AKA AKASAKA

5

Will Kaguya and Miyuki find a way to see each other sooner rather than later over summer vacation? And is tweeting really an effective way to communicate with your crush? Then, Kaguya's overprotective staff try to prevent her from going to the fireworks festival with the rest of the student council, Miyuki and Kaguya both try to find a way to enroll in the same elective class, and someone tries to celebrate someone else's birthday with *style*!

Some people believe the stars determine your compatibility.

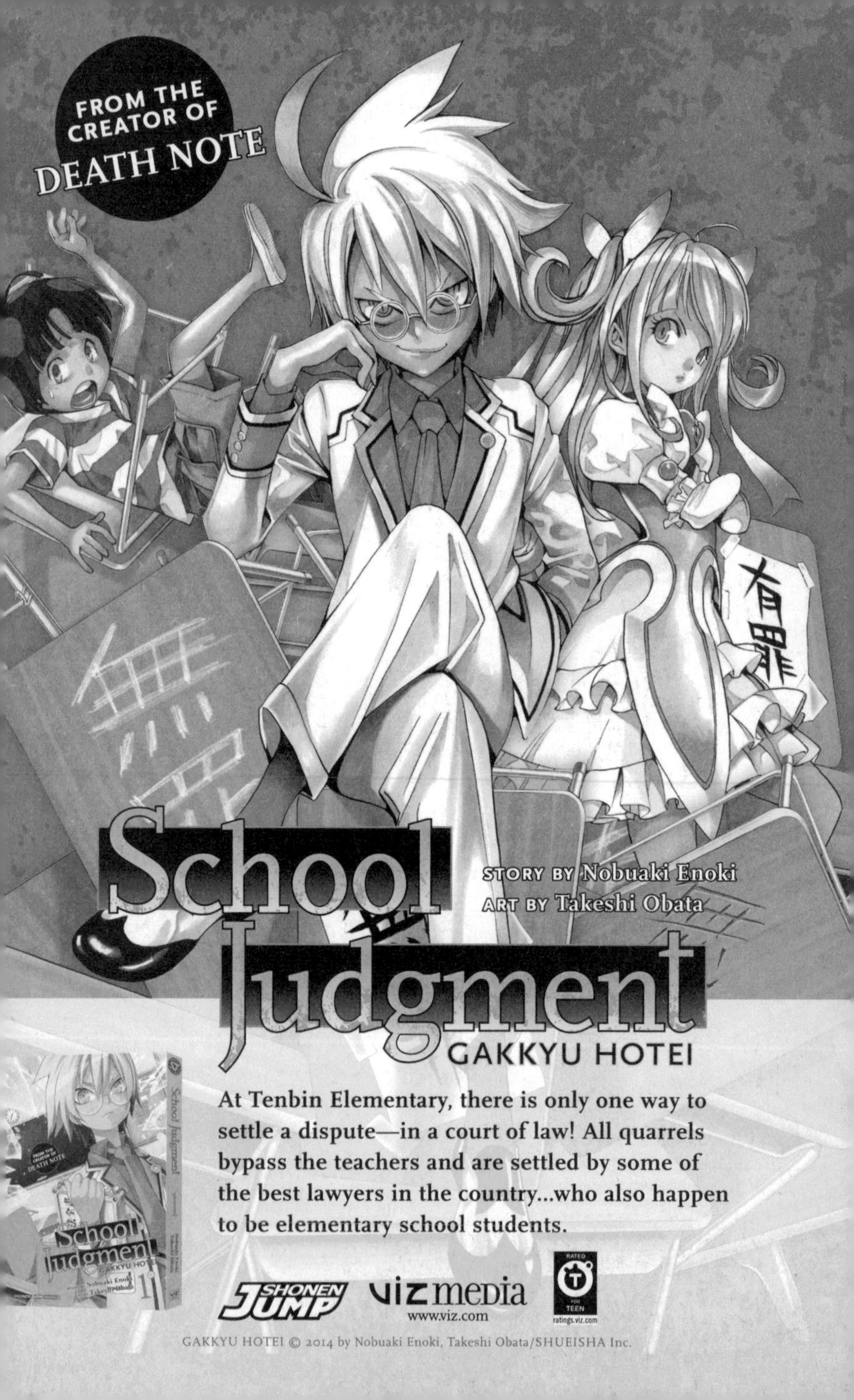
FROM THE CREATOR OF DEATH NOTE
有罪
School Judgment
STORY BY Nobuaki Enoki
ART BY Takeshi Obata
GAKKYU HOTEI
At Tenbin Elementary, there is only one way to settle a dispute—in a court of law! All quarrels bypass the teachers and are settled by some of the best lawyers in the country...who also happen to be elementary school students.
SHONEN JUMP
VIZ media
www.viz.com
RATED T FOR TEEN
ratings.viz.com
GAKKYU HOTEI © 2014 by Nobuaki Enoki, Takeshi Obata/SHUEISHA Inc.

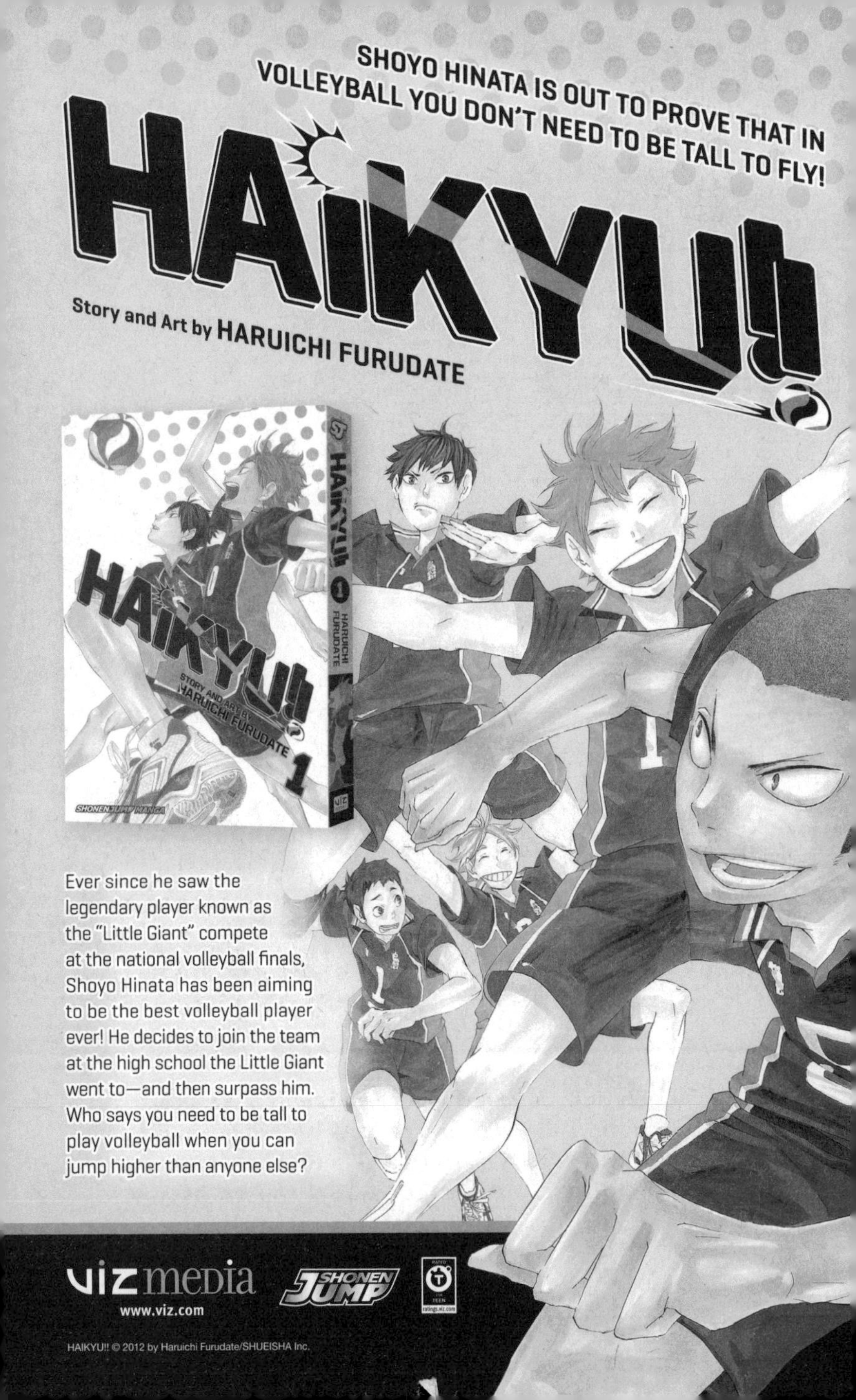
SHOYO HINATA IS OUT TO PROVE THAT IN VOLLEYBALL YOU DON'T NEED TO BE TALL TO FLY!
HAIKYU!!
Story and Art by HARUICHI FURUDATE
HAIKYU!! 1
HARUICHI FURUDATE
STORY AND ART BY HARUICHI FURUDATE
SHONEN JUMP MANGA
Ever since he saw the legendary player known as the "Little Giant" compete at the national volleyball finals, Shoyo Hinata has been aiming to be the best volleyball player ever! He decides to join the team at the high school the Little Giant went to—and then surpass him. Who says you need to be tall to play volleyball when you can jump higher than anyone else?
viz media
www.viz.com
SHONEN JUMP
RATED T TEEN
ratings.viz.com
HAIKYU!! © 2012 by Haruichi Furudate/SHUEISHA Inc.

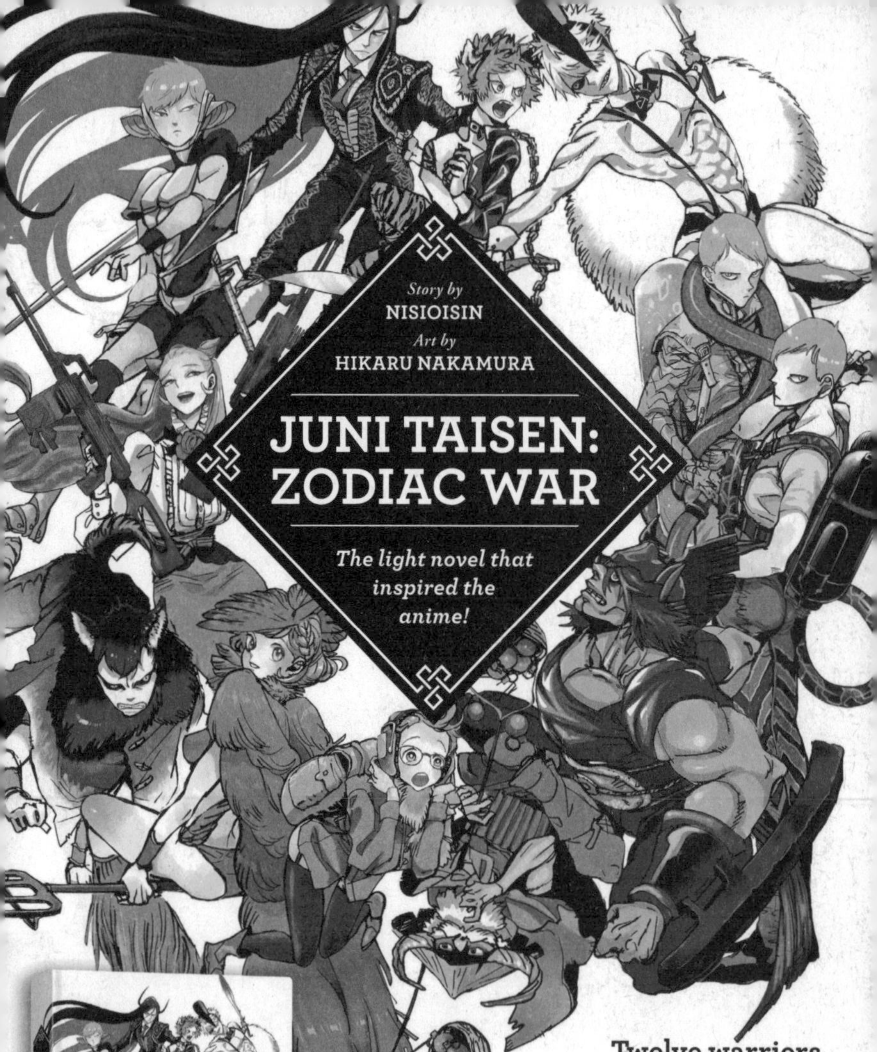
Story by
NISIOISIN
Art by
HIKARU NAKAMURA
JUNI TAISEN:
ZODIAC WAR
The light novel that inspired the anime!

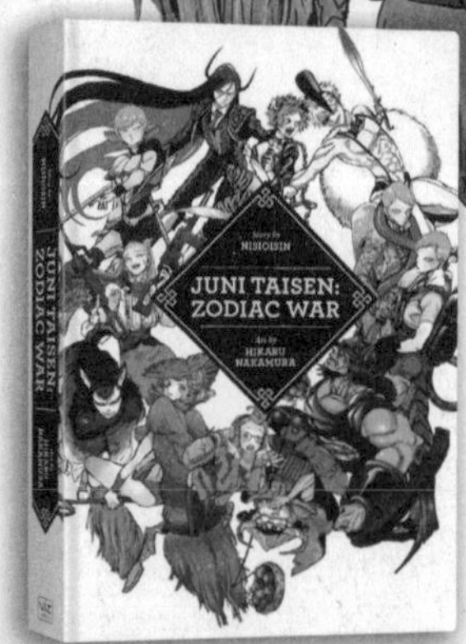
Story by
NISIOISIN
JUNI TAISEN:
ZODIAC WAR
Art by
HIKARU
NAKAMURA